W9-BIB-055

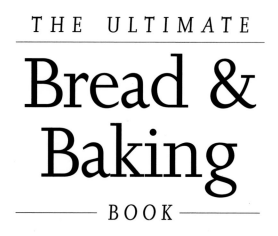

THE ULTIMATE Bread & Baking BOOK

THE ULTIMATE Bread & Baking BOOK

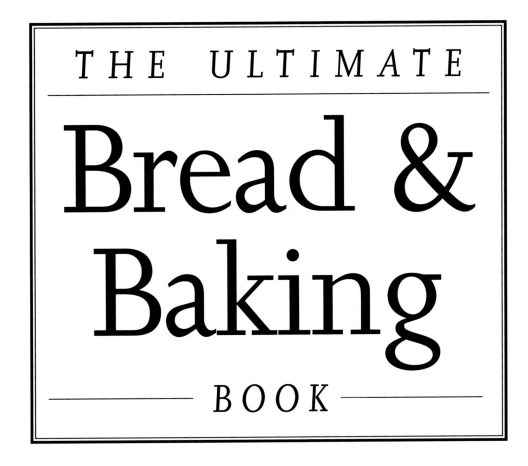

SHELTON BOOKS

TO ALAN, BOBBY & NICKY

The material in this book has previously appeared in
The Bread Book (Conran Octopus, 1993) and
The Baking Book (Conran Octopus, 1996).

The text and recipes of The Bread Book have been revised
and updated especially for this edition.

First published in the US in 1999 by Shelton Books
Conran Octopus Ltd
2-4 Heron Quays
Docklands
London E14 4JP

Text copyright © Linda Collister 1993, 1996, 1999
Photography copyright © Anthony Blake 1993, 1996, 1999
Design and layout copyright © Conran Octopus 1993, 1996, 1999

Linda Collister and Anthony Blake assert the moral right to be identified
as the author and photographer of this work. All rights reserved.

Designer: Paul Welti
Editors: Beverley Le Blanc and Norma MacMillan
Commissioning Editor: Louise Simpson
Editorial Assistant: Jane Chapman
Production: Julia Golding
Cover, 1-11, 210-211 & 360-368 designed by Haldane Mason Ltd
and typeset by SX Composing DTP Ltd

ISBN 1-84091-125-5

Typeset by Servis Filmsetting Ltd (1993), Peter Howard (1996)
Printed in China

CONTENTS

AN INTRODUCTION TO BREAD

Our increasingly hectic lifestyles, and family and work commitments keep us constantly on-the-go, leaving little time for the simpler pleasures in life. Baking a loaf of bread has to be, without a doubt, one of those such pleasures. For what could be more wholly satisfying than creating and baking your own bread? Bread-making is a past-time well within everyone's grasp and this book will show you just how easy it can be!

Anthony Blake and Linda Collister share a common passion for well-made bread, but have come together from different backgrounds to work on this book. Linda has a classic cook's training, having worked in Paris and Italy, while Anthony draws upon his life-long interest in food, which increased as he photographed some of the world's greatest chefs at work.

In the year-and-a-half that Linda and Anthony traveled throughout Europe and America, they encountered many bread-making enthusiasts, all of whom generously shared their secrets and tips. Welcomed by bakers and millers of all ages and experience, in both private and professional kitchens, Linda and Anthony's travels proved a thorough success, as this book demonstrates.

The first invaluable lesson in successful bread-making is that you cannot make good bread without good flour. Mass-produced, bleached, and highly refined flours often lead to disappointing results. High-quality flour with real flavor is easily available from small, independent millers. Organic, stoneground flours are also sold in good health food stores and delicatessens. Once you have started baking with well-produced flours, you will find the flavor and texture of your loaves vastly superior to those made with most supermarket flours.

The second important lesson of bread-making is that haste makes waste, not taste. For example, most of the bread recipes in this book are made with cool or lukewarm liquid, and then left to rise at cool to normal room temperature. This is because a slowly risen dough produces a loaf with a deeper flavor—don't be tempted to rush! The texture will also be improved, resulting in chewier bread with far fewer air bubbles. All in all, a slowly risen dough makes a more satisfying loaf, which will stay fresh for longer, too.

Bread-making does not actually require a great amount of skill. As long as you do not kill the yeast by using liquid that is too hot, there is very little that can go wrong. In addition, unlike pastry- and cake-making, which needs a light touch, dough kneading only requires time and effort. Once you begin baking bread, you won't want to stop, as you discover the endless variety to experiment with, all shapes and sizes, with different textures and tastes. This book contains a selection of just some of those delicious bread varieties from around the world—all guaranteed to inspire you to begin baking bread for yourself, your family, and friends.

BASIC BREADS

It is immensely satisfying to bake an honest, flavorful loaf of bread with a rich, tantalizing aroma. Good, nourishing bread has been held in high esteem since the age of the Pharaohs, and rightly so. The bread you eat today is a slice of social history. The basic ingredients, used by those ancient Egyptians, have remained unchanged – flour, salt, water, and usually leavening – although today we can choose from a dozen different flours, enrich the water with milk, eggs, or fat, and use fresh or dried yeasts, chemical leavening agents, or the natural yeasts produced in a sourdough. Our modern bread can be as fancy or simple, sophisticated or rustic as we choose.

This chapter contains complete instructions and photographs for each stage in the recipe for making a basic loaf of bread. Although bread-making is neither complex nor tricky, you do have to take many variables into account. I bake bread every day, yet I can never be absolutely sure of the result. Much depends on the weather and the kitchen temperature, the kind of flour, the type and age of the yeast, and even the hardness of the water. My aim is that you learn what looks, tastes, smells, and feels right.

OPPOSITE AND ABOVE
Baguettes are a traditional bread for the French

To the old saying that all you need to make good bread is time, warmth, and love, I would add practice. Once you have mastered a basic recipe – and it will take three or four batches to get the correct feel – you can experiment. Take risks – play around with various shapes, change the flavor and texture of the crumb by mixing flours and grains, or vary the crust with different toppings and glazes. The classic French baguette, for example, has a high proportion of crust to crumb, yet the crust is thin and razor-sharp, the crumb moist and light. You will soon learn that this result is achieved in the shaping, finishing, and baking of the loaf, and that a similar bread dough handled in a different manner is used to make soft, floury baps, a favorite Scottish breakfast roll.

Anthony Blake and I have watched many fine bakers in several countries make bread, and each has a special, individual method. Some bakers start with a "sponge" – yeast, liquid, and some of the flour – while others add all the liquid to the flour at once, and others add all the flour to the liquid. Some bakers swear by ice water; others use quite warm water. Some like hot conditions, while others prefer the refrigerator for the fermentation and rising of the dough. I prefer a loaf made with very little fresh yeast, flavorful flour, cool water, a fair amount of sea salt, and a long rising time in a cool spot. It is this slow fermentation of the dough that produces a well-flavored, chewy, even sturdy loaf that, as it matures, assumes a rich, complex flavor and is slow to stale.

Try the recipes and find what works best for you.

POINTS TO REMEMBER

Before you begin, read these points and The Basic Loaf recipe. These points explain why some of my recipes are made differently than recipes found in other books. For information on the chemistry of bread-making, read Harold McGee's *On Food and Cooking: The Science and Lore of the Kitchen* (Charles Scribner's Sons, 1984).

– Yeast is an organism that needs moisture, warmth, and sugar or flour to stimulate its growth. As it multiplies, it produces carbon dioxide, which makes dough rise.

– Temperature is crucial to yeast; if the water or liquid you add to it is too hot the yeast will be killed, too cool and its growth will be inhibited – which is actually often desirable if you want a slow rising. According to conventional wisdom, the ideal temperature is between 95°F and 105°F, termed lukewarm.

– The yeast will grow quickly if the dough is left to rise in a warm, draft-free spot. In a cool place, however, the dough will rise more slowly. Therefore rising times can vary from about 1 hour to overnight. I find that the cooler rising temperature gives a better-tasting bread, which is why most of my recipes leave the dough to rise at cool to normal room temperature. Choose a spot which is about 60°F, such as an unheated pantry.

– The quantity of liquid and flour you add varies depending on the flour and conditions, such as the heat and humidity of the kitchen. You may need a little more or a little less than the recipe states to achieve the desired dough consistency. In many recipes I've given a range for the amount of flour.

– To measure flour, scoop a dry-measure cup directly into the bag or canister. Level off the excess. If you prefer to weigh the flour, one cup will weigh 4 ounces (115g).

– I prefer fresh yeast to active dry yeast because it gives loaves a deeper flavor and I find the fresh easier to use. However, most recipes will work with active dry yeast and recipes usually include directions for both types (for detailed instructions; see page 18).

– My recipes call for either flaked (not crystal) sea salt or kosher salt because I prefer the flavor. If you use regular fine table salt, decrease the amount by half.

– Kneading (page 16) is vital for good, even-textured, well-shaped bread. Kneading helps to develop the gluten in the flour, which is necessary to support the carbon dioxide produced by the yeast. Kneading also incorporates air into the dough and ensures that the yeast is evenly distributed throughout so the loaf rises evenly.

– Dough is usually kneaded by hand for 10 minutes, or in a large, stationary mixer using a dough hook. However, I have never found that kneading dough in a food processor does it much good – and, as with all mechanical methods of kneading, it is easy to over-knead, which does more harm than good by breaking down gluten strands.

– The dough should be left to rise covered with a damp linen or cotton (but not terry-cloth) dish towel, or sheet of plastic wrap to prevent a dry crust forming, which can leave hard lumps in the finished loaf. The loaf will be heavy if it is not left to rise for long enough, though over-rising is more of a problem than slight under-rising. If a dough is seriously distended by being left to rise too long, it collapses when baked.

– Punching down the risen dough disperses the gas bubble for uniform texture and crumb.

– I do not usually specify what to use for greasing pans and baking sheets. Some bakers use melted lard, vegetable oil, or non-stick sprays; I prefer melted unsalted butter because doughs do not absorb butter as they do oil, and the loaf is less likely to stick as it bakes.

– Baking in a hot, preheated oven (usually 400°F or higher) kills the yeast quickly (which is what you want to have happen at this point) and prevents over-rising. The hotter the oven, the crisper the crust will be.

– Bread is baked through when it sounds hollow when tapped on the underside. Most breads are turned out of the baking pans onto the wire racks to cool, which prevents the steam from the loaf making the crust soggy underneath.

THE BASIC LOAF

INGREDIENTS

Makes 1 large loaf

- 3 cups (350g) unbleached white bread flour
- 3 cups (350g) whole-wheat bread flour, preferably stone-ground
- 2 tablespoons (15g) coarse sea salt, crushed or ground
- 1 0.6-oz cake fresh yeast (15g), or 1 envelope active dry yeast (2½ teaspoons) plus ½ teaspoon sugar
- 2 cups (430ml) lukewarm water
- extra flour for dusting and sprinkling

a large baking sheet, lightly greased

This is how to make a fine-tasting, good-looking loaf of bread. The combination of white bread flour (preferably stone-ground and unbleached) and whole-wheat (preferably stone-ground) makes a loaf that is easy to work, but with great flavor and a good texture. It is shaped into an oval and simply baked on a cookie sheet, rather than in a loaf pan. Although you may use a loaf pan if you like (see instructions for shaping in *A Plain White Loaf*, page 24), I find this free-form shape easier and more attractive.

This basic method, which first creates a "sponge," is the same for most yeast doughs. Many of the recipes in this book will refer back to the techniques illustrated and explained below and overleaf. This loaf will keep for up to five days, and can be frozen for one month.

In very cold weather, warming the bowl of flour in a 250°F oven for 5 to 8 minutes, or microwaving on high for ½ to 1½ minutes (be sure to use a microwave-safe bowl), depending upon the amount of flour, helps the yeast start working.

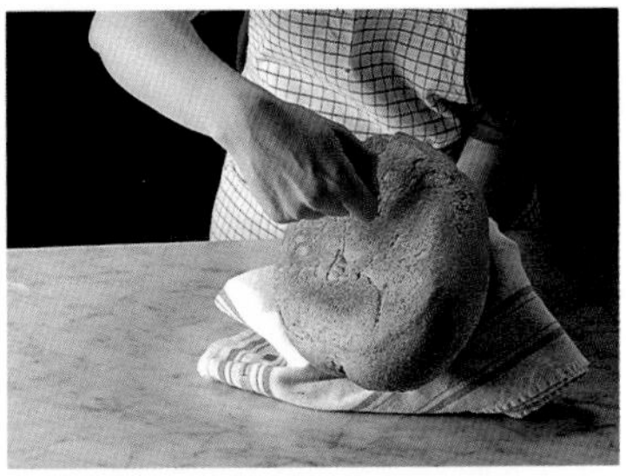

TO TEST IF THE LOAF IS BAKED THROUGH, CAREFULLY TURN IT UPSIDE DOWN AND TAP IT WITH YOUR KNUCKLES; A THOROUGHLY BAKED LOAF SOUNDS HOLLOW. IF THE LOAF SOUNDS DENSE OR HEAVY, BAKE IT FOR 5 MINUTES LONGER AND TEST AGAIN. TRANSFER THE BREAD TO A WIRE RACK TO COOL COMPLETELY.

Fresh Yeast Method

Professional bakers use the sponge method shown in steps 1 through 7 on page 16 to test whether the yeast is alive and working – growing and multiplying rapidly – before they add large quantities of flour, which will be wasted if the yeast is dead. If the batter does not become spongy, throw it out and begin again; the yeast is probably too old, or was killed by too hot water.

This sponge technique also has the advantage of lightening the heavier loaves. It is a time-consuming technique, so many experienced home bakers prefer to skip this step, but I think it is a good idea for anyone new to bread-making to use this technique until your knowledge of yeast's characteristics becomes second nature.

The aroma of freshly baked bread will fill the kitchen when the loaf comes out of the oven. This perfectly baked loaf has a good crisp crust and a well-flavored, chewy crumb.

The Basic Loaf Step-by-Step Directions

MIX TOGETHER THE WHITE FLOUR, WHOLE-WHEAT FLOUR, AND THE SALT IN A LARGE BOWL. IN VERY COLD WEATHER WARM THE BOWL OF FLOUR (SEE PAGE 15). THIS WILL HELP THE YEAST START WORKING.

1 CRUMBLE THE CAKE OF FRESH YEAST INTO A SMALL BOWL WITH YOUR FINGERS. (IF USING ACTIVE DRY YEAST, SEE PAGE 18.)

2 MIX ABOUT 1/4 CUP OF THE MEASURED LUKEWARM WATER WITH THE YEAST UNTIL SMOOTH.

3 MAKE A WELL ABOUT 6 INCHES WIDE IN THE CENTER OF THE FLOUR. ADD THE YEAST MIXTURE.

4 POUR THE REST OF THE LUKEWARM WATER INTO THE WELL.

5 DRAW A LITTLE FLOUR INTO THE WELL AND MIX THOROUGHLY WITH THE LIQUID. GRADUALLY MIX IN MORE FLOUR UNTIL YOU HAVE A THICK, SMOOTH BATTER IN THE WELL.

6 SPRINKLE THE BATTER WITH A LITTLE WHITE FLOUR TO PREVENT A SKIN FROM FORMING.

7 LET THE BATTER STAND FOR ABOUT 20 MINUTES TO SPONGE. IT WILL BECOME AERATED AND FROTHY AND EXPAND NEARLY TO FILL THE WELL IN THE SPONGE.

8 GRADUALLY MIX THE REST OF THE FLOUR IN THE BOWL INTO THE BATTER WITH YOUR HANDS.

9 GATHER THE DOUGH INTO A BALL. IT SHOULD BE FIRM AND LEAVE THE SIDE OF THE BOWL CLEANLY. IF DRY, ADD LUKEWARM WATER, 1 TABLESPOON AT A TIME; IF STICKY, ADD FLOUR, 1 TABLESPOON AT A TIME.

10 TURN DOUGH OUT OF THE BOWL ONTO A LIGHTLY FLOURED WORK SURFACE AND KNEAD FOR 10 MINUTES. TO KNEAD, FIRST STRETCH THE DOUGH AWAY FROM YOU.

11 THEN GATHER THE DOUGH BACK INTO A BALL.

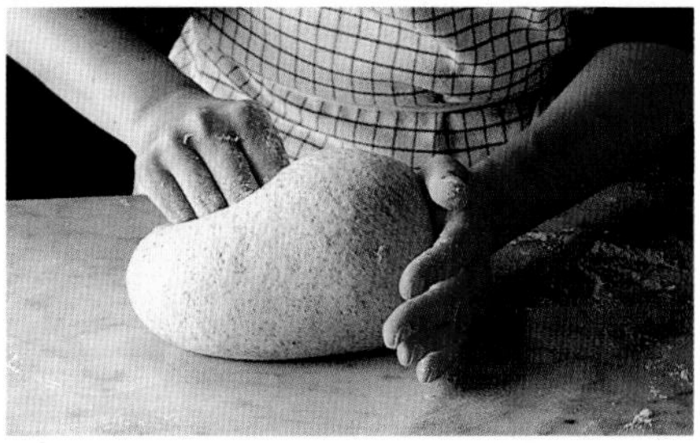

12 GIVE THE DOUGH A QUARTER TURN, THEN CONTINUE REPEATING THESE THREE MOVEMENTS.

13 AS DOUGH IS KNEADED, IT CHANGES TEXTURE TO BECOME VERY SMOOTH AND ELASTIC. IT LOOKS ALMOST GLOSSY. SHAPE THE DOUGH INTO A SMOOTH BALL.

14 WASH, DRY AND OIL THE BOWL. RETURN DOUGH TO BOWL AND TURN IT OVER SO THE TOP IS OILED TO PREVENT STICKING. COVER THE BOWL WITH A DAMP DISH TOWEL.

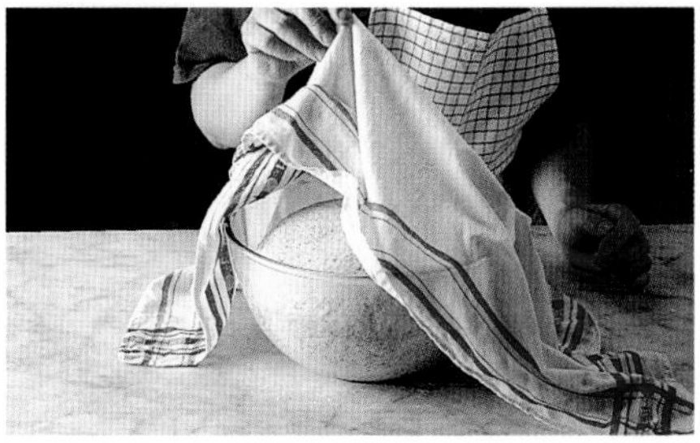

15 LET THE DOUGH RISE, OR PROOF, AT ROOM TEMPERATURE (ABOUT 70°F), AWAY FROM DRAFTS, UNTIL DOUBLED IN SIZE, WHICH USUALLY TAKES 1½ TO 2 HOURS.

16 THE DOUGH IS PROPERLY RISEN WHEN YOU CAN PRESS THE TIP OF YOUR FINGER INTO IT AND THE DOUGH DOES NOT SPRING BACK.

17 PUNCH DOWN THE DOUGH WITH YOUR KNUCKLES. THIS BREAKS UP LARGE CARBON DIOXIDE POCKETS AND REDISTRIBUTES THE GAS SO YOU GET AN EVEN-TEXTURED LOAF.

18 TO MAKE A FREE-FORM LOAF, ON A LIGHTLY FLOURED SURFACE, SHAPE THE DOUGH BY GENTLY KNEADING IT INTO AN OVAL 8 x 4 INCHES.

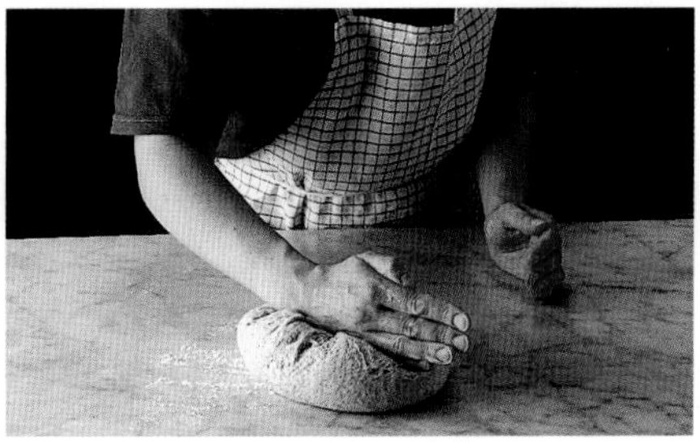

19 WITH THE EDGE OF YOUR HAND, MAKE A DEEP CREASE LENGTHWISE DOWN THE CENTER OF THE DOUGH.

20 ROLL THE SIDES OF THE DOUGH OVER TO MAKE A FAT SAUSAGE-SHAPE. TUCK THE SHORT ENDS UNDER AND PINCH ALL SEAMS TOGETHER TO SEAL THEM.

21 ROLL THE DOUGH OVER ON THE WORK SURFACE SO THE SEAM IS UNDERNEATH AND THE TOP LOOKS SMOOTH AND EVENLY SHAPED. (THE OVAL WILL MEASURE ABOUT 9 x 4 INCHES.)

22 PUT LOAF, SEAM DOWN, ONTO A GREASED BAKING SHEET. MAKE ½-INCH DEEP DIAGONAL SLASHES ON TOP. COVER WITH A DAMP DISH TOWEL; LET RISE UNTIL DOUBLED IN SIZE, 1½ TO 2 HOURS.

Baking Instructions

DURING THE LAST 15 MINUTES OF THE RISING TIME, HEAT THE OVEN TO 425°F. UNCOVER THE LOAF AND SPRINKLE THE TOP WITH ABOUT 1 TABLESPOON OF WHOLE-WHEAT FLOUR. BAKE THE LOAF FOR 15 MINUTES, THEN REDUCE THE OVEN TEMPERATURE TO 375°F AND CONTINUE BAKING FOR ANOTHER 20 TO 30 MINUTES, UNTIL THE LOAF SOUNDS HOLLOW WHEN TAPPED UNDERNEATH (PAGE 15).

Method for Active Dry Yeast

If you are using active dry yeast, it must be reconstituted before it will work. Reconstitute the yeast by sprinkling it over a small bowl containing ¼ cup warm water (105°F to 115°F), or an amount specified in a recipe, and ½ teaspoon granulated sugar.

STIR THE YEAST, SUGAR AND WATER UNTIL THE YEAST IS DISSOLVED.

YOU SHOULD HAVE A LUMP-FREE LIQUID. LEAVE IT TO BECOME FOAMY.

This is how reconstituted active dry yeast looks when it is foamy and ready to use. If your yeast does not look like this after 15 minutes, throw it out and begin with another, fresher envelope of yeast. It is a good idea to check the yeast's expiration date before opening.

After 5 to 10 minutes, the mixture should look very foamy. (If after 15 minutes the yeast is not foamy, it is inactive, either because it is too old or because it has been killed by water that was too hot. Throw the mixture out and start again with another, fresher envelope of yeast.) Dry yeast that is near its expiration date or taken from an open container will be slow to work, if it works at all, and the dough may take longer to rise than the times given in specific recipes. Add the foamy yeast mixture to a well in the flour and make the sponge as described in the fresh yeast method. Continue making the dough from step 8 of the fresh yeast method (see page 16).

Using Rapid-rise Dry Yeast

Rapid-rise active dry yeast can be used in all recipes where ordinary active dry yeast is specified. Simply sprinkle the contents of the envelope of yeast directly into the flour with all the other dry ingredients (omitting the sugar for the yeast). Skip the sponging stage, and mix all the liquid into the flour at once to make the dough.

WHAT WENT WRONG? COMMON PROBLEMS IN BREAD-MAKING

CRUST IS SOFT, PALE, AND SOGGY.
– Not baked long enough, or the oven temperature was too low.
– If a loaf does not sound hollow when tapped underneath, return it to the oven for 5–10 minutes longer. To make the crust crisper, place the loaf directly on the oven rack.

LOAF IS CRUMBLY AND DRY.
– Baked for too long, or the oven temperature was too high.
– Too much flour was used in the dough.

LOAF HAS UNINTENDED, LARGE HOLES.
– Over-kneaded in a food processor or electric mixer.
– If made by hand, the dough was under-kneaded (page 16).
– Risen dough was not punched down thoroughly before shaping (page 17).

CRUST IS DETACHED FROM CRUMB.
– Risen dough was not punched down thoroughly before shaping (page 17).
– Dough was not rolled tight enough while being shaped for a loaf pan (page 24).

DOUGH DIDN'T RISE, OR ROSE POORLY.
– Yeast was used past the expiration date on the envelope (page 18).
– Liquids to be mixed with yeast were too hot and killed the yeast. Liquid must be lukewarm (95°F–105°F), which is often described as blood heat or hand-hot.
– Dough was left to rise in a spot that was too hot. This is a particular danger with dough left to rise in a stainless steel bowl, especially when it is placed in an oven with a pilot light or on a stovetop.

BREAD TASTES YEASTY AND DAMP.
– Too much yeast was used. Take particular care measuring fresh yeast.
– Not baked long enough. If the loaf does not sound hollow when unmolded and tapped underneath, bake for 5–10 minutes longer. You can put it directly on the oven rack.

BREAD IS SOGGY, FLAT, AND DENSE.
– Too much liquid was added when making the dough and there was not enough flour to absorb it.
– Dough was not kneaded long enough, nor thoroughly enough (see this page).

LOAF COLLAPSED IN OVEN.
– Dough was left too long during second rising and it became over-risen. Dough should only double in size, or as specified in the recipe.

FREE-FORM LOAVES (Page 17) AND SHAPED LOAVES (Page 26) SPREAD DURING BAKING.
– Dough was too soft or too warm when it was shaped.

LOAF CRACKED ALONG ONE SIDE OR ROSE UNEVENLY.
– Loaf was subjected to uneven heat. It was placed too far to one side, or too near a hot spot in the oven. Check the oven manufacturer's handbook for correct rack and position.
– If you have an "eccentric" oven, turn loaf regularly while it bakes.
– Too much dough in the loaf pan, or the pan was too small.

TYPES OF FLOUR

Organic corn ready for grinding at Philipsburg Manor (page 69).

Although wheat flour is the most common variety used for making bread, you should familiarize yourself with the wide range of flours ground from other grains – these are the flours that can vary the flavor and add more texture to your loaves.

Whatever flour you buy, I urge you to search out both the stone-ground and unbleached varieties whenever possible. Your breads will have a deeper, fuller flavor.

In the following glossary, I have included other grain products important to bread-making, as well as flour storage tips (see right).

ALL-PURPOSE FLOUR is a blend of high-gluten hard wheat and low-gluten soft wheat, and is suitable for a wide range of baking needs. The flour is milled from the endosperm of the wheat berry, and contains neither the bran nor the germ. U.S. law requires that any flour not containing the germ of the wheat must have certain nutrients added back in, resulting in a flour labeled "enriched."

BARLEY FLOUR, ground from pearl barley (the grain stripped of husks and germ), imparts to breads a moist, cakelike quality with a malty aftertaste. Low in gluten, it needs to be combined with wheat flour. Adding 10 to 15 percent barley flour to sourdough, rye, and plain whole-wheat doughs makes for especially robust loaves.

BARLEY FLAKES can be cooked as a breakfast cereal or added to wheat flour for bread doughs (see Barley flour above).

BRAN is the outer layer or husk of the wheat berry. It is what gives whole-wheat flour its characteristic color. Unprocessed bran, or miller's bran, is often added to bread doughs, as well as muffin or pancake batters for extra fiber.

BULGHUR (some times spelt bulgur) is wheat berries that have been first steamed, then dried and cracked into either coarse, medium, or fine pieces, the latter often used in bread-making.

UNBLEACHED BREAD FLOUR, or bleached, formulated with practically all hard-wheat flour, has a high proportion of protein to starch. As the dough is kneaded, the protein develops into gluten, the firm, elastic structure that allows breads to rise. Available in whole-wheat or white.

BUCKWHEAT flour does not come from a true cereal but rather from a grass belonging to the sorrel family. The speckled gray-brown flour, ground from the buckwheat groat, has a distinct, slightly bitter flavor, and when mixed with wheat flour produces bread with a pungent, earthy flavor, a soft crust, and a moist, fine crumb. Buckwheat flour is also used in blinis, pancakes, and Japanese soba noodles.

CAKE FLOUR is a fine-textured, soft-wheat flour, with little gluten, and is used where a tender, delicate crumb is desired, as in cakes.

CORNMEAL is ground from dried whole kernels of yellow, white, or blue field corn, and can be milled fine or coarse. Stone-ground is preferable. Degerminated cornmeal has been sieved to remove the germ for longer shelf life. When incorporated into doughs, cornmeal creates a loaf with a grainy, somewhat dry crumb, and a slightly sweet flavor.

COARSE YELLOW CORNMEAL is the key ingredient in the well-known Italian polenta.

CORN FLOUR is finely ground cornmeal from the whole corn kernel and can be mixed with wheat flour for bread-making.

CORNSTARCH is ground from the heart or the endosperm of the corn kernel. Silky in texture, it's used as a thickener and in small quantities, to lighten flour for pastry-making.

MASA HARINA is cornmeal finely ground from white corn kernels that have been soaked in lime water before being dried. It is a major ingredient in tortilla making.

VITAL WHEAT (also known as gluten flour) is made from wheat flour and contains pure gluten, ranging from 70 to 100 percent. Gluten gives bread dough its elasticity and

Fresh stone-ground cornmeal.

allows it to rise. Added to a dough, vital wheat gluten gives it additional resiliency.

MILLET FLOUR is ground from whole millet and is rich in protein, vitamins, and minerals but lacking in gluten. It is used for making flat breads and griddle cakes, and when mixed with wheat flour, produces bread with a buttery, slightly sweet taste, a smooth, thin crust, and a moist, dense crumb.

ROLLED OATS, known commonly as oatmeal, are oat groats that have been hulled, steamed, and flattened into flakes. They can be ground into a coarse meal, or can be added as they are to bread doughs for extra fiber and nutrients.

STEEL-CUT OATS, often called Scotch or Irish oatmeal, are made by cutting the groats (hulled whole oat kernels) into pieces with steel rollers. Used for Scottish Griddle Oatcakes (page 72), they may also be added to bread doughs.

OAT FLOUR, finely ground from oat groats, contains no gluten. When mixed with wheat flour for bread-making, it contributes a firm crust, chewy texture, and a sweet, nutty flavor. Not widely available.

RYE FLAKES are cooked, rolled rye berries (the whole grain), similar to rolled oats. A small amount mixed into bread doughs adds a chewy texture and a slightly tangy flavor.

RYE FOUR adds a distinctive tangy, slightly sour flavor to breads, as well as a chewy texture. Since it contains little gluten, it is usually combined with higher protein flours (usually wheat) to increase elasticity and lighten the dough.

SELF-RISING FLOUR is a blend of all-purpose flour, baking powder, and salt, and is often used in the southern U.S. for corn bread and biscuits.

SEMOLINA FLOUR is finely ground from the endosperm of hard durum wheat. It is not the same as semolina meal which is coarsely ground from spring or winter wheat. Semolina flour adds texture and a strong wheat flavor to breads, and is also used for making pasta.

SOY FLOUR is high in protein and fat, contains no gluten, and is fifteen times richer in calcium and iron than wheat. Ground from toasted soybeans, it is used as a nutrition booster in many foods. For bread-making, a small amount mixed with wheat flour adds a mild almond flavor, a spongy crust, and a moist, fine crumb. Soy flour will cause baked goods to brown faster, so baking times or temperatures may need to be adjusted.

SPELT FLOUR is not a modern hybrid wheat, but rather its ancient ancestor. Although it can be substituted for regular wheat flour in any recipe, the usual rule is to use about 25 percent less liquid since the hydration rate of spelt flour is much higher than wheat. Also, the gluten in spelt flour is fragile, so over-mixing or kneading will produce a flat loaf.

STONE-GROUND flours have a higher nutritional value and better taste than those ground by high-speed steel rollers or hammers. The slow-moving stones crush the grain without tearing the germ and without generating heat that destroys vitamins and enzymes. The texture of stone-ground flour can range from coarse to powdery, depending on the amount of sieving the flour receives at the mill.

WHEAT GERM, the seed or embryo of the wheat kernel or berry, is high in nutrients, especially B vitamins. Its high oil content causes rancidity if it is not refrigerated. Available raw or toasted, wheat germ provides a nutrition boost to baked goods.

WHOLE-WHEAT FLOUR makes excellent breads because of its high gluten content and sweet, nutty taste. It includes the fibrous bran and nutritious germ oil from the wheat kernel or berry.

81% WHOLE-WHEAT FLOUR has had 19% of the husk and bran removed from the wheat berry, leaving only a very small amount of the germ and bran in the flour. This flour is not available retail in the U.S., although some specialty mills may be able to grind it to specification. Whole-wheat flour available in this country is labeled simply whole-wheat and includes all of the bran and germ.

CRACKED WHEAT can be fine, medium, or coarse cut, and is made by cracking the dried wheat berry between rollers. It is an excellent addition to bread doughs.

WHEAT FLAKES are cooked, rolled wheat berries, and can be used in the same way as rolled oats.

FLOUR STORAGE

All flours should be kept in airtight containers, or place the bag of flour in a plastic bag. If you remove the flour from its bag, be sure to label and date the container. All-purpose and white bread flour can be stored at 70°F for up to six months. Any flour, wheat, or otherwise that contains part of the germ from the grain will easily turn rancid because of the oil content. Tightly wrap these flours and refrigerate or freeze for up to three months. Let the flour come to room temperature before using.

TOPPINGS

Dough can be rolled in seeds or nuts after the first shaping and before the second rising, or glazed and then sprinkled with a topping just before baking. Some toppings scorch easily, so be ready to lower the oven temperature or cover the bread with foil after 15 to 20 minutes baking if the top is browning too quickly.

Fried sweet doughs (Page 92) are usually sprinkled with or rolled in confectioners' sugar, granulated or superfine sugar, or a ground cinnamon and sugar mixture after draining on paper towels.

1 Cornmeal
2 Wheat flakes
3 Fresh herbs, such as rosemary
4 Sunflower seeds
5 Barley flakes
6 Sea salt
7 Sesame seeds
8 Cracked wheat
9 Flax seeds
10 Oats
11 Caraway seeds
12 Grated cheese
13 Rye flakes
14 Poppy seeds
15 Plain top

GLAZES

Applied to the dough just before or just after baking, a glaze changes the appearance and taste of the crust, as well as its texture. A good, wide pastry brush (one that doesn't shed) is essential, and two thin coats of glaze give a better result than one thick one.

If you glaze the dough before baking, take care that you do not glue the dough to the rim of the loaf pan or to the baking sheet; this will not only give you a problem when you turn out the baked bread, but will hinder the "spring" as the bread tries to expand in the oven. You will get a cracked or strangely shaped result.

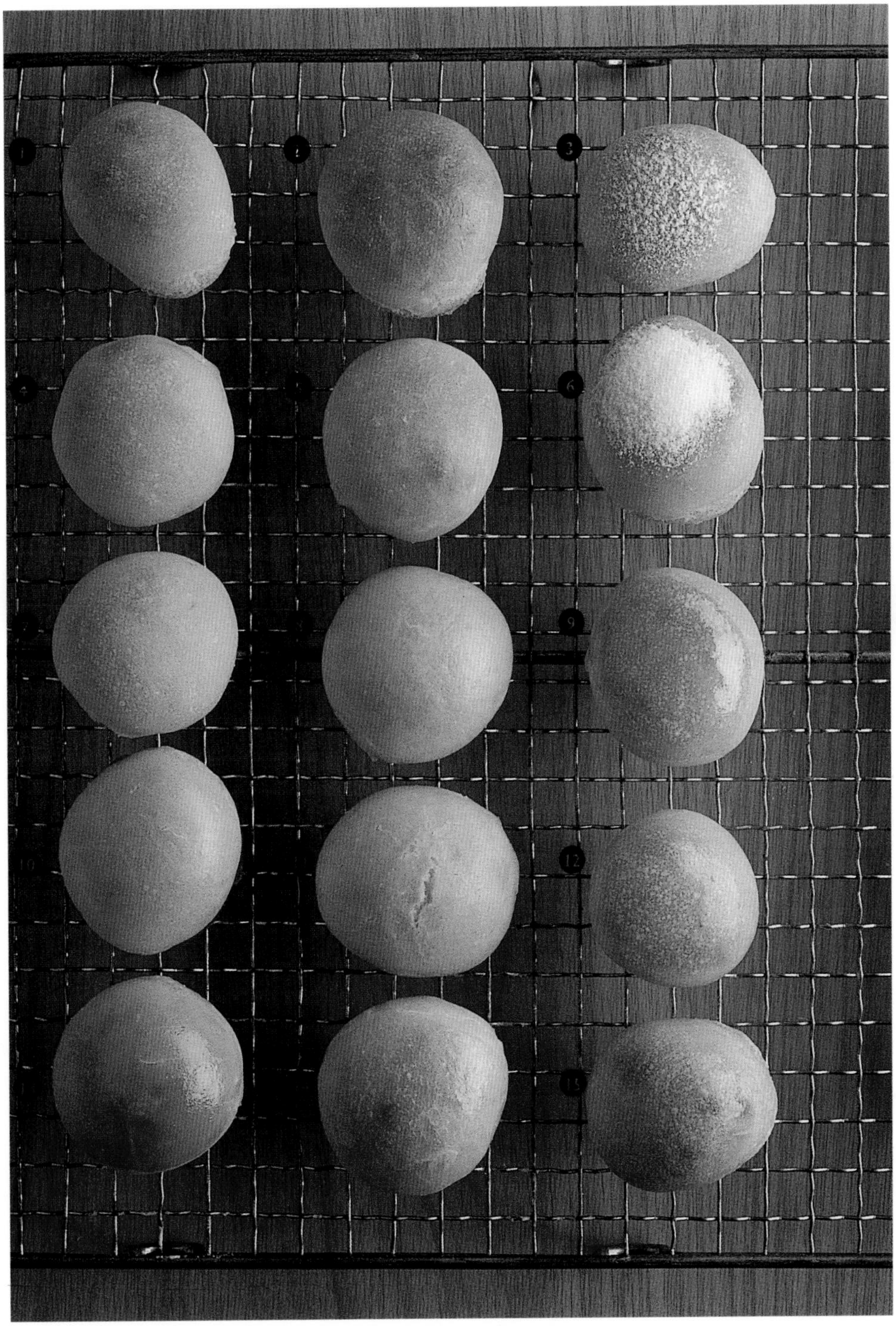

1 Unglazed plain loaf
2 Brushed with 1 egg white beaten with ¼ teaspoon sea salt before baking
3 Dusted with flour before baking
4 Brushed with water before baking
5 Brushed with whole milk before baking
6 Dusted with granulated sugar before baking
7 Brushed with 2 teaspoons sea salt dissolved in 1 cup (230ml) water before baking
8 Brushed with half-and-half before baking
9 Brushed with olive oil after baking
10 Brushed with 1 whole egg beaten with ¼ teaspoon salt before baking
11 Brushed with light or heavy cream before baking
12 Rubbed with a butter wrapper after baking
13 Brushed with 1 egg yolk beaten with a large pinch of sea salt before baking
14 Brushed with olive oil before baking
15 Brushed with a sweet glaze (3 tablespoons granulated sugar dissolved in 3 tablespoons hot milk) after baking

INGREDIENTS

Makes 2 small loaves

6 cups (680g) unbleached white bread flour

2 tablespoons (15g) coarse sea salt, crushed or ground

1 0.6-oz cake fresh yeast (15g), or 1 envelope active dry yeast (2½ teaspoons) plus ½ teaspoon sugar

2 cups (430ml) water from the cold tap

extra flour for dusting

2 loaf pans, about 8½ × 4½ × 2¾ inches, lightly greased

A PLAIN WHITE LOAF

This basic recipe for white bread can be used to make puffy loaves, or formed into some traditional English styles of loaves – for example, a large cottage. Coburg, porcupine, or rumpy loaf – or divided into rolls. (See page 26 for shaping breads.) You can also try the toppings and glazes on pages 22 and 23 to alter the taste and appearance of the baked loaf. This loaf will keep for four days and can be frozen for one month.

Make the dough as for The Basic Loaf (page 16) using 5 cups (570g) of the white flour. If the dough is sticky, work in small amounts of the remaining flour. Knead the dough, place it in a clean, lightly greased bowl, turn the dough over so the top is oiled, then cover it with a damp dish towel and let it rise at room temperature, away from drafts. Because of the cool temperature of the water, the dough will take longer to double in size than does the dough for The Basic Loaf – up to 2½ hours.

Punch down the risen dough and turn it out onto a lightly floured work surface. Cut the dough in half. Gently knead the dough, then pat or, with a floured rolling pin, roll it into a rectangle as wide as the pans are long, about ½ inch thick. Beginning with a short side, tightly roll up the pieces of dough, pinching the edges together as you roll, then pinch the seam closed. Tuck the ends under. Place the dough, seam sides down, in the prepared pans. The pans should be half filled.

Cover the pans with damp dish towels and let the doughs rise at room temperature until doubled in size – about 1 hour. (Do not let the doughs overproof and become enormous, however, or they will collapse during baking.) During the last 15 minutes of rising, heat the oven to 450°F.

Uncover the loaves and sprinkle the tops lightly with flour. Using a very sharp knife or razor blade, either make one deep slash lengthwise down the center of the loaves to form a split, or make two diagonal slashes across the tops.

Bake for 15 minutes. Reduce the oven temperature to 400°F. Bake for another 10 to 15 minutes. To test if a loaf is baked, turn it out of the pan and tap it with your knuckles; a thoroughly baked loaf sounds hollow when tapped underneath. Unmold the bread onto wire racks and cool completely.

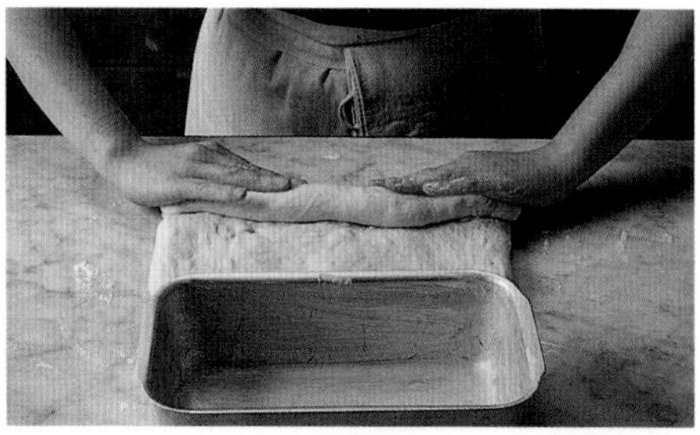

TO SHAPE THE DOUGH TO FIT THE PAN, ROLL IT UP, PINCHING THE EDGES.

PINCH THE SEAM CLOSED AND TUCK THE ENDS UNDER.

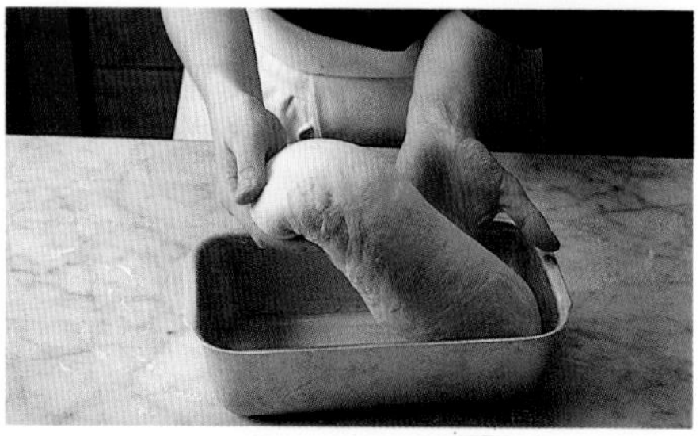

PLACE THE LOAF, SEAM SIDE DOWN, INTO THE PAN. THE PAN SHOULD BE HALF-FULL.

FOR A SPLIT-LOAF SHAPE, MAKE A DEEP SLASH LENGTHWISE DOWN THE CENTER.

OATMEAL ROLLS

INGREDIENTS

Makes 16

- $2\frac{3}{4}$ cups (230g) rolled oats
- $1\frac{3}{4}$ cups (395ml) milk
- 1 cup (115g) whole-wheat bread flour, preferably stone-ground
- 1 cup (115g) unbleached white bread flour
- $3\frac{1}{2}$ teaspoons (10g) coarse sea salt, crushed or ground
- 1 0.6-oz cake fresh yeast (15g), or 1 envelope active dry yeast ($2\frac{1}{2}$ teaspoons) plus $\frac{1}{2}$ teaspoon sugar
- 2 tablespoons lukewarm water
- extra flour for dusting
- beaten egg or half-and-half for glazing
- extra rolled oats for sprinkling

2 baking sheets, lightly greased

Oats add texture and a distinct mealy taste that you either like or loathe. Oat bread is in vogue on both sides of the Atlantic as I write this, due to the possible connection between a diet high in oat bran and lowered blood cholesterol levels. However, many commercial oat breads taste soapy or cakelike. I suggest you use organic oats for the best flavor. In England, I buy either Jordan's or Mornflake oats.

These rolls are good with soup and are excellent toasted. Eat them the day they're baked, or freeze when cooled. The dough can also be shaped into one medium-size loaf and baked free-form. (For shaping, see The Basic Loaf, page 17.) Allow more time for a single loaf to bake.

Soak the oats in the milk in a large, covered bowl for 2 hours. In a second large bowl, mix together the whole-wheat flour, the white flour, and salt. After the oats have soaked, crumble the fresh yeast into a small bowl and mix with the lukewarm water until smooth. If using dry yeast, mix the granules and the sugar with the lukewarm water, and let stand until foamy, 5 to 10 minutes (see page 18).

Stir the yeast mixture into the soaked oats and stir this mixture into the flour. Mix well to make a soft dough. If the dough is slightly crumbly, add more water, 1 tablespoon at a time, until the dough comes together. If the dough is sticky, gradually knead in more flour, 1 tablespoon at a time, until the dough leaves your hands and the sides of the bowl cleanly. The amount of liquid and flour needed in this recipe varies, depending on the kind of oats and the type of flours you use.

Turn out the dough onto a lightly floured work surface and knead for 10 minutes, or until smooth and elastic. Put the dough into an oiled bowl, and turn the dough over so the top is oiled. Cover with a damp dish towel. Let rise at room temperature, away from drafts, until doubled in size, about 1 hour.

Punch down the risen dough. Turn out the dough onto a lightly floured work surface. Weigh the dough and divide it into sixteen equal pieces, or roll it into a fat rope and cut into sixteen even pieces. Shape each piece into a roll by making a rough ball of dough and cupping your hand over the ball so your fingertips and wrist touch the work surface. Gently rotate your hand so the dough is rolled around and smoothed into a neat roll.

Space the rolls well apart on the prepared baking sheets. Cover lightly with damp dish towels and let rise at room temperature until almost doubled in size, 30 to 45 minutes. During the last 15 minutes of rising, heat the oven to 425°F.

Remove the dish towels. Lightly brush the rolls with the chosen glaze. Sprinkle with oats. Bake the rolls for 20 minutes, or until they are browned and sound hollow when tapped underneath. Transfer to a wire rack and cool completely.

THE OATS WILL LOOK VERY SLOPPY AND SOFT AFTER THEY HAVE SOAKED IN THE MILK FOR 2 HOURS.

ROTATE YOUR HAND SO THE DOUGH IS ROLLED AROUND AND SMOOTHED INTO A NEAT ROLL.

TRADITIONAL BRITISH SHAPES

Most of these shapes are typically British and have a long and colorful history. Whenever possible, I'll provide a bit of background material. To make these shapes, use the dough for The Basic Loaf (page 15) or A Plain White Loaf (page 24) and let it rise once, then punch down the dough.

Appealing to the eyes as well as the palate, these homemade breads have been shaped into traditional British-style loaves. The basket includes a Sesame Snail, a Bloomer loaf, two Coburg loaves, and two Porcupine loaves. The round Coburg loaf, baked free-form with a cross cut in the top, was, according to Elizabeth David, originally a four-cornered bread, sometimes called a skull. The porcupine shape is really self-explanatory. The directions for making each shape are explained and illustrated here and on the following two pages.

ROLL OUT THE DOUGH ON A LIGHTLY FLOURED WORK SURFACE WITH A LIGHTLY FLOURED ROLLING PIN TO A RECTANGLE 1 INCH THICK.

STARTING FROM A SHORT END, ROLL UP THE DOUGH LIKE A JELLY ROLL, PINCHING IT TOGETHER AFTER EACH ROLL.

AFTER DUSTING THE LOAF WITH WHITE FLOUR, BRUSH THE SLITS WITH SALT WATER (PAGE 23)

Bloomer

Makes one large loaf

Considerable controversy surrounds the origin of this shape, according to the late food writer Elizabeth David. It may have gotten its name because it was baked without a pan, and was thus allowed to "bloom" unhindered in the oven. Another version tells us that the loaf resembled the pantaloons worn by Mrs. Amelia Bloomer, an American, who brought them to England and made them popular as the practical garb for bicycling. Stories aside, the bloomer is shaped into a long, fat loaf with flat ends and deep crosswise slashes on the top.

Roll out the punched-down dough with a floured rolling pin into a large rectangle, about 1 inch thick. Starting with a short side, tightly roll up the dough like a jelly roll, pinching it together after each roll. Push the ends of the roll of dough toward the center to make a short, thick roll. Pinch the seam to seal and tuck the ends under neatly. These fiddly measures help prevent air pockets from forming in the loaf.

Slide a lightly greased baking sheet under the loaf, cover with a damp dish towel, and let rise at room temperature, away from drafts, until doubled in size, 1 to 1½ hours. During the last 15 minutes of rising, heat the oven to 450°F.

Using a very sharp knife, make six deep slashes across the top of the loaf, being careful not to drag the knife. Dust the loaf with white flour, then brush the slits with salt water (page 23). Bake for 15 minutes. Lower the oven temperature to 400°F and bake for another 25 to 35 minutes, or until the loaf sounds hollow when tapped underneath.

MAKE ONE DEEP CUT THROUGH THE MIDDLE, THEN MAKE TWO SHORT CUTS INTO THE CENTER.

OR, USE KITCHEN SCISSORS TO MAKE FOUR DEEP CUTS AT RIGHT ANGLES.

COBURG

Makes two medium-size loaves

On a lightly floured work surface, quickly knead the punched-down dough for a few seconds. Divide the dough in half. Shape each piece into a neat ball. Place each ball on a greased baking sheet. Cover with a damp dish towel and let rise at room temperature, away from drafts, until doubled in size, 1 to 1½ hours.

During the last 15 minutes of rising, heat the oven to 450°F. Using a very sharp knife, slash a deep cross through the top of each ball of dough, making one deep cut through the middle, then two short ones in the center. (Or, using kitchen scissors, make four cuts at right angles.) Brush with salt water (page 23), then dust with flour. Bake for 25 to 30 minutes, or until the loaves sound hollow when tapped underneath. If the loaves are browning too quickly, lower the oven temperature to 400°F.

Porcupine or Rumpy

Makes two medium-size loaves

Shape the punched-down dough into two balls, as for the Coburg (above). Place on greased baking sheets, cover with damp dish towels, and let rise at room temperature, away from drafts, until doubled in size, about 1 to 1½ hours. During the last 15 minutes of rising, heat the oven to 450°F.

Using a very sharp knife, slash the top of the dough several times to make a checkerboard pattern. You could also snip the dough using kitchen scissors. Brush the dough with a glaze (page 23).

Bake for 25 to 30 minutes, or until the loaves sound hollow when tapped underneath. If the loaves brown too quickly, lower the oven temperature to 400°F.

WITH A SHARP KNIFE, SCORE A CHECKERBOARD PATTERN ON TOP OF THE RISEN LOAF.

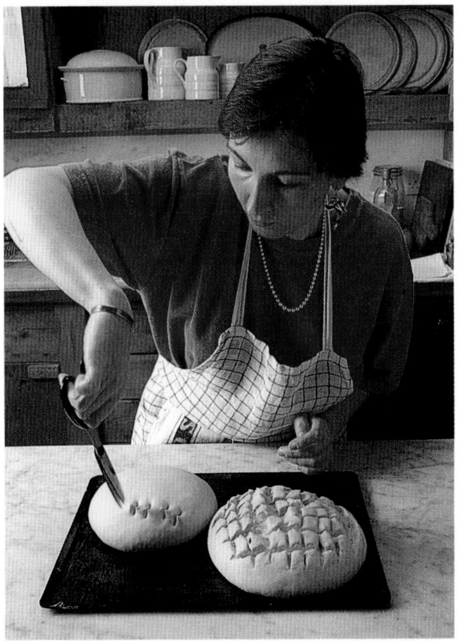

OR, USE KITCHEN SCISSORS TO MAKE NEAT ROWS OF SNIPS.

SESAME SNAIL

Makes one large loaf

Once again, punch down the risen dough – usually white (page 24) for this loaf, but there is no reason why you cannot use any other shade of dough. With your hands, roll the dough on a lightly floured surface into a rope about 3 inches thick and 25 inches long. Coil the dough into a snail shape, twisting the rope as you lift it, and tuck the ends under. Slide a greased baking sheet under the dough, pressing it back into shape if necessary. Cover with a damp dish towel and let rise, away from drafts, until almost doubled in size, about 1 hour. During the last 15 minutes, heat the oven to 450°F.

Brush the dough with water, then sprinkle with 1 to 2 tablespoons black or white sesame seeds, or a mixture of both. Gently prick the loaf around the sides with a fork. Bake for 15 minutes. Reduce the oven temperature to 400°F. Bake another 25 to 30 minutes, or until the loaf sounds hollow when tapped underneath.

In a North African bakery I found a similar loaf flavored with star anise; it was unusual and very good. To make that version, use a spice mill or clean coffee grinder to grind 2 whole star anise and 1 tablespoon black or white sesame seeds to a fine powder. This should give you a total of 2 tablespoons, which you add to the flour along with the salt. Make the white dough as directed (page 15), then let rise and shape as for the Sesame Snail. After brushing with water and sprinkling with sesame seeds, gently prick the loaf around the sides with a fork, then bake as for the Sesame Snail.

USING YOUR HANDS, ROLL OUT THE DOUGH ON A LIGHTLY FLOURED WORK SURFACE TO A ROPE ABOUT 3 INCHES THICK AND 25 INCHES LONG.

Right COIL THE DOUGH INTO A SNAIL SHAPE, TWISTING THE ROPE AS YOU LIFT IT. TUCK THE ENDS UNDER.

COTTAGE LOAF

INGREDIENTS

Makes 1 large loaf

3 cups (340g) unbleached white bread flour

3 cups (340g) whole-wheat bread flour, preferably stone-ground

2 tablespoons (15g) coarse sea salt, crushed or ground

1 0.6-oz cake fresh yeast (15g), or 1 envelope active dry yeast (2½ teaspoons) plus ½ teaspoon sugar

about 1¾ cups (400ml) water from the cold tap

extra flour for dusting

1 egg, beaten, for glazing

a large baking sheet, lightly greased

SECURE THE BALLS OF DOUGH BY PUSHING TWO FINGERS AND A THUMB THROUGH THE MIDDLE.

CAREFULLY BRUSH THE LOAF WITH THE CHOSEN GLAZE.

SCORE ALL AROUND THE BOTTOM BALL OF DOUGH. REPEAT ALL AROUND THE TOP BALL.

This very distinctive bread is always a round loaf with a smaller ball of dough pressed into the center, like a topknot. For the best taste I like to use a dough with at least 50 percent whole-wheat flour, but if you are after a "purer" look, the dough for A Plain White Loaf (page 24) is fine, too.

For the best shape the dough must be quite firm, so be ready to work in a little extra flour if necessary. It is also worth remembering that as the yeast multiplies it produces carbon dioxide and liquid (alcohol), so the dough will become softer after rising. It is best to do the final rising at cool room temperature to preserve the shape.

There are two different methods for assembling this bread. Home bakers tend to fashion the loaf by shaping the dough into two balls, putting the smaller on top, then fixing them together by pushing a finger through the middle of both balls before leaving the loaf to rise. Professional bakers, however, prefer to shape the balls and let them rise separately. They then gently flatten both balls and attach them by pushing two fingers and a thumb joined together through the middle. This technique produces the most reliable shape. Finish the loaf with either an egg glaze or a saltwater glaze (page 23) before baking. This loaf keeps for four days and can be frozen for one month.

Make the dough as for The Basic Loaf (page 16), using the white and whole-wheat flours, salt, yeast, and water. Knead the dough, place in a clean, greased bowl, turn the dough over, then cover it with a damp dish towel and let rise at room temperature, away from drafts, until doubled in size, 1½ to 2 hours.

Punch down the risen dough and turn it out onto a lightly floured work surface. Cut off one-third, then shape both the small and larger pieces of dough into balls. Place the balls well apart on the prepared baking sheet and cover with a damp dish towel. Let rise at room temperature until puffy but not quite doubled in size, usually 30 to 40 minutes. Heat the oven to 450°F.

Gently flatten each ball and put the smaller ball on top of the larger one. Push two fingers and a thumb joined together into the middle of the dough to join the pieces. Let stand for 5 to 10 minutes; if left for much longer, the loaf takes on a "drunken" look.

Brush the loaf with the chosen glaze, then vertically score around the edges of the top and bottom balls with a small sharp knife or razor blade. Bake for 15 minutes. Lower the oven temperature to 400°F. Bake for another 20 to 30 minutes, or until the loaf sounds hollow when tapped underneath. Transfer to a wire rack and cool completely.

RIGHT Freshly baked cottage loaves at Wreford's Bakery (page 177).

BRAIDED LOAF

INGREDIENTS

Makes 1 large loaf

- 6 cups (680g) unbleached white bread flour
- 1 teaspoon sugar
- 1 0.6-oz cake fresh yeast (15g), or 1 envelope active dry yeast (2½ teaspoons) plus ½ teaspoon sugar
- 1¾ cups (430ml) lukewarm milk
- 2 teaspoons salt
- 2 tablespoons (30g) butter
- 1 extra large egg, beaten
- extra flour for dusting
- half-and-half or beaten egg for glazing
- 2 tablespoons poppy seeds

a large baking sheet, lightly greased

Although you can use a basic all-white dough (page 24) or a dough made with a combination of whole-wheat and white flours (page 15), this slightly richer white dough, made with milk and an egg and sprinkled with poppy seeds, is the one that made my mother's Irish cook Annie famous before the Second World War.

To keep a good, even shape, the dough should not be too soft, and do not be tempted to put the dough to rise in a warm spot. This loaf will stay fresh for two to three days at room temperature, and it can be frozen for one month.

Mix together 1½ cups (170g) of the flour and the sugar in a large bowl. Make a well in the center of the flour and crumble in the fresh yeast. Pour the lukewarm milk over the yeast and mix until combined. If using dry yeast, mix the granules and the additional ½ teaspoon sugar with the milk in a separate bowl and let stand until frothy, 5 to 10 minutes (see page 18). Then pour the yeast mixture into the well in the flour.

Using your hands, work the flour in the bowl into the milk and yeast mixture to make a smooth batter (page 16). Cover with plastic wrap and let stand at room temperature for about 30 minutes until spongy.

Mix most of the remaining flour with the salt in another large bowl. Rub in the butter with your fingertips until the mixture looks like coarse crumbs. Stir the egg into the yeast sponge, then add the sponge to the flour mixture. Mix to form a fairly firm, rather than a soft or sticky, dough, adding as much of the remaining flour as is necessary, about 1 tablespoon at a time.

Turn out the dough onto a lightly floured work surface and punch down with your knuckles. Knead for 10 minutes, until the dough is quite firm, silky-smooth, and elastic. Put the dough into the washed and lightly greased bowl and turn the dough over so the top is oiled. Cover with a damp dish towel and let stand at room temperature, away from drafts, until doubled in size, 1 to 1½ hours.

Punch down the risen dough and turn it out onto the lightly floured work surface. The dough should be quite pliable, but not soft. It should hold its shape well – if not, work

AFTER ABOUT 30 MINUTES THE BATTER WILL BE SPONGY (FOREGROUND). THEN MIX MOST OF THE REMAINING FLOUR WITH THE SALT IN A LARGE BOWL. RUB IN THE BUTTER WITH YOUR FINGERTIPS.

WHEN THE BUTTER IS RUBBED IN THE FLOUR MIXTURE WILL LOOK LIKE COARSE CRUMBS.

AFTER THE DOUGH HAS RISEN, TURN IT OUT OF THE BOWL AND PUNCH IT DOWN.

DIVIDE THE DOUGH INTO THREE EQUAL PIECES. ROLL EACH PIECE OF DOUGH INTO A LONG ROPE.

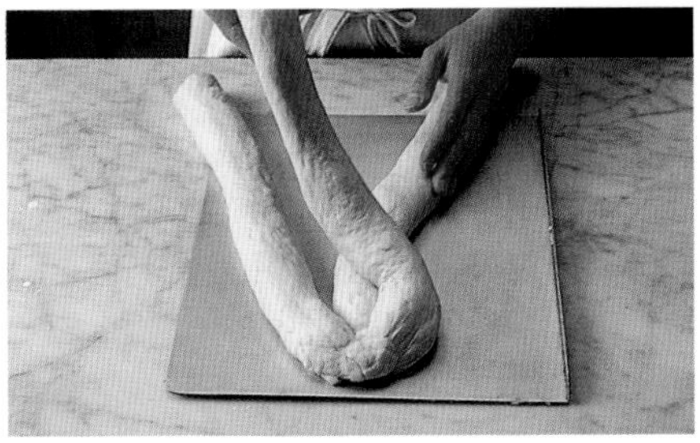

TO BRAID THE DOUGH, ARRANGE THE ROPES SIDE BY SIDE AND SLIGHTLY APART ON THE BAKING SHEET. PINCH THE ENDS TOGETHER FIRMLY. LIFT THE LEFT STRAND OVER THE CENTER STRAND.

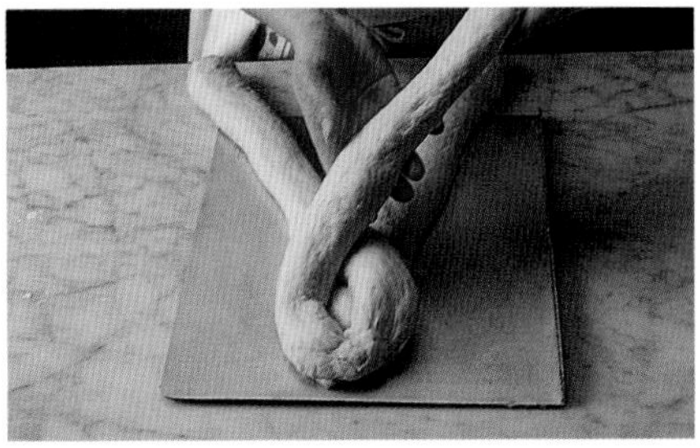

LIFT THE RIGHT STRAND OVER THE NEW CENTER STRAND.

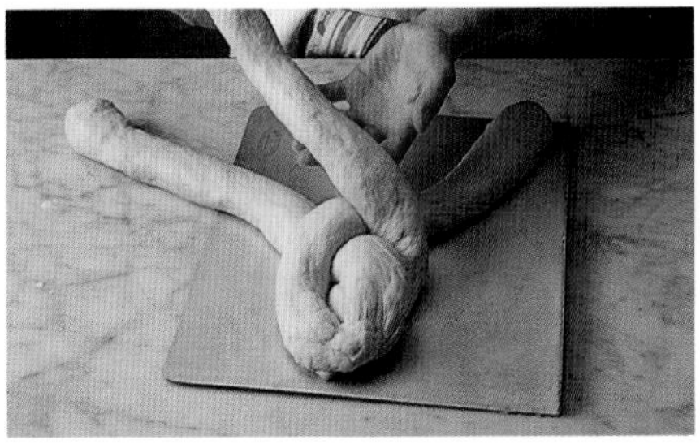

THEN LIFT THE NEW LEFT STRAND OVER THE NEW CENTER STRAND. REPEAT THIS PROCESS UNTIL ALL THE STRANDS ARE BRAIDED.

PINCH THE ENDS TOGETHER TO SEAL THEM. TUCK UNDER BOTH ENDS FOR A NEAT FINISH.

CAREFULLY BRUSH THE RISEN LOAF WITH LIGHT OR HEAVY CREAM, HALF-AND-HALF, OR BEATEN EGG TO GLAZE IT.

in a little more flour. Weigh the dough and divide it into three equal pieces, or roll it into a fat rope and cut into thirds.

Using your hands, roll each piece into a rope 16 inches long. Lay the three ropes on the prepared baking sheet, then braid the strands together neatly, but not too tightly. Take care not to stretch the dough unduly. Tuck the ends under and pinch to seal.

Cover with a damp dish towel and let stand at room temperature until almost doubled in size, about 1 hour. It is important not to overproof this loaf. During the last 15 minutes of rising, heat the oven to 450°F.

Carefully brush the loaf with the chosen glaze, then sprinkle with the poppy seeds. Bake for 15 to 20 minutes or until golden. Reduce the oven temperature to 400°F. Bake for another 20 minutes, or until the loaf sounds hollow when tapped on the bottom. Transfer to a wire rack and cool completely.

BAGUETTES

INGREDIENTS

Makes 3 loaves
5 cups (570g) unbleached white bread flour, preferably stone-ground
1 cup (110g) cake flour
2 tablespoons (15g) coarse sea salt, crushed or ground
1¾ cups (430ml) water from the cold tap
1 0.6-oz cake fresh yeast (15g)
extra flour for dusting
2 teaspoons salt dissolved in 1 cup (230ml) water for glazing

a large linen dish towel, floured
a large baking sheet, lightly greased

The traditional French stick loaf – with a shiny crust so crisp it breaks into razor-sharp shards and a fine-tasting, chewy interior with irregular holes – is rapidly disappearing. It is becoming difficult to find even in France, let alone anywhere else. It is also difficult to reproduce at home. In fact, you should probably not attempt this recipe unless you are an experienced bread maker. The best flour for baguettes is French and imported in bulk for bakeries and restaurants, rather than for home bakers. The oven temperature is crucial, too – domestic ovens are rarely hot enough – and, for a crusty crust, jets of steam are also vital. The best homemade loaves are made with a blend of stone-ground unbleached white bread flour and cake flour, and the oven is misted with water during baking.

Chef Pierre Koffmann, from the Michelin three-starred La Tante Claire restaurant in London, taught me how to achieve the correct temperature for the ingredients. He says the room temperature, the flour temperature (usually the same as the room temperature), and the water temperature must all total the number 190. This means if the kitchen is 72°F (a usual kitchen temperature), and the flour the same, the water must be chilled to 46°F. On a warm day it is best to use ice water. Pierre also showed me how to make the dough using what French bakers call the Polish method. The yeast and water mixture is made into a thin batter with an equal quantity of flour. It is then left to rise before continuing with the dough.

You can buy metal baguette pans, but good bakers regard them with contempt: "Avoid the loaf with that pattern of little dots underneath." Large dish towels are cheaper to use and work better for shaping the loaves. It is best to eat these loaves on the day they are made, and they do not freeze well.

Combine 4 cups (455g) bread flour, the cake flour, and the salt in a large bowl. Calculate the room and flour temperatures (see above) and chill the 1¾ cups of water so all the numbers add up to 190. Crumble the fresh yeast into a small bowl. Add 2 tablespoons of the chilled water, stir until smooth, then stir in the remaining water. Put 3 cups of the flour and salt mixture in another large bowl. Make a well in the center of the flour mixture and add the yeast mixture. Gradually work the flour into the liquid, using your hand, to make a sloppy batter (page 16).

Cover with a damp dish towel, or put the bowl into a large plastic bag and tie closed. Let stand for 4 to 5 hours at room temperature, away from drafts. The batter will become frothy, rise up in the bowl, then collapse back down.

Work in the rest of the flour mixture, plus as much of the remaining bread flour (about ¼ cup at a time) as is necessary to form a very soft dough. Turn out the dough onto a lightly floured work surface and knead for 10 minutes, or until the dough becomes firmer and springy, adding more bread flour if needed.

Wash, dry, and oil the bowl. Place the dough in the bowl and turn the dough over so the top is oiled. Cover with a damp dish towel and let rise at cool room temperature until doubled in size, 1½ to 2 hours.

Punch down the dough. Weigh the dough and divide it into three equal pieces, or roll

A sliced baguette, with its soft, irregular crumb, and a country-style loaf ready for the start of a simple meal. Even though the baguette has lost some of its flavor, it still appears on most tables every day in France.

RIGHT pedal power has transported a baguette fresh from the local baker's.

USE YOUR HAND TO MIX THE YEAST MIXTURE AND FLOUR TO MAKE A SLOPPY BATTER.

WHEN LEFT TO RISE, THE BATTER WILL BECOME FROTHY AND RISE UP IN THE BOWL.

AFTER 3 TO 5 HOURS RISING, THE BATTER WILL COLLAPSE BACK DOWN.

WORK IN THE REMAINING FLOUR MIXTURE PLUS THE REMAINING BREAD FLOUR TO FORM A SOFT DOUGH.

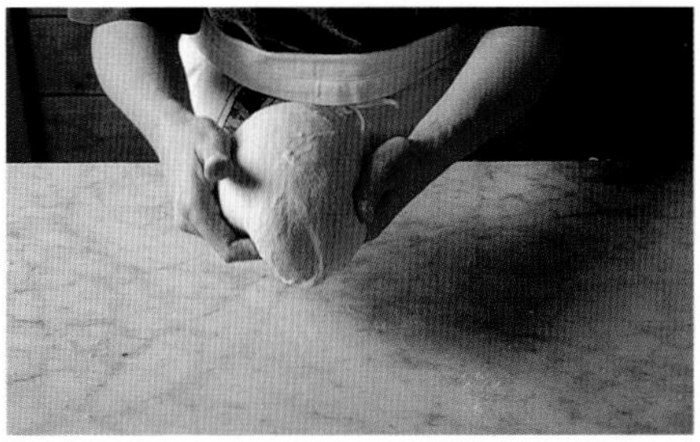

KNEAD THE DOUGH ON A LIGHTLY FLOURED WORK SURFACE FOR 10 MINUTES UNTIL IT BECOMES FIRMER AND SPRINGY.

ROLL OUT EACH PIECE OF DOUGH ON A LIGHTLY FLOURED WORK SURFACE INTO A CYLINDER, ABOUT 12 × 3 INCHES.

ARRANGE THE SHAPED LOAVES BETWEEN THE FOLDS OF THE FLOURED DISH TOWEL.

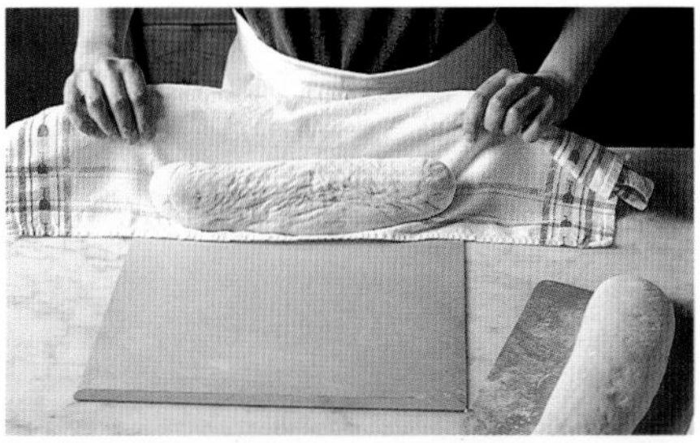

USE THE DISH TOWEL TO HELP ROLL LOAVES ONTO THE LIGHTLY GREASED BAKING SHEET.

USING A SHARP KNIFE, QUICKLY SLASH THE TOP OF EACH LOAF SEVERAL TIMES.

it into a fat rope and cut it into thirds. Roll each piece into a cylinder, about 12 x 3 inches. Fold the floured dish towel lengthwise to make three accordion-like creases or pleats. Arrange the pieces of dough between the folds so the loaves will keep their traditional baguette shape while they rise. Cover with a damp dish towel and let rise at cool room temperature until doubled in size, about 1 hour.

During the last 15 minutes of rising, place the baking sheet on an oven rack in the lowest position and heat the oven to 450°F.

Remove the damp dish towel and roll or lift the loaves onto the prepared baking sheet without crowding. It is best to bake the last loaf after the first two come out of the oven. Using a sharp knife or razor blade, quickly slash the top of each loaf several times, then brush with the salt water glaze.

Put the loaves in the oven, then spray the oven sides and bottom with water. Bake the loaves for 20 minutes, brushing them with salt water and spraying the oven sides and bottom with water after 10 minutes. At the end of 20 minutes, spray the oven again with water and reduce the oven temperature to 400°F.

Bake for another 5 to 10 minutes, until the loaves are crisp and they sound hollow when tapped underneath. Cool the loaves on a wire rack. Increase the oven temperature to 450°F, and bake the third loaf as described.

NOTE: You can use 1 envelope rapid-rise active dry yeast (2½ teaspoons), but I do not recommend using ordinary active dry yeast. Add the rapid-rise yeast to the 3 cups of flour followed by all the chilled water.

BRIDGE ROLLS

INGREDIENTS

Makes 36

6 cups (680g) unbleached white bread flour

4 teaspoons sugar

2 tablespoons (15g) coarse sea salt, crushed or ground

4 tablespoons (60g) unsalted butter, chilled and diced

1 0.6-oz cake fresh yeast (15g), or 1 envelope active dry yeast (2½ teaspoons) plus ½ teaspoon sugar

1¾ cups (400ml) lukewarm milk

1 large egg, beaten

extra flour for dusting

extra milk for brushing

2 large baking sheets, lightly greased

These are the small, soft-crusted rolls with a sweetish, light crumb that I remember from children's parties. They are an ideal sandwich roll filled and packed for picnics and lunch boxes. Eat within twenty-four hours of baking or freeze for up to one month.

On a vacation in Maine, I made the rolls a little larger than in this recipe and filled them with the local lobster meat mixed with mayonnaise for "Maine lobster rolls" – sheer heaven!

Put 5 cups (570g) flour, the sugar, and salt in a large bowl. Using your fingertips, rub the butter into the flour until the mixture looks like fine crumbs. Make a well in the center of the flour.

Crumble the fresh yeast into a small bowl. Add 4 tablespoons milk and mix until smooth. If using dry yeast, mix the granules and the additional ½ teaspoon sugar with the milk and let stand until foamy, 5 to 10 minutes (see page 18).

Add the yeast mixture to the well in the flour, then mix in the remaining milk and the beaten egg. Work in the flour that is in the bowl to make a soft, but not sticky dough, adding as much of the remaining flour as is necessary, about ¼ cup at a time.

Turn out the dough onto a well-floured work surface and knead for 10 minutes, or until smooth and elastic. Return the dough to the washed and greased bowl, and turn the dough over so the top is oiled. Cover the bowl with a damp dish towel and let rise at room temperature, away from drafts, until doubled in size, about 2 hours. (It is the milk and slow rising time that gives the rolls a fine, light crumb.)

Punch down the risen dough, roll it into a fat rope, and divide it into thirty-six equal

USING YOUR FINGERTIPS, RUB THE BUTTER INTO THE FLOUR UNTIL THE MIXTURE LOOKS LIKE FINE CRUMBS.

WORK IN THE FLOUR IN THE BOWL TO MAKE A SOFT, BUT NOT STICKY DOUGH, ADDING AS MUCH OF THE REMAINING FLOUR AS NECESSARY.

SHAPE EACH PIECE OF DOUGH INTO AN OVAL BY FIRST ROLLING IT INTO A CYLINDER.

SQUEEZE EACH PIECE WITH THE EDGES OF YOUR HANDS TO MAKE THE ENDS SLIGHTLY POINTED. ARRANGE APART ON THE LIGHTLY GREASED BAKING SHEETS.

LIGHTLY BRUSH THE RISEN ROLLS WITH THE MILK. IT IS BETTER TO BRUSH THE ROLLS LIGHTLY TWICE THAN ONCE HEAVILY.

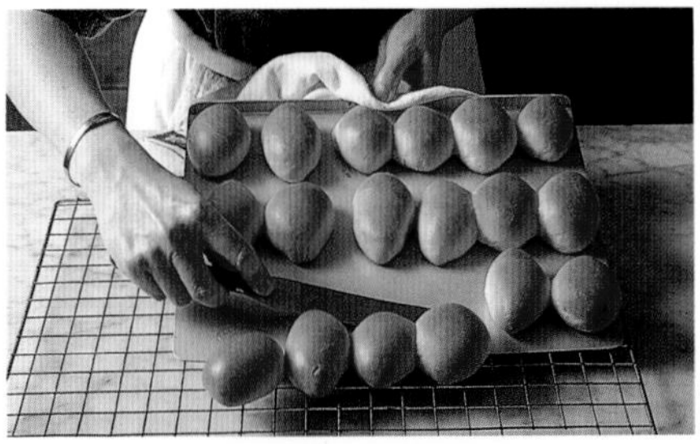

TRANSFER THE BAKED ROLLS TO WIRE RACKS. COVER WITH DRY DISH TOWELS SO THE CRUSTS REMAIN SOFT. LET THE ROLLS COOL COMPLETELY.

pieces. Shape each piece into an oval by first rolling it on the work surface into a cylinder, then roll the dough on the work surface with both of your hands to make pointed ends. Place the rolls slightly apart on the prepared baking sheets. Cover with damp dish towels and let the rolls rise at room temperature until doubled in size, 30 to 45 minutes. During the last 15 minutes of rising, heat the oven to 450°F.

Lightly brush the rolls with milk. Bake for 5 minutes. Lower the oven temperature to 400°F. Bake for another 5 to 10 minutes, or until the rolls are browned and sound hollow when tapped underneath.

Transfer the rolls to a wire rack. Cover with dry dish towels to keep the crusts soft and let cool completely.

For my wedding reception, I served guests small bridge rolls with a selection of fillings. I think you will find these rolls delicious with any filling you use.

BAPS

INGREDIENTS

Makes 12

6 cups (680g) unbleached white bread flour

2 tablespoons (15g) coarse sea salt, crushed or ground

¼ cup (60g) lard, diced

1 0.6-oz cake fresh yeast (15g), or 1 envelope active dry yeast (2½ teaspoons)

1 teaspoon sugar

1¾ cups (430ml) mixed lukewarm milk and water

extra flour for dusting

extra milk for glazing

2 baking sheets, lightly greased

Traditional Scottish scenes.

RIGHT Flour-topped baps and shiny softies ready for a traditional Scottish breakfast.

Breakfast and afternoon tea are the best meals of the day in Scotland. Breakfast is my idea of a superb feast, with oatmeal porridge, Loch Fyne kippers, good tea, homemade marmalade, plus floury, white, soft-crusted oval baps, warm from the oven, and Aberdeen Butteries (page 202).

When I worked in Scotland, I enjoyed the baps from Leiths in Ballater, Aberdeenshire, and they are still my favorite. The shape, size, and crumb of baps vary from baker to baker in Scotland, but the basic mixture and the techniques are the same. They use equal quantities of milk and water to give a fine, soft crumb, dust the baps with flour, then cover them with a cloth after baking to produce a soft top, rather than a tough or crisp crust. Many bakers add a little lard to the dough, too, to add extra flavor and improve the texture.

For hill walkers and stalkers, baps are wonderful, filled with grilled strips of bacon and a fried egg, then wrapped in plastic wrap or foil, ready for a fresh-air breakfast. Baps should be eaten warm when they are baked, but can be frozen for one month.

Mix 5 cups (570g) of the flour and the salt in a large bowl. Using your fingertips, rub the lard into the flour until the mixture looks like fine crumbs. Make a well in the center of the flour.

Crumble the fresh yeast into a small bowl. Stir in the sugar and 2 tablespoons of the lukewarm milk and water mixture until smooth. If using dry yeast, mix the granules and the sugar with 2 tablespoons of the liquid and let stand until foamy, 5 to 10 minutes (see page 18).

Add the yeast mixture and remaining milk and water to the well and mix in the flour in the bowl to make a very soft dough, adding as much of the remaining flour as is necessary, about ¼ cup at a time. If necessary, add a little more water, but the dough should not stick to your fingers or the sides of the bowl.

Turn out the dough onto a lightly floured work surface and knead for 10 minutes or until it looks and feels smooth and silky, adding a little more flour if necessary to prevent sticking. Put the dough back in the washed and lightly greased bowl, and turn the dough so the top is oiled. Cover with a damp dish towel and let rise, away from drafts, until doubled in size, about 1 hour in a warm kitchen, or 1½ hours at room temperature, or overnight in a cold pantry or the refrigerator.

PAT EACH PIECE OF DOUGH INTO AN OVAL ABOUT $4\frac{1}{2} \times 3$ INCHES. PLACE EACH BAP ON THE BAKING SHEET AS IT IS SHAPED.

SIFT A FINE LAYER OF FLOUR OVER THE BAPS. THEN LET THEM RISE UNTIL DOUBLED IN SIZE, ABOUT 30 MINUTES.

JUST BEFORE BAKING, SIFT A SECOND LAYER OF FLOUR OVER THE BAPS, THEN PRESS YOUR THUMB INTO THE CENTER OF EACH.

ABOVE RIGHT A hearty stalker's breakfast of freshly baked bap filled with a fried egg and bacon.

Punch down the risen dough. Turn out the dough onto a lightly floured work surface and knead it for a few seconds.

Weigh the dough and divide it into twelve equal pieces, or roll it into a fat rope and cut it into twelve even pieces. With floured fingers, pat each piece of dough into an oval, about $4\frac{1}{2} \times 3$ inches. Place well apart on the prepared baking sheets. Lightly brush the baps with milk, then sift a fine layer of flour over them. Let rise at room temperature until doubled in size, about 30 minutes, taking care not to let the baps over-proof. While the baps are rising, heat the oven to 425°F.

Sift another fine layer of flour over the baps, then press your thumb into the center of each. This technique makes the surface flattish, rather than domed. Bake immediately for 15 minutes, until golden and cooked underneath. Transfer to wire racks, cover with dry dish towels, and let cool for a few minutes before eating.

VARIATION: SOFTIES OR MORNING ROLLS

Use the same dough as for baps to make the soft rolls known as softies or morning rolls. Shape into smooth rolls by rolling each ball on the work surface under your cupped hand. Then cover and let rise as directed above. Before baking, brush with a little light or heavy cream. Bake in a 425°F oven for 20 minutes, or until golden brown. Brush again with cream after removing from the oven. Transfer to wire racks, cover with dry dish towels, and leave to cool. Serve warm or leave to cool completely.

LIGHTLY BRUSH THE RISEN SOFTIES WITH CREAM JUST BEFORE BAKING.

AS SOON AS THE SOFTIES COME OUT OF THE OVEN, BRUSH AGAIN WITH CREAM.

CORNISH OR DEVONSHIRE SPLITS

INGREDIENTS

Makes 22
- 6 cups (680g) unbleached white bread flour
- 2 tablespoons (15g) coarse sea salt, crushed or ground
- 1 0.6-oz cake fresh yeast (15g), or 1 envelope active dry yeast (2½ teaspoons)
- 1 teaspoon granulated sugar
- 1¾ cups (430ml) lukewarm milk
- ½ cup (110g) unsalted butter, diced
- extra flour for dusting
- confectioners' sugar for dusting
- a large baking sheet, floured

Joe Roskilly drives the family's herd of Jersey and Guernsey cows to the milking parlor.

In England, these buns, with their soft, sweet crust and light, moist crumb, are eaten warm, split open and spread with clotted cream and treacle, raspberry jam, or golden syrup. The cream and treacle combination, favored by Rachel Roskilly, who makes the best clotted cream I have ever tasted from her Jersey/Guernsey herd at St. Kevern, on The Lizard in Cornwall, is called "thunder and lightning." Clotted cream isn't readily available in the U.S., nor is treacle, but you could make an approximation of this wonderful combination by blending crème fraîche with dark molasses to taste.

Serve splits after they have cooled to warm. Eat within one day or freeze for up to one month.

Mix together the flour and salt in a large bowl. If it is a chilly day, gently warm the flour (page 15). Crumble the fresh yeast into a medium-size bowl. Mix with the sugar and 2 tablespoons of the milk until smooth. If using dry yeast, mix the granules and the sugar with 2 tablespoons of the milk and let stand until foamy, 5 to 10 minutes (see page 18).

Stir the rest of the milk into the yeast mixture, followed by 1½ cups (170g) of the flour, until smooth. Cover with plastic wrap and let stand at room temperature until frothy, about 30 minutes.

Using your fingertips, rub the diced butter into the remaining flour until the mixture looks like fine crumbs. Mix in the frothy yeast sponge to make a soft, but not too sticky, dough. If the dough is dry and crumbly, add a little more milk or water, 1 tablespoon at a time, until the dough comes together. If the dough sticks to your fingers, work in extra flour, 1 tablespoon at a time.

MIX THE BUTTER AND FLOUR MIXTURE WITH THE FROTHY YEAST SPONGE UNTIL THE DOUGH IS SOFT BUT NOT STICKY. IF THE DOUGH STICKS TO YOUR FINGERS, WORK IN ABOUT 1 TABLESPOON FLOUR.

CUP YOUR HANDS OVER A BALL OF DOUGH SO YOUR FINGERTIPS AND WRIST TOUCH THE WORK SURFACE. ROTATE YOUR HAND, SHAPING THE DOUGH INTO A SMOOTH ROLL.

ARRANGE THE ROLLS ON THE FLOURED BAKING SHEET SO THEY ALMOST TOUCH EACH OTHER.

AS SOON AS THE ROLLS COME OUT OF THE OVEN, SIFT CONFECTIONERS' SUGAR OVER THEM. TRANSFER TO WIRE RACKS AND COVER WITH DRY DISH TOWELS. COOL TO WARM.

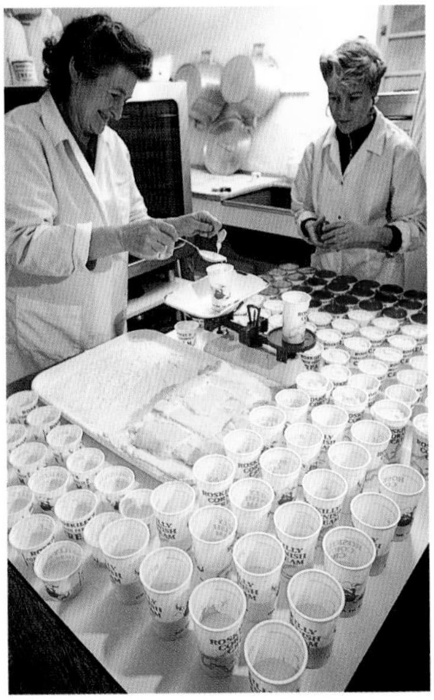

Rachel Roskilly (left) and an assistant fill pots with rich, thick clotted cream from her family dairy. Rachel's clotted cream is an essential ingredient in local cream teas.

RIGHT *A mouth-watering Cornish split filled with Rachel's clotted cream and homemade strawberry jam is a Cornish specialty. Neighboring Devonians also claim this rich treat as their own, calling it a Devonshire split.*

Turn out the dough onto a lightly floured work surface and knead for 10 minutes until smooth and elastic. Put the dough into an oiled bowl, and turn the dough over so the top is oiled. Cover with a damp dish towel. Let rise at room temperature, away from drafts, until doubled in size, 1 to 1½ hours.

Punch down the risen dough with your knuckles. Turn out the dough onto a floured surface and knead for about 10 seconds only. Weigh the dough and divide it into twenty-two equal pieces, or roll it into a fat rope and cut it into twenty-two even pieces. Shape each piece into a smooth roll by rolling it on the work surface under your cupped hand. Arrange the rolls on the prepared baking sheets so they almost touch each other. Cover lightly with damp dish towels and let rise at room temperature until almost doubled in size, about 45 minutes. During the last 15 minutes of rising, heat the oven to 425°F. Bake the splits for 15 to 20 minutes, or until golden. Remove the sheets from the oven and immediately sift confectioners' sugar over the splits. Transfer to wire racks and cover with dry dish towels to keep the crusts soft until cooled to lukewarm, then serve.

SPELT BREAD

INGREDIENTS

Makes 2 large loaves
- 13 cups (1.5kg) spelt flour
- 2 0.6-oz cakes fresh yeast (30g), or 2 envelopes active dry yeast (5 teaspoons) plus 1 teaspoon sugar
- 5 cups (1.2 liters) lukewarm water
- 2½ tablespoons (20g) coarse sea salt, crushed or ground
- 2 tablespoons sunflower or light olive oil
- 2 tablespoons sunflower seeds for sprinkling (optional)

2 loaf pans, about 10 x 5 x 3 inches, lightly greased

The flour made from spelt, an ancient wheat grain (page 21), has a distinct, nutty flavor quite different from the wheat flour with which we are familiar. Clare Marriage (left), who has experimented with sacks upon sacks of different flours in more than twenty years of bread making at Doves Farm, is emphatic in her claim that spelt flour "makes the tastiest bread I've ever eaten." It certainly makes a loaf with a nuttier, wheatier taste than most. The flour seems to benefit from the very wet dough of the Grant method (page 44); the flavor develops, and the open texture with plenty of air pockets is very appealing. It also means fewer crumbs when the loaf is sliced.

This recipe is adapted from Clare's Doves Farm Spelt Bread recipe. It tastes best the day after baking and keeps for up to five days. It can also be frozen for one month.

Put the flour into a large bowl and make a well in the center. Crumble the fresh yeast into a medium-size bowl. Pour half the water into the yeast and stir until smooth. If using dry yeast, mix the granules and the sugar with half the water and let stand until foamy, 5 to 10 minutes (see page 18).

Dissolve the salt in the remaining water, then stir in the oil. Pour the yeast mixture into the well in the flour and roughly mix the flour from the bowl into the yeast mixture, using your hand. Add the remaining liquid and mix vigorously with your hand for 5 minutes. Although the dough starts out soft and sticky, it will become smooth and elastic as you work it and will leave the sides of the bowl cleanly. (If not, mix in a little additional flour.) Divide the dough between the two prepared pans. They should be half full. Smooth each top with a damp pastry brush or with moistened fingers, gently easing the dough into the corners. Sprinkle with the sesame seeds, if desired.

Cover each pan with a damp dish towel and let rise at warm room temperature, away from drafts, for 35 to 45 minutes, until the dough rises to just below the top of the pans. During the last 15 minutes of rising, heat the oven to 400°F.

Bake for 45 to 50 minutes, until the loaves sound hollow when unmolded and tapped underneath. The loaves will have flattish tops. Turn them out onto wire racks to cool.

NOTE: This bread can also be baked in four greased 8½ × 4½ × 2¾-inch loaf pans. Baking time will be 30 to 35 minutes.

Michael and Clare Marriage of Doves Farm, near Hungerford in Oxfordshire, England, with the organically grown grains they use for their stone-ground flours.

MIX THE DOUGH FOR 5 MINUTES. IT WILL BECOME SMOOTH AND ELASTIC.

WHOLE-WHEAT LOAF

INGREDIENTS

Makes 1 large loaf
6 cups (680g) whole-wheat bread flour, preferably stone-ground
2 tablespoons (15g) coarse sea salt, crushed or ground
1 0.6-oz cake fresh yeast (15g), or 1 envelope active dry yeast (2½ teaspoons) plus ½ teaspoon sugar
1¾ cups (430ml) lukewarm water
2 teaspoons olive oil, vegetable oil, or melted butter
extra flour for dusting
a baking sheet, lightly greased

Stone-ground whole-wheat flour makes a very good bread – slightly dense, with plenty of flavor and a chewy crust. You know when you have eaten a slice that you will not feel hungry for a while. This bread is ideal for always-starving teenagers, as it really does fill them up – and healthfully!

This is not, however, a bread for an absolute beginner to try, since whole-wheat flour is difficult to work and knead. But once you get used to the heavy texture, it is not at all scary. If you are new to bread making and want to try a whole-wheat loaf, I suggest you bake The Grant Loaf (page 44) first for a very easy whole-wheat bread. Another alternative is to use The Basic Loaf recipe (page 15) and gradually increase the quantity of stone-ground whole-wheat bread flour each time you make the recipe, simultaneously decreasing the amount of white bread flour, until you are using only whole-wheat flour.

The oil or melted butter makes the loaf less crumbly, and also helps it keep longer. As with many breads in this chapter, this loaf improves on keeping and tastes best the day after it is baked. It can also be frozen for one month.

THIS DOUGH WILL BE HEAVY, SLIPPERY-WET AND DIFFICULT TO WORK WHEN IT IS FIRST TURNED OUT FOR KNEADING.

SHAPE THE DOUGH INTO A SMOOTH BALL. PLACE ON THE LIGHTLY GREASED BAKING SHEET AND LET RISE A SECOND TIME AT ROOM TEMPERATURE UNTIL DOUBLED IN SIZE, 1½ TO 2 HOURS.

Prepare the dough as for The Basic Loaf (page 16), using the flour, salt, fresh yeast, and water, and adding the oil or melted butter with the last of the water. If using dry yeast, mix the granules and the sugar with 4 tablespoons of the water and let stand until foamy, 5 to 10 minutes (see page 18). Pour the yeast mixture into the well in the flour.

The dough will seem heavy and slippery-wet at first, but do not be tempted to add more flour at this stage. As you knead the dough and the water is absorbed by the flour, it will gradually become less sticky, although kneading will be hard work at first.

Knead for 10 minutes, until the dough becomes softer and very elastic and pliable, but not sticky or crumbly. If the dough is crumbly, add 1 tablespoon of water at a time, until the dough comes together. If the dough is very sticky after the 10 minutes, knead in additional flour, 1 tablespoon at a time, thoroughly working in each addition before adding more.

Put the dough into a lightly greased bowl and turn the dough over so the top is oiled. Cover with a damp dish towel and let rise at room temperature, away from drafts, until doubled in size, 1½ to 2 hours.

Punch down the dough. Turn out the dough onto a floured work surface and knead for 1 minute, then shape the dough into a ball. Put the ball of dough on the prepared baking sheet and cover with a damp dish towel. Let rise at room temperature until doubled in size, about 1 hour. During the last 15 minutes of rising, heat the oven to 425°F.

Uncover the loaf and snip the top with scissors or slash it with a sharp knife or razor blade to make a cross. Bake the loaf for 15 minutes, until lightly browned. Reduce the oven temperature to 350°F. Bake for another 20 to 25 minutes, until the loaf sounds hollow when tapped underneath. If the loaf sounds dense or heavy, bake it for another 5 minutes, then test again. Transfer the bread to a wire rack to cool completely.

The water-powered Letheringsett Mill supplied local Norfolk communities with freshly ground flour from 1802 until 1944 when it was abandoned and left to deteriorate. It remained unused until 1982 when a conservation trust undertook the repairs and restoration.

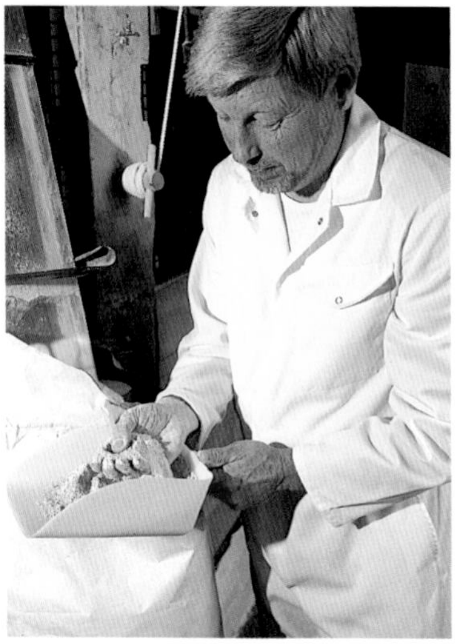

After leaving the Royal Navy, miller Mike Thurlow (above) moved to the mill in 1987 as the tenant-miller and completed the restoration to bring the mill back to working order. The educational demonstrations he gave then for local schoolchildren proved to be a learning experience for him as well because he knew nothing about milling when he first walked into the mill. Today, several London chefs have regular orders for his stone-ground whole-wheat flours.

Local farmers supply many of the grains Mike uses to grind his malted grain and several grades of whole-wheat flours.

MY FAVORITE LOAF

INGREDIENTS

Makes 1 large loaf

- 1⅓ cups thick wheat flakes
- 2 cups (230g) whole-wheat bread flour, preferably stone-ground
- 2 cups (230g) unbleached white bread flour
- 2 tablespoons (15g) coarse sea salt, crushed or ground
- 1 0.6-oz cake fresh yeast (15g), or 1 envelope active dry yeast (2½ teaspoons) plus ½ teaspoon sugar
- 1¾ cups (430ml) lukewarm water
- 1–2 teaspoons olive oil or melted butter
- extra flour for dusting

a loaf pan, about 10 × 5 × 3 inches, lightly greased

This is the loaf I come back to time and time again. However much I enjoy making and eating plenty of different styles and types of bread, I find everyone really appreciates the flavor and texture of this loaf. In England, I like to make this bread with a combination of three flours from Letheringsett Mill (left), which miller Mike Thurlow grinds to my specifications. However, the coarse-ground whole-wheat flour he grinds for me is difficult to come by in the States, so I've substituted wheat flakes ground to a medium-coarse meal in a food processor.

Like most whole-wheat breads, this one matures and tastes best one or two days after baking. Store wrapped at room temperature or freeze for up to one month.

Put the wheat flakes and 1 tablespoon of the whole-wheat flour in a food processor. Process 30 to 60 seconds until the flakes are ground to a medium-coarse meal. Put the meal into a large bowl and stir in the remaining whole-wheat flour, the white flour, and the salt. Make a well in the center of the flour mixture.

Crumble the fresh yeast into a small bowl. Add 4 tablespoons of the lukewarm water and stir until smooth. If using dry yeast, mix the granules with the lukewarm water and sugar and let stand until foamy, 5 to 10 minutes (page 18).

Pour the yeast mixture into the well in the flour. Stir the remaining lukewarm water and the oil or butter into the yeast mixture and draw a little of the flour mixture into the well and mix thoroughly. Gradually mix in enough of the flour that is in the bowl to make a smooth, thick batter. Cover the bowl with a damp dish towel and let stand about 20 minutes to form a frothy sponge.

Mix in the remaining flour that is in the bowl, adding as much additional whole-wheat flour as is necessary, about 1 tablespoon at a time, to form a fairly wet dough. Work the dough until it leaves the sides of the bowl cleanly. Then turn it out onto a lightly floured work surface and, with floured hands, knead the dough for 10 minutes. The dough will gradually become firmer and smoother as the water is absorbed by the wheat-flake meal, so don't be tempted to add more flour than is absolutely necessary.

Place the dough in the washed and lightly greased bowl and turn the dough over. Cover and let rise at room temperature until doubled in size, about 2 hours.

Turn out the dough onto a lightly floured work surface and punch it down. Shape it into a loaf to fit the prepared pan (see A Plain White Loaf, page 24). Cover it with a damp dish towel or plastic wrap and let rise until doubled in size, about 1½ hours. During the last 15 minutes of rising, heat the oven to 450°F.

Bake the loaf for 15 minutes. Reduce the oven temperature to 400°F. Bake for another 30 to 35 minutes, or until the loaf sounds hollow when unmolded and tapped underneath. Unmold the loaf onto a wire rack to cool completely.

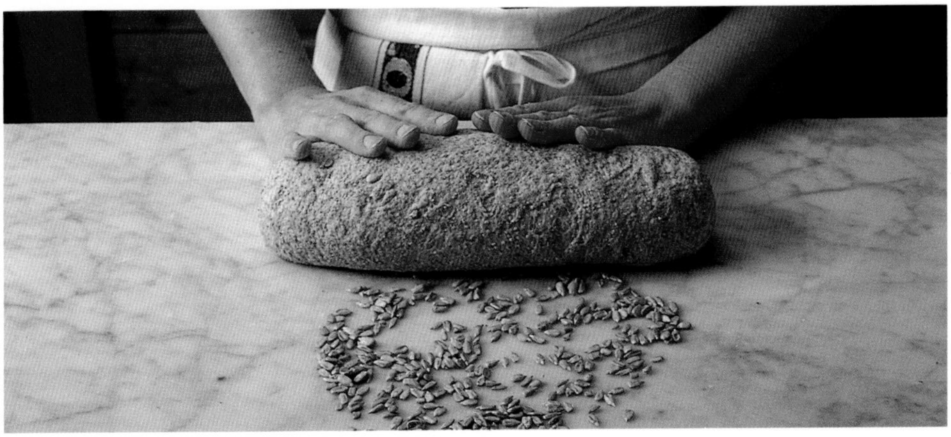

FOR EXTRA FLAVOR AND TEXTURE, ADD 2 TABLESPOONS SHELLED SUNFLOWER SEEDS TO THE FLOURS AND SALT. ROLL THE DOUGH IN EXTRA SHELLED SUNFLOWER SEEDS AFTER IT IS SHAPED.

THE GRANT LOAF

INGREDIENTS

Makes 1 large loaf

6 cups (680g) organic whole-wheat bread flour, preferably and stone-ground

1 teaspoon coarse sea salt, crushed or ground

2½ cups (570ml) lukewarm water

1 0.6-oz cake fresh yeast (15g) (see Notes)

1 teaspoon packed brown sugar or honey

a loaf pan, about 10 × 5 × 3 inches, lightly greased and warmed (see Notes)

In 1944, Doris Grant published a simple recipe for a delicious, wholesome bread in her book, Your Daily Bread (Faber & Faber). Ever since, generations of bakers influenced by her have enjoyed making and eating homemade bread. This recipe is the answer to those who claim that bread-making is too difficult or too time-consuming. The dough requires no kneading and has just one short rising period, in the pan. The majority of the bakers I have talked to say they caught the bread-making bug from trying the Grant recipe.

Once again the secret is to start with a good quality stone-ground whole-wheat flour, and to make sure the dough is elastic and slippery when you finish mixing it. The texture of this bread is moist and light, even though it appears quite dense, and the bread keeps well (the taste improves, too). I have halved Mrs. Grant's original quantities and increased the rising time from 20 minutes, as my loaves seem to need 30 to 35 minutes.

Mix 5 cups (570g) of the flour and the salt in a large bowl. In very cold weather, warm the bowl of flour in a 250°F oven for 5 to 8 minutes, or microwave on high for 1 to 1½ minutes. Make a well in the center of the flour.

Put 3 tablespoons of the lukewarm water in a small bowl, crumble in the fresh yeast, and mix until smooth. Stir in the sugar or honey. Let stand for 10 to 15 minutes, until the mixture is thick and frothy.

Pour the yeast mixture and the remaining lukewarm water into the well in the flour. Mix vigorously with your hand for 1 to 2 minutes, working in the flour from the sides to the center, until the dough feels elastic and comes cleanly away from the sides of the bowl. Add as much of the remaining flour as is necessary, about ¼ cup at a time. Doris Grant described the correct texture as "slippery."

Put the dough into the prepared pan and cover with a damp dish towel. Let stand in a warm place for 20 to 35 minutes, until the dough rises to within ½ inch of the top of the pan. While the dough is rising, heat the oven to 400°F.

Bake for 35 to 40 minutes, until the loaf sounds hollow when unmolded and gently tapped underneath. Transfer the bread to a wire rack to cool completely.

NOTES: You can also make this loaf using 1 envelope rapid-rise dry yeast (2½ teaspoons), but I have never been happy with the result when I have used ordinary active dry yeast. For the method, see page 18.

This bread can also be baked in two 8½ × 4½ × 2¾-inch loaf pans. The baking time will be 30 to 35 minutes.

MIX THE *WET DOUGH VIGOROUSLY* IN THE BOWL FOR 1 TO 2 MINUTES, *WORKING* IN THE FLOUR FROM THE SIDES TO THE CENTER. CONTINUE MIXING UNTIL THE DOUGH FEELS ELASTIC AND COMES CLEANLY *AWAY* FROM THE SIDES OF THE BOWL.

Award-winning baker Viola Unruh and her husband, Henry, outside their farmhouse.

VIOLA'S LIGHT WHOLE-WHEAT BREAD

INGREDIENTS

Makes 4 small loaves
3½ cups (800ml) water
2 0.6-oz cakes fresh yeast (30g), or 2 envelopes active dry yeast (5 teaspoons)
5 tablespoons (60g) sugar
5 tablespoons (70g) vegetable shortening or softened butter
2½ tablespoons (20g) coarse sea salt, crushed or ground
2¾ cups (310g) whole-wheat bread flour
about 8 cups (900g) unbleached white bread flour
3 tablespoons vital wheat gluten
1 large egg, beaten
extra flour for dusting

4 loaf pans, about 8½ × 4½ × 2½ inches, greased

"Just the kind of bread you like to eat," said one of the judges as Viola Unruh beat two hundred other home bakers to win the 1990 Kansas Festival of Breads Contest, sponsored by the Kansas Wheat Commission.

"My recipe was so simple I never thought I would win against some of the fancier breads," said Viola as she rapidly made yet another batch of four loaves. She swears by vital wheat gluten and Hudson Cream Flour (page 48) to produce a light, fine loaf that looks great. Viola started making bread when she married Henry 45 years ago. The quantity of bread, as well as the quality, is important when you live on a remote corn farm with 3,200 head of cattle in Montezuma, Kansas – and you have to feed your sons and farm workers, who can demolish a batch of bread in just one meal.

This recipe uses the sponging technique, which Viola prefers for all her breads. "You get a better loaf," she says, adding that if you mix and knead bread dough by hand, rather than with a dough hook on a machine, "the texture is much finer."

I have made this bread without the vital wheat gluten, and the recipe still works well. Gluten is found at health-food stores or may be purchased by mail order (see List of Suppliers, page 360). Viola keeps her whole-wheat flour in the freezer to prevent it from becoming rancid in the Kansas heat. This loaf keeps for two days, or it can be frozen for one month.

Warm ½ cup (115ml) of the water to lukewarm. Crumble the fresh yeast into the lukewarm water in a small bowl and stir until smooth. If using dry yeast, mix the granules and the lukewarm water in a small bowl, stir in a teaspoon of the sugar, and let stand until foamy, 5 to 10 minutes (see page 18).

Heat the rest of the water to about 150°F and pour it over the shortening or butter, sugar, and salt in a large bowl. Stir until melted and slightly cooled.

Stir in the whole-wheat flour, followed by about half of the white flour and the vital wheat gluten. Mix thoroughly together. (Viola uses a slotted spoon.) Add the yeast mixture and stir well. Beat in the egg. Beat this sloppy batter for 3 minutes, then cover with plastic wrap and let stand until it becomes spongy, about 10 minutes.

Uncover the sponge and gradually work in some of the remaining white flour, a handful at a time, until the dough is firm enough to turn out onto a lightly floured work surface. Then knead in enough of the remaining flour, very little at a time, until the dough is no longer sticky. Knead the dough for 10 minutes, until it is firm and pliable enough to flop from hand to hand. The exact amount of flour will depend on the flour itself and the temperature in the kitchen. Put the dough back into the bowl (there is no need to oil the bowl). Cover with plastic wrap or a damp dish towel and let rise until doubled in size, about 1 hour in a warm Kansas kitchen. Turn out the risen dough onto a lightly floured work surface. Punch it down and lightly knead, working the dough from hand to hand for 2 to 3 minutes.

Divide the dough into four equal pieces. Shape each piece into a rough ball, then place in the prepared pans. Cover with damp dish towels or plastic wrap and let rest for 10 minutes, which makes the dough easier to shape. Flour the work surface. Remove the dough, one piece at a time, and roll out with a lightly floured rolling pin into a rectangle measuring about 11 x 9 inches, and about ½ inch thick. Starting with a short side, roll up tightly like a jelly roll, then pinch the seam to seal tightly. Return to the loaf pan, seam side down, and tuck the ends under, pinching to seal. Repeat with the remaining dough. Cover the loaves again and let rise until doubled in size, about 45 minutes. During the last 15 minutes of rising, heat the oven to 400°F. Bake the loaves for 10 minutes, then lower the over temperature to 350°F. Bake the loaves for about 25 minutes longer, or until they sound hollow when unmolded and tapped underneath. Turn out the loaves from the pans onto wire racks. Rub the crusts with a butter wrapper and let cool completely.

Viola recommends serving her delicious bread with homemade apricot jam.

LIKE ALL GOOD BAKERS, VIOLA ASSEMBLES AND MEASURES ALL HER INGREDIENTS BEFORE SHE STARTS MIXING. HERE SHE BEATS THE EGG IN A MUG.

SHE POURS HOT WATER OVER VEGETABLE SHORTENING, SUGAR, AND SALT, STIRRING TO MELT THE SHORTENING AND DISSOLVE THE SUGAR.

SHE ADDS THE EGG TO A MIXTURE OF SHORTENING, WATER, SUGAR, YEAST, AND FLOUR. SHE BEATS IT WITH A SLOTTED SPOON TO MAKE A SLOPPY BATTER.

THE BATTER IS COVERED WITH PLASTIC WRAP AND LEFT FOR ABOUT 10 MINUTES UNTIL IT BECOMES SPONGY.

VIOLA THEN USES HER SLOTTED SPOON TO BEAT IN ENOUGH OF THE REMAINING WHITE FLOUR TO MAKE A FIRM DOUGH.

SHE TURNS OUT THE DOUGH ONTO A LIGHTLY FLOURED WORK SURFACE AND KNEADS IT FOR 10 MINUTES, ADDING ADDITIONAL FLOUR, UNTIL THE DOUGH IS NO LONGER STICKY.

AFTER KNEADING, THE DOUGH BECOMES FIRM AND PLIABLE. THE DOUGH IS RETURNED TO THE BOWL, COVERED WITH PLASTIC WRAP, AND LEFT TO RISE.

AFTER THE DOUGH HAS DOUBLED IN SIZE, VIOLA REMOVES THE PLASTIC WRAP, TURNS OUT THE DOUGH AND WORKS IT FROM HAND TO HAND FOR 2 TO 3 MINUTES.

USING A KNIFE, VIOLA CUTS THE DOUGH INTO QUARTERS.

EACH PORTION OF DOUGH IS THEN SHAPED INTO A ROUGH OVAL, PLACED IN THE GREASED PANS AND LEFT TO REST, COVERED, FOR 10 MINUTES.

WORKING WITH ONE PORTION OF DOUGH AT A TIME, VIOLA ROLLS IT OUT TO A RECTANGLE MEASURING ABOUT 11 × 9 INCHES, AND ABOUT ½ INCH THICK.

SHE THEN ROLLS UP THE DOUGH LIKE A JELLY ROLL AND PUTS IT IN THE PAN FOR A SECOND RISING. AFTER THE DOUGH DOUBLES IN SIZE, IT IS PUT IN THE OVEN TO BAKE FOR ABOUT 35 MINUTES, OR UNTIL IT SOUNDS HOLLOW WHEN TAPPED UNDERNEATH.

HUDSON CREAM WHOLE-WHEAT BREAD

INGREDIENTS

Makes 2 large loaves
- 2 0.6-oz cakes fresh yeast (30g), or 2 envelopes active dry yeast (5 teaspoons)
- 1 cup (230ml) lukewarm water
- 1 cup (230ml) lukewarm milk
- ⅓ cup (110g) whipped or spun honey
- 9–10 cups (1–1.1kg) white-wheat or whole-wheat bread flour, preferably stone-ground
- 2 large eggs, beaten
- 2 tablespoons (15g) coarse sea salt, crushed or ground
- extra flour for dusting
- 4 tablespoons (60g) butter, lard or vegetable shortening, diced

2 loaf pans, about 10 × 5 × 3 inches, lightly greased

Talking to finalists and prize winners of bread-making competitions in the States, I discovered that many swore by Hudson Cream Flour (see List of Suppliers, page 360). One cook in West Virginia who used it for her prize-winning biscuits said, "I want to pass down to my children good morals, good values, and Hudson Cream Flour."

The printed cambric flour bags sold at the mill and by mail order (the flour comes in paper sacks) are sought after for making aprons like the one Viola Unruh is wearing on page 45. Stafford County Flour Mill in Kansas, where this flour is milled, can be seen three miles away from the road, the silos rising from the farmland like a huge block of apartments. Founded in 1905 by a German immigrant, the mill stayed in the same family until 1986; the current president, Al Brensing, has worked there for more than 55 years. The dairy image (the company logo is a Jersey cow) and "cream" brand name refer not to the color of the flour, available bleached or unbleached, but to the very smooth texture, due to the hard red winter wheat from which it is milled. Their organic unbleached flour and white wheat flours (a new type of whole-wheat flour) are slowly finding a market. Look in grocery stores in Pennsylvania, Indiana, Ohio, Kentucky, Tennessee, and West Virginia, as well as in Kansas.

This recipe, using Hudson Cream whole-wheat flour, has won many prizes. A loaf of this bread disappeared very quickly when I took it to a luncheon with friends. It is a moist loaf that keeps well and improves with age. It can be frozen for up to one month.

Crumble the fresh yeast into a large bowl. Add the lukewarm water and stir until dissolved. Stir in the milk and honey. Using your hand or a wooden spoon, beat in 4½ cups (500g) of the flour and the eggs. The original recipe says to beat for one hundred strokes, which takes 2 to 3 minutes. Cover with a damp dish towel and let rest at room temperature until spongy, 20 to 30 minutes. If using dry yeast, mix the granules with half the lukewarm water and half the honey, and let stand until foamy, 5 to 10 minutes (page 18). Add the remaining water and honey, plus the milk, and continue to make a sponge.

Uncover the sponge and mix in the salt, followed by the remaining flour, about ½ cup at a time, until the dough is no longer sticky. The exact amount will depend on the flour you use. Turn out the dough onto a lightly floured work surface and knead for 10 minutes, gradually working in the butter and additional flour, if necessary. When the dough looks and feels smooth and pliable, return it to the washed and lightly greased bowl, and turn the dough over so the top is oiled. Cover with a damp dish towel and let rise at room temperature, away from drafts, until doubled in size, 1 to 1½ hours.

Punch down the risen dough and divide in half. Cover with a damp dish towel and let rest for 10 minutes. Shape the portions into loaves to fit the prepared pans (see A Plain White Loaf, page 24). Cover the pans with damp dish towels and let the dough rise at room temperature until doubled in size, about 1 hour. During the last 15 minutes of rising, heat the oven to 375°F.

Bake the loaves for 10 minutes. Reduce the oven temperature to 350°F. Bake for another 20 to 30 minutes, or until the loaves sound hollow when unmolded and tapped underneath. Turn out the loaves from the pans and transfer to wire racks and cool.

NOTE: Whipped or spun honey is solid and nearly white in color. It is found at most health-food stores.

USING YOUR HAND, BEAT HALF THE FLOUR AND THE EGGS INTO THE YEAST MIXTURE.

CONTINUE ADDING FLOUR UNTIL THE DOUGH IS NO LONGER STICKY.

MALTED WHEAT LOAF

INGREDIENTS

Makes 1 large loaf
5–6 cups (570–680g) whole-wheat bread flour, preferably stone-ground
¾ cup (85g) malted wheat flakes
2 tablespoons (15g) coarse sea salt, crushed or ground
1 0.6-oz cake fresh yeast (15g), or 1 envelope active dry yeast (2½ teaspoons) plus ½ teaspoon sugar
1¾ cups (400ml) lukewarm water
1 tablespoon olive oil, vegetable oil or melted butter
extra flour for dusting

a loaf pan, about 10 × 5 × 3 inches, lightly greased

A combination of whole-wheat flour and malted wheat flakes makes a well-textured loaf with a naturally sweet taste. If you prefer, you could use old-fashioned graham flour instead, or replace one-third of the whole-wheat flour with unbleached white bread flour. Another variation is to shape the dough into a Cottage Loaf (page 29), and to glaze it with beaten egg and sprinkle it with cracked wheat before baking.

This bread makes very good toast, which my family enjoys for breakfast. The loaf will keep for four days and can be frozen for one month.

Make the dough as for The Basic Loaf (page 16), using 5 cups (570g) of the flour, the wheat flakes, salt, yeast, and water, and adding the oil or melted butter with the last of the water. If using dry yeast, mix the granules and the sugar with 2 tablespoons of the water and let stand until foamy, 5 to 10 minutes (see page 18), then pour the yeast mixture into the well in the flour. If the dough is sticky, work in small amounts of the remaining flour. Knead the dough, then place it in a clean, lightly greased bowl. Turn the dough over so the top is oiled, then cover it with a damp dish towel and let it rise at room temperature, away from drafts, until doubled in size, 1¼–1½ hours.

Punch down the risen dough, then turn it out onto a lightly floured work surface. Shape into a loaf to fit the prepared pan (page 24). If you like, make a split loaf shape by cutting a deep slash lengthwise in the top of the loaf using a sharp knife. Cover the pan with a damp dish towel and let the dough rise at room temperature until doubled in size, about 1 hour. During the last 15 minutes of rising, heat the oven to 450°F.

Bake for 15 minutes. Reduce the oven temperature to 400°F and bake for a further 25 to 30 minutes, or until the loaf sounds hollow when unmolded and tapped underneath. Turn out the loaf from the pan and transfer to a wire rack to cool.

It is not surprising that cultures around the world start the day with bread for breakfast. Both whole-wheat and white breads made with enriched flour are an excellent source of niacin, riboflavin, and thiamin, vital vitamins necessary for good health. Breads also contain starch, minerals, and varying amounts of roughage. Serve bread fresh or toasted for breakfast.

GERMAN THREE-GRAIN BREAD

INGREDIENTS

Makes 2 small loaves

Makes 2 small loaves

3 tablespoons (30g) steel-cut oats
4 cups (455g) unbleached white bread flour
1⅔ cups (170g) rye flour
3 tablespoons (30g) flax seed
2 tablespoons (15g) coarse sea salt, crushed or ground
1¼ cups (280ml) lukewarm water
⅔ cup (140ml) lukewarm milk
1 0.6-oz cake fresh yeast (15g), or 1 envelope active dry yeast (2½ teaspoons) plus ½ teaspoon sugar
extra flour for dusting
extra milk for glazing
extra flax seed for sprinkling

a large baking sheet, lightly greased

This is a flavorful loaf made from wheat and rye flours with oats and flax seed, which are available by mail order at health-food stores. They are popular in German baking. This loaf is superb with cured meats, hard cheeses, or smoked fish, and pickles. It tastes best after it has matured for a day and it can be frozen for one month.

Grind the oats in a food processor to the texture of bulgur wheat. In a large, warmed bowl, stir together 3½ cups (400g) white flour, the rye flour, oats, flax seed, and salt. Mix together the water and milk. Put 4 tablespoons of this mixture into a small bowl. Crumble in the fresh yeast and mix until smooth. Add 2 tablespoons of the dry ingredients and stir to make a thick paste. Let stand until frothy and spongy-looking, about 10 minutes. (This won't rise as much as other sponges.) If using dry yeast, mix the granules and the sugar with 4 tablespoons lukewarm liquid and let stand until foamy, 5 to 10 minutes (see page 18).

Make a well in the dry ingredients and add the yeast mixture and the remaining liquid. Mix to form a firm dough, adding as much of the remaining white flour as is necessary, about 1 tablespoon at a time.

Turn out the dough onto a lightly floured work surface and knead thoroughly for 10 minutes, or until smooth and elastic. Put the dough into a lightly oiled bowl and turn the dough over so the top is oiled. Cover with a damp dish towel. Let rise at room temperature, away from drafts, until doubled in size, 2 to 3 hours.

Punch down the risen dough. Shape into 2 small ovals (page 17). Arrange the loaves on the prepared baking sheet. Cover with a damp dish towel and let rise at room temperature until doubled in size, about 1 hour. During the last 15 minutes of rising, heat the oven to 425°F.

Using a sharp knife or a razor blade, make a slash lengthwise down the center of each loaf. Brush with milk to glaze, then sprinkle with the additional flax seed. Bake for 30 to 40 minutes, or until the bread sounds hollow when tapped on the underside. Transfer to a wire rack or two racks to cool completely. Wrap tightly in aluminium foil and let rest at room temperature for one day so the flavors mature.

SPRINKLE FLAX SEED OVER THE SLASHED LOAVES JUST BEFORE BAKING.

Traditionally dressed Bavarians take a break from their shopping in a Munich market. Breads made with rye flour and flax seed are eaten with full-flavored cured meats and smoked fish.

There are few days when Kansas home economist Cindy Falk does not bake a loaf of bread for her family. Multi-grain Harvest Bread and Pioneer Bread (page 52) are two of her flavor-packed loaves. Both have the nutritional bonus of being high in protein. Cindy teaches bread-making in local schools, and her children are following in her footsteps. Here her daughter helps her measure water before starting a fresh batch of dough.

MULTI-GRAIN HARVEST BREAD

INGREDIENTS

Makes 4 small loaves
- 1½ cups (340ml) water
- 4 tablespoons (60g) butter
- 2 tablespoons packed dark brown sugar
- 2 tablespoons molasses
- ¼ cup (40g) cracked wheat
- ¾ cup (85g) whole-wheat bread flour, preferably stone-ground
- 2 tablespoons (20g) nonfat dry milk powder
- ⅓ cup (40g) soy flour
- ¼ cup (30g) yellow cornmeal
- ¼ cup (20g) rolled oats
- 6 tablespoons (40g) rye flour
- 6 tablespoons (40g) barley flour or amaranth flour
- ⅓ cup (40g) oat flour (see introduction)
- 2 tablespoons (15g) coarse sea salt, crushed or ground
- 1 0.6-oz cake fresh yeast (15g), or 1 envelope active dry yeast (2½ teaspoons) plus ½ teaspoon granulated sugar
- 3½–4½ cups (395–500g) unbleached white bread flour
- 1 large egg, beaten

- 4 loaf pans, about 7 × 5 × 3 inches, lightly greased

Cindy Falk, a home economist with the Kansas Wheat Commission, lives in Onaga, in northeast Kansas, up toward Nebraska. Her house has wonderful views of the hills and of the fields her husband farms in his spare time. In 1826, Cindy's ancestors came to the States from a dairy farm in Neuchâtel, Switzerland, an area famed for its wine and cheese. This area of Kansas, with its rolling green hills and fields, reminded them of home more than any other part of the state.

Cindy has been making bread since she was eleven years old and has won countless awards at state fairs and national cooking contests, which may not be surprising as her mother is another prize-winning baker. Now Cindy's children win competitions, too. Derek, the fourteen-year-old, cans fruits and vegetables and makes wonderful cakes, while Laura, aged eleven, has won prizes for her Portuguese Sweet Breads (page 138).

This is Cindy's blue-ribbon recipe from the 1992 Kansas State Fair, and it's a flavorful, high-protein loaf. Make the oat flour by processing 5 tablespoons old-fashioned rolled oats in a blender or food processor using the pulse switch until the oats are floury. Eat this blue-ribbon recipe the day it is baked, or the day after; do not refrigerate, or it will go stale more quickly.

Heat together the water, butter, brown sugar, and molasses in a medium-size saucepan over moderate heat for about 2 minutes, stirring frequently, until it is very warm (125°F to 130°F). Stir in the cracked wheat. Remove from the heat and let stand for 5 minutes, stirring occasionally, until the liquid is lukewarm.

In a large bowl, stir together the whole-wheat flour, milk powder, soy flour, cornmeal, rolled oats, rye flour, amaranth or barley flour, oat flour, and salt. (Warm the flours if it is a cold day; see page 15.) Crumble the fresh yeast into a small bowl. Add 2 tablespoons of the lukewarm cracked-wheat mixture and mix until smooth. If using dry yeast, mix the granules and the granulated sugar with 2 tablespoons of the lukewarm cracked-wheat mixture and let stand until foamy, 5 to 10 minutes (see page 18).

Add the yeast mixture and the cracked-wheat mixture to the flours in the bowl along with 3½ cups (395g) of the white flour and beat with your hand or a wooden spoon for

This loaf is excellent for slicing and using for sandwiches.

2 minutes. Add the egg and about ¼ cup of the white flour, then beat for 2 minutes more. Gradually mix in as much of the remaining flour as necessary, about ¼ cup at a time, to make a soft dough that forms a ball and leaves the sides of the bowl cleanly. The exact amount of flour needed will vary depending on the type of flour and the temperature.

Lightly oil your hands and the work surface. Turn out the dough and knead for 10 to 12 minutes until smooth, elastic, but still slightly sticky. The oil stops the dough from sticking as you knead; adding extra flour at this stage would make the loaf tough and dry. Cover the dough with the upturned bowl, or return it to the washed and lightly greased bowl, turn the dough so the top is oiled, and cover with a damp dish towel. Let the dough rise at room temperature, away from drafts, until doubled in size, 1 to 1½ hours.

Punch down the dough and divide into four. Cover with a damp dish towel or plastic wrap and let rest for 10 minutes. On a lightly floured work surface, shape the loaves by rolling each piece with a lightly floured rolling pin from the center onward into a rectangle, about 15 x 7 inches. The dough should be about ¼ inch thick. Starting from a short end, roll up the dough tightly – pushing the dough together and pinching the seams after each roll – so you have a short, fat roll. Seal the ends of the roll with the edge of your hand, pushing down to the counter. Fold the ends under, and pinch to seal.

Put one roll seam side down into each prepared pan to ensure a loaf with an even shape and no large pockets of air or "floating" crust. (Cindy has a quick method for shaping loaves not intended for competitions: Press the lump of punched-down dough into a heavily greased pan. Turn the dough out, then slide it back into the pan so that the side that was underneath is now on top. Cindy covers the second piece of dough with a damp dish towel or plastic wrap while shaping the first to prevent it from drying out.) Cover the pans with damp dish towels or plastic wrap and let the dough rise at room temperature until doubled in size, about 1 hour. During the last 15 minutes of rising, heat the oven to 375°F.

Bake the loaves for 25 to 30 minutes, until they are golden and sound hollow when unmolded and tapped underneath. Transfer the loaves to wire racks and cool completely.

CINDY ROLLS OUT EACH PORTION OF DOUGH, ROLLING FROM THE CENTER OUTWARD INTO A RECTANGLE.

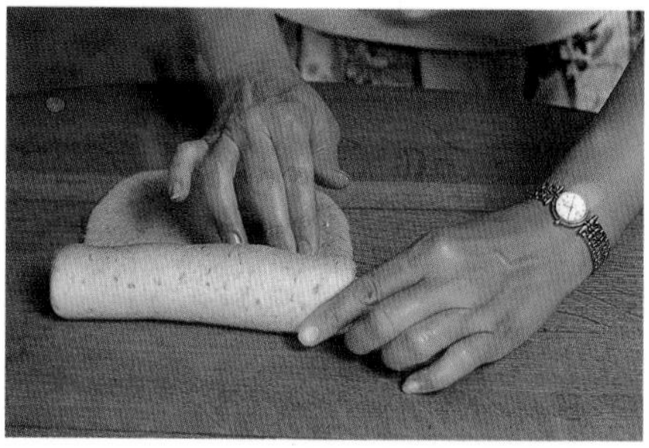

STARTING FROM A SHORT END, SHE THEN ROLLS UP THE DOUGH, SEALING AND PINCHING THE EDGES TOGETHER AFTER EACH ROLL.

PIONEER BREAD

This is Cindy Falk's recipe for "a healthy daily bread dating from Kansas's settler days." Baked in round cake pans, this is a delicious loaf, very nutritious, with a light, but chewy texture. It is best on the day it is baked, or the day after. It toasts and freezes well.

Cindy uses this recipe to teach local schoolchildren just how good homemade bread tastes, as well as to illustrate how American settler history is bound with the land and cultivation. This recipe reflects Kansas's nickname – the

INGREDIENTS

Makes 2 medium loaves
½ cup (65g) yellow cornmeal
¼ cup packed (50g) dark brown sugar
2 tablespoons (15g) coarse sea salt, crushed or ground
4 tablespoons vegetable oil
1 cup (230ml) boiling water
2 0.6-oz cakes fresh yeast (30g), or 2 envelopes active dry yeast (5 teaspoons) plus ½ teaspoon granulated sugar
½ cup (115ml) lukewarm water
1 cup (230ml) water from the cold tap
1⅓ cups (165g) whole-wheat bread flour, preferably stone-ground
¾ cup (85g) rye flour
5–6 cups (570–680g) unbleached white bread flour
extra flour for dusting
3 tablespoons sunflower seeds
extra cornmeal for sprinkling
2 deep 9-inch round cake pans or springform cake pans, lightly greased

Sunflower State – as well as its reputation as America's breadbasket.

Cindy also teaches the children how to measure accurately, and sets a timer for the kneading, rising, and baking times.

Combine the cornmeal, brown sugar, salt, oil, and boiling water in a large bowl to soften the cornmeal and dissolve the sugar and salt. The oil prevents the loaf from being crumbly when sliced.

Crumble the fresh yeast into a small bowl and stir in the lukewarm water until smooth. If using dry yeast, mix the granules and the ½ teaspoon granulated sugar with the lukewarm water and let stand until foamy, 5 to 10 minutes (see page 18).

Add the cold tap water to the cornmeal mixture, then add the yeast mixture and stir well. Using your hand or a wooden spoon, beat in the whole-wheat and rye flours, mixing well. Gradually stir in the white flour, a handful at a time, adding just enough to make a dough that is moderately stiff and leaves the sides of the bowl cleanly. (Cindy prefers a dough that is slightly too soft, rather than too stiff, as "you get a nicer bread.")

Turn out the dough onto a lightly floured work surface and knead for at least 10 minutes until smooth and elastic, using only enough additional flour to prevent sticking. (Cindy says she kneads her bread for 25 minutes for competitions, to improve the volume and texture.)

Sprinkle the sunflower seeds over the dough and knead for a couple of minutes to incorporate them evenly throughout the dough.

Put the dough into the washed and lightly greased bowl, turning the dough so the top is oiled. Cover with a damp dish towel or plastic wrap and let rise in a warm place, away from drafts, until doubled in size, about 1 hour.

Punch down the risen dough with your fist. Lightly oil your hands and the work surface to avoid needing extra flour, which can make streaks in the finished loaf. Sprinkle the greased pans with a little extra cornmeal. Turn out the dough and divide it into two equal pieces. Shape each piece into a ball. Then roll it into a pear-shaped oval so one end is narrower than the other.

Put a loaf in each pan, putting the narrow end in first and letting the wider end form the top. Cover with damp dish towels or plastic wrap and let rise at room temperature, away from drafts, until almost doubled in size, about 1 hour. During the last 15 minutes of rising, heat the oven to 375°F.

Using a sharp knife or razor blade, slash the top of each loaf in a star pattern, or use kitchen scissors to snip a star pattern. Bake the loaves for 35 to 45 minutes, or until they are well browned and sound hollow when unmolded and tapped underneath. If the loaves stick to the pans, let them stand for 5 minutes so the steam loosens the bottom, then try again. Transfer the loaves to wire racks and cool completely.

Pioneer Bread has a soft crust and a well-textured crumb. Cindy recommends serving it with a salad and, in fact, she often serves it with her mother's award-winning meatball, pasta, and red pepper salad.

FLAT BREADS

The international collection of breads in this chapter includes the oldest and simplest of all breads to make. Leavened or unleavened, flat breads can be crisp or chewy, plain or rich. They are generally quick to make and cook in minutes, if not seconds, either on top of the stove or in a red-hot oven.

Traditionally cooked on a hot, flat iron plate over a flame, many of these breads have been made for centuries by travelers and nomads, linking the cultures of the world. Pita Bread (page 62) and Lavash (page 63), both from the Middle East, for example, are close cousins of the Naan (page 61) and Chapati (page 56) of India; Branch Bread (page 64) from Scandinavia is a second cousin to Griddle Oatcakes (page 72) of Scotland, Maddybenny Fadge (page 70) of Northern Ireland, and Manx Potato Cakes (page 70).

In some cultures in the Middle East, and in parts of Asia, flat breads have the dual purpose of being a basic dietary staple and of replacing plates and silverware, making them essential for every meal. For example, grilled meat kabobs and koftas are enclosed in pita breads so they can be eaten out of hand. Naan and chapatis have been designed to scoop food from the plate to the mouth.

OPPOSITE Making an Indian flat bread. ABOVE Enjoying a stuffed pita-bread.

Flat breads cooked on top of the stove traditionally require a griddle, a large, flat cast-iron round pan, although you can use a heavy aluminum, or even a nonstick griddle, or a tava, a slightly concave, heavy iron cooking pan used throughout India. (Look for this pan in stores selling Indian foods and cookware.) Even a shallow, cast-iron frying pan works well. Good, heavy-duty baking sheets that will not buckle in extreme heat are essential for flat breads which are to be baked in the oven, such as pitas.

The recipes for Hoe Cakes (page 69), Pita Bread (page 62), Maddybenny Fadge (page 70), and Manx Potato Cakes (page 70) are ideal for new bread makers because they do not require any special equipment or skill. They are also "fun" recipes to make.

One point to remember when making flat breads is to make sure the oven is free from grease and debris before heating it to the maximum setting for pitas and the like. I forgot to check this once and when I opened the door to put in a batch of pitas I was greeted by clouds of smoke.

So if you are as dismayed as I am by the flat breads available in the supermarket, try your hand at the recipes here; I know the results will please.

INDIAN FLAT BREADS

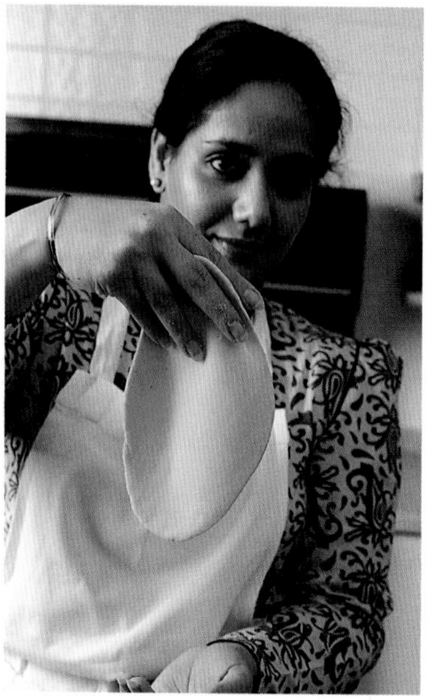

Jagdessh Sohal demonstrates her fail-proof technique for making Indian flat breads.

Whether it is the oval, white naan from the Punjab, the flat, chewy, unleavened chapati, or the flaky, rich paratha of northern India, a flat bread is eaten with every meal in India.

Although I cook a lot of Indian food, I had never thought of making Indian flat breads at home until I met Jagdessh Sohal. Jagdessh was born in Bombay and came to England in 1976, when she married. For the past few years she has been a consultant to Sharwood, a company specializing in Asian foods, making sure their large range of Indian prepared dishes and products is authentic. Jagdessh explained to me that these breads are purposely kept simple in flavor to act as a foil for the rich or spicy dishes in the meal. She also explained which bread to serve with which type of dish; or example, chapatis, pooris, and parathas, are best served with lentil dishes, and naans are best with dry-cooked meat or vegetable dishes, such as tandooris and kebobs. These breads play an important part in the meal, acting as a staple and as a means of scooping up food, often making forks and spoons unnecessary.

To test the heat of a tava, or your frying pan or griddle, before cooking Chapatis (below) and Parathas (page 60), Jagdessh says to sprinkle a good pinch of flour on it. When the tava is the correct temperature, the flour browns in 3 seconds. If it takes longer, the tava is too cool, and if the flour burns instantly, she says to let the tava cool slightly before beginning to cook the breads.

NOTE: The recipes for chapatis, pooris, and parathas call for ghee, a form of clarified butter, although clarified butter or melted unsalted butter can be substituted. Ghee is the fat used most often in Indian cooking. It has a high smoking point, which makes it ideal for sautéing and frying. The distinct, almost caramelized, flavor (a bit like unsweetened, condensed milk) is produced as the butter simmers and the water evaporates. It can be purchased in food shops specializing in Indian foods, or it's easy to prepare at home. To make ghee, melt 2 cups (230g) of unsalted butter in a small saucepan over low heat. Simmer for about 15 minutes, or until the white milk solids on the bottom of the pan turn golden. Watch carefully for the color change. The simmering time will depend on the amount of water in the butter. Once the particles have turned golden, strain the mixture through a strainer lined with cheesecloth. Let the ghee cool, then pour it into a jar with a tight-fitting lid. Refrigerate it for up to six months or freeze it for up to a year.

CHAPATIS

INGREDIENTS

Makes 8

2¼ cups (255g) sifted whole-wheat pastry flour

⅔–¾ cup (165ml) water

1 teaspoon salt

extra flour for shaping

ghee (see above), clarified butter or melted butter for brushing

a tava, large cast-iron frying pan, or heavy griddle

These are flat, unleavened disks made with atta, a very fine whole-wheat flour available in Indian stores. As an alternative, Jagdessh suggests using the whole-wheat flour sold for making pastry, with the coarser bits of bran sifted out, and I find this works just as well. She makes ten to fifteen chapatis every night for dinner, cooking them on an ungreased tava, a concave iron pan, on top of the stove. My cast-iron frying pan makes a good substitute, as does a griddle. Jagdessh also uses a special rolling pin that is thicker in the middle, but a regular one works just fine. Eat chapatis warm.

Put the flour in a medium-size bowl. Add 3 tablespoons of the water and roughly mix together, then add the salt. Mix briefly, then add a further 4 tablespoons water. Mix with your fingertips or a spoon, until the flakes of dough start to come together. Gradually work in additional water, about 1 tablespoon at a time, to make a very sticky dough. Jagdessh's method is to pour the water into her cupped hand, sprinkling it over the dry dough at the side of the bowl and working it in, discarding any excess water. After you've made this dough several times, you will be able to master her traditional technique.

Using unfloured knuckles, knead the dough in the bowl very thoroughly. When the dough feels firm and elastic, but still slightly sticky, cover the bowl with a dish towel and let stand for 5 to 10 minutes. The dough should become firmer and no longer sticky.

Put a little flour in a shallow dish. Using floured fingers, pull off egg-size pieces of dough. Between your floured palms, roll each piece of dough into a ball. Flatten each ball into a disk with a lump in the middle by rotating the dough between the palm of one hand and the fingers of the other hand. Use your fingers to press and gently pull out the rim, turning the dough to make a circle. The disk will be about 2½ to 3 inches in diameter.

Press the disk into the dish of flour to lightly coat it on both sides. Then roll it out with a rolling pin into a circle about 7 inches across and ⅛ inch thick. (Jagdessh likes to stretch the dough more by flipping it from hand to hand.)

Heat the tava, frying pan, or griddle over moderately high heat until very hot, but do not add any oil or the kitchen will fill with smoke. When the pan is the proper temperature, a pinch of flour sprinkled into the pan will brown in 3 seconds. Cook a chapati in the pan for about 30 seconds, or until the color of the upper surface changes. Using your fingers or a thin-bladed metal spatula, flip the chapati over so the speckled, cooked surface is on top. Cook for about 30 seconds longer. Flip it over again and use a dry dish towel to press down the edges of the chapati as it rises and puffs up, so the bread cooks evenly. Flip the chapati again and repeat with the other side. Lift out of the pan, place on a clean dish towel, and lightly brush the top with ghee, clarified butter, or melted unsalted butter. As you cook them, keep the chapatis hot on a baking sheet in a 250°F oven, loosely covered with foil. Serve hot.

JAGDESSH USES HER FINGERS TO MIX TOGETHER THE FLOUR AND 3 TABLESPOONS WATER.

SHE SPRINKLES EXTRA WATER THROUGH HER CUPPED HANDS INTO THE DOUGH IF IT IS DRY.

THE FLAKES OF DOUGH COME TOGETHER AS IT IS MIXED.

USING UNFLOURED KNUCKLES, SHE KNEADS THE DOUGH IN THE BOWL.

USING FLOURED FINGERS, JAGDESSH PULLS OFF EGG-SIZE PIECES OF DOUGH.

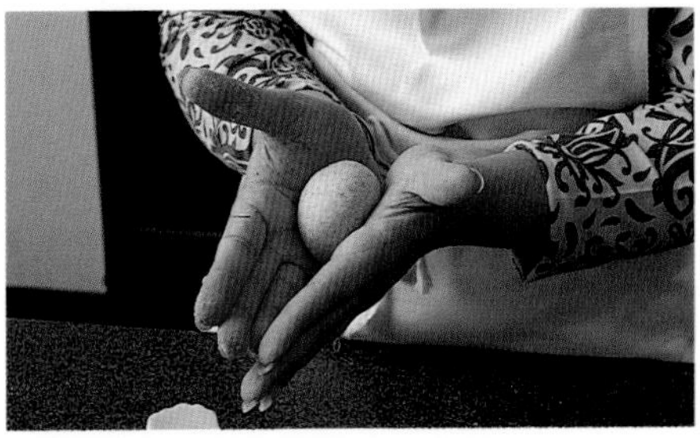

SHE SHAPES EACH PIECE OF DOUGH INTO A BALL BY ROLLING IT BETWEEN HER FLOURED PALMS.

OPPOSITE
No Indian meal is complete without a selection of flat breads to accompany the exotically spiced dishes. In Indian homes, the breads are often used for scooping up foods, removing the need for forks and spoons. When Indian food is served in Western homes or in restaurants, however, it is usually eaten with silverware. This meal includes naan (foreground), as well as chapatis (middle), and parathas (background).

TO SHAPE A CHAPATI, JAGDESSH ROTATES A BALL OF DOUGH BETWEEN HER PALM AND FINGERS.

SHE THEN USES HER FINGERS TO PRESS AND GENTLY PULL OUT THE RIM, TURNING THE DOUGH TO MAKE A CIRCLE.

USING AN INDIAN-STYLE ROLLING PIN, SHE ROLLS THE FLOURED DOUGH INTO A 7-INCH CIRCLE.

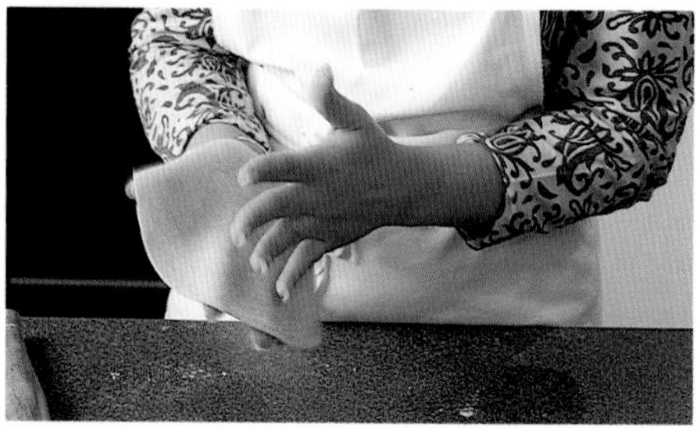
SHE THEN FLIPS THE CIRCLE FROM HAND TO HAND SEVERAL TIMES TO STRETCH THE DOUGH.

SHE USES HER FINGERS TO FLIP THE CHAPATI OVER AFTER IT HAS COOKED FOR 30 SECONDS.

USING A FOLDED DISH TOWEL, JAGDESSH PRESSES DOWN ON THE PUFFED AREAS OF THE CHAPATI SO IT COOKS EVENLY.

POORIS

INGREDIENTS

Makes 8

1 recipe Chapati dough (page 56)
additional flour for shaping
vegetable oil for frying

a heavy, deep, 10-inch frying pan

These use the same dough as chapatis, but they are smaller and puffed up like pillows because they are cooked in hot fat rather than in a dry pan. For a lighter dough, use half unbleached all-purpose flour and half sifted whole-wheat pastry flour. Some cooks also like to add 1–2 tablespoons of ghee (page 56) to the dough for extra richness.

Prepare the dough and shape and roll it as for Chapatis, making the circles only 5 inches in diameter. Heat about 1 inch of oil in the frying pan over moderately high heat until it reaches 375°F. Add one poori to the oil. At first it will sink to the bottom of the pan, then it will float and begin to puff up. Turn it over using two slotted spoons or a large skimmer and a metal spoon. Spoon some oil over the top, then turn it over again. It will puff up more after turning. This whole cooking process will take about 1½ minutes. The poori will puff up like an overstuffed pillow and be very lightly speckled with brown.

Using the two spoons, lift the poori from the oil and let it drain a second or so over the pan, then transfer to paper towels to drain completely. Repeat with the remaining pooris. Serve each poori immediately after it is fried and drained.

PARATHAS

INGREDIENTS

Makes 8

1 recipe Chapati dough (page 56)

additional flour for shaping

ghee (page 56), clarified butter, or melted unsalted butter

a tava, a cast-iron frying pan, or a heavy griddle

A cooked paratha contains crisp layers of rich dough.

Parathas are made in a similar way to chapatis, with the same dough, but they are flakier and richer. The chapati dough is brushed with ghee, folded several times, and cooked with more ghee on a tava, or frying pan, or a griddle to make a crisp, rich, flaky bread. Serve parathas as soon as possible after cooking.

Prepare and divide the dough as for Chapatis. Roll each piece of dough into a ball. Press the ball of dough in a small bowl of flour, turning it over so it is lightly dusted on all sides. Roll out the dough into a circle, about 6 inches across.

Lightly brush about 2 teaspoons ghee, clarified butter, or melted unsalted butter over each circle of dough. Fold each into thirds like an envelope – top third down and bottom third up. Fold the ends in to make a square package of dough. Dip all sides of the dough in the flour. Roll out the package with a rolling pin, turning the dough to make a 7-inch square about ⅛ inch thick. It is traditional to flip the square from hand to hand a couple of times to stretch the dough.

Heat a tava, frying pan, or griddle until very hot, but do not add any oil. When the tava, frying pan, or griddle is the proper temperature, a pinch of flour sprinkled into the pan will brown in 30 seconds. Cook the paratha in the hot pan for 30 seconds. Flip it over and cook the second side about 30 seconds. Turn the paratha over again and brush the top with ghee, clarified butter, or melted unsalted butter. Turn the paratha over and brush the other side as before. The cooked paratha should be crisp, speckled with brown patches, and slightly puffy. As you cook them, keep the parathas warm on a platter or baking sheet in a single layer, uncovered, in a 250°F oven.

TO DEVELOP THE FLAKY LAYERS, JAGDESSH FOLDS THE DOUGH LIKE AN ENVELOPE. SHE THEN FOLDS THE ENDS IN TO MAKE A SQUARE PACKAGE OF DOUGH.

SHE DIPS ALL SIDES OF THE DOUGH INTO FLOUR BEFORE SHE ROLLS IT OUT.

SHE FLIPS THE DOUGH BETWEEN HER HANDS SEVERAL TIMES TO STRETCH IT.

SHE SPREADS MELTED GHEE ON EACH SIDE OF THE PARATHA AS IT COOKS. YOU CAN ALSO USE MELTED CLARIFIED BUTTER OR REGULAR BUTTER. IT IS THE EXTRA FAT THAT GIVES THE PARATHA ITS RICHNESS.

NAAN

INGREDIENTS

Makes 8

1 ⅔ cups (250g) self-rising flour

2 tablespoons plain yogurt

1 teaspoon salt

about ½ cup (115ml) lukewarm water

Naan is a Punjabi leavened bread made with white flour and yogurt, which ferments the dough and adds flavor. Jagdessh prefers to use the chemical leavening agents in self-rising flour, rather than yeast, to raise this bread.

These breads are traditionally baked in a clay oven sunk into the ground, called a tandoor*, few Indian homes – let alone houses in England or the U.S. – possess a* tandoor*, so Jagdessh cooks her naan under a very hot broiler. Other home cooks use heated baking sheets in an oven heated on the maximum setting, but Jagdessh says her method works best – and I can vouch that the results are excellent. Jagdessh also makes flavored naan. She rolls out the dough and brushes it lightly with melted ghee (page 56) as below. Then she presses cumin or sesame seeds or a little minced onion into the dough before broiling.*

Serve naan warm.

Combine the flour, yogurt, and salt in a large bowl. Add the lukewarm water, 1 tablespoon at a time, working it into the flour mixture with your fingers and bringing the flakes of dough together. Add just enough water to make a soft, slightly sticky dough.

Knead the dough roughly in the bowl for a couple of seconds, then cover with a damp dish towel and let stand in a warm spot so the dough ferments, about 1 hour. During the last 15 minutes of standing time, heat the broiler and broiler pan.

Flour your fingers and pull off a piece of dough about the size of an egg. Between your palms, form the dough into a ball, then roll it out with a rolling pin on an unfloured work surface into an oval 8 to 9 inches long and about ⅓ inch thick. Repeat with the remaining dough to make eight naan.

Put one naan on the hot broiler pan and broil, about 3 to 4 inches from the source of heat, until it puffs up and is speckled with brown spots. Naan cook very quickly, in about 30 seconds, so watch it constantly. Turn it over and cook the second side. Repeat with the remaining seven naan.

JAGDESSH ADDS WATER THROUGH HER FINGERS UNTIL THE DOUGH IS SOFT AND SLIGHTLY STICKY.

USING FLOURED FINGERS, SHE PULLS OFF EGG-SIZE PIECES OF DOUGH.

SHE ROLLS OUT EACH BALL OF DOUGH INTO AN OVAL, 8 TO 9 INCHES LONG.

SHE BROILS THE NAAN FOR ABOUT 30 SECONDS ON EACH SIDE UNTIL IT IS PUFFED AND SPECKLED WITH BROWN. IT IS THEN READY TO SERVE.

Middle Eastern Breads

Claudia Roden, who has written the definitive book on Middle Eastern food, A New Book of Middle Eastern Food *(Viking, 1986), says that for some in the Middle East, bread, more than any other food, is considered a direct gift from God. Middle Eastern and Indian flat breads must be first cousins, as there are so many similarities. The crackerlike lavash, although leavened with yeast, is cooked rapidly on a very hot, ungreased pan, as are chapatis. Pita bread, also made with yeast, is like naan – thin, soft, and flat – and it is cooked rapidly, in the oven, where it puffs up spectacularly. Like Indian breads, lavash and pitas are used for scooping up dips and sauces. Pitas, which have an inside "pocket," can also be stuffed with meat, kabobs, vegetables, or felafel.*

PITA BREAD

INGREDIENTS

Makes 12

1 0.6-oz cake fresh yeast (15g), or 1 envelope active dry yeast (2½ teaspoons) plus ½ teaspoon sugar
1¼ cups (280ml) lukewarm water
1 tablespoon olive oil
about 4 cups (455g) unbleached white bread flour
1 teaspoon salt
extra flour for dusting

several heavy baking sheets

Pita bread, the daily bread of the Middle East, should not be flabby or leathery, as are many commercial versions. If your pitas are tough, replace half of the bread flour with unbleached all-purpose flour to reduce the gluten content. This will make the flour mixture softer and the baked pitas more tender. Cool pitas for at least 10 minutes before eating, or cool them completely and store in plastic bags or freeze.

Crumble the fresh yeast into a large bowl. Mix in 4 tablespoons lukewarm water until smooth. If using dry yeast, mix the granules and the sugar with the lukewarm water and let stand until foamy, 5 to 10 minutes (page 18). Stir the remaining lukewarm water and the olive oil into the yeast mixture.

Add a handful of the flour and the salt to the yeast mixture in the large bowl, beating with your hand to make a smooth batter. Add enough of the remaining flour, a handful at a time, to make a soft dough. As you begin to add the flour, first beat the batter with your hand or a wooden spoon; as the dough becomes firmer, vigorously knead in the flour with lightly floured hands, working in the bowl. The dough should eventually become soft and not sticky. Turn out the dough onto a lightly floured work surface and let it rest for about 5 minutes.

Knead the dough with lightly floured hands until it becomes smooth, silky, shiny, and firm, but still elastic, adding more flour as needed. (My Turkish friend Zeynep says it should feel like a baby's bottom.) Wash and dry the bowl and oil it. Put the dough in the bowl and turn the dough over so the top is oiled. Cover with a damp dish towel. Let the dough rise at room temperature until doubled in size, about 1½ hours.

Punch down the dough, and turn it out onto a lightly floured work surface. Weigh the dough and divide it into twelve equal pieces, or roll it into a fat rope and cut it into twelfths. Roll each piece between your palms into a rough ball. Smooth the balls by bringing the sides down underneath the ball and pinching them together. Place the balls

A PITA BREAD BEGINS TO PUFF UP AFTER IT HAS BEEN IN THE OVEN FOR 1 MINUTE.

AFTER 2 MINUTES IT PUFFS EVEN MORE.

on the work surface, cover with a dry dish towel or sheet of plastic wrap, and let rest for 10 minutes. This helps the dough to relax, making it easier to roll out.

Using a very lightly floured rolling pin, roll out each ball on a very lightly floured work surface into a round, about 6 inches across and ¼ inch thick. (If they are too thin they will become crisp, like crackers, when baked.) Rolling them out takes a bit of practice because the dough will spring back. Lay the dough rounds on floured dish towels or a floured baking sheet and let rise at room temperature until doubled in size, about 30 minutes. During the last 15 minutes of standing, heat the oven to 500°F. Place a baking sheet on each shelf of the oven to heat up. (Nonstick ones work well, as do well-seasoned old baking sheets. If you have only newer ones, they may need to be very lightly greased.)

Wearing very thick oven mitts, transfer a round to each very hot baking sheet and lightly mist or sprinkle it with water to keep it pale. Bake for 2 minutes, without opening the door. After checking that it hasn't browned too much, bake for another minute or so (depending on how hot your oven gets) until the pita is firm, yet still pale. If the pita starts to brown before it is firm, lower the oven temperature slightly. Transfer the pitas to a wire rack and let stand until just warm. Then cover with a dry dish towel or plastic wrap to keep the crust soft. Bake the remaining rounds in the same way.

LAVASH

This bread is rolled so thin it cooks rapidly to make a bubbly, crisp cracker. If it puffs up like pita or naan, roll the circles thinner (let rest for 10 minutes first). Serve the same day, with mezze (appetizers), such as baba ghanoush, stuffed grape leaves, hummus, taramasalata, and tabbouleh.

INGREDIENTS

Makes about 15

- 1 cup (110g) whole-wheat pastry flour, preferably stone-ground
- 3 cups (340g) unbleached white bread flour
- 1 teaspoon salt
- 1 0.6-oz cake fresh yeast (15g), or 1 envelope active dry yeast (2½ teaspoons) plus ½ teaspoon sugar
- about 1¼ cups (280ml) lukewarm water
- extra flour for dusting

a griddle or cast-iron frying pan

Stir together the flours and salt in a large bowl. Make a well in the center of the flour mixture. Crumble the fresh yeast into another bowl and stir in half of the lukewarm water until smooth. If using dry yeast, mix the granules and the ½ teaspoon sugar with the lukewarm water and let stand until foamy, 5–10 minutes (page 18). Add the yeast mixture to the well in the flour. Stir in the flour from the bowl with your hand or a wooden spoon to make a soft, but not sticky dough. If the dough is dry and crumbly, add as much of the remaining water as needed, one tablespoon at a time.

Turn out the dough onto a lightly floured work surface and knead for about 5 minutes until smooth. Put the dough back into the bowl, cover with a damp dish towel and let rise at room temperature, away from drafts, until doubled in size – about 1 hour. Punch down the dough and turn out onto a floured work surface. Weigh the dough and divide into 15 equal egg-size pieces, or roll it into a fat rope and divide into 15 pieces. Shape into smooth balls as for Pita Bread (left), cover with a dry dish towel or sheet of plastic wrap and let rise for 30 minutes.

Working with one ball at a time, roll out each as thinly as possible on a very lightly floured surface to make an almost translucent round, about 5 inches across, using as little flour as possible. Heat the griddle or frying pan until very hot. Gently dust off any excess flour (the flour will scorch in the pan, causing black specks – you may need to wipe out the pan after cooking each). Cook the round for about 1 minute, then flip it over and briefly cook the other side (30 seconds at the most) – the bread should be lightly browned on top of the bubbles which have formed. Remove with a spatula to a wire rack to cool. Cook the remaining dough in the same way, rolling out the next one as soon as the previous one has been removed from the griddle to cool. If your griddle is large enough, you can cook two breads at once. Cool in single layers on wire racks.

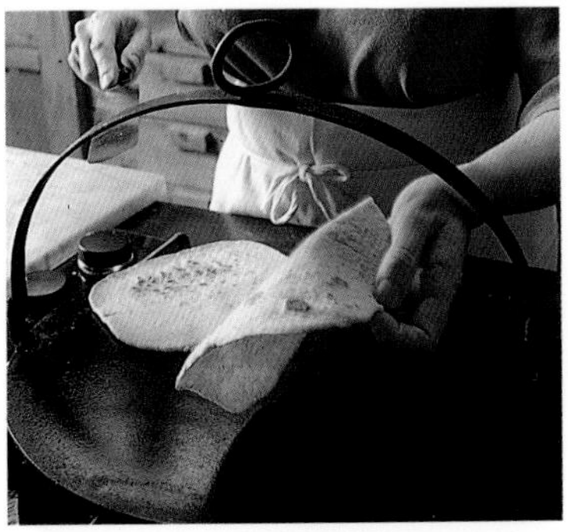

REMOVE EACH LAVASH FROM THE GRIDDLE WHEN THE TOPS OF THE BUBBLES ARE LIGHTLY BROWNED.

BRANCH BREAD

INGREDIENTS

Makes 12

1 cup (110g) rye flour

1 cup (110g) whole-wheat bread flour, preferably stone-ground

2½ cups (340g) unbleached all-purpose flour

1½ teaspoons salt

½ teaspoon sugar

1¼ cups (280ml) milk

2 tablespoons (30g) unsalted butter

extra flour for dusting

coarse sea salt for sprinkling

2 baking sheets, lightly greased

USING A SHARP KNIFE, CUT A SERIES OF CHEVRONS IN THE DOUGH.

I have my friend Stephen Pouncey to thank for this Icelandic recipe, which he gleaned and translated on a deer-stalking trip in Sweden. Branch bread is a crispbread – made without yeast, and designed to keep. If you are in a hurry, however, choose another recipe, as these take some time to roll and bake. When rolling out the dough, it should be as thin as a flower petal.

Branch bread is good to serve with soups, pâtés and dips. It is also excellent for feeding to teething babies (without the salt topping). After cooling, store carefully in an airtight container because these are very fragile. They will keep for up to one month.

Mix together the flours, salt, and sugar in a large bowl. Make a well in the center.

Heat the milk in a small saucepan over moderately low heat until small bubbles appear around the edges. Remove the milk from the heat and stir in the butter. When the butter has melted, pour the hot liquid into the well in the flour mixture. Stir the flours into the liquid using a wooden spoon. As soon as the dough becomes cool enough to handle, work it into a smooth dough with your hands, pressing the dough together to eliminate any lumps, as if making shortbread, rather than kneading it.

Turn out the dough onto a lightly floured work surface and cover with the upturned bowl; the dough should still be warm. Let the dough rest for 30 minutes. Heat the oven to 425°F.

Divide the dough into twelve equal pieces. Roll out each piece as thinly as possible into a round. Using a 9- to 9½-inch dinner plate as a guide, trim the dough; discard the scraps. Using a sharp knife, cut a series of chevrons in the dough: once baked these will make a spruce tree design. Transfer one round to each prepared baking sheet, lifting it carefully, or sliding the baking sheet underneath.

Brush the dough very lightly with water and sprinkle with coarse salt to taste. Bake two breads at a time until lightly browned and crisp, 8 to 10 minutes. Keep your eye on them, as they bake very quickly. Transfer the breads to wire racks to cool completely. Repeat with the remaining dough.

During the baking, the chevrons in branch bread open out to look like the branches of a spruce tree.

Quaintly old-fashioned, toasted crumpets remain a favorite afternoon teatime treat. Serve them with hot with good-quality butter.

CRUMPETS OR "LES ÉPONGES"

INGREDIENTS

Makes about 18

- 2 cups (230g) unbleached white bread flour
- 1⅔ cups (230g) unbleached all-purpose flour
- ¾ teaspoon cream of tartar
- 1 0.6-oz cake fresh yeast (15g), or 1 envelope active dry yeast (2½ teaspoons) plus ½ teaspoon sugar
- 2¼ cups (510ml) lukewarm water
- 3½ teaspoons (10g) coarse sea salt, crushed or ground
- ½ teaspoon baking soda
- ⅔ cup (140ml) lukewarm milk

a griddle or cast-iron frying pan
4 crumpet rings, about 3½ inches diameter, greased

Well-made crumpets – light, with large air holes, and very tasty – are absolutely scrumptious. The rubbery commercial ones I have found in England are travesties best avoided. In the States, English muffins resemble crumpets more than they do our English muffins, but crumpets have a moist, almost damp crumb. Crumpets are eaten whole, not split in two, either hot from the griddle or toasted, and spread with butter. Do not stint on the butter. Crumpets also freeze well, and you can toast them straight from the freezer. Les éponges is what a young French friend calls these crumpets, and the name has stuck.

Fellow food writer Elaine Hallgarten gave me a copy of The Modern Baker Confectioner and Caterer, *by Master Baker John Kirkland, published in 1907, and his advice and recipe remain invaluable. I have found the combination of flours in this recipe works well.*

Sift together the flours and cream of tartar into a large bowl. Crumble the fresh yeast into a medium-size bowl. Mix in the lukewarm water until smooth. If using dry yeast, mix the granules and the sugar with ¾ cup (170ml) lukewarm water and let stand until foamy, 5 to 10 minutes (page 18). Stir in the remaining lukewarm water.

Mix the yeast mixture into the flour to make a very thick, but smooth batter, beating vigorously with your hand or a wooden spoon for 2 minutes. Cover the bowl with plastic wrap and let stand in a warm spot until the batter rises and then falls, about 1 hour.

Add the salt and beat the batter for about 1 minute. Then cover the bowl and let stand in a warm spot for 15 to 20 minutes, so the batter can "rest."

Dissolve the baking soda in the lukewarm milk. Then gently stir it into the batter. The batter should not be too stiff or your crumpets will be "blind" – without holes – so it is best to test one before cooking the whole batch.

Heat an ungreased, very clean griddle or frying pan over moderately low heat for about 3 minutes until very hot. Put a well-greased crumpet ring on the griddle. Spoon or pour ⅓ cup of the batter into the ring. The amount of batter will depend on the size of your crumpet ring.

As soon as the batter is poured into the ring, it should begin to form holes. If holes do not form, add a little more lukewarm water, a tablespoon at a time, to the batter in the bowl and try again. If the batter is too thin and runs out under the ring, gently work in a little more all-purpose flour and try again. Once the batter is the proper consistency, continue with the remaining batter, cooking the crumpets in batches, three or four at a time. As soon as the top surface is set and covered with holes, 7 to 8 minutes, the crumpet is ready to flip over.

To flip the crumpet, remove the ring with a towel or tongs, then turn the crumpet carefully with a spatula. The top, cooked side should be chestnut brown. Cook the second, holey side of the crumpet for 2 to 3 minutes, or until pale golden. The crumpet should be about ¾ inch thick. Remove the crumpet from the griddle. Grease the crumpet rings well after each use.

BEAT THE BATTER VIGOROUSLY WITH YOUR HAND UNTIL IT IS THICK AND SMOOTH.

GENTLY STIR IN THE MILK MIXTURE.

SPOON OR POUR ABOUT ⅓ CUP BATTER INTO EACH GREASED CRUMPET RING.

USING A DISH TOWEL, EASE OFF THE RING WHEN THE UPPER SURFACE IS HOLEY.

USING A SPATULA, FLIP THE UNMOLDED CRUMPET OVER AND COOK FOR 2 TO 3 MINUTES LONGER. THE HOLEY SIDE SHOULD BE PALE GOLDEN.

A cozy afternoon tea with homemade muffins (front) and crumpets in front of a roaring fire is just the thing to brighten up a damp, cold British winter's day.

A plate of freshly made pikelets is kept warm next to the fire. Pikelets are the northern cousins of crumpets, traditionally made in Derbyshire, Yorkshire, and Lancashire. They are cooked on a griddle like crumpets, but without the restraining rings. As a result, they look like small, thin pancakes.

To make pikelets, use the ingredients for Crumpets (page 65), but increase the amount of milk to 1¼ cups (280ml). Make the batter the same way, then drop 2 tablespoons batter in pools directly onto a hot, ungreased griddle or cast-iron frying pan. Cook for about 3 minutes on each side. This should yield about 30 pikelets.

ENGLISH MUFFINS

Early in the 20th century, Master Baker John Kirkland (page 65) wrote that these muffins are different in almost every respect from crumpets: "Muffins are thick, extremely lightly fermented dough cakes, not holey or tough, three inches across and almost two inches thick." He recommends using flour with a moderately strong gluten level for best results, and I find that this mixture of flours works well.

The dough is very soft indeed, and that, along with the three risings, gives these muffins their lightness. They are nothing like the rubbery raisin and bran ones sold commercially, or the really disappointing "sourdough English muffins" I came across in New England supermarkets. To American tastes, these will not be what is usually expected in an English muffin; English muffins in the States are more like our crumpets. But please do try this recipe; it's not at all difficult and the results are truly delicious.

INGREDIENTS

Makes 8

3 cups (340g) unbleached white bread flour

¾ cup (110g) unbleached all-purpose flour

3½ teaspoons (10g) coarse sea salt, crushed or ground

1 0.6-oz cake fresh yeast (15g), or 1 envelope active dry yeast (2½ teaspoons)

½ teaspoon sugar

1 cup (230ml) lukewarm water

⅔ cup (140ml) lukewarm milk

extra flour for dusting

rice flour, cornstarch or cornmeal for dusting

2 or 4 baking sheets

a griddle or cast-iron frying pan

The "proper" way to eat English muffins is to open them slightly with a fork at the middle joint, toast them on both sides, and then tear them open with the fork and spread thickly with butter. Store them wrapped at room temperature or freeze them.

Mix the flours with the salt in a large bowl and warm the bowl of flour (page 15). This will help the yeast start working and give the muffins their light texture.

Crumble the fresh yeast into a small bowl. Mix in the sugar and half of the lukewarm water until smooth. If using dry yeast, mix the granules and the sugar with half of the lukewarm water and let stand until foamy, 5 to 10 minutes (page 18).

Make a well in the warmed flour. Add the yeast mixture, the remaining lukewarm water, and the milk and mix with your hand to make a very soft, slightly sticky dough. Turn out the dough onto a lightly floured work surface and knead with floured hands for 10 minutes until the dough is soft, elastic, smooth, and no longer sticky. Shape the dough into a ball.

Return the dough to the bowl. Cover with a damp dish towel. Let rise in a warm spot, away from drafts, until doubled in size, about 1 hour.

Punch down the dough and turn it out onto a lightly floured surface. Knead it again for 5 minutes. John Kirkland recommends dipping your hands in a little lukewarm water for this stage. Return the dough to the bowl and cover again. Let rest for 30 minutes.

Divide the dough into eight pieces. According to John Kirkland, "The usual method is to squeeze the dough through a ring made by the thumb and forefinger of one floured hand," and this is the method I use. Squeeze off the ball of dough and drop it onto a baking sheet well dusted with rice flour, cornstarch, or cornmeal. Sprinkle the dough with more rice flour, cornstarch, or cornmeal. Cover the tray of muffins with another baking tray, then a damp dish towel. Let rise in a warm spot for 30 minutes.

Heat an ungreased griddle or frying pan about 2 minutes over moderate heat until moderately hot. With a metal spatula, invert the muffins, three at a time, onto the hot griddle. Cook about 12 minutes or until the undersides are golden brown. Turn the muffins over and cook 10 to 12 minutes longer, or until the second side is browned and the sides of the muffins spring back when pressed. Transfer the muffins to a warm serving platter and wrap with a dry dish towel to keep warm. Wipe out the griddle or pan with a cloth and continue cooking the remaining muffins.

USE YOUR HANDS TO MIX A VERY SOFT, SLIGHTLY STICKY DOUGH.

DIVIDE THE DOUGH INTO BALLS BY SQUEEZING IT THROUGH YOUR THUMB AND FOREFINGER.

COVER THE DOUGH WITH A BAKING SHEET, THEN A TOWEL AND LET RISE.

USING A SPATULA, FLIP OVER EACH MUFFIN SO BOTH SIDES ARE GOLDEN BROWN.

HOE CAKES

"Do not think of making this recipe unless you have good bacon fat," says Caroll Boltin, adamantly. "They will be tasteless." She has spent many years researching the American pioneers and their early settlements in New York State's Hudson Valley.

"This was a fast way to have bread in colonial times. It was cheap, easy, and quick, and everyone had bacon fat in the larder." The simple, gritty cornmeal batter was cooked over the open fire in a flat garden hoe – hence the name – and eaten immediately with soup or a vegetable stew.

This is Caroll's recipe, which she often makes at Philipsburg Manor, a historic restoration in North Tarrytown, New York, to illustrate what 17th-century life was like. To cook the cakes, wealthier settlers would have used a spider, a kettle with built-in legs that sat in the fireplace, but a heavy cast-iron frying pan on the stove top works just as well for the modern cook.

Be sure to eat these cakes while they're still hot; they do not keep well.

The water-powered mill at Philipsburg Manor (right), on the Pocantico River at North Tarrytown, New York, has been grinding and selling cornmeal since early in the 18th century. Here, miller Peter Curtis employs a traditional grinding method similar to those used by the Manor's earliest millers.

INGREDIENTS

Makes about 12

1¾ cups stone-ground yellow cornmeal
½ teaspoon salt
about ⅔ cup (140ml) boiling water
bacon fat for cooking

a heavy cast-iron frying pan

Mix together the cornmeal and salt in a small bowl, then stir in enough of the boiling water to make a sloppy batter that barely holds its shape. Let stand for 5 minutes.

Heat a frying pan on the stove over moderately high heat or over the glowing embers of a fire – there should be no flames – until hot, about 2 minutes.

Add plenty of bacon fat or vegetable oil to the hot pan so it is about ¼ inch deep. Heat the fat about 2 to 3 minutes until the surface is rippling and a small bit of the batter bubbles as soon as it is dropped into the fat. Drop the batter by generous tablespoons into the pan. Do not crowd the pan; the cakes should be cooked in batches. Cook the cakes until the undersides are golden and crisp, 1 to 2 minutes. Flip the cakes over with two slotted spatulas and cook the other side 1 to 2 minutes until browned and crisp. Transfer to paper towels to drain. Adjust the heat as necessary to maintain the temperature of the fat, and continue to cook the remaining cakes.

NOTE: You'll need about ⅔ cup of bacon fat to cook these in, about the amount rendered from 1 pound (455g) of bacon.

MADDYBENNY FADGE

INGREDIENTS

Makes 18
2 cups (455g) cooked mashed potatoes
2 tablespoons (30g) unsalted butter, diced
½ teaspoon salt
about ¾ cup (110g) unbleached all-purpose flour
extra flour for dusting
bacon fat or vegetable oil for frying

a griddle or heavy cast-iron frying pan

This recipe comes from Rosemary White, of Maddybenny Farm, Portrush, Northern Ireland. I met her when she won the Great Irish Breakfast award for her farmhouse bed and breakfast a few years ago; the judge had said, "Her breakfast was magnificent, and the presentation faultless." To win the prize, Rosemary prepared her famous Ulster Fry – lean, crisp bacon, meaty sausages, mushrooms, apple rings, and eggs accompanied by fadge, the local potato cakes, and her Maddybenny Wheaten Bread (page 81). The secret of a good breakfast, Rosemary says, is freshness. "I never start to cook for my guests in the morning until I see the whites of their eyes." Serve fadge hot.

Put the mashed potatoes in a large bowl. Add the butter and salt. Knead in the flour, adding just enough to bind the potatoes, making a soft, but not sticky dough. Too much flour will make the dough tough. Cover and chill for several hours or overnight.

Roll out the dough with a lightly floured rolling pin on a lightly floured work surface to a ¼ inch thickness. Cut into triangles or squares. Heat a griddle or cast-iron frying pan over moderately high heat. Add a little bacon fat or oil to the griddle, just enough to prevent the fadge from sticking. Cook the fadge in batches until brown on one side, about 1 minute. Turn the fadge over and cook the second side until brown. Keep warm in a 250°F oven while cooking the remainder. Add more fat to the griddle as needed.

NOTE: The exact amount of flour needed for this recipe and Manx Potato Cakes (below) depends on the consistency of the mashed potatoes. The dough should be soft, but not sticky. Do not mash the potatoes or make the dough in a food processor – the machine will make the results gluey and disgusting.

ROLL OUT THE DOUGH ON A LIGHTLY FLOURED WORK SURFACE, THEN CUT IT INTO TRIANGLES OR SQUARES.

RIGHT
A sizzling farmhouse breakfast of fadge, crisp bacon, mushrooms, and a sunny-side-up egg.

MANX POTATO CAKES

INGREDIENTS

Makes about 9
2 cups (455g) cooked mashed potatoes
2 tablespoons (30g) unsalted butter
½ teaspoon salt, or to taste
plenty of black pepper
1 large egg, beaten
¼ cup (30g) shredded aged Cheddar cheese
about ¾ cup (110g) self-rising flour
bacon fat or vegetable oil for frying

My Manx grandmother (from the Isle of Man), who prided herself on keeping a good table and larder, made these potato cakes for high tea to go with ham and poached eggs. These are richer than Maddybenny Fadge (above). Eat immediately after cooking.

Prepare the dough as for Maddybenny Fadge (above), adding the black pepper, egg, and cheese to the potatoes with the salt and butter. There is no need to chill this dough.

Pull off nine egg-size pieces of dough and roll them between your palms, flouring your hands to prevent sticking, if necessary. Flatten the dough balls to make thin cakes, about 3 inches across and ¼ inch thick.

Heat a griddle or cast-iron frying pan over moderately high heat. Add a little bacon fat or oil to the griddle, just enough to prevent the cakes from sticking. Fry the cakes in batches until golden brown, crispy, and slightly puffed, about 3 minutes. Turn the potato cakes over with a metal spatula and cook the second side about 3 minutes longer, until crisp. Add more fat to the griddle as needed.

BLINIS

Blinis are light, crumbly, flavorful, yeast-leavened pancakes. Their intense, slightly bitter taste comes from the speckled gray-brown buckwheat flour. Traditionally, blinis should be eaten with sour cream or melted butter and Beluga or pressed caviar, but these days lumpfish roe, salmon caviar, chopped hard-boiled egg, and/or smoked fish are more usual – and easier on the budget. Eat these while still warm.

INGREDIENTS

Makes about 12 blinis

- 1 0.6-oz cake fresh yeast (15g), or 1 envelope active dry yeast (2½ teaspoons)
- 1 teaspoon sugar
- ¾ cup (170ml) lukewarm water
- 1 large egg, separated
- 1¼ cups (140g) buckwheat flour
- 1 teaspoon salt
- ¾ cup (170ml) lukewarm milk
- butter or lard for frying

a heavy frying pan, crêpe pan, or griddle

Crumble the fresh yeast into a large bowl. Mix in the sugar and 4 tablespoons lukewarm water until smooth. If using dry yeast, mix the granules and the sugar with ¼ cup of the lukewarm water and let stand until foamy, 5 to 10 minutes (page 18).

Whisk the remaining lukewarm water and the egg yolk into the yeast mixture. Whisk in the flour and salt to make a very thick batter. Cover with a damp dish towel. Let rise in a warm place, away from drafts, until doubled in volume, 1½ to 2 hours.

Whisk in the lukewarm milk to make a batter the consistency of thick heavy cream. Cover again and let stand in a warm place until small bubbles appear on the surface, about 1 hour. Beat the egg white in a small bowl with an electric mixer until it forms stiff peaks, then gently fold it into the batter with a rubber spatula.

Heat a crêpe pan, frying pan, or griddle pan over moderate heat until moderately hot, 1½ to 2 minutes or until your palm held 1½ inches above the pan feels warm after 15 seconds. Swirl 1 teaspoon of the butter into the pan. When the butter has melted, spoon a scant ¼ cup of batter into the pan and gently spread the batter with the back of a spoon to make a 4-inch pancake. Cook until the edges of the blini have set and small bubbles form on the surface, 2 to 3 minutes. Turn the blini over with a spatula and cook the second side for about 2 minutes, or until dry and the top springs back when pressed lightly in the center with your fingertips. Keep warm in a 300°F oven, uncovered, in a single layer, while cooking the remaining batter. Add more butter to the pan as needed.

WHISK THE BATTER UNTIL IT IS VERY THICK.

WHISK IN THE LUKEWARM MILK. THE BATTER SHOULD BE THE CONSISTENCY OF HEAVY CREAM.

COOK EACH BLINI UNTIL THE UPPER SURFACE HAS SET, 2 TO 3 MINUTES, THEN TURN THE BLINI OVER WITH A SPATULA AND COOK THE SECOND SIDE ABOUT 2 MINUTES. CONTINUE UNTIL ALL BLINIS ARE COOKED.

GRIDDLE OATCAKES

INGREDIENTS

Makes about 12 oatcakes
1⅓ cups (230g) steel-cut oats
½ teaspoon salt
2 tablespoons (30g) meat drippings, bacon fat, or lard, melted
6–8 tablespoons (85–115ml) boiling water
flour for rolling and cutting

a griddle or large cast-iron frying pan
2 jelly-roll pans fitted with wire racks

Scottish oatcakes are thin, crumbly, brittle-crisp biscuits made from oats ground into a meal (not a flour), salt, good, flavorful meat drippings or bacon fat, and hot water. As there is no leavening, the lightness comes from the steam produced during cooking. The shortness and the taste depend on the fat used – bacon fat adds a good flavor.

Oatcake expert F. Marian McNeill declared, in The Scots Kitchen *(Edinburgh: Blackie, 1929), "Oatcakes are especially good with herring, sardines, cheese, buttermilk, or broth, or spread with butter and marmalade to complete the breakfast." That is surely true, but today you are more likely to see oatcakes in the Scottish Highlands served at tea time with butter, homemade raspberry jam, or a heather honey. In fancy restaurants Scottish soft cheeses are sometimes offered with oatcakes, although these are rarely homemade.*

Medium-ground steel-cut oats are commonly used in the Highlands for oatcakes. In the States, the steel-cut oats sold are usually the coarse-ground type. Even the oats labeled fine-ground are coarser than Scottish medium-ground oats, so I've found it necessary to grind the oats briefly in a food processor to obtain the proper texture. This takes just a minute or so, though.

Triangular curly-edged oatcakes are cooked on a griddle, while a circular variety is baked in the oven.

You need to be careful when making oatcakes because they are likely to become crumbly as you roll them out. If this happens, you can add a few drops of hot water, or gently warm the dough in a very low oven if it has stiffened. According to Master Baker John Kirkland (page 65), "The springing effects [the expansion of the dough when baked] in their turn are modified for good or evil according to the manner in which the dough has been manipulated. If properly handled, the dough will be short and plump. If badly treated, [it will be] thin and hard."

Put the oats in a food processor and grind until they turn to a coarse meal, like the texture of fine bulgur wheat. Mix together the oats and salt in a medium-size bowl. Stir in the melted drippings, bacon fat, or lard with a metal spatula. Mix in 5 tablespoons of the boiling water, then add additional water as needed until the mixture binds together. It should be firm, not too sticky, and not crumbly. Gently knead for a few seconds to bring together into a dough.

Divide the dough in half. Quickly roll out the first half on a very lightly floured work surface using a lightly floured rolling pin, to a round about 10 inches across and ¼ inch thick. Use your fingers to press in and reform the edges if they start to crack or crumble. Cut the round into 6 triangles. Repeat with the other portion of dough. Let the dough triangles dry, uncovered, for 20 minutes.

Heat the oven to 300°F. Heat a griddle or frying pan over moderately low heat for about 3 minutes, until moderately hot; your palm will feel warm when held 1½ inches above the griddle after about 30 seconds. To speed up the cooking process you can use two griddles or frying pans, or a griddle and a frying pan – whatever you have – if you like. Do not grease the griddle.

USING A SHARP KNIFE, CUT THE ROLLED-OUT DOUGH INTO SIX TRIANGLES

COOK THE TRIANGLES UNTIL THE EDGES START TO CURL UPWARD.

Cook the triangles in batches, about three at a time, spaced apart, on the griddle, until they curl upward, 5 to 6 minutes. Turn them over with a metal spatula and cook the second side for about 4 to 5 minutes, until they become paler in color and are firm. Transfer to the wire racks on the jelly-roll pans in single layers. When all the oatcakes are cooked, place the jelly-roll pans with the oatcakes in the oven to dry out for about 20 minutes. (Catherine Brown, an authority on Scottish cooking, says that to remove excess moisture, oatcakes used to be dried in a special toaster in front of the fire.) Remove the oatcakes from the oven and take the racks off the pans. Let them cool completely and then store them in airtight containers.

PUPUSAS

INGREDIENTS

Makes 8

2 cups (230g) masa harina (tortilla flour)

½ teaspoon salt

3 tablespoons fresh lime juice

½–¾ cup (115-170ml) water from the cold tap

¾ cup (85g) shredded aged Cheddar cheese

TOPPING:

2½ cups (230g) finely shredded white cabbage

1 cup (110g) finely shredded carrots

a little ground black pepper, to taste

1 teaspoon salt

½ cup (110ml) white wine vinegar

1 tablespoon chopped fresh oregano

½–1 teaspoon chopped fresh hot chili pepper, to taste

a heavy cast-iron frying pan or griddle

A ready-to-eat pupusa with the pickled vegetable topping.

Anà Sylvia Landeverde, a young professional cook from El Savador, showed Anthony Blake and me how to make her country's national dish of cornmeal griddle cakes, which are flavored with cheese and topped with chili-pickled cabbage and carrots. They were delicious, and were scoffed down as they came off the griddle.

Prepare the pickled topping at least 2 hours before you plan to eat. Mix all the topping ingredients together, then cover and let stand at room temperature for 2 hours. Stir well before using.

To prepare the griddle cakes, mix together the masa harina, salt, lime juice, and enough water to make a stiff, clammy dough. Work it together lightly with your fingertips until you have a smooth ball. If the dough is crumbly, add 1 tablespoon water; if it is sticky, work in a little more masa harina. Cover the dough and let stand for 30 minutes.

Weigh the dough and divide into eight equal pieces. Take one piece and slap it palm to palm to make a fairly thick cake about 3 inches in diameter and about 1 inch thick.

Place 1 tablespoon of the cheese in the center of each cake, pressing it firmly. Pinch the edges of the dough together over the cheese, then roll it in your hands so the cheese is securely enclosed. Using your hands, flatten the ball to make a rough disk 5 inches across and about ¼ inch thick, patting it and turning it with your palms, trying to make sure the cheese doesn't break through the dough. Keep shaped pupusas covered with plastic wrap while you repeat the process with the remaining dough.

Heat the oven to 250°F to keep the cooked pupusas warm on a platter, uncovered, while the others cook. (These take a few minutes to cook, so to speed up the process you can use two griddles or two frying pans, thus cooking four pupusas at once.)

Heat the griddle or pan over moderately high heat about 3 minutes, until moderately hot. Lightly brush the griddle with oil. Cook the griddle cakes, two at a time if they fit in your griddle or pan, turning them frequently, reducing the heat if necessary, until the cheese melts and they are speckled with brown and slightly puffy, about 5 minutes. Brush the griddle or pan with oil as needed. When they are all cooked, top with the pickled vegetables and serve immediately.

ANÀ PUTS THE SHREDDED CHEESE IN THE CENTER OF THE THICK DOUGH CAKE.

ANÀ TRANSFERS THE HOT PUPUSA TO A PLATE.

QUICK BREADS

The varied breads in this chapter are called quick breads because the batters are simply mixed and then baked. No lengthy kneading or rising periods are necessary, so you can have freshly baked bread in a short time. They are all made without yeast, relying instead on chemical leavening agents (baking soda and baking powder), which rapidly produce bubbles of gas when they come in contact with moisture and warmth.

To leaven a dough or batter, baking soda, an alkali, must be combined with a slightly acidic dry ingredient like cream of tartar, or with an acidic liquid like buttermilk, sour milk, or a milk and yogurt mixture. Baking soda is also used when doughs contain brown sugar, molasses, any form of citrus, sour cream, or dried fruit. Baking powder is a ready-mixed combination of alkali and acid leavening agents. The gases that baking powder and baking soda produce help the dough to rise, although with not quite the same effect as yeast. Once mixed, the dough or batter is quickly shaped or spooned into the pan. There is no need for prolonged kneading with these breads, as the gluten in the flour should not be developed; for this reason, softer flours – all-purpose or self-rising flour (all-purpose flour with baking powder and salt added) – are used instead of strong, high-gluten bread flours. The finished dough should be baked immediately, while the leaveners are still active.

OPPOSITE *A morning's baking.* ABOVE *A bemused lad at afternoon tea.*

Most of these breads cook fairly rapidly, and you will find they have a denser texture than yeast breads and they stale more quickly. Enriching the dough with butter or oil, eggs, or fruit helps to produce a longer-keeping loaf.

These are sweet and savory breads to accompany meals, take along on picnics, have in the kitchen for ready snacks or serve with a cup of tea to revive sagging spirits late in the afternoon. Fresh Soda Bread (page 90) is a real morning treat, and Blueberry Muffins Hertz (page 78) are always welcomed for breakfast, as a snack, or in packed lunches. I often include Bacon Loaf (page 82) when I am planning the menu for a party, as it is good to serve with a selection of cheeses.

On chilly winter days, try the Herb Rolls (page 84) with steaming vegetable soups. The flavor of the fresh herbs and mild cream cheese makes this a great combination, which my family always enjoys.

NOTE: Adding extra baking powder or baking soda will not improve the texture. Rather, it will add a nasty chemical tang to the finished result, and the combination of bleached flour and too much of a leavening agent can often produce a chlorine aftertaste.

ITALIAN SEMOLINA BREAD

INGREDIENTS

Makes 1 large loaf
1 0.6-oz cake fresh yeast (15g)
½ cup (115ml) water from the cold tap
1⅔ cups (200g) unbleached white bread flour
1⅔ cups (280g) semolina flour
1 teaspoon salt
2 tablespoons (30g) butter, chilled and diced
1 tablespoon honey
1 egg, beaten
beaten egg for glazing

a baking sheet, greased

Durum wheat semolina flour, the kind used for pasta, makes a good-textured, fairly close loaf with a nice flavor. Because the flour is hard, with a higher gluten content than even bread flour, I think it is best to mix it with white or whole-wheat bread flour to prevent the loaf from being tough. Good Italian grocers and wholefood markets should stock semolina flour.

Crumble the yeast into a small bowl and mix to a smooth liquid with the water. Mix the flours and salt together in a large mixing bowl. Add the diced butter and rub in using the tips of your fingers to make fine crumbs. Stir the honey and egg into the yeast liquid, then add to the flour mixture and mix to a soft but not sticky dough. Turn onto a lightly floured work surface and knead thoroughly for 10 minutes. Shape the dough into a ball, return it to the bowl, and cover. Let it rise at normal room temperature for 1–1½ hours or until the dough has doubled in bulk.

Punch down the risen dough with your knuckles and turn it onto a very lightly floured work surface. Shape the dough into an oval (see page 78) and place on the prepared baking sheet. Cover with a damp dish towel and let rise as before until doubled in size – about 1 hour.

Preheat the oven to 375°F.

Brush the risen loaf with beaten egg to glaze, then bake for 30–35 minutes or until the bread sounds hollow when tapped on the base. Transfer to a wire rack to cool. Eat within 24 hours, or toast, or freeze for up to 3 months.

NOTE You can use 1 package (¼oz/7g) active dry yeast instead of fresh yeast, dissolving it in warm water. For rapid-rise dry yeast, mix it with the flours and salt. Rub in the butter. Mix the water with the honey and egg, then proceed with the recipe.

OPPOSITE Eating al fresco in Paghezzana, Italy.

BLUEBERRY MUFFINS HERTZ

INGREDIENTS

Makes 12
1 cup (140g) unbleached all-purpose flour
1 cup (140g) whole-wheat flour, preferably stone-ground
7 tablespoons (85g) sugar
1 tablespoon baking powder
a large pinch of salt
1¼ cups (280ml) milk
¼ cup (60ml) soy oil
1 extra large egg, beaten
2 teaspoons lemon juice
1¼ cups (140g) fresh or frozen blueberries

a 12-cup muffin pan, well greased or lined with paper muffin cases

OPPOSITE *A selection of sweet quick breads. Left to right (front): Tina's Breakfast Loaf, Date and Apple Loaf (page 83), and Smithy Loaf (page 81). On tray: Gingerbread (page 80) and Blueberry Muffins Hertz.*

American muffins bear no resemblance to English muffins; they are made with all-purpose flour and baking powder rather than from a yeast batter, and are baked in muffin pans instead of being cooked on a griddle. They look, and can taste, rather like cupcakes, or what we Brits call "fairy cakes," though they are less sweet, and have a moist, spongy crumb and a light texture. The best homemade muffins are a world away from the sawdust-dry, dense commercial variety, and wild blueberry muffins are the best of all.

My husband's mother, Annette Hertz, welcomed me into the family as only an all-American mother can. She enthusiastically introduced me to Maine's finest bounty – fresh seafood, rich ice cream, and the exquisite-tasting wild blueberries that she uses to make muffins for her grandchildren. This is her recipe, using a mixture of all-purpose and whole-wheat flours. (Annette uses a 50/50 flour blend that she buys from her supermarket.)

Maine wild blueberries are small, about the size of fresh currants, intensely flavored, and slightly tart, with more depth of taste than the fatter, cultivated ones. As fresh blueberries are only available for a few weeks, you can use frozen blueberries, straight from the freezer, out of season. The blueberries can also be replaced with fresh red currants, cranberries, huckleberries, pitted cherries, blackberries, diced apple, or dried fruits and nuts.

You can also experiment with spices – try cinnamon, nutmeg, pumpkin-pie spice, or add a bit of grated fresh lemon or orange rind. Or try one of the freshly ground spice mixtures on page 150. The oil can be replaced with an equal quantity of melted unsalted butter for a richer taste. Muffins should be eaten warm from the oven, or at least on the day of baking. They can also be frozen for one month.

Heat the oven to 400°F. Mix together the flours, sugar, baking powder, and salt in a large bowl. Whisk together the milk, oil, egg, and lemon juice in a medium-size bowl. Stir the milk mixture into the dry ingredients until almost combined. Quickly but gently fold in the blueberries with a rubber spatula; the mixture should still look lumpy. Overmixing will make the muffins tough. Spoon the batter into the prepared muffin pan, filling each two-thirds full.

Bake the muffins for 20 to 25 minutes, or until they have a distinct cracked peak in the middle and are golden brown and firm to the touch. A wooden pick inserted in the center of a muffin should come out clean. If the muffins seem slightly wet or soft, bake a few minutes longer. Cool the muffins in the pan for about 1 minute. Turn them out on to a wire rack to cool for a few minutes.

Blueberry Muffins Hertz are delicious served warm.

TINA'S BREAKFAST LOAF

INGREDIENTS

Makes 1 large loaf
½ cup (110g) unsalted butter, softened
¾ cup packed (170g) dark brown sugar
1⅔ cups (255g) unbleached all-purpose flour
2 teaspoons baking soda
a pinch of salt
1 cup + 2 tablespoons (260ml) sour cream
1 large egg
TOPPING:
3 tablespoons packed light brown sugar
2 teaspoons ground cinnamon
½ cup (60g) roughly chopped walnuts

a loaf pan, about 10 × 5 × 3 inches, lightly greased and bottom lined with waxed paper

This recipe dates back to the late seventies, when I was working in Paris. It comes from Tina Ujlaki, now the food editor of Food & Wine *magazine in New York City, who used to make this simple and satisfying cake as an antidote to all the elaborate, rich French pâtisserie we consumed while we were there. This cake is a favorite of Tina's family. I enjoy serving it warm for breakfast with freshly brewed coffee.*

Heat the oven to 350°F. Mix all the topping ingredients in a small bowl with your fingertips until blended.

To make the cake: Beat together the butter and sugar with an electric mixer at high speed, or with a spoon, until the mixture is pale yellow and fluffy. Sift together the flour, baking soda, and salt on to a sheet of waxed paper. Whisk together the sour cream and eggs in a small bowl. Add the flour mixture and the sour cream mixture to the butter and sugar and mix on low speed, or stir just until the batter is thoroughly combined. The batter will be quite soft.

Spoon half the batter into the prepared pan. Sprinkle half of the topping over the batter. Spoon the remaining batter into the pan. Evenly sprinkle the remaining topping over the batter and press it lightly into the surface.

Bake the cake for 45 to 55 minutes, or until it is lightly browned and a wooden pick inserted in the center comes out clean. Cool the cake in the pan on a wire rack for about 5 minutes.

Carefully turn the cake out of the pan, remove the waxed paper from the bottom, and put upright on a serving platter. Then cut into slices and serve warm.

GINGERBREAD

INGREDIENTS

Makes 1 large loaf

- 1⅔ cups (230g) unbleached self-rising flour
- 1 teaspoon baking soda
- 1 tablespoon ground ginger
- 1 teaspoon ground cinnamon
- 1 teaspoon pumpkin-pie spice
- ½ cup (110g) unsalted butter, chilled and diced
- ⅓ cup (110g) dark unsulfured molasses
- ⅓ cup (110g) golden syrup (see Note)
- ½ cup + 2 tablespoons packed (110g) light brown sugar
- 1¼ cups (280ml) milk
- 1 extra large egg, beaten

a loaf pan, about 10 × 5 × 3 inches, greased and bottom lined with waxed paper

In my time as a pastry chef I have made many gingerbreads, but this is the most wonderful, sticky, spicy gingerbread I've ever tasted. It is dark, moist, well-spiced, not particularly sweet, and the flavor is unhampered by fruit or nuts. For the best flavor, let the gingerbread age a couple of days before eating. Enjoy it thickly sliced, with butter or slices of cheese.

Heat the oven to 350°F. Sift the flour, baking soda, and spices into a large bowl. Rub in the butter with your fingertips until the mixture looks like fine crumbs. In a small saucepan, heat the molasses with the syrup until melted, then let cool to lukewarm. Meanwhile, in another small pan, dissolve the sugar in the milk over a low heat, stirring. Whisk the milk into the flour mixture, then whisk in the molasses mixture followed by the egg. When thoroughly combined, you should have a thin batter.

Pour the batter into the prepared pan. Bake for 50 to 60 minutes, or until a skewer inserted off center comes out clean. (As the gingerbread bakes it will bubble up and rise, then fall, leaving a large, moist depression.) Let cool completely in the pan. Turn the cake out of the pan and remove the paper. Wrap the cake in waxed paper and then in foil.

NOTE: Golden syrup is found in jars or cans in most gourmet shops or better supermarkets.

WHISK THE BATTER UNTIL IT IS SMOOTH. IT SHOULD BE FAIRLY THIN.

BAKE UNTIL A SKEWER INSERTED OFF CENTER COMES OUT CLEAN.

Homemade gingerbread is an old-fashioned treat that still has great appeal. The flavor will be at its best if you bake this a couple of days before serving.

SMITHY LOAF

INGREDIENTS

Makes 1 medium loaf

1 cup + 2 tablespoons (260ml) water
2 cups (340g) golden raisins
½ cup (110g) unsalted butter
½ cup + 2 tablespoons packed (110g) light brown sugar
2 teaspoons pumpkin-pie spice
1 teaspoon baking soda
a pinch of salt
1⅔ cups (230g) unbleached all-purpose flour
1 teaspoon baking powder
2 large eggs, beaten

a loaf pan, about 7 × 5 × 3 inches, greased and bottom lined with waxed paper

I'm not sure where this recipe came from originally, but it was given to me by Malcolm Appleby, who is a distinguished silversmith – hence the loaf's name. Malcolm lives in Scotland, in what was once a railway station. This recipe reminds me of the teas he serves on his station platform in sight of his herb garden and the "bulb" garden (made from colored lights). Malcolm has the most marvelous sense of humor, and I always smile when I make this good loaf. Eat this bread the day after it's made, sliced and buttered.

Heat the oven to 350°F. Bring the 1 cup of water to a boil in a large saucepan. Add the raisins, butter, sugar, pumpkin-pie spice, baking soda, and salt. Lower the heat and simmer gently for 5 minutes, stirring occasionally to combine the ingredients, until the raisins have plumped and the butter is melted. Let the mixture cool slightly. Stir in the flour and baking powder until well combined, then stir in the beaten eggs. Scrape the batter into the prepared pan and smooth the surface.

Bake the loaf for 40 to 50 minutes, or until a wooden pick inserted in the center comes out clean. Completely cool the loaf in the pan on a wire rack. Then turn it out and wrap with waxed paper and then foil.

STIR IN THE FLOUR AND BAKING POWDER UNTIL WELL COMBINED.

SCRAPE THE BATTER INTO THE PREPARED LOAF PAN.

Maddybenny Wheaten Bread

MADDYBENNY WHEATEN BREAD

INGREDIENTS

Makes 1 medium loaf
6 cups (680g) whole-wheat bread flour, preferably stone-ground
1 tablespoon baking soda
1 tablespoon sugar
2 teaspoons salt
3–3¾ cups (710–850ml) buttermilk
extra flour for dusting

a baking pan, about 13 × 9 inches, greased

Another of Rosemary White's delicious and easy recipes from Northern Ireland (see her recipe for fadge on page 70). Here, four loaves are baked in one pan and then broken apart after baking. Any spare loaves can be frozen, well wrapped, for up to one month.

Heat the oven to 425°F. Stir together the flour, baking soda, sugar, and salt in a large mixing bowl. Make a well in the center. Add 3 cups (710ml) of the buttermilk. Using a metal spatula, mix the flour into the buttermilk to form a soft, but not sticky dough. Depending on the flour, you may need to add more buttermilk, 1 tablespoon at a time.

As soon as the dough comes together, turn it out on to a lightly floured work surface. With lightly floured hands, knead the dough gently for a few seconds, just until the dough looks even and has no floury patches. It still should look quite lumpy. Place the dough in the prepared pan and, with lightly floured hands, press it gently into the corners. Cut a deep cross on top with a sharp knife to score four equal rectangular sections. Bake the bread for 35 to 45 minutes, or until it has a firm, brown crust.

Turn out the bread on to a wire rack. Cover it with a clean dish towel, tucking the ends of the towel under the bread loosely. Let it cool to warm, if you wish, or cool it completely. Cut or break into four loaves.

A selection of savory quick breads. Left to right: Beer Bread (opposite), Herb Rolls (page 84), Bacon Loaf, and Maddybenny Wheaten Bread (page 81).

BACON LOAF

INGREDIENTS

Makes 1 large loaf

4 oz (110g) thick-sliced bacon, diced (about 1 cup)

2½ cups (340g) unbleached all-purpose flour

2 teaspoons baking powder

freshly ground black pepper, to taste

a large pinch of salt

¾ cup (170g) unsalted butter, chilled and diced

4 oz (110g) thickly sliced lean ham, diced (about 1 cup)

4 large eggs, beaten

a loaf pan, about 10 × 5 × 3 inches, greased

This richly flavored loaf smells so tantalizing in the oven, it's difficult to wait until it is cool enough to slice. Although the recipe comes from an American relative in Boston, I like to make it with thickly sliced smoked English bacon and a thick slice of good ham. In the States, if you can't get English bacon, use thick-sliced double-smoked bacon, available from a good butcher or gourmet foods store. This loaf is best on the day it is made.

Heat the oven to 350°F. Put the bacon into a cold frying pan and fry over moderately high heat for 5 minutes, stirring frequently, until crisp. Remove from the heat.

Sift together the flour, baking powder, pepper, and salt into a large bowl. Rub in the butter until the mixture looks like fine crumbs. Make a well in the center.

Stir the bacon and the bacon fat into the flour mixture. Add the ham and eggs, and stir to form a stiff batter. Spoon the batter into the prepared pan and smooth the surface. Bake the loaf for 45 to 55 minutes, or until it is lightly browned and a wooden pick inserted into the center comes out clean. Let cool in the pan on a wire rack for 5 minutes. Turn out the loaf on to the rack. Eat warm or let cool completely.

STIR IN THE CRISP BACON, HAM, AND EGGS TO MAKE A STIFF BATTER.

SPOON THE STIFF BATTER INTO THE PREPARED LOAF PAN.

DATE AND APPLE LOAF

INGREDIENTS

Makes 1 small loaf
½ cup (110g) unsalted butter, softened
½ cup + 2 tablespoons packed (110g) light brown sugar
2 large eggs, beaten
¾ cup (110g) unbleached self-rising flour
¾ cup (110g) whole-wheat flour, preferably stone-ground
1 cup (110g) chopped walnuts
¾ cup (110g) chopped pitted dates
¾ cup (110g) peeled and grated apple
about 2 tablespoons milk

a loaf pan, about 7 × 5 × 3 inches, greased and bottom lined with waxed paper

Use a well-flavored, tart apple for this slightly sweet loaf. In England I like this best made with Bramley cooking apples. In the States I suggest using Rhode Island greenings, Jonathans, Ida Reds, or a good, firm Granny Smith apple. The quantity of milk needed will depend on the flour you choose. This bread is tasty sliced and spread with butter or cheese.

Heat the oven to 350°F.

Beat together the butter and sugar in a large bowl with an electric mixer at high speed, or with a spoon, until light and fluffy. Beat in the eggs one at a time. With mixer on low speed, stir in the flours, walnuts, dates, and apples. Stir in enough milk to make a batter that clings to a wooden spoon, but falls when the spoon is tapped. Spoon the batter into the prepared pan.

Bake the loaf for 1 to 1¼ hours, or until a wooden pick inserted in the center comes out clean. Cool the loaf in the pan on a wire rack for 10 minutes. Then turn out the loaf on to a wire rack, remove the waxed paper from the bottom, and cool completely.

Make Date and Apple Loaf (above) in the fall when apples are at their best.

BEER BREAD

INGREDIENTS

Makes 1 small loaf
3¼ cups (455g) whole-wheat flour, preferably stone-ground
1 tablespoon baking powder
½ teaspoon salt
1 teaspoon honey
1½ cups (340ml) full-flavored dark ale

a loaf pan, about 7 × 5 × 3 inches, well greased

A very quick loaf, this takes just over an hour from start to finish. Eat it with a good aged cheese, such as Cheddar, or with a soup. I prefer to use very coarse Irish wheaten flour, which I am able to buy in Ireland (it isn't available anywhere else), but regular whole-wheat flour, or whole-wheat pastry flour will work fine too. Your choice depends on how coarse or fine-textured you like your bread.

This bread is a British favorite, but it may not be to everyone's taste. If your family or friends are not fond of beer, you should probably choose another recipe. Eat this loaf the day you make it, or toast it later. It can also be frozen for one month.

Heat the oven to 350°F. Mix together the whole-wheat flour, baking powder, and salt in a large mixing bowl. Stir in the honey and ale to make a heavy, wet dough.

Spoon the dough into the prepared pan and smooth the surface.

Bake the bread for 40 to 50 minutes, or until golden brown and a pick inserted in the center comes out clean. Turn out on to a wire rack and let cool completely.

HERB ROLLS

INGREDIENTS

Makes 8

- $3\frac{1}{4}$ cups (455g) unbleached self-rising flour
- 1 teaspoon salt
- freshly ground black pepper, to taste
- 1 cup (230g) cottage cheese
- 1 large egg
- 2 tablespoons chopped fresh herbs, such as chives, parsley, and thyme
- about 1 cup (230ml) milk
- extra flour for dusting
- extra milk for brushing

a baking sheet, greased

Fresh herbs are vital for this recipe – dried herbs simply won't do. The rolls look rough and craggy, which is part of their charm. The flavor goes well with winter vegetable soups, as well as with salads. Eat these warm with butter. The rolls can be kept in a plastic bag for a day, and they freeze well for up to one month.

Heat the oven to 350°F. Sift together the flour, salt, and pepper into a large bowl.

Put the cottage cheese, egg, and herbs into a blender or food processor. Process until smooth. If you don't have a blender or food processor, finely mince the herbs, then combine with the cottage cheese and egg in a bowl and whisk until well blended and as smooth as possible.

Stir the cheese mixture into the flour using a metal spatula. Add just enough of the milk to make a soft but not sticky dough.

Turn the dough out on to a lightly floured work surface and lightly knead four to six times until it is fairly smooth. Divide the dough into eight equal pieces. Gently shape each piece into a rough ball. Arrange them spaced apart on the prepared baking sheet. Brush the rolls with milk. Bake for about 25 minutes, or until they turn golden brown and sound hollow when tapped underneath. Transfer to a wire rack to cool slightly.

Lovage, tansy, bee balm, and summer savory are among the more unusual aromatic herbs and plants, dating from the 17th century, flourishing in the kitchen garden of Philipsburg Manor (page 69). The combination of chives, parsley, and thyme in the ingredients for Herb Rolls (above) makes the most of readily available herbs, but it is only a suggestion. Use any mix of herbs you like, as long as they are fresh. Oregano or marjoram would be lovely instead of thyme, and you could use basil leaves in place of the parsley.

When Europeans arrived in New England in the 17th century, corn was growing in abundance, and they soon adapted many Native American recipes for cooking and baking the indigenous crop. Ever since, cornmeal has been a staple in American kitchens and corn bread, in numerous regional guises, is popular all across the country.

My selection of cornmeal recipes (right) includes Corn Dabs (below), a colonial recipe baked in corn-stick pans, and in individual antique rectangular molds with crisp bacon pieces added, and Corn Bread (page 86).

For the best cornmeal, search out small local mills who stone-grind the corn. Buy it in small quantities and, for freshness, keep it in the refrigerator or freezer.

Freshly baked corn bread is on the menu at Windham Hill Inn, in West Townshend, Vermont.

CORN DABS

This recipe is an authentic heirloom from colonial America, and may be a surprise to modern tastes. Although the corn dabs look like corn sticks, they are much denser and coarser, and they will not rise because they do not use any leavening.

"Leavening agents did not arrive until 1820," explains food historian Caroll Boltin (page 69). "White flour was scarce, so the cornmeal used alone would give a gritty texture." However, the dabs remain moist and creamy on the inside, thanks to the addition of sour cream – an example of the Dutch settlers' influence in New York State's Hudson Valley.

These plain and simple dabs were eaten with rich oyster or clam stews and fish soups – a good combination. They are a nice change from today's more usual, sweeter baked cornmeal muffins and breads. Eat them while they're still warm.

Heat the oven to 425°F.

INGREDIENTS

Makes 7

- ¾ cup (170ml) boiling water
- 1 cup + 2 tablespoons (140g) yellow cornmeal
- ¼ cup (60ml) sour cream
- 1 large egg, beaten
- 1 tablespoon melted bacon fat or butter
- ¼ teaspoon salt (optional)
- plenty of extra bacon fat for greasing pan

a cast-iron corn-stick pan, greased

Pour the boiling water over the cornmeal in a large bowl. Mix well with a fork. Then add the sour cream. Mix thoroughly and let stand for 10 minutes to soften the cornmeal. Put the corn-stick pan on a baking sheet and place in the oven to heat up for 10 to 15 minutes, until pan is just smoking.

Stir the egg, bacon fat or butter, and salt into the batter. Stir in the crumbled bacon too, if you wish. Pour the batter into a large glass measuring cup for easier handling.

Open the oven door and pull the rack with the corn-stick pan on it toward you. Generously brush the melted bacon fat or butter into the hot corn-stick pan. Return it to the oven for a couple of minutes to heat the fat. Pour the batter into the molds to almost full – the batter should sizzle when it hits the very hot fat. Bake the dabs for 15 minutes, or until crusty and golden and just slightly puffed, and the edges pull away from the pan; a wooden pick inserted in the center should come out clean. Turn out the dabs immediately.

NOTE: Three strips of bacon will render enough fat for the recipe and for greasing the pan; you can also crumble the cooked bacon and add it to the batter for more flavor in the dabs.

CORN BREAD

INGREDIENTS

Makes 9 squares

- 1 cup (140g) unbleached all-purpose flour
- 1 cup + 2 tablespoons (140g) yellow cornmeal
- ¼ cup (50g) sugar
- 4 teaspoons baking powder
- ½ teaspoon salt
- 1 cup (230ml) milk
- 2 large eggs, beaten
- 1 tablespoon melted butter
- 1 teaspoon caraway seeds

an 8-inch square cake pan, greased

This is Caroll Boltin's favorite recipe for corn bread. "The caraway seeds are an authentic colonial addition," says Caroll, who has researched American settlers (see page 69). "It reflects the Dutch influence on cooking here in the Hudson Valley of New York State."

Heat the oven to 375°F.

Stir together the flour, cornmeal, sugar, baking powder, and salt in a large bowl. Add the milk, eggs, and melted butter and stir well to make a smooth batter. Stir in the caraway seeds. Scrape the batter into the prepared pan and smooth the surface.

Bake the bread for 20 to 25 minutes, or until the corn bread is golden, firm to the touch, and has shrunk from the corners of the pan, and a wooden pick inserted in the center comes out clean. Cool the corn bread on a wire rack for 10 minutes, then turn it out on to a platter. Serve warm, cut into squares.

NOTE: If you prefer to make corn muffins, bake the batter in a twelve-cup muffin pan, greased or lined with paper or foil liners.

CAROLL BEATS CARAWAY SEEDS INTO THE CORN BREAD BATTER.

SHE SCRAPES THE BATTER INTO THE PREPARED CAKE PAN. THE CORN BREAD IS THEN READY TO BE BAKED.

PHOEBE LETT'S TREACLE BREAD

INGREDIENTS

Makes 2 small loaves

- 4¾ cups (680g) whole-wheat flour, preferably stone-ground
- 1⅔ cups unbleached all-purpose flour
- 1 tablespoon raw brown sugar, such as Demerara
- 2 teaspoons salt
- 2 teaspoons baking soda
- 1½ teaspoons ground ginger
- 4 tablespoons (60g) butter, well chilled and diced
- 3–3¼ cups (690–710ml) buttermilk
- 3 tablespoons dark unsulfured molasses
- 1 large egg, beaten
- extra flour for shaping
- sesame seeds for sprinkling (optional)

2 loaf pans, about 7 × 5 × 3 inches, or 8-inch layer cake pans, greased and bottom lined with waxed paper

I love making this simple and well-flavored Irish loaf – it smells wonderful, and has become a picnic favorite. This recipe is a specialty of Phoebe Lett, who lives in Enniscorthy, County Wexford, in Ireland. Phoebe and her husband Bill are tremendous hosts; after spending five minutes with them you feel you've known them a lifetime.

A restaurant in Wexford serves an excellent first course – triangles of this warm treacle bread with Cashel Blue cheese (an Irish blue cheese) melted on top, surrounded by a good salad with a nicely tart dressing. Or simply eat this bread sliced, with butter and cheese.

Since treacle isn't widely available in the U.S., I've adapted this recipe to use dark unsulfured molasses, but you can use treacle instead.

Heat the oven to 400°F.

Stir together the flours, sugar, salt, baking soda, and ginger in a large bowl. Rub in the butter with your fingertips, or cut in with a pastry blender, until the mixture looks like fine crumbs.

Whisk together 3 cups (690ml) buttermilk, the molasses, and egg in a medium-size bowl. Quickly stir the buttermilk mixture into the dry ingredients using a wooden spoon. The dough should be heavy and slightly sticky; if there are dry crumbs, add a little more buttermilk, one tablespoon at a time.

Flour your hands and gently knead the dough in the mixing bowl until it comes together – a few seconds only. It will still look rough and lumpy. Divide the dough in half and shape each half into an oval (or a round, if using round pans). Put one piece into each pan and press the dough into the corners. Sprinkle the tops with the sesame seeds if you wish, and press them firmly into the loaves so they don't fall off when the loaves are turned out.

Bake the loaves for 10 minutes, then reduce the oven temperature to 350°F and bake for another 35 to 40 minutes. (Cover the loaves loosely with a sheet of foil if they brown too quickly.) When they are done, the loaves will have a crunchy crust and be well-risen; when tapped underneath, they will sound hollow.

Turn the loaves out, remove the waxed paper from the bottoms, and cool completely on wire racks. Wrap in waxed paper and then foil, and keep at room temperature for a day before slicing. The extra loaf can be frozen up to one month.

THE DOUGH SHOULD REMAIN ROUGH AND LUMPY AFTER IT HAS BEEN GENTLY KNEADED. DIVIDE IT IN HALF, SHAPE INTO OVALS AND PLACE IN THE PANS.

Treacle bread is best simply served with butter, as here, or with cheese. Sesame seeds add extra texture.

TOP
John Doyle (right) discusses the day's events on the farm with his nephew, while Mary's bread bakes in the cast-iron pot. Extra ashes have been placed on top of the pot so the bread bakes evenly.
ABOVE
After about 40 minutes, Mary removes the perfectly baked bread.

BASIC BROWN BREAD

Phoebe Lette (page 87) insisted we visit Mary Curtis, whom she calls "a true country woman – her bread is supreme." Mary and her husband farm at Bree in Country Wexford, Ireland. In 1989 she won the Farmers Journal Farm Woman of the Year award in an impressive competition that involved cooking an entire meal in front of an audience, making an evening gown (not in public), and changing the wheel on a farm vehicle against the clock. With four grown-up children who still come home each weekend, the Curtises "go through a lot of bread," and Mary bakes three loaves at a time to make the best use of her forty-year-old, oil-fired Rayburn oven.

"No two days will I make the same bread – I'll add sesame, poppy, or caraway seeds, or thyme and sage to go with soups,' she says. Mary grows her own vegetables and herbs, and uses the full-fat unpasteurized milk from her own cows to make buttermilk. When it comes to flour she prefers Odlums cream flour ("cream" meaning unbleached) and Abbey stone-ground wholemeal (whole-wheat) flour, which she calls "good and coarse."

To bake a batch of brown bread in the traditional way – in a cast-iron pot suspended over the red embers of an open fire – Mary walked across a couple of fields, over a stile, and under a barbed-wire fence to visit her next-door neighbors, Pat and John Doyle, farming brothers well into their eighties. The open-fire method was regularly used in rural areas of Ireland for baking until the 1950s and, as Mary has discovered, it bakes wonderful, slightly smoky bread; the closed pot traps the steam inside to produce a softer than usual crust.

The Doyles prepared the fire a good hour before the bread was put in to bake, so the flames had died down and the embers glowed red. Then they suspended a massive, solid iron pot on a chain from a swing arm and heated it until moderately hot.

"To test the pot, sprinkle a little flour inside. It should change color slowly," she says. "If it turns black instantly, swing the pot away from the fire for a few minutes." Mary placed her shaped brown loaf into the pot, covered the pot with its heavy lid, then heaped hot ashes on top of the lid so the loaf would cook evenly.

After 40 minutes spent chatting about old times on the farm, she checked on the bread's progress – it looked wonderful. The cooked loaf was wrapped in a cloth to soften the crust, left to cool, then eagerly devoured.

Here is Mary's recipe for brown bread, adapted for more modern kitchens. This loaf is best eaten within twenty-four hours.

INGREDIENTS

Makes 1 medium loaf

- 2½ cups (340g) whole-wheat flour, preferably stone-ground
- ¾ cup (110g) unbleached all-purpose flour
- ½ cup (30g) wheat bran
- 2½ tablespoons (15g) wheat germ
- 1 teaspoon baking soda
- 1 teaspoon salt
- 2 tablespoons (30g) butter or margarine, chilled and diced
- 1¼–1¾ cups (280–430ml) buttermilk
- extra flour for dusting

a large baking sheet, well floured

Heat the oven to 425°F. Mix together the flours, bran, wheat germ, baking soda, and salt in a large bowl. Rub in the margarine or butter using your fingertips, lifting the mixture high above the bowl to aerate the dough, until it looks like fine crumbs.

Stir in enough of the buttermilk to make a stiff dough; it will look a bit rough. Turn the dough out on to a well-floured work surface and quickly knead it with the heel of your hand, pushing the dough from the middle out and then pulling it back. Use your other hand to rotate the dough as you knead it. As soon as the dough looks smooth, shape it into a flat disk. Place the loaf on the prepared baking sheet. Sprinkle with flour and cut a deep cross in the loaf. Bake the bread for 35 to 45 minutes, or until the loaf is crusty, browned, and sounds hollow when tapped underneath. Transfer to a wire rack and cool completely.

NOTE: Mary Curtis gave me an old recipe for buttermilk from the days when every farm made its own buttermilk and butter. You need to start a buttermilk "plant," which will ferment milk. Cream 2 0.6-oz cakes fresh yeast (30g) with 2½ tablespoons (30g) sugar in a large bowl until smooth. Gradually stir in 5 cups (1.15 liters) lukewarm milk. Cover the bowl with a dish towel and let stand for a couple of days at room temperature. The mixture should smell and taste like buttermilk. Line a strainer with a double thickness of cheesecloth and strain the mixture. Refrigerate the buttermilk, and it is ready to use. (It will keep for one day, covered.) The residue in the cheesecloth can be used to make the next batch of buttermilk. Rinse the residue in the cheesecloth with lukewarm water, then put it into a clean container, preferably one scalded in boiling water. Add a generous teaspoon of sugar, mix, add the milk, and proceed as before.

USING HER FINGERTIPS, MARY RUBS IN THE MARGARINE.

ALL THE INGREDIENTS ARE STIRRED TO MAKE A STIFF DOUGH.

USING THE HEEL OF HER HAND, MARY KNEADS THE DOUGH.

SHE PATS THE LOAVES INTO FLAT DISKS.

PROUD MARY'S LOAVES ARE READY FOR THE OVEN.

SHE TESTS A LOAF BY TAPPING IT ON THE BOTTOM.

SODA BREAD

INGREDIENTS

Makes 4 large triangles
3¼ cups (455g) unbleached self-rising flour, white or whole-wheat
1 teaspoon sugar
1 teaspoon salt
2 tablespoons (30g) butter, well chilled and diced
about 1½ cups (340ml) buttermilk
fat or oil for cooking

a large, heavy cast-iron frying pan with a lid or baking sheet to cover

This is Mary Curtis's recipe for soda bread, the traditional bread of Ireland, which is quickly made from self-rising flour and buttermilk and cooked on top of the stove in a heavy cast-iron frying pan. "It's a quick way to have fresh bread, and it's good and puffy and fluffy," says Mary. Make sure the pan is large enough to turn the bread with ease – otherwise cook it in two batches or use two frying pans. Eat this bread while it's still warm.

Heat the pan over moderately low heat while you make the dough. Sift together the flour, sugar, and salt into a large bowl. Rub in the butter with your fingertips or cut in with a pastry blender, lifting the mixture a few inches above the bowl and letting it fall to aerate the dough, until the mixture looks like fine crumbs. Stir in enough buttermilk to just moisten the dry ingredients and to make a soft, light, and fluffy dough; don't overwork the dough. Quickly turn it out on to a floured surface and knead four to five times until the dough comes together and forms a smooth ball. Pat out to a disk about 1 inch thick. Cut the disk in quarters.

Lightly brush the pan with oil. Put the bread into the heated pan, cover, and cook over moderately low heat for 15 to 20 minutes, turning the triangles over two or three times so they cook evenly. The finished bread should be golden brown and well risen. Remove the bread from the pan, transfer to a wire rack, and wrap with a dry dish towel until ready to serve.

MARY RUBS IN THE BUTTER, LIFTING THE FLOUR MIXTURE ABOVE THE BOWL.

USING FLOURED FINGERS, SHE PATS THE DOUGH INTO A FLAT DISK.

USING A SHARP KNIFE, SHE CUTS THE DOUGH INTO QUARTERS.

THE DOUGH QUARTERS ARE COVERED WHILE THEY COOK.

AFTER 5 MINUTES' COOKING, MARY FLIPS OVER THE QUARTERS TO ENSURE EVEN COOKING.

SHE PLACES THE COOKED BREAD ONTO A WIRE RACK.

OPPOSITE
Soda bread from a local bakery, along with cheese, farmhouse butter, and a fruit tart, made a simple, impromptu picnic when Anthony and I were in Co. Cork, Ireland.

Country Butter

COFFEE

FRIED DOUGHS

"Where can you find a really good doughnut these days?" lamented an elderly friend as she recalled her favorite childhood treat. A good doughnut is light, flavorful, and made from kneaded dough, perhaps filled with plenty of proper fruit jam, cooked in lard or a good vegetable oil, then coated in crunchy white sugar. Such doughnuts may no longer be easy to find commercially, but they are not at all difficult to make.

I'm quite conservative about what I eat for breakfast and was about to help myself to a bowl of granola at the Windham Hill Inn in West Townshend, Vermont, when innkeeper Linda Busteed appeared with a plate of freshly cooked doughnuts. My in-laws jumped for joy. "Positively the finest you'll ever taste," they said, being long-term fans of Windham Hill's cooking. They were right (see Megan's Potato Doughnuts, page 98), but they didn't guess the secret of their lightness (mashed potatoes).

Doughnuts and fried doughs originated as the last scraps of a big batch of bread dough. The pieces would be sweetened and cut, or filled with fruit or jam, and then fried – either as a treat for the children, or as a necessity for a quickly cooked breakfast, as Lois Keller explains (page 101). For Ina McNeil (page 102), fry breads are an essential part of the early fall powwows (large gatherings of Native Americans). Although she travels all over the U.S. to cook sweet and savory fry breads in huge quantities for these events, she still makes them regularly for her family. Lois Keller's German Whole-Wheat Grebble (page 101) is similar to Ina's baking-powder dry bread (through handled in a very different way), but Lois' dough is formed into twisted strips.

OPPOSITE Freshly made doughnuts, New Orleans style. *ABOVE* Doughnuts frying.

Doughnuts and fried doughs can be rich, such as the brioche-like Fancy Ring Doughnuts (page 97) or the Dutch Oliebollen (page 100), or quick and simple, like The Fry-Bread Queen's Fry Bread. But either way, homemade doughnuts are a treat indeed.

TIPS FOR FRYING DOUGHS

– Use good quality, fresh vegetable oil (lard or solid white vegetable shortening can also be used), cool the oil, and strain it after each use through a coffee filter or strainer lined with white paper towels. If necessary, skim the oil with a skimmer or a long-handled, fine strainer between batches of doughnuts to remove any charred crumbs, which will ruin both the taste and appearance of your doughnuts.

– To avoid accidents, don't fill the pan more than one-third full with oil – it will bubble up when you add the doughnuts. Keep the lid close by to cover the fat should it ever catch fire, and never leave the pan unattended.

– For the best results, the oil should have reached the correct temperature – 350°F on a frying or candy thermometer. Many electric fryers have a built-in thermostat. To test the temperature if you don't have a thermometer, drop a cube of bread in the oil. It should brown in 40 seconds at that heat. If the oil is too cool, the doughnut will sink to the bottom, absorb the oil, and become greasy. If the oil is too hot, the outsides will be hard and overcooked while the centers are still raw.

– Fry the doughnuts (which should be at room temperature) a few pieces at a time – don't crowd the pan.

– Turn the doughnuts over frequently with a skimmer or slotted spoon so they cook and brown evenly. Adjust the heat under the oil and test its temperature between batches; reheat it, if necessary.

– Remove the doughnuts with a fry basket or a slotted spoon, a skimmer, or a pair of long-handled tongs, then drain on plenty of paper towels. Eat as soon as possible – they don't keep and can't be frozen.

JAM DOUGHNUTS

INGREDIENTS

Makes about 12

4–4½ cups (455–510g) unbleached white bread flour
1 teaspoon salt
1 0.6-oz cake fresh yeast (15g), or
1 envelope active dry yeast (2½ teaspoons)
3 tablespoons (40g) sugar
1 cup (230ml) lukewarm milk
2 large eggs, beaten
2 tablespoons (30g) butter, melted and cooled
extra flour for dusting
about ¼ cup raspberry or strawberry jam
oil for deep-frying
extra sugar for sprinkling
a 2½-inch round biscuit or cookie cutter
a pastry brush

1–2 large baking sheets, lightly floured
a deep-fat fryer or large Dutch oven

I like homemade raspberry or strawberry jam in the center of my doughnut, but a nice tart apricot conserve, chunky, dark marmalade, or even a little mincemeat left from Christmas can be substituted. This dough is flavorful and very light. The secret to making these doughnuts is to seal the cut circles of dough thoroughly so the filling doesn't leak out during cooking. Eat the same day for best texture and taste.

Mix together 4 cups (455g) flour and the salt in a large bowl. Make a well in the center of the flour. Crumble the fresh yeast into the well. Add the sugar and 2 tablespoons of the lukewarm milk. Mix until the liquid is smooth. Add the remaining milk to the well. If using dry yeast, mix the granules with 2 tablespoons of the lukewarm milk and 2

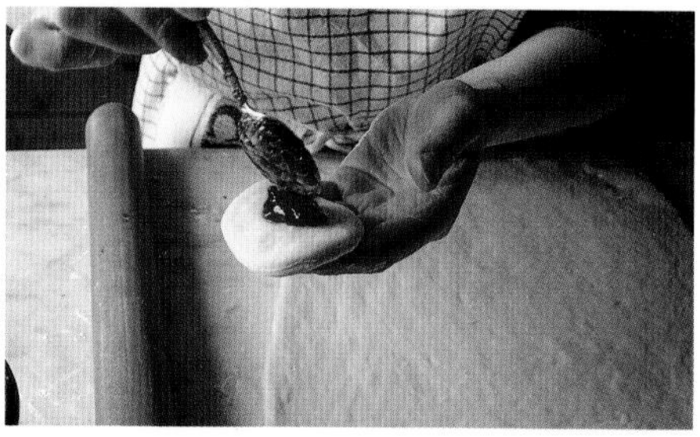

SPOON ABOUT 1 TEASPOON OF JAM IN THE CENTER OF ONE DOUGH ROUND.

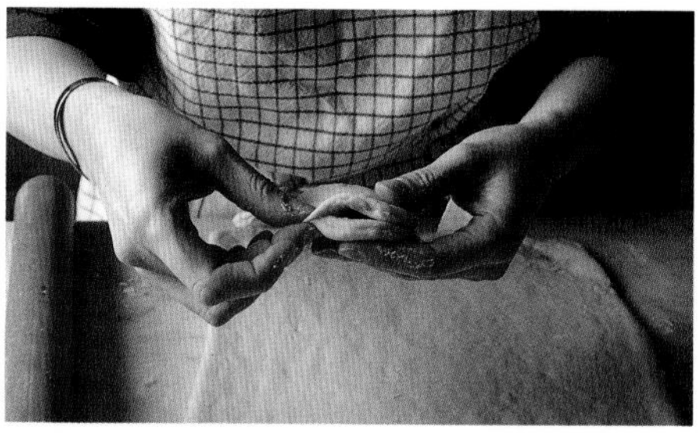

COVER WITH A SECOND DOUGH ROUND AND PRESS AND PINCH THE EDGES TOGETHER TO SEAL THOROUGHLY.

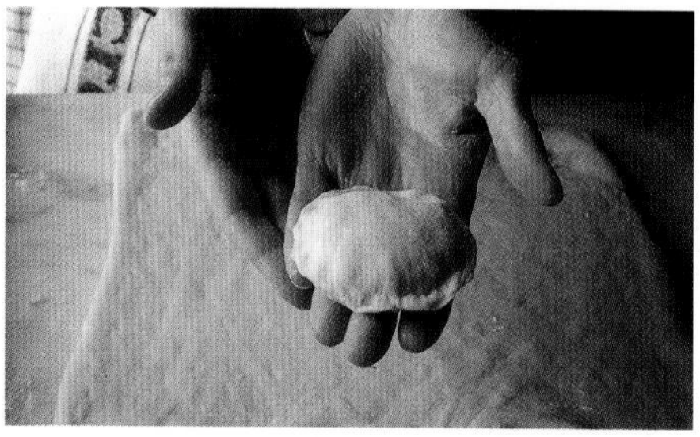

THE FILLED DOUGHNUT SHOULD BE SEALED ALL AROUND SO JAM DOESN'T LEAK OUT DURING FRYING.

LIFT THE DOUGHNUTS OUT OF THE HOT OIL WHEN THEY ARE WELL BROWNED AND PUFFED.

Made with flavorful and very light dough, these jam-filled doughnuts will be popular with children and adults. For extra sweetness, you can gently roll the doughnuts in granulated sugar, coating both sides, instead of just sprinkling the tops.

tablespoons sugar in a small bowl and let stand until foamy, 5 to 10 minutes (page 18). Add the yeast mixture to the well in the flour along with the remaining milk and sugar.

Add the eggs and butter to the well. Mix these liquid ingredients together. Work in the flour to make a soft, but not sticky dough. If there are crumbs of dry dough, add a little extra milk, 1 tablespoon at a time. If the dough sticks to your fingers, work in extra flour, 1 tablespoon at a time.

Turn out the dough onto a lightly floured surface and knead until smooth and elastic, about 10 minutes, adding a little more flour as needed to prevent sticking. Clean and dry the bowl and oil it lightly. Put the ball of dough back into the bowl and turn it over. Cover and let rise, until doubled in size, about 2 hours.

Punch down the risen dough. Turn out onto a lightly floured surface and knead for a few seconds. With a lightly floured rolling pin, gradually roll out the dough to about ½ inch thick. When rolling out the dough, let it rest periodically to relax the dough.

Cut out rounds with the floured biscuit or cookie cutter. Re-roll the scraps and cut; you should have about 24 rounds.

Spoon about 1 teaspoon of jam in the center of one round. Brush the edges with a little water. Cover with a second round and press and pinch the edges together to seal thoroughly. Repeat with the remaining dough. Place on lightly floured baking sheets, spacing them apart, and cover lightly with a dry dish towel. Let rise at warm room temperature, away from drafts, until almost doubled in size, about 20 minutes.

Meanwhile, pour the oil into the deep-fat fryer or Dutch oven to a depth of about 3 inches. Slowly heat until the oil registers 350°F on a frying thermometer (see page 93). Lower three doughnuts into the hot oil with a slotted spoon. Fry the doughnuts, turning them frequently, until well browned and puffed, about 10 minutes. Lift out the doughnuts and drain on paper towels. Fry the remaining doughnuts in batches. While still warm, sprinkle the doughnuts with granulated sugar. Let cool.

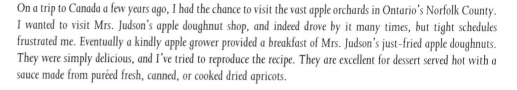

ONTARIO APPLE DOUGHNUTS

INGREDIENTS

Makes about 14
1 batch Jam Doughnuts dough (page 94)
1 large Granny Smith apple
1 tablespoon water
sugar to taste
ground cinnamon, grated lemon or orange rind, golden raisins, or chopped walnuts or pecans (optional)
oil for deep-frying
ground cinnamon mixed with sugar for sprinkling
1–2 baking sheets, lightly floured

a deep-fat fryer or large Dutch oven

On a trip to Canada a few years ago, I had the chance to visit the vast apple orchards in Ontario's Norfolk County. I wanted to visit Mrs. Judson's apple doughnut shop, and indeed drove by it many times, but tight schedules frustrated me. Eventually a kindly apple grower provided a breakfast of Mrs. Judson's just-fried apple doughnuts. They were simply delicious, and I've tried to reproduce the recipe. They are excellent for dessert served hot with a sauce made from puréed fresh, canned, or cooked dried apricots.

Prepare the Jam Doughnut dough through the first rising. While the dough is rising, peel, core, and thickly slice the apple. Place in a small saucepan with the water, cover, and cook very slowly, stirring occasionally, until the apple is very soft. Add granulated sugar to taste, and small amounts of any of the optional flavoring ingredients.

Punch down the dough, transfer to a lightly floured work surface, and knead for a few seconds. Gradually roll out the dough with a rolling pin to a large rectangle, about ½ inch thick, letting the dough rest periodically. With a floured knife, cut the dough into 3-inch squares. Re-roll the scraps and cut into squares. Place 1 teaspoon of the apple filling into the center of each square. Brush the edges lightly with water. Fold each square in half diagonally over the filling to form a triangle. Seal by pressing and pinching the edges together. Place the triangles, spaced apart, on lightly floured baking sheets. Let rise, uncovered, at warm room temperature, away from drafts, until almost doubled in size, 20 to 30 minutes.

Meanwhile, pour the oil into the deep-fat fryer or Dutch oven to a depth of about 3 inches. Slowly heat over moderate heat until the oil registers 350°F on a frying thermometer (see page 93).

Place three dough triangles in the fry basket and lower into the hot oil, or slip them, one at a time, into the oil with a slotted spoon. Do not crowd the pan. Fry the doughnuts, turning them often so they brown evenly, until nicely puffed and golden, about 5 minutes. Lift out the doughnuts with the fry basket or slotted spoon and place on paper towels to drain. While still warm, sprinkle the doughnuts with cinnamon-sugar. Fry the remaining doughnuts in batches. Eat the same day.

For a delicious dessert, serve these apple doughnuts while they are still warm with apricot purée and crème fraîche.

PLACE ONE TEASPOON OF THE APPLE FILLING IN THE CENTER OF EACH DOUGH SQUARE.

FOLD EACH SQUARE OVER THE FILLING TO FORM A TRIANGLE.

FANCY RING DOUGHNUT

WORK THE BUTTER INTO THE DOUGH, SQUEEZING THE TWO TOGETHER UNTIL THOROUGHLY COMBINED

RIGHT Fancy Ring Doughnut

INGREDIENTS

Makes 18

- 4 cups (455g) unbleached white bread flour
- 1 teaspoon salt
- 1 0.6-oz cake fresh yeast (15g), or 1 envelope active dry yeast (2½ teaspoons)
- ¾ cup (170ml) milk, at room temperature
- 5 tablespoons (60g) granulated sugar
- 4 large eggs, at room temperature, beaten
- ½ cup (110g) butter, at room temperature
- extra flour for dusting
- oil for deep-frying
- confectioners' sugar for sprinkling

- a 3-inch doughnut cutter, or a 3-inch round biscuit or cookie cutter and a ½-inch round cutter
- 1–2 large baking sheets, lightly floured
- a deep-fat fryer or large Dutch oven

The dough here is very rich – it's a type of brioche – and it makes the lightest, finest-textured doughnuts. After chilling and shaping the dough, gently bring it back to warm room temperature before frying to avoid a heavy, soggy result. Eat these the day they are made.

Stir together the flour and salt in a large bowl. Crumble the fresh yeast into a small bowl. Stir in 2 tablespoons of the milk until smooth. If using dry yeast, mix the granules with 2 tablespoons of the milk and ½ teaspoon of sugar in a small bowl and let stand until foamy, 5 to 10 minutes (page 18).

Mix the sugar into the flour mixture. Make a well in the center of the flour and pour in the yeast mixture, the remaining milk, and the beaten eggs. Using your hand, combine all the ingredients in the well, then gradually work in the flour from the bowl to make a smooth batter. Beat the batter with your hand, pulling and stretching it, for about 10 minutes. The dough will be very sticky at this stage. Cover the bowl with a damp dish towel and let stand at room temperature, away from drafts, until doubled in size, about 1½ hours.

Punch down the dough with floured knuckles. Keeping the mixture in the bowl, work the butter into the dough, squeezing the two together until thoroughly combined. The dough should look smooth and glossy, with no streaks, and should be somewhat sticky.

Cover the bowl with a damp dish towel and refrigerate for at least 4 hours or until doubled in size (the dough can be left in the refrigerator overnight at this point).

Punch down the dough – it should be quite firm. Turn out the dough onto a floured work surface. Roll out the dough with a floured rolling pin to a circle about 1 inch thick. Using the floured doughnut cutter or the large floured biscuit or cookie cutter, stamp out circles. If using the biscuit or cookie cutter, use the smaller cutter to stamp out a round in the center of each. Re-roll the scraps and centers and cut: you should have about 18 rings. Place the rings, spaced apart, on floured baking sheets. Let rise, uncovered, away from drafts, until they have doubled in size and warmed to room temperature, 30 minutes to 1 hour.

Meanwhile, pour the oil into the deep-fat fryer or Dutch oven to a depth of about 3 inches. Slowly heat until the oil registers 350°F on a frying thermometer. Lower about three rings of dough into the hot oil. Fry the doughnuts, stirring from time to time and turning the rings, for about 5 minutes, or until golden brown. Lift the doughnuts out with the fry basket or slotted spoon and drain on paper towels. Cook the remaining doughnuts in batches. Sprinkle the doughnuts, while still warm, with the confectioners' sugar. Let cool.

MEGAN'S POTATO DOUGHNUTS

These are the best doughnuts I've ever tasted. Last summer my in-laws introduced me to the beautiful Windham Hill Inn, in West Townshend, Vermont, during their annual visit to the Marlboro music festival. These were so wonderful I asked innkeeper Linda Busteed for the secret. "Potatoes and spice, and Megan," she replied giving the credit to her assistant, Megan McCooey. Eat these the day you make them.

INGREDIENTS

Makes 14

- 1 cup (230g) freshly cooked mashed potatoes
- 3¼–4 cups (455–570g) unbleached all-purpose flour
- 1 cup (200g) granulated sugar
- 1 tablespoon baking powder
- ½ teaspoon grated nutmeg
- ½ teaspoon ground ginger
- 3 tablespoons (40g) butter, softened and cut into small pieces
- 2 large eggs, beaten
- 1 cup (230ml) milk
- a few drops of vanilla extract
- extra flour for dusting
- oil for deep-frying
- confectioners' sugar for sifting

- a 3-inch doughnut cutter, or a 3-inch round biscuit or cookie cutter and a ½-inch cutter
- a deep-fat fryer or large Dutch oven

Put the potatoes into a large bowl (they should be free of lumps and at room temperature). Add 3¼ cups (455g) of the flour, the sugar, baking powder, and spices. Add the butter, eggs, milk, and vanilla, and mix thoroughly to make a soft, biscuit-like dough. If necessary, add more flour, 1 tablespoon at a time, until the dough holds together.

Turn out the dough onto a floured work surface. Knead for about 1 minute, or until just smooth. Roll out the dough with a floured rolling pin to an 8-inch circle about 1 inch thick. Cut out rounds using the floured doughnut cutter or the larger floured biscuit or cookie cutter. If using the biscuit or cookie cutter, stamp out the center of each round – to make a ring – using the floured smaller cutter. Re-roll the trimmings and cut out more rings. If you wish, the center rounds can also be fried.

Pour the oil into the deep-fat fryer or Dutch oven to a depth of about 3 inches. Slowly heat over moderate heat until the oil registers 350°F on a frying thermometer (see page 93). Place about three rings of dough in a fry basket and lower the basket into the hot oil, or slip the rings, one at a time, into the hot oil with a slotted spoon. Don't overcrowd the pan. Fry the rings, turning frequently so they brown evenly, for about 8 minutes, or until puffy and golden brown. Lift the rings out with the fry basket or slotted spoon and place on paper towels to drain. Sift confectioners' sugar over the doughnuts, and let cool. Fry the remaining doughnuts in batches.

Serve these spicy doughnuts and the fried centers with freshly brewed coffee.

Innkeeper and cook Linda Busteed rises early each morning to prepare freshly baked goods for her guests. These light potato doughnuts are served at least once a week. Here she is cutting out a batch in her sunny kitchen.

Gnocci fritti are best served warm sprinkled with freshly grated Parmesan cheese.

GNOCCI FRITTI

This is a savory fried dough from Italy. The dough is cut into squares, which puff up to resemble pillows as they cook. Gnocci fritti are eaten warm, dusted with Parmesan cheese, accompanied by thin slices of good prosciutto. This recipe will serve eight or ten as a first course. These take some time to fry, about 30 minutes, so you may want to invite guests into the kitchen to eat them freshly cooked.

INGREDIENTS

Makes about 32

- 5 cups (570g) unbleached white bread flour
- 1 teaspoon salt
- 1 0.6-oz cake fresh yeast (15g), or 1 envelope active dry yeast (2½ teaspoons) plus ½ teaspoon sugar
- 1¼ cups (280ml) mixed lukewarm milk and water
- 1 tablespoon olive oil
- extra flour for dusting
- oil for deep-frying
- freshly grated Parmesan cheese or coarse sea salt for sprinkling

a deep-fat fryer or large Dutch oven

Mix together the flour and salt in a large bowl. Make a well in the center of the flour. Crumble the fresh yeast into a small bowl. Stir in 2 tablespoons of the warm liquid until smooth. Then stir in the rest of the liquid and the olive oil. If using dry yeast, mix the granules with 2 tablespoons of the warm liquid and the sugar and let stand until foamy, 5 to 10 minutes (page 18). Stir in the rest of the warm liquid and the olive oil.

Add the yeast mixture to the well in the flour. Mix in the flour from the bowl to make a fairly firm dough. If necessary, add a little more warm water, 1 tablespoon at a time, if the dough seems dry and won't come together.

Turn out the dough onto a lightly floured work surface and knead for 5 minutes. The dough should be glossy and elastic. Cover the ball of dough with the upturned bowl and let stand at room temperature for 30 minutes. The dough will rise slightly and become quite pliable. Punch down the dough with floured knuckles. With a lightly floured rolling pin, roll out the dough on a lightly floured work surface to about ¼ inch thick.

With a floured, large, sharp knife, cut the dough into 2-inch squares. Re-roll and cut the scraps, or fry the odd-shaped pieces. Cover the dough squares with dry dish towels so they don't form a hard crust.

Pour the oil into the deep-fat fryer or Dutch oven to a depth of about 3 inches. Slowly heat over moderate heat until the oil registers about 350°F on a frying thermometer (see page 93). In the time this takes, the dough will have risen slightly. Place about four squares of dough in the fry basket and lower the basket into the hot oil, or slip them, one at a time, into the hot oil with a slotted spoon. Don't overcrowd the pan. Fry the dough squares, turning them frequently, until they are puffed and evenly golden brown, about 4 minutes. Lift out the squares with the fry basket or slotted spoon and place on paper towels to drain. Keep warm on a baking sheet in a 250°F oven. Fry the remaining squares in batches. Arrange the warm squares on a serving dish. Sprinkle with Parmesan cheese or salt and serve immediately with prosciutto.

Enjoy oliebollens Dutch style as a snack. The dough is very rich, so they also make a delicious dessert if served with a scoop of vanilla ice cream.

OLIEBOLLEN

INGREDIENTS

Makes 14

2½ cups (280g) unbleached white bread flour

½ teaspoon salt

1 0.6-oz cake fresh yeast (15g), or 1 envelope active dry yeast (2½ teaspoons)

2 teaspoons sugar

1¼ cups (280ml) lukewarm milk

finely grated rind and juice of ½ lemon

⅓ cup (60g) currants

⅓ cup (60g) raisins

1 Golden Delicious apple

extra flour for dusting

oil for deep-frying

extra sugar for rolling

2 baking sheets, lightly floured

a deep-fat fryer or large Dutch oven

These Dutch doughnuts are very light and moist, and are flavored with plenty of dried fruit, chopped apple, and lemon. The cooked puffy doughnuts are rolled in sugar while still hot.

Mix the flour and salt in a large bowl. Make a well in the center of the flour. Crumble the fresh yeast into a small bowl. Stir in the sugar and half the lukewarm milk until smooth. If using dry yeast, mix the granules with the sugar and half the lukewarm milk and let stand until foamy, 5 to 10 minutes (page 18). Pour the yeast mixture into the well. Mix in a little of the flour in the bowl to make a thin batter. Cover the bowl with a dry dish towel or plastic wrap and let stand until spongy, about 20 minutes (page 16).

Add the remaining milk and the lemon rind and juice to the well and mix thoroughly with the yeast mixture. Gradually work in the remaining flour in the bowl with your hands to make a very soft, quite sticky dough.

Knead the dough very thoroughly in the bowl by slapping it up and down with your hand for 10 minutes. It should stiffen somewhat, yet still be a bit sticky, and come away in one piece from the side of the bowl.

Sprinkle the currants and raisins over the dough. Quickly peel, core, and dice the apple into ¼-inch pieces (you should have about 1 cup). Sprinkle over the dough. Work the dried fruit and apple into the dough by gently squeezing the mixture through your fingers until the fruits are evenly distributed, but not crushed. Cover the bowl with a damp dish towel. Let rise at room temperature, away from drafts, until doubled in size, about 1 to 1½ hours. Meanwhile, pour the oil into the deep-fat fryer or Dutch oven to a depth of about 3 inches. Slowly heat the oil over moderate heat until it registers 350°F on a frying thermometer (see page 93). Punch down the dough with floured knuckles. Using an ice cream scoop, scoop up a rough ball of dough and drop it into the hot oil. Add three more balls of dough to the pan and fry, turning them over occasionally, until golden brown and puffed up, 7 to 8 minutes. Keep the remaining dough covered while these fry. Lift the doughnuts out with the fry basket or a slotted spoon and place on paper towels to drain. While still warm, roll the doughnuts in sugar to coat and let cool. Fry the remaining dough in batches. Eat the doughnuts the day they are made.

WHOLE-WHEAT GREBBLE

INGREDIENTS

Makes 22

1⅓ 0.6-oz cakes fresh yeast (20g), or 1½ envelopes active dry yeast (3¾ teaspoons)
½ cup (110ml) lukewarm water
¼ cup packed (50g) light brown sugar or 2½ tablespoons honey
about 5¼ cups (600g) whole-wheat bread flour, preferably stone-ground
½ teaspoon baking soda
1½ cups (340g) cottage cheese
2 large eggs, beaten
2 tablespoons (30g) butter, melted
2 teaspoons salt
extra flour for dusting
oil for deep-frying
confectioners' sugar for sprinkling

a deep-fat fryer or large Dutch oven

This German recipe has been passed down to Lois Keller through her husband Jerry's family. Its origins lie in the ingenuity of farmers' wives, she explained. "They used to mix up their bread dough at night, wrap the warmed bowl in blankets – don't forget, this was before central heating and winter nights were very cold – and leave the dough to rise overnight. In the morning, they could fry the dough quickly in lard to make a good, fresh breakfast." The Keller family lives near Ellis in west-central Kansas on a 5,000 acre farm of mixed crops – wheat, corn, and beans – and "nodding donkeys" (oil wells). Lois is an amazing woman. She works in the fields all day drilling oil or driving the combine, then cooks a massive meal for everyone. After dinner, she is still hard at work. "Some people knit in the evening, but I hand-clean some of our wheat." Lois grinds the wheat in a machine that resembles a huge coffee grinder, making it as coarse or as fine as she likes. It takes 3 or 4 minutes to grind 1½ pounds of wheat kernels, which is enough for a loaf of bread. This dough can also be shaped and made into light, slightly sweet rolls (for shaping and baking instructions, see Oatmeal Rolls, page 25).

Crumble the yeast into a small bowl. Stir in the warm water and the sugar or honey until smooth. If using dry yeast, sprinkle the granules over the warm water. Stir in the sugar or honey and let stand until foamy, 5 to 10 minutes (page 18).

Mix together half the flour with the baking soda, making a well in the center. Blend the cottage cheese, eggs, butter, and salt until smooth. Pour this mixture into the well. Add the yeast mixture to the food processor or blender and process briefly. Tip this into the well and mix together, working in the flour from the sides until the dough comes together and is soft, but not sticky.

Turn it out onto a floured surface. Flour your hands and knead the dough for 10 minutes until it is firm, smooth, and elastic, only adding extra flour to prevent it from sticking. Put the ball of dough back into the washed, dried, and oiled bowl and turn it over. Cover with a damp dish towel and let stand at warm room temperature, away from drafts, until doubled in size, about 1 hour.

Pour the oil into the deep-fat fryer or Dutch oven to a depth of about 3 inches. Slowly heat over moderate heat until the oil registers 350°F on a frying thermometer (page 93).

Punch down the dough and divide into twenty-two pieces. Using a floured rolling pin, roll each piece into an oval about ¼ inch thick. Cut a slit lengthwise down the center of each dough oval, cutting almost to the edges. Shape the ovals by twisting the ends of each in opposite directions. Place about three dough twists in a fry basket and lower the basket into the hot oil. Fry the grebbles, turning constantly, for about 2 minutes, or until puffed, golden brown, and crispy. Lift out the grebbles with the fry basket and drain on paper towels. Eat immediately dusted with confectioners' sugar.

BELOW RIGHT Grebbles can be sprinkled with confectioners' sugar just before serving.

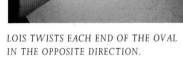

LOIS TWISTS EACH END OF THE OVAL IN THE OPPOSITE DIRECTION.

THE FRY-BREAD QUEEN'S FRY BREAD

INGREDIENTS

Makes about 20 large diamonds

- 4 cups (680g) unbleached all-purpose flour
- scant 1 cup (100g) dry milk powder
- ½ cup (100g) sugar
- 3 tablespoons baking powder
- 2 teaspoons salt
- 1¼–1½ cups (280–340ml) water from the cold tap
- extra flour for dusting
- oil for deep-frying

a deep-fat fryer or large Dutch oven

Ina McNeil is the great-granddaughter of Chief Sitting Bull of Little Bighorn fame. She is also known as the "fry-bread queen" because of her cooking at huge powwows and feasts.

On the Sioux reservation where Ina was born, along the North/South Dakota border, women compete to make the best fry bread for powwows. The meetings are large, and making enough fry bread can involve using up to 35 pounds of flour. "This recipe is very quick," Ina says. "My mother says that the mood you are in will determine how your fry bread will turn out. So be happy and people will enjoy your bread and be happy, too."

Ina grew up watching her mother and grandmother make fry bread, so she learned to cook by sight and touch, rather than by using exact measurements. The secret of a good fry bread, she says, is not to overwork the dough when you knead it. Make sure it feels elastic and springy.

Mix the flour, powdered milk, sugar, baking powder, and salt in a large bowl. Make a well in the center. Add 1¼ cups (280ml) water to the well. Gradually mix in the flour in the bowl with your hand to make a soft biscuit-like dough. It should not be dry or stiff. If the dough seems sticky, add flour, 1 tablespoon at a time. If too dry, add water, 1 tablespoon at a time.

Pour oil into the deep-fat fryer or Dutch oven to a depth of about 3 inches. Slowly heat over moderate heat until the oil registers 350°F on a frying thermometer (see page 93).

Turn out the dough onto a lightly floured work surface. Roll with a lightly floured rolling pin or pat out the dough to a large rectangle, about ¼ inch thick. With a floured, sharp knife, cut the dough into 4- to 5-inch triangles or diamond shapes. Re-roll the scraps and cut. Cut a slit along the center of each piece with a small knife, cutting through the dough and almost to the edges, to help the middle cook at the same rate as the edges. Shake or brush off the excess flour.

Place a couple of triangles of dough in the fry basket and lower the basket into the hot oil, or drop the dough one piece at a time into the oil with a slotted spoon, without crowding the pan.

Fry the pieces of bread, turning them so they cook evenly, until they puff and are browned, about 2 minutes. Lift the pieces out with the fry basket or slotted spoon and place on paper towels to drain. Eat while still warm.

INA DROPS A DOUGH TRIANGLE INTO THE HOT OIL TO FRY.

BEFORE STARTING TO FRY, INA TESTS THE OIL'S TEMPERATURE BY DROPPING IN A SMALL PIECE OF DOUGH. "IT SHOULD PUFF UP AND RISE TO THE SURFACE IMMEDIATELY," SHE SAYS.

Right DRAIN FRY BREAD ON PAPER TOWELS AS SOON AS IT IS REMOVED FROM THE HOT OIL.

Right INA SHAPES A PIECE OF ROLLED-OUT DOUGH BY THROWING IT FROM HAND TO HAND TO FLATTEN IT INTO A ROUND THE SIZE OF A SIDE PLATE.

Far Right INA FRIES THE YEAST FRY BREAD ONE PIECE AT A TIME. AS SHE DRAINS A HOT, JUST-FRIED BREAD ON PAPER TOWELS, SHE PREPARES TO FRY ANOTHER.

YEAST FRY BREAD WITH RAISINS

INGREDIENTS

Makes about 20

1 0.6-oz cake fresh yeast (15g), or 1 envelope active dry yeast (2½ teaspoons)
2½ tablespoons (30g) granulated sugar
2 cups (455ml) lukewarm water
1 large egg, beaten
2 tablespoons vegetable oil
2 teaspoons salt
3 tablespoons (30g) raisins
6½ cups (750g) unbleached white bread flour
extra flour for dusting
oil for deep-frying
confectioners' sugar for sprinkling

a deep-fat fryer or large Dutch oven

Ina McNeil (opposite) adds raisins to this yeast dough and fries it as a favorite snack for her grandchildren.

When I visited Ina with Anthony Blake she made this fry bread (without raisins and confectioners' sugar). We ate it like a taco, filled with chili-spiced meat, bean sauce, lettuce, tomatoes, grated cheese, and salsa. How we feasted! As Ina explained, "You are not invited to a Native American's home unless they can feed you."

Crumble the fresh yeast into a large bowl. Whisk in the sugar and lukewarm water until smooth. Let stand 15 minutes, until foamy. If using dry yeast, mix the granules with the sugar and water and let stand until foamy, 5–10 minutes (page 18).

Whisk the egg, oil, and salt into the yeast mixture. Stir in the raisins. Stir in half the flour to make a sloppy batter. Work in enough of the remaining flour to make a soft, sticky dough.

Turn out the dough onto a lightly floured surface. Knead for 5 minutes, until smooth and elastic, using the heel of your hand to stretch out the dough. Shape it into a ball. Wash, dry, and oil the bowl. Put the dough in the bowl, and turn it over so the top is oiled. Cover with a dish towel and let rise at room temperature, away from drafts, until doubled in size, about 1 hour.

Punch down the dough in the bowl, then shape it into a ball again. Cover and let rise again at room temperature, away from drafts, until doubled in size, about 1 hour.

Pour enough oil into the deep-fat fryer or Dutch oven to reach to a depth of about 3 inches. Slowly heat over moderate heat until the oil registers 350°F on a frying thermometer (page 93).

Punch down the dough. With floured hands, pinch off an egg-size piece of dough. Flatten into a disk, then toss it from hand to hand, pulling it out into a round the size of a bread plate. (Ina shapes and fries the dough one piece at a time.) Place the dough into a fry basket and lower the basket into the oil, or slip the round into the oil with a slotted spoon. Fry the round about 1 minute on each side, turning it over with a slotted spoon. It should puff up instantly. Remove from the oil and drain on paper towels. Sprinkle with confectioners' sugar and eat immediately.

1979
San Cosma®
CLASSICO

SAVORY BREADS

For far too long even good restaurants served bland and boring bread. If you were lucky, the melba toast might be nicely browned and crisp. Bread was necessary, but not important enough to merit a special baker or source. Now top chef-owners vie to offer the biggest choice of savory breads, presenting customers with ever-expanding breadbaskets and even loaded carts to confuse indecisive diners.

The selection of savory breads you can make is virtually endless, requiring only a good basic dough and some imagination. Kneading fruity, slightly peppery extra-virgin olive oil into a plain white dough and letting it rise slowly produces a flavorful, mellow loaf with a light, open texture and a thin, tearable crust (see Pugliese, page 106). Working olives – black, green, or those stuffed with anchovies, almonds, or pimientos – into a dough makes a bread that is particularly good to eat with Mediterranean dishes, or to use for sandwiches. A fabulous tomato bread can be made with sun-dried tomatoes, or sun-dried tomato purée. However, avoid using ordinary tomato paste, which tends to make a pretty loaf, but one that lacks flavor or is too sweet. Adding smoked tomatoes to bread is the latest fashion – very esoteric.

OPPOSITE Italian Pugliese
ABOVE Outdoor Italian bread oven.

You can make powerfully flavored savory loaves simply by spreading a basic dough with sliced yellow or red onions that have been sautéed until soft in olive oil and seasoned with plenty of fresh thyme. Then you roll up the dough like a jelly-roll, enclosing the onions as a filling. Another idea is to twist pieces of dough around while roasted garlic cloves to make savory rolls. Pesto sauce made from fresh basil in season, cilantro, crisp cracklings left from a pork roast, or cracked black peppercorns can also be used as flavorings for wonderful savory breads. Serve a thick slice with a bowl of soup for a satisfying, nourishing meal.

In this chapter, I use enriched brioche dough – often thought of as only a breakfast bread – to make a flavorful cheese loaf (see Brioche de Gannat, page 113) and as a rich and spectacular bread casing for a whole Brie (see Alyson Cook's Brie en Brioche, page 115). This may be served warm with a salad for a main course, or as part of a buffet spread.

Pissaladière (page 115), Flamiche aux Maroilles (page 120), Tarte Flambée (page 116), and Focaccia (page 110) are made from flattened doughs that act as plates, or trays, for a topping or filling. The crust can be thin, crisp, and crunchy, or soft, deep, and chewy. Scattered on top of or pushed into the dough are herbs, salt, and cheese, or an elaborately rich mixture, such as ratatouille.

Any of these doughs will lend itself to endless experimentation, though I am not a fan of too-trendy combinations, like tandoori pizza or Caribbean pizza, topped with pineapple and ham.

PUGLIESE

INGREDIENTS

Makes 1 very large loaf
13 cups (1.5kg) unbleached white bread flour
3½ tablespoons (30g) coarse sea salt, crushed or ground
2 0.6-oz cakes fresh yeast (30g), or 2 envelopes active dry yeast (5 teaspoons)
1 teaspoon sugar
3¾–4½ cups (850–990ml) lukewarm water
⅔ cup (140ml) extra virgin olive oil
extra flour for dusting

a large baking sheet, floured

A Tuscan hillside covered with olive trees. It is the fruity taste of golden-green extra-virgin and virgin olive oils from this part of Italy that flavors many Italian breads. If you buy a good-quality oil, you will be rewarded with authentic-tasting breads. It is not worth using a cheaper substitute.

This soft-crumbed yet chewy, white olive-oil bread with a pale, thin crust is based on one I tasted in Puglia, Italy. Store this bread, wrapped, at room temperature for two to three days.

Mix together the flour and salt in a large mixing bowl. Make a well in the center of the flour. Crumble the fresh yeast into a small bowl. Stir in the sugar and 3 tablespoons of the lukewarm water until smooth. Let stand for 5 minutes, or until it starts to become foamy. If using dry yeast, mix the granules and the sugar with 3 tablespoons of the lukewarm water and let stand until foamy, 5 to 10 minutes (page 18).

Pour the yeast mixture into the well in the flour, adding most of the remaining lukewarm water. Roughly mix in the flour from the bowl with your hand or a wooden spoon. Then mix in the olive oil and continue mixing until the dough comes together. If the dough remains dry and crumbly, gradually add the remaining water, 1–2 tablespoons at a time, as necessary; the dough should be soft, but not sticky, and should hold its shape. Turn out the dough on to a lightly floured work surface. Knead for 10 minutes until it becomes very smooth and elastic.

Shape the dough into a ball. Wash, dry, and oil the bowl. Return the dough to the bowl, and turn the dough over so the top is oiled. Cover with a damp dish towel and let rise at cool to normal room temperature, away from drafts, until the dough has doubled in size, 3½ to 4 hours (this will depend on the temperature of the room and the dough). Gently turn out the dough on to the prepared baking sheet, without punching it down. Gently pull out the sides of the dough, then tuck them underneath to make a neat, pillow-like round loaf. Do this several times, but do not knead the dough, punch it down, or turn it over.

Cover the dough with a damp dish towel and let rise, away from drafts, until almost doubled in size, 1 to 1½ hours. During the last fifteen minutes of rising, heat the oven to 450F. Lightly dust the loaf with flour. Bake the bread for 12 minutes. Then lower the oven temperature to 375F and bake for 25 to 35 minutes longer, or until the loaf is nicely browned and sounds hollow when tapped underneath. Transfer the loaf to a wire rack and cool completely.

VARIATIONS: PUGLIESE WITH TOMATOES AND BASIL Chop the contents of one 8-ounce (230g) jar well-drained sun-dried tomatoes packed in olive oil. Chop enough fresh basil to yield ½ cup. Knead the tomatoes and basil into the dough when it is smooth and elastic, just before the first rising. Proceed with the recipe as above.

PUGLIESE WITH OLIVES Roughly chop 6 to 9 ounces (170–255g) pitted black or green olives, or stuffed green olives; the more you use, the more pronounced the flavor will be. Knead the olives into the dough when it is smooth and elastic, just before the first rising. Proceed with the recipe as above.

TUCK THE SIDES UNDERNEATH TO MAKE A TIDY, PILLOW-LIKE ROUND.

SOFT-CRUMBED PUGLIESE IS DELICIOUS EATEN FRESH SOON AFTER BAKING.

Fresh basil, juicy, sun-ripened tomatoes, and mozzarella cheese are the natural partners for freshly baked ciabatta.

CIABATTA

INGREDIENTS

Makes 2 loaves

6 cups (680g) unbleached white bread flour

2 0.6-oz cakes fresh yeast (30g)

2 cups (430ml) water from the cold tap

⅔ cup (140ml) extra virgin olive oil

2 tablespoons (15g) coarse sea salt, crushed or ground

extra flour for sprinkling and dusting

2 baking sheets, heavily floured

This Italian loaf comes from the area around Lake Como in the north, and it is supposed to resemble a slipper. In any case, it is free-form – simply poured out of the bowl in which it has risen on to the baking sheet in a rough and ready rectangular loaf. It has large holes, and a soft but chewy, floury crust. I find that many commercial loaves taste of stale olive oil or lack the pungency of good extra-virgin oil.

Finding a good recipe for this bread was difficult, and I made about thirty before I was happy with the results. Taking advice from chef Pierre Koffmann, I adapted his baguette recipe (page 32), adding a good quantity olive oil to the dough, and altering the final consistency. As with the baguettes, it is not easy to achieve a perfect result the first time, even though the final loaf should taste very good. I have not had good results with either regular or rapid-rise active dry yeast, so I have only included instructions for using fresh yeast.

Put 4 cups (455g) flour into a large bowl. Make a well in the center of the flour. Crumble the fresh yeast into a small bowl. Stir in ½ cup (110ml) of the water until smooth. Pour the yeast mixture into the well in the flour. Then add the remaining water to the well and mix. Mix the flour from the bowl into the yeast mixture in the well with your hand or a wooden spoon to make a very sticky batterlike dough. Using your hand, beat the mixture for 5 minutes until very elastic. Cover the bowl with a damp dish towel and let rise at room temperature, away from drafts, for 4 hours. The dough will rise up enormously, so check that it does not stick to the dish towel.

Punch down the dough. Add the oil and salt to the dough and mix briefly with your hand. Then gradually work the rest of the flour into the dough with your hand to make a soft, quite sticky dough. When the dough is smooth and the flour has been thoroughly combined, cover the bowl with a damp dish towel and let rise at room temperature, away from drafts, until doubled in size, about 1 hour.

Using a very sharp knife, divide the dough in half, disturbing the dough as little as possible. Do not punch it down or try to knead or shape the dough at all. Tip a portion of dough on to each prepared baking sheet, nudging it with a spatula, to form two rough-looking rectangular loaves, about 1 inch thick. Sprinkle the loaves with flour and let rise, uncovered, at room temperature, away from drafts, until doubled in size, 45 minutes to 1 hour. During the last 15 minutes of rising, heat the oven to 425F.

Bake the loaves for about 35 minutes, or until they are browned and sound hollow when tapped underneath. Transfer the loaves to wire racks to cool. They are best eaten warm and fresh, or they can be frozen for up to one week.

TIP A PORTION OF DOUGH ONTO EACH PREPARED BAKING SHEET TO FORM ROUGH-LOOKING RECTANGULAR LOAVES, ABOUT 1 INCH THICK. YOU MAY HAVE TO USE A SPATULA TO NUDGE THE DOUGH INTO SHAPE.

GRISSINI

INGREDIENTS

Makes about 46

- 3 cups (340g) whole-wheat bread flour, preferably stone-ground
- 1 cup (115g) unbleached white bread flour
- 2 teaspoons salt, or more to taste
- 1 0.6-oz cake fresh yeast (15g), or 1 envelope active dry yeast (2½ teaspoons) plus ½ teaspoon sugar
- 1 cup (230ml) lukewarm water
- ¼ cup (60ml) olive oil
- extra flour for dusting

2 large baking sheets, lightly greased

Napoleon was so fond of what he called les petits bâtons that he had them sent daily by post to his court. These thin, crunchy breadsticks are made from a simple yeast dough enriched with a little olive oil or lard. In England, I prefer making grissini with 85 percent brown flour, a whole-wheat flour that has had some of the wheat germ removed; it produces a texture somewhere between white and whole-wheat flour. This flour is not available in the States, so I've used a combination of flours. You can vary the proportions to your taste. Children particularly like the Parmesan variation. Another idea is to sprinkle the dough with sesame seeds, poppy seeds, or coarse sea salt before baking.

Once you get the hang of making grissini, the thin strips of dough can be rapidly rolled, pulled, and stretched by hand to form sticks. The distinctly nonuniform look of the finished result is very appealing. These go well with soups, salads, and antipasti, as well as dips, and are a wonderful replacement for the often-dreadful party nibbles. Store them in an airtight tin.

Mix together the whole-wheat flour, the white flour, and salt in a large bowl and make a well in the center. Crumble the fresh yeast into a small bowl and stir in half the water until smooth. If using dry yeast, mix the granules and the sugar with half the water and let stand until foamy, 5 to 10 minutes (see page 18).

Add the yeast mixture to the well in the flour and mix in enough of the flour in the bowl to make a thick batter. Let stand for 20 minutes to sponge (page 16). Add the remaining water and the oil and mix to form a fairly firm dough. If the dough is sticky, work in small amounts of the remaining whole-wheat flour.

Turn out the dough on to a lightly floured work surface and knead for 10 minutes, or until it is smooth and elastic.

Return the dough to the washed and greased bowl and turn the dough over so the top is oiled. Cover with a damp dish towel and let rise at room temperature, away from drafts, until just doubled in size, about 1 hour. It is better to slightly underproof this

ROLL OUT THE DOUGH ON A LIGHTLY FLOURED WORK SURFACE TO A RECTANGLE ABOUT ¼ INCH THICK.

CUT THE RECTANGLE IN HALF LENGTHWISE, THEN SLICE EACH RECTANGLE CROSSWISE INTO STRIPS ½ INCH WIDE.

USING YOUR HANDS, ROLL OUT AND STRETCH EACH STRIP UNTIL IT IS ABOUT 10 INCHES LONG. PLACE ON THE LIGHTLY GREASED BAKING SHEETS.

HALFWAY THROUGH THE BAKING TIME, TURN THE GRISSINI OVER SO THEY BROWN EVENLY.

dough than to overproof it. During the last 15 minutes of rising, heat the oven to 450F.

Punch down the risen dough. Roll it out on a lightly floured work surface with a lightly floured rolling pin to a large rectangle about ¼ inch thick.

Using a sharp knife, cut the rectangle in half lengthwise to make two long, narrow rectangles. Slice each rectangle crosswise into strips ½ inch wide. Using your hands, roll and stretch each strip until it is about 10 inches long. Place on the prepared baking sheets. Work as quickly as possible, as the grissini should be baked as soon as they are shaped. Do not give the dough a second rising.

Bake the grissini for 12 to 20 minutes, depending on how crispy you like them. Turn them over halfway through baking so they brown evenly. Transfer the grissini to wire racks to cool completely.

VARIATIONS: PARMESAN GRISSINI Add ½ cup (60g) freshly grated Parmesan cheese to the flour with the salt. Then proceed with the recipe.
TOMATO GRISSINI Add 2 tablespoons drained and chopped oil-packed sun-dried tomatoes to the kneaded dough before letting it rise.

Serve grissini for nibbling with pre-dinner drinks or as part of a first course. Ideal accompaniments include fruity black olives and rich unsalted butter.

FOCACCIA

INGREDIENTS

Makes 1 large loaf
1 0.6-oz cake fresh yeast (15g), or
  1 envelope active dry yeast
  (2½ teaspoons) plus ½ teaspoon sugar
1¼ cups (280ml) water from the cold tap
6–7 tablespoons extra virgin olive oil
about 4½ cups (500g) unbleached white
  bread flour
2 teaspoons salt
extra flour for dusting
2 teaspoons coarse sea salt for sprinkling

a large roasting pan, about 10 × 14
  inches, greased

This version of focaccia, flavored with olive oil and salt, comes from Genoa, Italy. Although it is made in a roasting pan, you can shape the dough into one or two rounds and bake them on jelly-roll pans. The crumb is open, light, and moist, and the crust thin and full of flavor – never soggy and rubbery, or too crisp and dry. The thickness and flavorings are determined by the baker or the region.

Enjoy this bread on picnics, with salads and cold meats, or as a snack.

Crumble the fresh yeast into a large bowl. Stir in ½ cup of the water until smooth. Then stir in the remaining ½ cup water and 3 tablespoons of the oil. If using dry yeast, heat half of the water to lukewarm. Mix the yeast granules and the ½ teaspoon sugar with the lukewarm water and let stand until foamy, 5 to 10 minutes (page 18). Stir in the remaining water and 3 tablespoons oil.

With your hand or a wooden spoon, beat half the flour and the 2 teaspoons salt into the yeast mixture. Work in enough of the remaining flour to make a very soft, but not sticky dough. Turn out the dough on to a floured work surface and knead for 10 minutes until very smooth and silky. Wash, dry, and oil the bowl. Return the dough to the bowl, and turn the dough so the top is oiled. Cover and let rise at room temperature, away from drafts, until doubled in size, about 2 hours.

Punch down the dough. Turn out the dough on to a lightly floured work surface and roll it out with a lightly floured rolling pin to a rectangle the same size as your roasting pan. Lift the dough into the pan and pat it into the corners. Cover with a damp dish towel and let rise at room temperature, away from drafts, until not quite doubled in size, 45 to 60 minutes. Dimple the dough by pressing your fingertips into it firmly so it is marked with indentations about ½ inch deep. Cover and let rise at room temperature until doubled in size, 1 to 1½ hours. During the last 15 minutes, heat the oven to 425F.

Drizzle the remaining olive oil over the dough so the dimples are filled, then sprinkle with the coarse salt. Put the focaccia in the oven, then spray the oven sides and bottom with water (avoiding the light bulb). This helps produce a good, moist bread. Bake for 5 minutes, then spray the oven sides and bottom again. Bake about 20 minutes longer until the focaccia is golden brown. Lift the focaccia on to a wire rack and eat while still warm.

DIMPLE THE DOUGH BY PRESSING YOUR FINGERTIPS INTO IT FIRMLY SO IT IS MARKED WITH INDENTATIONS ABOUT ½-INCH DEEP.

A simple loaf of focaccia can turn into a feast when served as an antipasto with Italian salami, a bowl of homemade Italian vinegar-and-olive-oil dressing, and additional coarse salt to sprinkle over the bread. To serve Italian style, dip hunks of the bread in the dressing or into fruity olive oil. A carafe of crisp, dry Italian wine is all that is needed to complete the feast. The focaccia dough also makes a good base for a deep-crust pizza, but if you use it for pizza, do not dimple the dough or give it the third rising.

A selection of olive-oil flavored breads is an essential part of most Italian family feasts.

VARIATIONS: CHOPPED OLIVE FOCACCIA Work ⅔ cup (85g) chopped pitted black oil-cured or Kalamata olives into the dough toward the end of the kneading time. Proceed as opposite, dimpling the dough and letting it rise. Drizzle with the oil, but omit the salt topping. Bake as opposite.

ROSEMARY FOCACCIA Add 1 tablespoon chopped fresh rosemary leaves to the dough with the last handful of flour. Then proceed with the kneading and rising. After you have dimpled the dough and it has risen, press small sprigs of fresh rosemary into the dough every 2 to 3 inches. Drizzle with the oil, but omit the salt topping, and bake as opposite. This smells heavenly as it bakes.

ROSEMARY-GARLIC FOCACCIA Prepare the dough as opposite, then dimple. Slice several garlic cloves into slivers. Press the garlic slivers into the dough. Cover and let rise as opposite. Press a few small sprigs of fresh rosemary into the dough. Drizzle with the oil, sprinkle with the salt topping, and bake as opposite.

RED-ONION FOCACCIA Prepare the dough as opposite, then dimple it and let it rise as directed opposite. Slice 2 small red onions into thin rings. Scatter the onion rings over the risen dough, then drizzle with the oil and sprinkle with the salt topping. Bake as opposite.

CHEDDAR CHEESE AND ONION LOAF

INGREDIENTS

Makes 1 large loaf

- 6 cups (680g) unbleached white bread flour
- 2 tablespoons (15g) coarse sea salt, crushed or ground
- 1 teaspoon mustard powder
- 1 0.6-oz cake fresh yeast (15g), or 1 envelope active dry yeast (2½ teaspoons) plus ½ teaspoon sugar
- 2 cups (420ml) water from the cold tap
- extra flour for dusting
- milk for glazing

FILLING AND TOPPING:

- 1 cup (110g) shredded aged Cheddar cheese
- ⅔ cup (85g) diced aged Cheddar cheese
- 1 medium onion, finely chopped
- 2 tablespoons vegetable oil
- 1 small onion, sliced in rings, for topping the loaf

a loaf pan, about 10 × 5 × 3 inches, greased

Made to eat warm or toasted with soups and salads, this bread is not for the faint-hearted. For a really full flavor, use a nutty, well-aged Cheddar cheese and strong onions; they will mellow and blend with the other ingredients during baking. It is important to roll up the dough tightly (page 26) to avoid gaps in the baked loaf.

Mix together the flour, salt, and mustard in a large bowl. Make a well in the center of the flour. Crumble the fresh yeast into a small bowl. Stir in half of the water until smooth. If using dry yeast, heat half of the water to lukewarm. Mix the yeast granules and the ½ teaspoon sugar to the lukewarm water and let stand until foamy, 5 to 10 minutes (page 18).

Pour the yeast mixture into the well in the flour. Mix enough of the flour from the bowl into the yeast mixture with your hand or a wooden spoon to make a thin, smooth batter. Sprinkle the batter with a little flour to prevent a skin forming. Cover the bowl with a damp dish towel and let stand until spongy and foamy, about 20 minutes.

Add the remaining water to the foamy batter and mix together. Gradually work in the flour from the bowl with your hand to make a soft, but not sticky dough. Turn out the dough on to a floured work surface and knead for 10 minutes, until smooth and elastic. Wash, dry, and oil the bowl. Return the dough to the bowl, and turn the dough over so the top is oiled. Cover with a damp dish towel and let rise at cool to normal room temperature, away from drafts, until doubled in size, about 2 hours.

Meanwhile, combine ¾ cup (85g) of the shredded cheese with all the diced cheese; the variety of textures makes the filling more interesting. Sauté the chopped onion in the oil over low heat until it is soft and begins to turn golden, 10 to 12 minutes. Let cool.

Punch down the dough and turn it out on to a floured work surface. Roll out the dough with a floured rolling pin into a 10 × 15-inch rectangle. Sprinkle the cheese mixture over the dough, leaving a ½-inch border at all edges. Top with the sautéed onion. Roll up

Full, robust flavors characterize Roquefort and Walnut Loaf (left) and Cheddar Cheese and Onion Loaf. If you prefer, add a slightly nutty taste and more texture to either loaf by using 4 cups (455g) whole-wheat bread flour and 2 cups (230g) unbleached white bread flour, rather than all white flour as in the recipe. You can also substitute pecans for the walnuts.

tightly from a short side like a jelly-roll to make a loaf 10 inches long. Place the loaf, seam side down, into the prepared pan, tucking under the ends so it fits. Cover and let rise at room temperature, away from drafts, until doubled in size, about 1 to 2 hours. During the last 15 minutes of rising, heat the oven to 400F. Brush the loaf with a little milk, then sprinkle with the remaining shredded cheese. Bake the loaf for 20 minutes. While the loaf is baking, blanch the onion rings in a pan of boiling water for 1 minute, then drain. Arrange the blanched onion rings on top of the loaf and bake 20 to 25 minutes longer until the loaf sounds hollow when unmolded and tapped underneath. Turn out the loaf on to a wire rack to cool completely.

ROQUEFORT AND WALNUT LOAF

INGREDIENTS

Makes 1 large loaf

- 1 batch dough for Cheddar Cheese and Onion Loaf (page 111)
- 5 oz (140g) Roquefort cheese
- 1 cup (110g) coarsely chopped walnuts
- milk for glazing

a loaf pan, about 10 × 5 × 3 inches, greased

A good spinach salad, with young, tender leaves, fried bacon lardons (thick, matchstick-size strips of bacon), and a hot piquant dressing made by deglazing the bacon pan with vinegar, is the ideal accompaniment to this bread. Any well-made blue cheese – by which I mean one that tastes more of creamy, ripe, buttery blue cheese than of salt – can be substituted for the ewes' milk Roquefort. When buying cheese, always ask for a taste.

Prepare the dough with the flour, salt, mustard powder, yeast, and water. Cover and let rise, away from drafts, until doubled in size, about 2 hours.

Turn out the dough on to a floured work surface. Roll out the dough with a floured rolling pin into a 10 × 15-inch rectangle. Crumble the Roquefort cheese over the dough, leaving a ½-inch border all around. Top with the walnuts.

Then roll up the dough from a short side like a jelly roll. Place the loaf, seam side down, in the prepared loaf pan, tucking under the ends. Cover and let rise at room temperature until doubled in size, 1 to 2 hours. During the last 15 minutes of rising, heat the oven to 400F. Brush the loaf with a little milk. Bake the loaf for 40 to 50 minutes, or until the loaf sounds hollow when unmolded and tapped underneath. Turn out the loaf on to a wire rack to cool completely.

BRIOCHE DE GANNAT

INGREDIENTS

Makes 1 large loaf
2½ cups (280g) unbleached white bread flour
1 teaspoon salt
freshly ground black pepper
1 0.6-oz cake fresh yeast (15g), or 1 envelope active dry yeast (2½ teaspoons) plus ½ teaspoon sugar
½ cup (115ml) lukewarm milk
2 eggs
4 tablespoons (60g) unsalted butter, melted
extra flour for dusting
1 cup (110g) shredded Cantal or Gruyère cheese
1 egg beaten with ½ teaspoon salt for glazing

a loaf pan, about 7 × 5 × 3 inches, greased

This cheese brioche comes from the small town of Gannat in the Auvergne region of France, where flavorful Cantal cheese is made. The brioche dough in this recipe is not as complicated or as rich in eggs and butter as the dough for Michel Roux's Brioche (page 203); the richness here comes from the cheese. This brioche is light in texture, and I think it is best eaten on the day it is baked. Otherwise, this loaf tastes good toasted. I serve it with cheese and salads, or slice it and melt cheese on top. I've adapted this recipe from French Regional Cooking, *by Anne Willan* (Morrow, 1979).

Mix together the flour, the salt, and pepper from several turns of the peppermill in a large bowl. Make a well in the center of the flour.

Crumble the fresh yeast into a small bowl. Whisk in the lukewarm milk until smooth. Whisk in the eggs just to break them up, then whisk in the butter. If using dry yeast, mix the granules and the ½ teaspoon sugar with the lukewarm milk and let stand until foamy, 5 to 10 minutes (page 18). Whisk the eggs and butter into the yeast mixture.

Pour the yeast mixture into the well in the flour. Gradually work the flour from the bowl into the liquid with your hand or a wooden spoon to make a soft, but not sticky dough, adding a little more flour as needed, 1 tablespoon at a time, to prevent the dough sticking to your fingers.

Turn out the dough on to a lightly floured work surface and knead for 10 minutes until smooth and elastic. Wash, dry, and oil the bowl.

Return the dough to the bowl, and turn the dough over so the top is oiled. Cover with a damp dish towel and let rise at cool to normal temperature, away from drafts, until doubled in size, 1½ to 2 hours.

Punch down the risen dough. Turn out the dough on to a lightly floured work surface and gently knead in the shredded cheese, reserving 2 tablespoons for sprinkling on top of the loaf just before baking. Shape the dough into a loaf to fit the loaf pan (page 24). Put the dough, seam side down, into the prepared pan, pinching and tucking under the ends so it fits. Then cover with a damp dish towel and let rise at room temperature, away from drafts, until it rises to the top of the pan, 1 to 1½ hours. During the last 15 minutes of rising, heat the oven to 400F.

Gently brush the dough with the egg glaze, taking care not to "glue" the dough to the sides of the pan. Then sprinkle with the reserved 2 tablespoons of cheese. Bake the bread for 35 to 45 minutes, or until the loaf is golden brown and sounds hollow when unmolded and tapped underneath. Turn out the brioche on to a wire rack to cool completely.

THE GLAZED LOAF IS TOPPED WITH THE RESERVED CHEESE.

THE BRIOCHE DOUGH BAKES INTO A SOFT, DELICATE CRUMB.

PROVENÇAL VEGETABLE TARTS

INGREDIENTS

Makes 2 tarts; each serves 6 to 8

- 3½ cups (395g) unbleached white bread flour
- 2 teaspoons salt
- 1 0.6-oz cake fresh yeast (15g), or 1 envelope active dry yeast (2½ teaspoons) plus ½ teaspoon sugar
- scant 1 cup (200ml) lukewarm milk
- 2 large eggs, beaten
- 4 tablespoons (60g) unsalted butter, softened
- 2 tablespoons chopped mixed fresh herbs, such as parsley, basil, thyme, rosemary, and oregano
- extra flour for dusting

RATATOUILLE FILLING:

- 3 tablespoons extra virgin olive oil
- 1 small onion, chopped
- 3 cloves garlic, chopped
- 1 red bell pepper, seeded and diced
- 5 plum tomatoes, peeled, seeded, and diced
- 1 small eggplant, cut into thick matchstick strips
- 2 zucchini, cut into thick matchstick strips
- 1 teaspoon chopped fresh thyme
- salt and freshly ground black pepper
- 2 oz (60g) Gruyère cheese, thinly sliced
- 2 large eggs, beaten
- ⅔ cup (140ml) heavy cream

2 deep 8- to 9-inch quiche pans or springform pans, lightly greased

I adore ratatouille, whether served hot with roast lamb or cold as a salad. It also makes a substantial filling for these crisp, rich, herby, bread-crust tarts, which I serve warm with a big green salad for a summer lunch.

To make the bread crust: Mix together the flour and salt in a medium-size bowl. Make a well in the center of the flour. Crumble the fresh yeast into a small bowl. Whisk in the lukewarm milk until smooth. If using dry yeast, mix the granules and the ½ teaspoon sugar with 4 tablespoons lukewarm milk and let stand until foamy, 5 to 10 minutes (page 18). Add the remaining milk. Whisk the eggs into the yeast mixture until well blended.

Pour the yeast mixture into the well in the flour. Work in the flour from the bowl, beating to make a smooth, soft, and slightly sticky dough. Knead the dough by pulling it up with your fingers and pushing it down in the bowl with the heel of your hand until very smooth and elastic, about 5 minutes. Beat in the butter and herbs until the dough is smooth, with no streaks of butter or herbs. Shape into a ball. Wash, dry, and oil the bowl. Return the dough to the bowl, and turn the dough over so the top is oiled. Cover and let rise at cool to normal room temperature until doubled in size, about 2 hours.

Meanwhile, make the filling. Heat the oil in a large, deep skillet. Add the onion and garlic and cook until tender but not browned, 7 to 10 minutes. Add the red pepper and cook, stirring frequently, for 5 minutes. Stir in the tomatoes, eggplant, zucchini, thyme, and salt and pepper to taste. Cook, stirring occasionally, about 10 minutes, or until the vegetables are tender but not mushy. Adjust the seasoning, and let cool.

Punch down the dough. Turn out the dough on to a floured work surface and divide into two equal portions. Roll out each portion with a floured rolling pin into an 11-inch round. Put one round into one of the pans, lining the base and sides by pressing the dough with your knuckles and fingers; the dough should be even with the top of the quiche pan, and it will extend up the side of a springform pan about 1 inch. Cover the dough with half of the cheese. Then fill with half the ratatouille. Line and fill the second pan with the remaining dough, cheese, and ratatouille.

Beat the eggs with the cream and a little salt and pepper to taste. Pour this mixture over the ratatouille in each pan, dividing equally, and using a fork to ease the vegetables apart; do not puncture the dough. Let stand, uncovered, away from drafts, until the dough starts to rise, about 15 minutes. Meanwhile, heat the oven to 400F. Bake the tarts for 30 to 35 minutes, or until they are golden brown and the fillings are set. Serve warm.

The ratatouille filling in this tart captures the sun-drenched flavors of the South of France. Juicy-ripe tomatoes, red bell peppers, eggplant, and zucchini, along with plenty of garlic, olive oil, and thyme combine to evoke images of summer along the Mediterranean. This tart is best served warm, so if you bake it in advance, reheat it in a 350F oven for 15–20 minutes.

RIGHT
The bottom round of dough should be six inches larger than the cheese.

FAR RIGHT
After Alyson wraps the cheese with the dough, she brushes it with the egg glaze. Serve this the day it is baked, ideally with a selection of salads. The brioche dough, however, can be made and the recipe assembled the night before you plan to serve this loaf, then covered with plastic wrap and chilled overnight. Remove from the refrigerator, unwrap, and cover with a dry dish towel. Let the brioche rise at normal to room temperature until the dough puffs up, as directed. (This can take up to four hours.) Then bake it as described in the recipe.

ALYSON COOK'S BRIE EN BRIOCHE

I will be honest. The main point of the trip Anthony Blake and I took to California was to see my best friend Alyson, who comes from Somerset, England. We met many years ago at The Cordon Bleu, in London. She now owns a classy catering business in Los Angeles and is cooking for Hollywood legends who like to dine at home in style. This is one of Alyson's most-frequently requested dishes. It is ideal for parties.

INGREDIENTS

Makes 1 very large loaf

- 1 0.6-oz cake fresh yeast (15g), or 1 envelope active dry yeast (2½ teaspoons) plus ½ teaspoon sugar
- 5 tablespoons (70ml) lukewarm milk
- 2 tablespoons (15g) coarse sea salt, crushed or ground
- 4½ cups (500g) unbleached white bread flour
- 6 large eggs, beaten
- 1 cup + 2 tablespoons (250g) unsalted butter, softened
- 2 teaspoons sugar
- extra flour for dusting
- a 2-lb (900g) whole Brie cheese, 8 to 9 inches in diameter
- 1 jar (about 12 oz/340g) spiced apricot chutney or mango chutney
- 1 egg beaten with ¼ teaspoon salt for glazing

a baking sheet lined with parchment paper

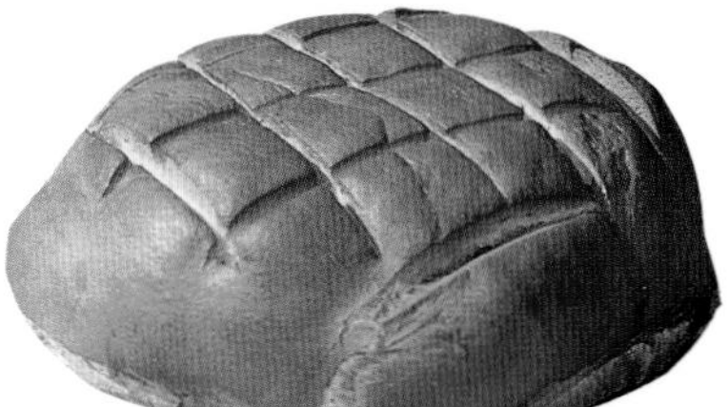

Make the brioche dough as for Michel Roux's Brioche (page 203), using the proportions listed here. Add the yeast mixture to the flour, then beat in the eggs and knead the dough; finally, work in the butter and sugar mixture. Chill the dough after the first rising until it is firm but not hard, 3 to 5 hours. Turn out the dough on to a lightly floured work surface. Cut off one-quarter of the dough and cover with a damp dish towel.

Measure the cheese, then roll out the large piece of dough with a lightly floured rolling pin into a round, about 8 inches larger than the cheese, and about ½ inch thick. Spread the chutney evenly over the top of the cheese. Gently place the cheese upside-down in the center of the dough circle. Trim the edges of the dough, if necessary, to neaten it. Roll out the reserved dough into a circle ½ inch larger than the cheese.

Lightly brush the top of the cheese with the egg glaze. Bring the dough up around the sides of the cheese, in toward the center, leaving some of the cheese exposed in the middle, and pressing gently so the dough adheres to the cheese. Brush the top of the dough with the egg glaze. Place the other dough round on top of the cheese and gently pat the dough to seal it.

Lightly flour your hands and turn the wrapped cheese upside-down on to the prepared baking sheet. If necessary, gently mold the sides into an even shape with your hands.

Lightly score the top in a diamond or checkered pattern with the tip of a sharp knife. Let rise, uncovered, at room temperature, away from drafts, until the dough puffs up, 30 to 45 minutes. During the last 15 minutes of rising time, heat the oven to 375F. Slide another baking sheet under the first to insulate the bottom so the brioche doesn't scorch.

Bake the brioche for 35 minutes, or until puffed and golden brown. Brush with the remaining egg glaze and bake 10 minutes longer. (Alyson says this gives a better finish than glazing before baking.) Transfer to a wire rack to cool completely.

TARTE FLAMBÉE

INGREDIENTS

Makes 2 thin tarts; each serves 2–3

4 cups (455g) unbleached white bread flour

1½ teaspoons salt

1 0.6-oz cake fresh yeast (15g), or

1 envelope active dry yeast (2½ teaspoons) plus ½ teaspoon sugar

1¼ cups (280ml) water from the cold tap

1 teaspoon vegetable oil or melted butter

extra flour for dusting

TOPPING:

8 oz (230g) slab bacon

1¼ cups (280ml) crème fraîche, or ⅔ cup (140ml) each sour cream and heavy cream

2 onions, very thinly sliced

freshly ground black pepper

2 baking sheets or jelly-roll pans, lightly greased

Matchsticks of bacon, called lardons, and crème fraîche are combined with very thinly sliced onions to make the traditional topping for this rich, crisp Alsatian tart. Take care to slice the onions as thinly as possible, or they will still taste raw after the short baking time. I suggest you use the thin slicing blade of a food processor, or a mandolin.

Tarte flambée, with a wafer-thin, crunchy crust and a rich, but simple, shallow topping of crème fraîche, thinly sliced onions, and bacon slivers, can be found in almost every café-bar and restaurant in the Alsace region of France. It makes a good, inexpensive snack or ample first course.

In Riquewihr, Anthony Blake and I found the A la Fontaine restaurant, where bakers cooked these tarts to order in an outside oven situated right in the midst of the diners. The oven, built in typical Alsace style, is long, thin, and fired by logs underneath. The wood fire gives the tarts a smoky taste and a crisp crust – and it cooks the dough rapidly. The baker transferred each baked tart from the oven to the logs underneath to "flambé" it for a few seconds before serving.

Thanks to Patricia Well's invaluable book, The Food Lover's Guide to France *(Workman, 1987), we also visited the Ferme Auberge, in Weiterswiller. You can eat tarte flambée to your heart's content at this working farm and inn, where owner Simone Bloch bakes the tarts in her 45-year-old oven. Shaped like a metal coffin, 1 foot deep and 8 feet long, the oven stands on a brick platform in her small kitchen. I watched as she rapidly assembled tarts measuring 12 × 18 inches. She also adds cheese or mushrooms on request. The day we were there, tarte flambée was the only item on the menu, and nobody complained as more and more tarts kept appearing at the tables. Folding up the tarts in local fashion and eating with our fingers, Anthony and I managed three between us.*

To make the crust: Mix together the flour and salt in a large bowl. Make a well in the center of the flour. Crumble the fresh yeast into a small bowl. Stir in the water until smooth.

If using dry yeast, heat ½ cup (110ml) of the water to lukewarm. Mix the granules and the ½ teaspoon sugar with the lukewarm water and let stand until foamy, 5 to 10 minutes (page 18). Mix in the remaining water.

Pour the yeast mixture into the well in the flour. Stir in the oil or melted butter. Mix enough of the flour from the bowl into the yeast mixture with your fingers or a wooden spoon to make a thin, smooth batter. Sprinkle the batter with a little flour to prevent a skin forming. Cover the bowl with a dish towel and let the batter stand until spongy and foamy, about 20 minutes.

Work the rest of the flour from the bowl into the batter with your hands or a wooden spoon to make a soft, not sticky dough. Turn out the dough on to a lightly floured work surface and knead for 10 minutes until smooth and elastic. Wash, dry, and oil the bowl. Return the dough to the bowl, and turn the dough over so the top is oiled. Cover with a damp dish towel and let rise at room temperature, away from drafts, until doubled in size, 1½ to 2 hours. During the last 15 minutes of rising, heat the oven to 450F and prepare the topping.

Cut the bacon into thick matchstick shapes, called lardons, discarding any rind. If using sour cream and heavy cream, mix them together.

Punch down the risen dough. Turn it out on to a lightly floured work surface and divide into two equal portions. Roll out half the dough with a lightly floured rolling pin to a very thin rectangle the same size as your baking sheet or jelly-roll pan.

Roll the dough up on the rolling pin and unroll on to the prepared baking sheets or jelly-roll pans to cover it completely. Do not worry if the dough stretches and flops over the edges, because they will be folded in before baking. Repeat with the second piece of dough on the second prepared baking sheet or pan.

Spread one sheet of dough with half of the crème fraîche or the cream mixture. Sprinkle with half of the sliced onions and half of the bacon; season with plenty of pepper, to taste. Fold over the edges to make a ½-inch border. Repeat the process with the second sheet of dough.

Bake the tarts for 12 to 15 minutes, or until the tarts are golden and the bases crisp. Eat immediately.

PISSALADIÈRE

INGREDIENTS

Makes 1 large pissaladière; serves 6–8

- 2¼ cups (255g) unbleached white bread flour
- 1½ teaspoons salt
- 1 0.6-oz cake fresh yeast (15g), or 1 envelope active dry yeast (2½ teaspoons) plus ½ teaspoon sugar
- ½ cup + 2 tablespoons (130ml) lukewarm milk
- 2 large eggs, beaten
- 7 tablespoons (100g) unsalted butter, softened
- extra flour for dusting

FILLING:

- 2½ 2-oz cans anchovy fillets packed in oil, drained
- ¼ cup (60ml) milk
- 14½-oz can plum tomatoes, drained
- 2 tablespoons tomato paste
- 2 tablespoons olive oil
- 2 cloves garlic, or to taste
- 1 tablespoon chopped fresh oregano
- salt and freshly ground black pepper
- sugar
- lemon juice
- about ½ cup (90g) pitted black olives
- extra olive oil for brushing

a baking sheet or jelly-roll pan, about 12 × 8 × 1 inch, greased

This is another recipe from my friend Alyson Cook (page 115). She says she likes to use a brioche dough for pissaladières because it is moister and richer than a plain white dough. She varies the topping, sprinkling capers over the traditional anchovies and tomatoes, or spreading lightly sautéed sliced onions on the dough before adding the tomato topping. Sometimes she replaces the oregano with fresh basil and then garnishes with fresh basil leaves. The black olives can be replaced with garlic slices.

To make the crust: Mix together the flour and salt in a large bowl. Make a well in the center of the flour. Crumble the fresh yeast into a small bowl. Stir in the lukewarm milk until smooth. If using dry yeast, mix the granules and the ½ teaspoon sugar with the lukewarm milk and let stand until foamy, 5 to 10 minutes (page 18).

Pour the yeast mixture into the well in the flour. Add the beaten eggs, mixing with your fingers or a small whisk to combine the ingredients. Gradually work in the flour from the bowl with your hands or a wooden spoon to make a very soft and quite sticky dough. Knead the dough by lifting it with one hand and slapping it against the sides of the bowl. Work in the softened butter by beating and slapping the dough up and down with your hand. Cover with a damp dish towel and let rise at room temperature, away from drafts, until doubled in size, 1½ to 2 hours.

Punch down the risen dough with your knuckles. Cover with a dish towel and chill until firm, but not hard, 4 to 5 hours.

Meanwhile, prepare the topping: Soak the anchovies in the milk for 15 to 20 minutes to remove some of the excess salt. Drain the anchovies and discard the milk. Purée the plum tomatoes in a blender or food processor with the tomato paste, olive oil, garlic cloves, and oregano leaves. Or, you may chop the plum tomatoes, garlic cloves, and oregano leaves by hand and stir in the tomato paste and olive oil. Season to taste with salt and pepper, sugar, and lemon juice. Heat the oven to 400F.

Turn out the dough on to a lightly floured work surface and roll out with a lightly floured rolling pin into a 12 × 8-inch rectangle, or a rectangle to fill the baking pan you are using. Roll up the dough on the rolling pin and transfer to the prepared baking pan. Press it on to the bottom of the pan and into the corners, squeezing out any bubbles of air trapped between the pan and dough. Spoon the tomato mixture over the dough and spread evenly, leaving a ½-inch border at all edges.

Arrange the drained anchovies in a criss-cross pattern over the top. Put an olive in the center of each diamond.

Bake the pissaladière for 20 to 25 minutes, or until the crust is golden brown and crisp. Remove from the oven and brush the rim of the crust with olive oil. Drizzle a little olive oil over the topping as well. Then cool to warm, cut into squares, and serve.

PRESS THE DOUGH INTO THE BOTTOM AND CORNERS OF THE PAN.

ANCHOVIES AND BLACK OLIVES ARE THE TRADITIONAL TOPPING FOR THIS PIZZA-LIKE FLAT TART.

Leek Tart (left) and Flamiche aux Maroilles are both made with a rich brioche dough crust, which makes an interesting change from more familiar piecrust.

FLAMICHE AUX MAROILLES

This is a savory cheese tart with a brioche crust. The ideal cheese for this is Maroilles, a strong, pungent, soft cheese with a brown rind that has been washed in beer as the cheese ripens. It is named after the town of Maroilles, in northern France, where it is made. However, Maroilles is next to impossible to find in the States, as it is almost never exported beyond the Continent. Edward Edleman, of the Ideal Cheese Shop, in New York City, suggested the following substitutes, in order of preference: Chaumes, Alsatian Muenster, Pont l'Evêque, Saint-Nectaire, Danish Esrom, or Appenzeller. Cooked leeks or onions may be used as substitutes for the cheese filling (see the subsequent recipe), but I prefer the version made with cheese. Serve flamiche warm from the oven, with a green salad.

INGREDIENTS

Makes 1 large tart; serves 6–8

*1 batch Pissaladière dough (page 117)**

FILLING:

8 oz (230g) Maroilles cheese (see introduction), rind removed and then thinly sliced

½ cup + 2 tablespoons (130ml) crème fraîche or heavy cream

1 large egg

1 large egg yolk

¼ teaspoon freshly grated nutmeg

salt and freshly ground black pepper

a deep 9- to 9½-inch quiche pan, springform pan or deep-dish pie plate, greased

Prepare the dough as for the Pissaladière. Cover with a damp dish towel and let rise at room temperature, away from drafts, until doubled in size, 1½ to 2 hours. Punch down, cover again, and chill until firm, but not hard, 4 to 5 hours.

Turn out the dough on to a lightly floured work surface. Roll with a lightly floured rolling pin into a 12-inch round. Wrap the dough around the rolling pin and lift it over the prepared quiche pan or pie plate. Gradually unroll the dough so it is draped over the pan, then press it gently with your fingers on to the bottom and up the sides to evenly line the pan; do not stretch the dough. Trim off any excess dough to make a neat crust.

Arrange the cheese in an even layer over the bottom of the dough. In a medium-size bowl, beat together the crème fraîche or cream with the egg and egg yolk, nutmeg, and plenty of black pepper and a little salt to taste, just until combined. Pour this mixture over the cheese. Let the tart rise at warm room temperature (75F), away from drafts, until it is puffy and the rim is almost doubled in size, 30 to 45 minutes. During the last 15 minutes of rising, heat the oven to 400F.

Bake the tart for 40 to 50 minutes, or until the filling is set and the crust is golden brown and crisp.

LEEK TART

INGREDIENTS

Makes 1 large tart; serves 6–8

1 batch Pissaladière dough (page 117)

FILLING:

2 lb (900g) leeks, trimmed

4 tablespoons (60g) butter

salt and freshly ground black pepper

½ cup + 2 tablespoons (130ml) crème fraîche or heavy cream

1 large egg

1 large egg yolk

a deep 9- to 9½-inch quiche pan or deep-dish pie pan, buttered

Prepare the dough as for Pissaladière (page 117). Cover with a damp dish towel and let rise at room temperature, away from drafts, until doubled in size, 1½ to 2 hours. Punch down the dough. Cover again and chill until firm, but not hard, 4 to 5 hours.

Meanwhile, prepare the filling. Halve lengthwise and thoroughly rinse the leeks of sand and grit. Drain them well, then thinly slice. Melt the butter in a large, heavy-bottomed frying pan with lid. Add the leeks and salt and pepper to taste, and stir. Cover with a disk of buttered parchment paper and the pan's lid and cook slowly until the leeks are very tender, but not browned, about 25 minutes. Let cool. Heat the oven to 400F. Turn out the dough on to a lightly floured work surface. Roll with a lightly floured rolling pin into a 12-inch round. Line the quiche pan or pie plate as for Flamiche aux Maroilles. Beat together the crème fraîche or cream, egg, and egg yolk in a medium-size bowl until just combined. Season lightly with salt and pepper. Spoon the leeks into the dough crust, then pour over the cream mixture. Let rise as Flamiche aux Maroilles. Heat the oven to 400F. Bake the tart for 40 to 50 minutes, or until the filling is set and the crust is golden brown and crisp. Serve warm.

ETHIOPIAN SPICE BREAD

INGREDIENTS

Makes 1 large loaf

6 tablespoons (85g) butter

2 tablespoons minced onion

1 clove garlic, minced

1½ tablespoons ground coriander

1 tablespoon ground fenugreek

1½ tablespoons sweet paprika

½ teaspoon freshly ground black pepper

½ teaspoon ground cinnamon

¼ teaspoon cayenne

a large pinch of freshly grated nutmeg

a large pinch of ground cloves

6 cups (680g) unbleached white bread flour

2 teaspoons salt

1 0.6-oz cake fresh yeast (15g), or 1 envelope active dry yeast (2½ teaspoons)

1½ cups + 2 tablespoons (370ml) lukewarm water

2½ tablespoons packed (30g) light brown sugar

extra flour for dusting

1 tablespoon (15g) butter, melted, for glazing

a baking sheet, lightly greased

I found this recipe in The Independent, *a British newspaper, and have made it regularly ever since. It was attributed to Dr. Fiona Pharoah, and my thanks go to her and Kumud, who gave it to her. I have altered the recipe amounts and method slightly, but the basic recipe is the same. The texture is light, the color inside is golden, and the flavor is mild, yet intriguing, developing to its best after 24 hours. Everyone likes this!*

Melt the butter in a small saucepan. Add the onion, garlic, and spices and cook over low heat, stirring constantly, for 2 minutes until the spices are fragrant and lose their raw taste. Remove from the heat and let cool slightly.

Meanwhile, mix together the flour and salt in a large bowl. Make a well in the center of the flour. Crumble the fresh yeast into a small bowl. Stir in the water until smooth, then stir in the sugar. If using dry yeast, mix the granules and 1 teaspoon of the sugar with ½ cup (110ml) of the water and let stand until foamy, 5 to 10 minutes (page 18). Add the remaining sugar and water.

Pour the yeast mixture into the well in the flour, followed by the spice and onion mixture. Mix enough flour from the bowl into the yeast mixture to make a medium-thick batter. Sprinkle the batter with a little flour to prevent a skin forming. Cover the bowl and let stand until the batter becomes spongy and foamy, about 20 minutes.

Work the rest of the flour from the bowl into the batter to make a fairly firm dough. Turn out the dough on to a lightly floured work surface and knead for 10 minutes until smooth and elastic, adding a little extra flour if the dough is sticky.

Return the dough to the bowl. Cover and let rise at room temperature, away from drafts, until doubled in size, about 2 hours. Punch down the dough. Break off a large walnut-size piece of dough and reserve. Turn out the dough on to a floured work surface and shape into a free-form loaf as for The Basic Loaf (page 17). Put the loaf on the prepared baking sheet. With a sharp knife, lightly score a cross on top of the loaf. Place the small nut of dough in the center of the cross. Cover and let rise at room temperature, away from drafts, until doubled in size, about 1 hour. During the last 15 minutes of rising, heat the oven to 375F. Bake for 40 to 50 minutes, or until the loaf is browned and sounds hollow when tapped underneath. Transfer to a wire rack. Brush with the melted butter and let cool.

BAGELS

INGREDIENTS

Makes 20

4 cups (455g) unbleached white bread flour

2 teaspoons salt

1 0.6-oz cake fresh yeast (15g), or 1 envelope active dry yeast (2½ teaspoons)

1 cup (230ml) mixed milk and water, at room temperature

1 teaspoon sugar

2 tablespoons (30g) butter, melted, or vegetable oil

1 large egg, separated

extra flour for dusting

sesame seeds or poppy seeds for sprinkling (optional)

3 baking sheets, greased

a steamer pot with a lid, or a large deep skillet, a wire rack and aluminum foil

The popularity of the bagel – literally, "a roll with a hole" – has spread from Jewish communities to the wide world. A bagel was just a bagel to me until I realized I had married into a family of American East Coast bagel mavens. Yet they particularly love those made by a man called Noah in, of all places, Berkeley, California. "Noah's bagels have Yiddish in their souls," I was told. "There's nothing like them in Brooklyn."

Noah Alper bakes 250,000 bagels a week in the college town of Berkeley, and I met with him in his College Avenue shop. He defined the archetypical bagel for me. "It's important that it's big, crusty on the outside, chewy inside, tasty, and with plenty of seeds. Of course you don't have to be Jewish to know what a good bagel tastes like." I've adapted his recipe to make bagels that are smaller than what is usually encountered, because that is what I prefer.

Bagels were first made centuries ago in Poland. Badly made, a bagel will be rubbery, heavy, and soggy. The best ones, like Noah's, are finished by hand. The added toppings can be poppy seeds, sesame seeds, onions, caraway seeds, salt, or, as a California curiosity, sunflower seeds.

Eat bagels sliced and plain, toasted and buttered, spread with a schmear (a liberal coating) of cream cheese, or with cream cheese and lox or smoked salmon, onions, and pickles. These bagels are best eaten as soon as possible after baking; otherwise cool, wrap in freezer bags, and freeze for up to one month. Remove from the bags and reheat straight from the freezer on the oven racks in a 350F oven for about 10 minutes before serving.

Mix together 3½ cups (400g) of the flour and the salt in a large bowl. Make a well in the center of the flour. Crumble the fresh yeast into a small bowl. Whisk in the milk mixture until smooth. Stir in the sugar. If using dry yeast, heat ½ cup (110ml) of the milk mixture to lukewarm. Mix the yeast granules and the sugar with the lukewarm liquid and let stand until foamy, 5 to 10 minutes (page 18). Stir in the remaining liquid.

Pour the yeast mixture into the well in the flour, followed by the melted butter or vegetable oil. Lightly beat the egg white until frothy, then add to the well and mix with a small whisk until thoroughly combined. Gradually work in the flour from the bowl with your hand or a wooden spoon to make a soft and pliable dough. Turn out dough on to a lightly floured work surface. Cover with the upturned bowl and let stand for 5 minutes.

Then knead for 10 minutes until the dough is smooth and elastic, adding the remaining flour as needed, 1 tablespoon at a time, to prevent sticking. Wash, dry, and oil the bowl

Noah Alper's bagel shop in Berkeley, California. Noah's method of bagel making – he steams his bagels before baking them, instead of poaching them – has caused something of a controversy among the bagel lovers of the Bay Area. Among his faithful followers, "super onion," with onion in the dough and sprinkled on top, is his best-seller.

A sumptuous brunch of fresh bagels with smoked salmon, cream cheese with snipped fresh chives, and just-brewed coffee.

Return the dough to the bowl, and turn the dough over so the top is oiled. Cover with a damp dish towel and let rise at room temperature, away from drafts, until doubled in size, 1½ to 2 hours.

Punch down the dough. Weigh the dough and divide it into twenty equal portions, or roll it into a 20-inch rope and cut into twenty 1-inch pieces. Using your hands, and only flouring them and the work surface if it is necessary to prevent the dough from sticking, roll each piece into a sausage about 6 inches long. Taper the ends, then join them securely together using a little cold water to make a neat ring. Arrange the bagels, well apart, on the prepared baking sheets. Cover with dry dish towels and let rise at room temperature, away from drafts, until almost doubled in size, about 45 minutes. During the last 15 minutes of rising, heat the oven to 400F.

Bring some water to a boil in the bottom of a steamer pot or half fill a large, deep skillet with water and bring to a boil. Reduce the heat so the water is simmering. Place the steamer rack or wire rack over the simmering water. Arrange three or four bagels at a time, spaced apart, on the steamer rack or wire rack and cover with the steamer lid or a dome-shaped piece of aluminum foil; keep the remaining bagels covered. Steam for 1 minute.

Transfer the bagels to the greased baking sheet. If you prefer, the bagels can be poached, three at a time, for 30 seconds each.

Beat the egg yolk with 2 teaspoons cold water. Brush the steamed or poached bagels with the egg glaze. Leave plain, or sprinkle with sesame or poppy seeds. Bake the bagels for 20 to 25 minutes, or until they are golden brown and puffed up. Transfer to wire racks to cool.

FRUIT AND NUT BREADS

When I was four years old, I was so proud of my new green gingham uniform dress I refused to take it off at the end of my first day at school, despite a large sticky patch on the back of my skirt. During the school break we had been given a glass of milk and a buttered currant bun with a sticky, shiny glaze. My new little friends told me the only way to eat the bun – which I had never seen the likes of – was to sit on it, then cram the squashed mass into my mouth in one go. I did not think of the consequences, but ate the bun as instructed. What fun – what a good bun! It came from the Victoria Bakery in Barnet High Street, in north London, a bakery renowned for its fruit and nut breads, spicy buns, and hot cross buns. This unfortunate introduction to sweet fruit breads did not deter my enthusiasm for them. I have been collecting the best recipes for years.

For centuries, breads made from soft, rich doughs were held in high esteem, and took the place of the cakes we eat today. They were flavored with raisins, currants, or other dried fruits, such as apricots, prunes, peaches, and pears, and sometimes with spice and nuts. The large breads were leavened with the yeast that was a by-product from brewing ale until chemical leavening agents became generally available. Today, it is almost as if we have come full cycle, and once again sweet fruited breads are in fashion; however, some consider them a luxurious treat due to the high calorie content from the sugar (both refined and in the dried fruit) and the fat they contain.

OPPOSITE and ABOVE
Sandra's Saffron Buns

In this chapter, I want to pass on my enthusiasm and introduce you to traditional and modern varieties of fruit and nut breads. The famous Chelsea Buns of London (page 131), Bara Brith (page 129) from Wales, and the similar Barm Brack (page 128) from Ireland are among the breads generations of home bakers have served at teatime, instead of a cake. More modern fruit and nut breads include Viola's Caramel Cinnamon Rolls (page 127) from America, the attractive Peach Couronne (page 134), and the light Hazelnut, Apricot, and Honey Loaf (page 133). If all these seem too sweet, try the Walnut Bread (page 136), which is excellent with a good farmhouse cheese.

These breads are easy to make and do not require much skill, so they're ideal for introducing children to bread-making. You will find that homemade fruit and nut breads, including the ever-popular sticky buns, are light, moist, and full of flavor. They really are worth making, because many of the commercial varieties have become dense, flavorless, and far too sweet.

SANDRA'S SAFFRON BUNS

INGREDIENTS

Makes 14

- 1 teaspoon saffron strands
- 2 tablespoons lukewarm water
- 4 cups (455g) unbleached white bread flour
- ½ teaspoon salt
- 7 tablespoons (85g) granulated sugar
- 1¼ cups (200g) mixed dried fruit such as dark and golden raisins and currants
- 2½ tablespoons (30g) chopped mixed candied citrus peel
- 1½ cups (170g) unsalted butter, chilled and diced
- 2 0.6-oz cakes fresh yeast (30g), or 2 envelopes active dry yeast (5 teaspoons)
- ¾ cup (170ml) lukewarm milk
- 2 tablespoons (30g) butter, melted
- 2½ tablespoons (30g) coarse granulated sugar or raw brown sugar such as Demerara

2 baking sheets, well greased

Quite by chance, Anthony Blake and I booked a fortnight's bed and breakfast stay at the house of one of Cornwall's finest bakers, named Sandra. She was apparently tireless, and relentlessly cheerful. No matter what time we looked into her kitchen, there she was baking, weighing warmed flour, rinsing dried fruit, kneading large balls of dough, and constantly checking the color of the loaves in the oven. Every day Sandra started at 5 A.M., finishing well after midnight, baking batch after batch of pungent saffron buns, which are her specialty, along with a few dozen pasties, and her standard white and whole-wheat loaves. We returned late after a day of photography to discover that, although Sandra had had a massive and shiny new oven installed after breakfast, she had not missed a beat with her baking.

Saffron is used a good deal in Cornish baking, despite the fact that the local saying "as dear as saffron" is all too apt. Good saffron is fabulously expensive because each saffron crocus produces only three stamens, which have to be laboriously plucked out with tweezers, and 4,000 stamens weigh only one ounce. Although nearly all our saffron now comes from Spain, until a hundred years ago it was grown extensively in England around the towns of Saffron Walden, in Essex, and Stratton, in Cornwall. For centuries, this expensive flavoring was used to make breads and cakes look and taste wonderfully rich. The best saffron buns, like these, are generously flecked with saffron filaments. As this dough is enriched with a fair quantity of butter, it takes quite a bit of time to rise, but the result is light textured, fine crumbed, rich, and highly aromatic. Eat the buns within two days of baking, spread with butter. These buns do not freeze well.

Put the saffron strands onto a heatproof saucer or in a small ovenproof skillet and toast in a 350°F oven for 10 to 15 minutes, or until their color darkens. Soak the saffron strands in the lukewarm water in a cup for at least 1 hour – it is best if you can leave it overnight.

Stir together the flour and salt in a large bowl. Stir in all but 1 teaspoon of the granulated sugar, all the dried fruit, and the mixed candied citrus peel. Rub in the butter with your fingertips until the mixture resembles fine crumbs.

Make a well in the center of the flour. Crumble the fresh yeast into a small bowl. Stir in the reserved 1 teaspoon sugar and half of the lukewarm milk. Let the yeast mixture stand for about 5 minutes, or until it starts to become foamy. If using dry yeast, mix the granules and the reserved 1 teaspoon sugar with half the lukewarm milk and let stand until foamy, 5 to 10 minutes (page 18).

Pour the saffron, its soaking liquid, and the yeast mixture into the well in the flour,

Golden yellow and studded with dark and golden raisins and currants, these saffron-flavored buns are best spread with creamy, unsalted butter or with cream cheese. The dough can also be shaped into one large loaf, which is ideal for slicing and toasting.

Above
SHAPE EACH PIECE OF DOUGH INTO A NEAT BUN BY ROLLING IT BETWEEN YOUR FLOURED PALMS.

Top
KNEAD THE DOUGH IN THE BOWL UNTIL IT IS VERY SMOOTH AND ELASTIC. PULL OFF FOURTEEN PIECES OF DOUGH.

adding most of the remaining lukewarm milk. Using your hand, mix the flour mixture from the bowl into the liquid in the well until the dough comes together. If the dough is dry and crumbly, gradually add more lukewarm milk, 1 tablespoon at a time; the dough should be soft, but not sticky. Knead the dough in the bowl for 10 minutes, working it thoroughly against the side of the bowl, until it is very smooth and elastic. Cover with a damp dish towel and let rise, away from drafts, until doubled in size. This heavy dough is slow to rise and can take as long as overnight in a cool room, or 3 to 4 hours in a warm kitchen.

Punch down the dough. Using lightly floured hands, one at a time, pull off fourteen equal-size pieces of dough and roll each between your palms to form neat buns. Or, roll the dough into a fat rope and cut into fourteen equal pieces. Using floured hands, shape each portion into a bun. Put on the prepared baking sheets, spaced well apart. Cover with a damp towel and let rise at warm room temperature (about 75°F) until doubled in size, about 2 hours. During the last 15 minutes of rising, heat the oven to 375°F.

Bake the buns for 15 minutes. Then lower the oven temperature to 350°F and bake for 5 minutes longer, or until the buns sound hollow when tapped underneath. Brush the hot buns with melted butter and sprinkle with coarse sugar. Then bake for 3 minutes longer. Transfer to wire racks to cool completely.

NOTE: You can also make a saffron loaf, instead of buns. After the first rising, shape the dough into a loaf (page 24) and put it, seam side down, into a well-greased 10 × 5 × 3-inch loaf pan. Let rise as above, then bake in a 375°F oven 40 minutes. Lower the oven temperature to 350°F and bake for 15 to 20 minutes longer, or until the loaf sounds hollow when unmolded and tapped underneath. Brush with melted butter and sprinkle with the coarse sugar. Then bake 3 minutes longer. Unmold onto a wire rack to cool.

GENTLY WORK THE CANDIED FRUIT AND ALMONDS INTO THE SOFT, RICH DOUGH

ABOVE RIGHT
Serve slices of sugar-crusted pougno for a delicious breakfast.

POUGNO

This bread, generously studded with fruits confits, or candied fruits – also called glacé or crystallized fruit – comes from the Provence region of southern France. The region is justly famous for preserving whole fruit, such as strawberries, mandarins, figs, tiny whole pineapples, and greengage plums, by cooking them in a concentrated sugar syrup. Pieces of fruit, such as pineapple rings, lemon and orange slices, and melon and pumpkin chunks, are also preserved in sugar. The confits are sold in the region's best grocers and confiseurs, and used for making cakes, breads, and pastries, as well as being eaten with a knife and fork at the end of a festive meal, usually Christmas.

Quality candied fruits are expensive because the preserving process is time-consuming and often done by hand. For the best flavor, do not used candied citrus peel from the supermarket. If you cannot get good candied fruit, use dark or golden raisins instead. In Provence, pougno is eaten for breakfast with bowls of very milky, strong coffee. It is best eaten within four days of baking, and can be frozen for up to one month.

INGREDIENTS

Makes 1 small loaf

2 cups (230g) unbleached white bread flour
½ teaspoon salt
1 0.6-oz cake fresh yeast (15g), or 1 envelope active dry yeast (2½ teaspoons)
2½ tablespoons (30g) sugar
2 tablespoons lukewarm milk
3 large eggs, beaten
extra flour for dusting
4 tablespoons (60g) butter, softened and diced
finely grated rind of 1 lemon and 1 orange
¾ cup (110g) finely chopped mixed candied fruits (see introduction)
½ cup (60g) roughly chopped blanched almonds
sugar for dredging

a baking sheet, greased

Stir together the flour and salt in a warmed medium-size bowl and make a well in the center of the flour. Crumble the fresh yeast into a small bowl. Stir in the sugar and lukewarm milk until smooth. Let the yeast mixture stand for about 5 minutes, or until it starts to become foamy. If using dry yeast, mix the granules and the sugar with the lukewarm milk and let stand until foamy, 5 to 10 minutes (page 18).

Pour the eggs and the yeast mixture into the well in the flour. Mix in the flour from the bowl with your hand or a wooden spoon to make a soft dough. Turn out onto a lightly floured surface and knead for 10 minutes, or until it becomes smooth, shiny, and elastic.

Using your hand, with fingertips splayed, gently beat the butter into the dough until incorporated. Add the grated lemon and orange rinds, working in the same way.

Shape the dough into a ball. Wash, dry, and oil the bowl. Return the dough to the bowl, and turn the dough over so the top is oiled. Cover with a damp dish towel and let rise at room temperature, away from drafts, until doubled in size, about 2 hours.

Punch down the dough, then turn out onto a lightly floured surface. Gently work in the candied fruit and almonds until thoroughly incorporated. Shape the dough into a disk about 1½ inches thick and put it on the prepared baking sheet. Cover lightly with a damp dish towel and let rise at room temperature (about 75°F) until doubled in size, about 1 hour. During the last 15 minutes of rising, heat the oven to 375°F. Bake the loaf for 15 to 20 minutes, or until it is golden and sounds hollow when tapped underneath. Dredge in the sugar, then transfer to a wire rack to cool completely.

VIOLA'S CARAMEL CINNAMON ROLLS

The lightest, moistest, and gooiest sticky buns ever! Viola Unruh (page 45) says the secret to these rolls is to let the sweet, rich, and airy dough rise three times. This old-fashioned American prairie kitchen recipe, her husband Henry's favorite, is an absolute treasure. The vital wheat gluten Viola includes in every batch is unobtainable in Great Britain, yet may be purchased at health-food stores or by mail order in the States (page 360). However, the results are just as enjoyable when the dough is made without it. In England I use good-quality unrefined Barbados muscovado sugar, but dark brown sugar works well, too. This recipe makes plenty of caramel topping. When the rolls have cooled, store them, well wrapped, at room temperature, and eat them within two days.

INGREDIENTS

Makes 15

1 0.6-oz cake fresh yeast (15g), or 1 envelope active dry yeast (2½ teaspoons)
½ cup (115ml) lukewarm water
¼ cup (50g) + 1 teaspoon granulated sugar
4 tablespoons (60g) butter, diced
¾ teaspoon salt
1¼ cups (280ml) hot water (about 150°F)
about 6 cups (680g) unbleached white bread flour
1½ tablespoons vital wheat gluten (optional)
1 large egg, beaten
extra flour for dusting

FILLING:
6 tablespoons (85g) butter, softened
7 tablespoons packed (85g) dark brown sugar
1 tablespoon ground cinnamon, or to taste

CARAMEL TOPPING:
1 cup packed (200g) dark brown sugar
½ cup (115ml) heavy cream

a roasting pan, about 13 × 9 inches, well greased
a baking sheet, lightly greased

To make the dough: Crumble the fresh yeast into a small bowl. Stir in the lukewarm water and the 1 teaspoon granulated sugar until smooth. Let the yeast mixture stand for 5 to 10 minutes, or until it starts to become foamy.

If using dry yeast, mix the granules and the 1 teaspoon sugar with the lukewarm water and let stand until foamy, 5 to 10 minutes (page 18).

Meanwhile, put the butter, the remaining granulated sugar, and the salt into a large bowl. Pour in the hot water and stir until the butter melts. Add 2 cups (230g) of the flour and the vital wheat gluten, if using, and beat together well with a wooden spoon until the mixture is very smooth. Pour in the yeast mixture and the egg and beat for 1 minute until well blended. Cover with a damp dish towel and let rest for 10 minutes.

Working in the bowl, gradually knead in 2 cups (230g) of the remaining flour to make a soft dough. Turn out the dough onto a lightly floured work surface and knead for 10 minutes, gradually working in as much of the remaining flour as is necessary, a handful at a time, to make a soft, but not sticky dough. Wash, dry, and oil the bowl.

Return the dough to the bowl, and turn the dough over to oil the top. Cover with a damp dish towel and let rise at room temperature, away from drafts, until doubled in size, about 1 hour. Punch down the dough. Leave the dough in the bowl, cover again and let rise again at warm room temperature (about 75°F) until almost doubled in size, about 1 hour.

Punch down the dough. Turn out onto a lightly floured work surface and knead for 1 minute. Cover with an upturned bowl and let rest for 10 minutes.

Meanwhile, make the filling: Beat the butter with the dark brown sugar and cinnamon in a medium-size bowl with a spoon or electric mixer until light and fluffy.

Roll out the dough on a lightly floured work surface with a lightly floured rolling pin into a 15 × 10-inch rectangle. Gently spread the filling over the rectangle, trying not to stretch the dough, spreading all the way to the edges. Then roll up tightly from a long side, like a jelly-roll. Cut the roll into fifteen even slices, each about 1 inch thick. Arrange the slices, with a cut side down, in the prepared baking pan, with the sides just touching. Cover with a damp dish towel and let rise at room temperature until doubled in size, about 45 minutes. (If the temperature is too warm, the filling will ooze out.) During the last 15 minutes of rising, heat the oven to 350°F.

Bake the rolls for 30 to 35 minutes, or until they are well risen and golden brown. (Viola recommends that you do not bake them too near the bottom of the oven.)

Meanwhile, make the caramel topping: Whisk the dark brown sugar and cream together in a small bowl until no lumps remain. Turn out the buns in one piece onto the baking sheet.

Pour the caramel topping into the baking pan. Tilt the pan so the topping covers the bottom evenly. Then slide the buns, upside-down, back into the pan on top of the caramel mixture. Return to the oven and bake 10 minutes longer. Remove from the oven and let the buns cool in the pan for 6 minutes. Invert the pan onto a baking sheet, so the caramel sauce is on top of the rolls. Pull the rolls apart to serve.

INVERT THE ROLLS ONTO A BAKING SHEET AND PULL APART TO SERVE.

BARM BRACK

This spicy loaf, dotted with currants, is from Ireland, where it was originally baked in a cast-iron pot suspended over a fire. Although now baked in conventional ovens, the bread is still made in a traditional round shape rather than as a loaf. The word "barm" in the name comes from the liquid ale yeast that was used to raise the dough before blocks of compressed yeast made bread-making easier.

Barm brack is a close cousin to bara brith (opposite), but it is sweeter and more cake-like. It keeps, well wrapped, for four or five days, or can be frozen for up to one month.

INGREDIENTS

Makes 1 loaf

- 4 cups (455g) unbleached white bread flour
- 1 teaspoon ground cinnamon
- 1 teaspoon pumpkin-pie spice
- 1 teaspoon salt
- 6 tablespoons (85g) butter, diced
- 7 tablespoons packed (85g) light brown sugar or granulated sugar
- 1 0.6-oz cake fresh yeast (15g), or 1 envelope active dry yeast (2½ teaspoons)
- ½ cup (115ml) lukewarm milk
- 2 large eggs, beaten
- extra flour for dusting
- 2 cups (280g) currants
- 1 tablespoon granulated sugar dissolved in 2 tablespoons boiling water for glazing

an 8-inch round, deep cake pan, greased

Put the flour, cinnamon, pumpkin-pie spice, and salt into a large bowl. Rub the butter into the flour with your fingertips until the mixture resembles fine crumbs. Stir in the sugar (reserve 1 teaspoon if using dry yeast). Make a well in the center of the flour mixture.

Crumble the fresh yeast into a small bowl. Stir in the lukewarm milk until smooth. If using dry yeast, mix the granules and the reserved 1 teaspoon sugar with the lukewarm milk and let stand until foamy, 5 to 10 minutes (page 18). Add the eggs to the yeast mixture and stir to mix. Pour the mixture into the well in the flour. Gradually work the flour from the bowl into the yeast and egg mixture to make a soft but not sticky dough. If the dough is dry and crumbly, add more milk or water, 1 tablespoon at a time. If the dough sticks to your fingers, add more flour, 1 tablespoon at a time.

Turn out the dough onto a lightly floured work surface and knead for about 10 minutes, until smooth and elastic. Gradually knead in the currants until evenly distributed, 4 to 5 minutes. Return the dough to the bowl (there is no need to oil the bowl for this recipe). Cover with a damp dish towel and let rise at room temperature, away from drafts, until doubled in size, 2 to 2½ hours.

Punch down the dough. Turn it out onto a floured surface and shape the soft dough into a round to fit the pan. Put the round into the prepared pan. Cover with a damp dish towel and let rise at room temperature, away from drafts, until doubled in size, 1 to 1½ hours. During the last 15 minutes, heat the oven to 400°F.

Bake the loaf for 50 to 60 minutes, or until it is browned and sounds hollow when unmolded and tapped underneath. If the loaf is browning too much during baking, cover loosely with butter wrappers or a sheet of foil.

Remove from the oven and brush with the hot, sweet glaze. Return to the oven for 2 minutes longer. Turn out onto a wire rack, glazed side up, and let cool completely.

ABOVE
Rich with currants, barm brack is served in Ireland for afternoon tea. It is just as delicious with a cup of coffee for a mid-morning snack.

RIGHT
Rural Ireland, where you can still see milk being transported by horse and cart, has a rich baking heritage. Accomplished home bakers keep traditional recipes alive, of which barm brack remains one of the most popular. More variations include golden raisins and candied citrus peel; if you wish, replace some of the currants with a tablespoon or two of diced candied peel.

A farmhouse afternoon tea: Teacakes For Toasting (page 130), Bara Brith, and Barm Brack (opposite).

BARA BRITH

The name of this speckled loaf from Wales means currant bread. I've also added dark and golden raisins and a bit of candied citrus peel for extra flavor. To avoid over-baking the loaf, be sure to check it after 30 minutes.

INGREDIENTS

Makes 1 large loaf

- 1⅓ cups (230g) mixed dried fruit, such as dark and golden raisins, currants, and chopped candied citrus peel
- 1½ cups (340ml) strong hot tea
- 4 cups (455g) unbleached white bread flour
- 5 tablespoons packed (60g) light brown sugar
- 1 teaspoon salt
- ½ teaspoon pumpkin-pie spice
- 1 0.6-oz cake fresh yeast (15g), or 1 envelope active dry yeast (2½ teaspoons)
- about 2 tablespoons lukewarm milk
- 4 tablespoons (60g) butter, melted and cooled

a loaf pan, about 10 × 5 × 3 inches, greased

Put the mixed dried fruit and candied citrus peel into a medium-size bowl. Add the hot tea and stir well. Cover with plastic wrap and let soak overnight at room temperature.

The next day, place the flour, brown sugar (reserve 1 teaspoon if using dry yeast), the salt, and the spice into a large bowl. Rub the brown sugar into the flour with your fingers to break up any lumps and to mix the ingredients. Make a well in the center of the flour mixture.

Crumble the fresh yeast into a small bowl. Stir in the lukewarm milk until smooth. If using dry yeast, mix the granules and the reserved 1 teaspoon brown sugar with the lukewarm milk and let stand until foamy, 5 to 10 minutes (page 18). Pour the yeast mixture into the well in the flour. Add the melted butter and the fruit mixture with all the soaking liquid and stir with a wooden spoon to mix with the yeast mixture. Mix the flour from the bowl into the yeast and fruit mixture to make a soft dough. If the dough is dry and crumbly, add a little more milk, 1 tablespoon at a time. If the dough sticks to your fingers, add more flour, 1 tablespoon at a time.

Gently knead the dough in the bowl for 5 minutes, or until the fruit is evenly distributed and the dough is elastic; it will be quite soft. Turn out the dough onto a sheet of waxed paper and wash, dry, and oil the mixing bowl. Return the dough to the bowl, and turn the dough over so the top is oiled. Cover with a damp dish towel and let rise at room temperature, away from drafts, until doubled in size, 1½ to 2 hours.

Punch down the dough. Turn out the dough onto a floured surface and shape into a loaf to fit the prepared pan (page 24). Put the loaf, seam side down, into the pan. Cover with a damp towel and let rise at room temperature, away from drafts, until doubled in size, 1 to 1½ hours. During the last 15 minutes, heat the oven to 400°F. Bake the loaf for 30 to 40 minutes, or until it sounds hollow when unmolded and tapped underneath. If the loaf is browning too quickly during baking, cover it loosely with foil. Turn the loaf out of the pan onto a wire rack to cool.

Right
REMOVE THE TEACAKES FROM THE OVEN WHEN THEY ARE GOLDEN BROWN AND PUFFED UP.
Far right
SERVE TOASTED TEACAKES SPREAD WITH BUTTER. TO TOAST THEM UNDER A HOT BROILER, TOAST THE TOP AND THE BOTTOM. SPLIT THE TEACAKES IN HALF AND TOAST THE CUT SURFACES.

TEACAKES FOR TOASTING

INGREDIENTS

Makes 8
1/3 cup (60g) currants
2 1/2 tablespoons (30g) chopped mixed candied citrus peel
2/3 cup (140ml) strong hot tea
about 2/3 cup (140ml) milk
1 0.6-oz cake fresh yeast (15g), or 1 envelope active dry yeast (2 1/2 teaspoons)
2 1/2 tablespoons (30g) sugar
4 cups (455g) unbleached white bread flour
1 teaspoon salt
4 tablespoons (60g) lard or butter, chilled and diced
extra flour for dusting
milk for brushing

2 baking sheets, greased

My mother, like her mother before her, comes into her own at teatime. She possesses a china cupboard stacked from floor to ceiling with exquisite tea services, including some porcelain so eggshell-thin it is almost transparent; she enjoys using it, despite the hazards. Each day, teatime is an important ritual, even if it is "just family."

My American husband is greatly amused by the quaintness of this almost bygone English custom, although he has succumbed to its soothing comforts – even if he does insist on black coffee, instead of tea.

The best way to toast teacakes is under a very hot broiler, or over the red-hot embers of an open fire. These teacakes stale quickly so eat within one day, or you can keep for two days if you plan to toast them. They can also be frozen for up to one month. Thaw at room temperature before toasting.

Put the currants and candied citrus peel into a small bowl. Pour in the hot tea, stir well, and let steep for 1 hour. Drain the fruit in a strainer set over a measuring cup. Add enough milk to the tea soaking liquid to make 1 1/4 cups (280ml).

Crumble the fresh yeast into a small bowl. Stir in the tea mixture until smooth. If using dry yeast, note the amount of tea soaking liquid left after the fruit is strained. Reserve the tea. Measure an amount of milk that when added to the tea will total 1 1/4 cups (280ml) of liquid. Heat the measured amount of milk in a small saucepan to lukewarm. Mix the dry yeast granules and 1 tablespoon of the granulated sugar with the lukewarm milk and let stand until foamy, 5 to 10 minutes (page 18). Then stir in the tea soaking liquid.

Mix together the flour and salt in a large bowl. Rub in the lard or butter with your fingertips until the mixture resembles fine crumbs. Stir in the sugar (the remaining 1 tablespoon if using the dry yeast) and the soaked currants and candied citrus peel. Make a well in the center of the flour mixture.

Pour the yeast mixture into the well. Mix the flour from the bowl into the liquid in the well with your hand or a wooden spoon to make a soft dough. Turn out the dough onto a lightly floured work surface and knead for 10 minutes until smooth and elastic.

Return the dough to the bowl. (There is no need to oil the bowl.) Cover with a damp dish towel and let rise at room temperature, away from drafts, until doubled in size, 1 1/2 to 2 1/2 hours, depending on the weather and the temperature of the room.

Gently punch down the dough. Turn out the dough onto a lightly floured work surface. Weigh the dough and divide it into eight equal pieces, or roll it into a fat rope and cut it into eight equal pieces. Shape each portion into a neat roll (see Oatmeal Rolls, page 25). Flatten each roll so it is about 5 inches wide and 3/4 inch thick. Arrange the teacakes on the prepared baking sheets, spaced well apart. Cover loosely with a damp dish towel and let rise at room temperature until almost doubled in size, about 45 minutes. During the last 15 minutes of rising, heat the oven to 400°F.

Glaze the teacakes with milk. Bake them for about 20 minutes until they are golden brown and puffed up.

Transfer to wire racks. Lightly dust each teacake with flour, then cover loosely with dry dish towels to keep the crusts soft. Let them cool completely.

CHELSEA BUNS

For about a hundred years, until its demise in 1839, the Chelsea Bun House was famous for its spicy, sugary, sticky buns. Situated in Bunhouse Place, off Pimlico Road, in London, the bakery was hugely fashionable, the place to be seen standing in line to buy a Chelsea bun. The owners also claimed to have invented the hot cross bun. In fact, the bakery's hot cross buns were in such demand that one Good Friday, thousands of people, including King George III, thronged down Ebury Street toward the shop. Eat these within two days of baking.

INGREDIENTS

Makes 9

- 4 cups (455g) unbleached white bread flour
- 1 teaspoon salt
- 3 tablespoons (40g) granulated sugar
- 1 0.6-oz cake fresh yeast (15g), or 1 envelope active dry yeast (2½ teaspoons)
- ¾ cup (170ml) lukewarm milk
- 1 extra large egg, beaten
- 4 tablespoons (60g) butter, melted
- extra flour for dusting

FILLING:

- 3 tablespoons (40g) butter, melted
- ⅓ cup packed (70g) light or dark brown sugar
- 1 cup (140g) mixed dried fruit, such as dark and light raisins, currants, and mixed candied citrus peel

STICKY GLAZE:

- 7 tablespoons packed (85g) light brown sugar
- 4 tablespoons (60g) butter
- ¼ cup (60ml) milk
- 2 tablespoons honey

an 8- to 9-inch square cake pan about 1½ inches deep, greased

To make the dough: Mix together the flour, salt, and half the sugar in a large bowl. Make a well in the center of the flour mixture. Crumble the fresh yeast into a small bowl. Stir in the remaining sugar and the lukewarm milk until smooth. If using dry yeast, mix the granules and the sugar with the lukewarm milk and let stand until foamy, 5 to 10 minutes (page 18).

Pour the yeast mixture into the well in the flour and mix enough flour from the bowl into the liquid with your hand or a wooden spoon to make a thick batter. Let stand until spongy, about 10 minutes. Beat the egg and melted butter into the spongy mixture with your hand or a small whisk. Gradually work in the flour from the bowl to make a soft, but not sticky dough. If the dough is dry, add water or milk, 1 tablespoon at a time.

Turn out the dough onto a lightly floured work surface and knead for 10 minutes until very smooth, elastic, and satiny. Wash, dry, and oil the bowl. Return the dough to the bowl, and turn the dough over so the top is oiled. Cover with a damp dish towel and let rise at room temperature, away from drafts, until doubled in size, about 1½ hours.

Punch down the dough. Turn out the dough onto a floured work surface and roll out with a floured rolling pin into a 16 × 9-inch rectangle, with a long side facing you.

For the filling: Brush the dough with the melted butter. Then sprinkle with the sugar, followed by the mixed dried fruit and the candied citrus peel, leaving a ½-inch border all around the edge. Starting from the long side, roll up the dough fairly tightly, like a jelly roll. Cut the roll into nine even pieces and arrange them, cut side down, in the prepared pan, touching but not squashed together. Cover the pan with a damp dish towel and let rise at room temperature, away from drafts, until almost doubled in size, 30 to 40 minutes. During the last 15 minutes of rising, heat the oven to 400°F.

To make the sticky glaze: Combine the brown sugar, butter, milk, and honey in a small saucepan and heat over moderately low heat, stirring frequently, until the butter melts and the sugar dissolves. Bring to the boil, then simmer for 1 minute. Pour the glaze over the risen buns. Bake the buns for 25 to 30 minutes, or until golden brown.

Cool in the pan for about 10 minutes, or until the topping is firm, but not set. Then transfer the buns to a wire rack set over a sheet of foil and let cool. If the topping is left too long and welds onto the pan, put the pan back in the oven until the topping softens again. Pull or tear the buns apart when they have cooled.

POUR THE STICKY GLAZE OVER THE RISEN BUNS, THEN BAKE.

COOL THE BUNS ON A WIRE RACK, THEN PULL OR TEAR APART TO SERVE.

GERMAN PEAR LOAF

INGREDIENTS

Makes 1 loaf

1 cup (170g) chopped dried pears
⅓ cup (60g) chopped dried figs
⅓ cup (60g) chopped pitted prunes
⅔ cup (140ml) apple or prune juice
⅔ cup (140ml) water from the cold tap
3½ cups (395g) unbleached white bread flour
⅔ cup (60g) rye flour
7 tablespoons packed (85g) light brown sugar
1 teaspoon salt
1 0.6-oz cake fresh yeast (15g), or 1 envelope active dry yeast (2½ teaspoons)
2 tablespoons lukewarm water
grated rind of 1 lemon
1 cup (110g) mixed chopped blanched almonds and hazelnuts
extra flour for dusting

a baking sheet, greased

A loaf packed with dried fruit and nuts, but not as rich, heavy, or moist as the densely fruited Hutzelbrot from Nuremberg (page 151). This is traditionally served with a glass of kirsch or fruit liqueur, but is equally good with coffee for breakfast. Eat within one week of baking, or freeze for up to one month.

Mix together the pears, figs, and prunes in a medium-size bowl. Add the apple or prune juice and cold water and stir well. Cover with plastic wrap and let soak overnight.

The next day, drain the fruit in a strainer set over a bowl. Put the fruit into a small bowl and cover with cling film. Set the fruit and the soaking liquid aside.

Put the white flour, rye flour, sugar (if using dry yeast, reserve 1 teaspoon of the sugar), and salt into a large bowl. Rub the ingredients together with your fingertips to break up any lumps of brown sugar and to combine the ingredients. Make a well in the center of the flour mixture.

Crumble the fresh yeast into a small bowl. Stir in the 2 tablespoons lukewarm water until smooth. If using dry yeast, mix the granules and the reserved 1 teaspoon sugar with the lukewarm water and let stand until foamy, 5 to 10 minutes (page 18).

Pour the yeast mixture and the reserved fruit soaking liquid into the well in the flour. Mix in the flour from the bowl with your hand or a wooden spoon to make a soft but not sticky dough. If the dough seems too wet and sticky, add more white flour, 1 tablespoon at a time. If the dough is dry, add more water, 1 tablespoon at a time.

Turn out the dough onto a lightly floured work surface and knead for 10 minutes or until smooth and elastic. Return the dough to the bowl. (There is no need to oil the bowl.) Cover with a damp dish towel and let rise at room temperature, away from drafts, until doubled in size, about 1½ hours.

OPPOSITE
Dried fruit sweetens and flavors the Hazelnut, Apricot, and Honey Loaf and the German Pear Loaf (center). I prefer to purchase dried fruits from a health-food store with a fast turnover (see also mail-order sources in the List of Suppliers, page 130). Look for moist, pliable fruit with a slightly tart, intense, fruity flavor, otherwise, the breads will be too sweet.

Punch down the dough. Turn out onto a lightly floured surface and press out into a rough rectangle. Sprinkle the soaked fruit, lemon rind, and nuts over the dough, then gently knead until they are evenly distributed, about 5 minutes. Shape the dough into an oval loaf (see The Basic Loaf, page 17) about 10 inches long. Place the loaf, seam side down, on the prepared baking sheet. Cover with a damp dish towel and let rise at room temperature, away from drafts, until it again doubles in size, 1–1½ hours. During the last 15 minutes of rising, heat the oven to 350°F.

Bake the loaf for 1–1¼ hours, or until it is golden brown and sounds hollow when tapped underneath. Transfer to a wire rack to cool completely.

HAZELNUT, APRICOT, AND HONEY LOAF

INGREDIENTS

Makes 2 small loaves
- 1 0.6-oz cake fresh yeast (15g), or 1 envelope active dry yeast (2½ teaspoons)
- ⅔ cup (140ml) lukewarm milk
- 1 tablespoon well-flavored honey
- ¾ cup (110g) roughly chopped dried apricots
- ⅔ cup (140ml) boiling water
- 4 cups (455g) unbleached white bread flour
- ¾ cup (85g) toasted and halved hazelnuts
- 1 teaspoon salt
- 2 tablespoons hazelnut oil, or 2 tablespoons (30g) butter, melted
- extra flour for dusting
- ⅔ cup (60g) rye flour

2 loaf pans, about 7 × 5 × 3 inches, greased

This recipe uses hazelnut oil, more expected on salads than in breads, along with a flavorful honey, such as orange blossom, heather, or wildflower. I was given this recipe by Shaun Hill of Gidleigh Park, in Devon, England. Eat this loaf within three days, or toast and serve with butter or cheese. It can be frozen for one month.

Crumble the fresh yeast into a small bowl. Stir in the lukewarm milk and honey until smooth. Let the yeast mixture stand 5 to 10 minutes, or until it starts to become foamy. If using dry yeast, mix the granules with the lukewarm milk and the honey and let stand until foamy, 5 to 10 minutes (page 18). Meanwhile, put the apricots into a small bowl. Pour in the boiling water and let soak for about 10 minutes, or until the fruit has plumped up and the water cooled to lukewarm. Mix together 3½ cups (400g) flour, the hazelnuts, and the salt in a large bowl and make a well in the center.

Pour the yeast mixture into the well in the flour mixture, followed by the hazelnut oil or melted butter, and the apricots and their soaking liquid. Mix together all the ingredients in the well with your hand or a wooden spoon. Then gradually work the flour from the bowl in to the liquid in the well to make a soft, but not sticky dough. If the dough sticks to your fingers, work in the rest of the flour, as needed, 1 tablespoon at a time.

Turn out the dough onto a lightly floured work surface and knead for 10 minutes until smooth and fairly firm. Return the dough to the bowl (there is no need to oil the bowl). Cover with a damp dish towel and let rise at room temperature, away from drafts, until doubled in size, 1½ to 2 hours.

Punch down the dough. Turn it out onto a surface covered with the rye flour. Divide it in half. Knead each portion in the rye flour for 1 minute, then shape into a loaf to fit one of the pans (see A Plain White Loaf, page 24). Put a loaf, seam side down, into each prepared pan. Cover with a damp dish towel and let rise at room temperature until almost doubled in size, about 45 minutes. During the last 15 minutes of rising, heat the oven to 425°F.

Bake the loaves for 35 to 40 minutes, or until they are golden brown and sound hollow

LET THE LOAVES RISE IN THE PAN UNTIL ALMOST DOUBLED IN SIZE.

This twisted ring with its unusual fruit and nut filling can be served as a coffee cake, or as a winter dessert. It is especially good with pouring cream, or vanilla-scented, lightly whipped heavy cream. The intricate-looking shape is surprisingly easy to make, but you should allow yourself plenty of time for your first attempt.

when unmolded and tapped underneath. Turn out onto a wire rack to cool completely.

PEACH COURONNE

Dried peaches plus raisins and walnuts make a deliciously tart filling for this pretty ring. The dried peaches can be replaced by an equal quantity of dried apricots, if you wish. Serve the couronne warm as a dessert, with cream if you like, or at teatime. Eat within one day, or freeze for only one week.

Place the peaches in a small bowl. Pour in the orange juice and let soak overnight.

To prepare the dough: Mix the flour and salt in a medium-size bowl. Rub in the butter until the mixture resembles fine crumbs. Make a well in the center of the flour mixture. Crumble the fresh yeast into a small bowl. Stir in the lukewarm milk until smooth. If using dry yeast, mix the granules and the ½ teaspoon sugar with the lukewarm milk and let stand until foamy, 5 to 10 minutes (page 18). Mix the egg into the yeast mixture.

Pour the yeast mixture and the egg into the well. With your hand, gradually work the

INGREDIENTS

Makes 1 large ring
¾ cup (110g) chopped dried peaches
⅔ cup (140ml) orange juice
2 cups (230g) unbleached white bread flour
½ teaspoon salt
3 tablespoons (40g) butter, chilled and diced
⅔ 0.6-oz cake fresh yeast (10g), or ⅔ envelope active dry yeast (2 teaspoons) plus ½ teaspoon granulated sugar
5 tablespoons (70ml) lukewarm milk
1 large egg, beaten
extra flour for dusting
2 tablespoons granulated sugar
2 tablespoons cold milk (optional)
FILLING:
6 tablespoons (85g) butter, softened
5 tablespoons packed (60g) light brown sugar
3½ tablespoons (30g) unbleached all-purpose flour
½ cup (60g) walnut pieces
6½ tablespoons (60g) raisins
grated rind of 1 orange

a baking sheet, greased

flour from the bowl into the liquid to make a soft, but not sticky dough. Turn out the dough onto a floured work surface and knead for 10 minutes until smooth, elastic, and satiny.

Shape the dough into a ball. Return it to the bowl. Cover with a damp dish towel and let rise at room temperature, away from drafts, until doubled in size, about 1 hour.

Meanwhile, prepare the filling: Drain the peaches, reserving the soaking liquid. Beat the butter and brown sugar in a medium-size bowl with an electric mixer on medium-high speed until fluffy. On low speed, beat in the flour, then the walnuts, raisins, orange rind, and peaches. Or, stir them in with a wooden spoon.

Punch down the dough. Turn out the dough onto a floured work surface and with a floured rolling pin roll out into a 12 × 9-inch rectangle. Spread the filling evenly over the dough. Roll the dough up fairly tightly from a long side, like a jelly roll. Gently roll the dough back and forth, stretching it, until it is 20 inches long.

Carefully cut the dough in half lengthwise. Working with the cut sides facing up, twist the halves together. Lift gently onto the prepared baking sheet and shape the twisted roll into a neat ring, twisting and pinching the ends together to close the ring. Cover loosely with a damp dish towel and let rise at room temperature, away from drafts, until doubled in size, about 1 hour. During the last 15 minutes of rising, heat the oven to 400°F.

Bake the ring for 20 to 25 minutes, or until firm and golden. Stir the sugar with the cold milk or 2 tablespoons of the reserved peach soaking liquid in a small saucepan and bring to a boil, stirring to dissolve the sugar. Remove the couronne from the oven and immediately brush with the hot glaze. Slide onto a wire rack to cool.

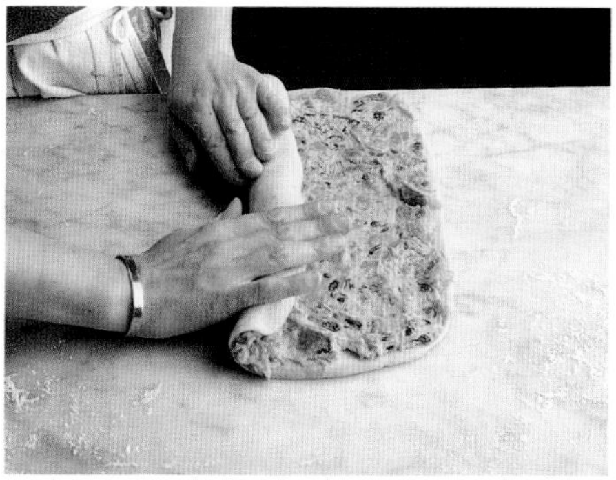

SPREAD THE FILLING EVENLY OVER THE DOUGH. ROLL UP THE DOUGH FROM A LONG SIDE, AS FOR A JELLY ROLL.

USING A VERY SHARP KNIFE, CAREFULLY CUT THE DOUGH IN HALF LENGTHWISE.

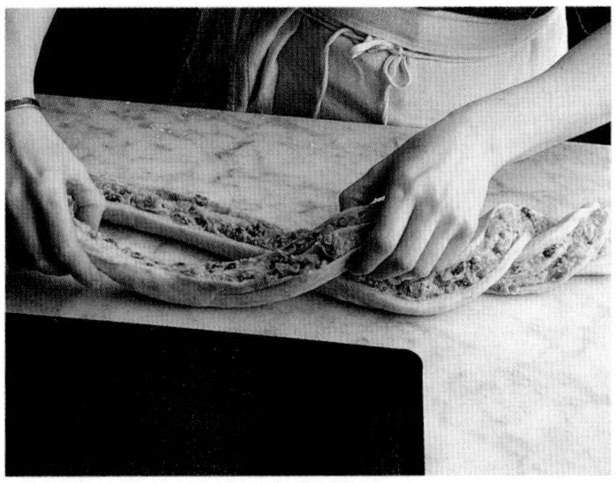

WORKING WITH THE CUT SIDES FACING UP, TWIST THE TWO HALVES TOGETHER.

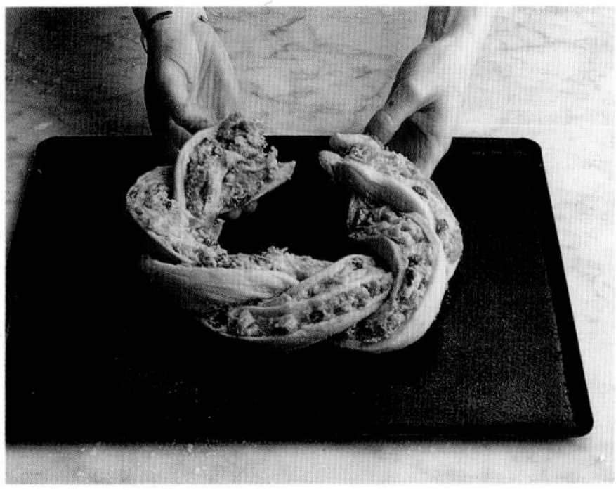

BRING THE ENDS OF THE DOUGH TOGETHER TO CLOSE THE RING. PINCH THEM TO SEAL.

LOIS'S FRUIT SLICE

INGREDIENTS

Makes 2 large fruit slices
1 0.6-oz cake fresh yeast (15g), or 1 envelope active dry yeast ($2\frac{1}{2}$ teaspoons)
½ cup (100g) + 2 teaspoons sugar
¾ cup (170ml) lukewarm water
1 cup (230ml) heavy cream
1 teaspoon salt
2 large eggs, beaten
2 tablespoons (30g) butter, melted
about 6 cups (680g) unbleached white bread flour
extra flour for dusting
FILLING:
1½ lb (680g) prune plums, halved and pitted, or 1¼ lb (570g) fresh berries, such as blueberries, blackberries, raspberries, and pitted sour cherries
1½ tablespoons cornstarch or 2 tablespoons tapioca
about 1½ cups (300g) sugar
CRUMBLE TOPPING:
¾ cup (110g) unbleached all-purpose flour
½ cup #aa 2 tablespoons (130g) sugar
½ cup (110g) butter, at room temperature

2 baking sheets with edges or jelly-roll pans, about 14 × 8 inches, greased

Here is another recipe from Lois Keller (page 103), who lives in the heart of America – indeed, she is almost exactly at America's center, if you fold the map in fourths. This recipe, from her husband's German family, uses white flour, and is one of the few recipes Lois makes with refined flour. (She prefers to grind her own flour from whole wheat kernels.) Lois likes to use the wild berries that grow around her farm, or the German purple-blue plums she also grows, which are packed with flavor. You may use the European type of plums called prune plums. Prune plums are small, dark purple, and usually freestone plums with pointed, not rounded, ends. Grown in California, the Pacific Northwest, Michigan, and New York State, they become available in August. This coffee cake is eaten with coffee for breakfast or mid-afternoon tea. It is best eaten within two days of baking.

To prepare the dough: Crumble the fresh yeast into a large bowl. Stir in the 2 teaspoons sugar and the lukewarm water until smooth. If using dry yeast, mix the granules and the 2 teaspoons sugar with the lukewarm water and let stand until foamy, 5 to 10 minutes (page 18). In a medium-size bowl, whisk the cream with the remaining sugar and the salt just until mixed. Whisk in the eggs and melted butter until well blended.

Add 1½ cups (170g) flour to the yeast mixture and mix in with your hand. Stir in the cream mixture. Then work in enough of the remaining flour to make a very soft dough. If the dough seems too sticky, work in a little extra flour, 1 tablespoon at a time. If the dough is dry and crumbly, work in a little extra water, 1 tablespoon at a time. Turn out the dough onto a lightly floured work surface and knead with floured hands for 10 minutes to form a smooth and satiny ball. The dough should be soft rather than dry or tough. Return the dough to the bowl. Cover with a damp dish towel and let rise at room temperature, away from drafts, until doubled in size, about 1 hour. During the last 15 minutes of rising, heat the oven to 350°F.

Meanwhile, prepare the filling. Mix together the plums, berries, or cherries, the cornstarch or tapioca, and sugar to taste in a large bowl. (If the fruit is very sweet you'll need less sugar than listed.) Cover and let stand while the dough is rising.

To prepare the crumble topping: Mix together the flour and sugar in a medium-size bowl. Using a fork, work in the butter to make coarse crumbs. Set aside.

Punch down the dough. Turn out the dough onto a floured surface and knead for 30 seconds. Divide the dough in half. Roll out each portion on a floured work surface with a floured rolling pin into a rectangle about ¼ inch thick, the same size as the prepared baking sheets or jelly-roll pans. Roll up the dough loosely on the rolling pin and unroll onto the sheets or pans, patting the dough with your hands into the corners, forming a slight rim on all sides. Spoon half the fruit filling evenly over each piece of dough. If using plums, arrange them cut-side up on the dough. Sprinkle half of the crumble topping evenly over each coffee cake. Bake the cakes for 30 to 35 minutes, or until the base is golden and firm. Serve warm with cream.

Lois Keller with a freshly baked fruit slice.

WALNUT BREAD

Toasting the walnut halves until lightly browned gives this loaf a dense, nutty flavor. Some bakers also add a tablespoon or two of walnut oil or melted butter with the last of the water. Eat this loaf within three days of baking, or freeze for up to one month.

Stir together the whole-wheat and white flours and the salt in a large bowl and make a well in the center. Crumble the fresh yeast into a small bowl. Stir in half of the lukewarm water and the honey until smooth. If using dry yeast, mix the granules and the honey with half of the lukewarm water and let stand until foamy, 5 to 10 minutes (page 18).

Walnut Bread variations in this photo include sliced Raisin Bread.

INGREDIENTS

Makes 2 medium loaves

4 cups (455g) whole-wheat bread flour, preferably stone-ground
2 cups (230g) unbleached white bread flour
2½ teaspoons salt
1 0.6-oz cake fresh yeast (15g), or 1 envelope active dry yeast (2½ teaspoons)
2 cups (460ml) lukewarm water
1½ tablespoons well-flavored honey
1 tablespoon walnut oil or melted butter (optional)
extra flour for dusting
2½ cups (230g) walnut halves, toasted, cooled and roughly chopped

1 or 2 baking sheets, greased

Pour the yeast mixture into the well in the flour. Mix in enough flour from the bowl with your hand to make a thick batter. Let stand until spongy, 10 to 15 minutes.

If necessary, reheat the remaining water to lukewarm. Pour the water into the sponge, along with the oil or melted butter, if using. With your hand or a wooden spoon, gradually work the flour from the bowl into the sponge to make a soft, but not sticky dough. If the dough sticks to your fingers, work in a little extra flour, 1 tablespoon at a time. If the dough is dry and crumbly, work in a little extra water, 1 tablespoon at a time. Turn out the dough onto a lightly floured work surface and knead for 10 minutes until smooth and elastic. Gently knead the walnuts into the dough until they are evenly distributed, about 2 minutes. Wash, dry, and oil the bowl.

Shape the dough into a ball. Return the dough to the bowl, and turn the dough over so the top is oiled. Cover with a damp dish towel and let rise at room temperature, away from drafts, until doubled in size, about 2 hours.

Punch down the dough. Turn it out onto a floured surface and knead gently for 1 minute. Divide in half. Shape each half into a neat ball and place on the prepared baking sheet(s). Cover with a damp dish towel and let rise at room temperature, away from drafts, until doubled in size, about 1½ hours. During the last 15 minutes of rising, heat the oven to 425°F. Cut three shallow slashes in the top of each loaf. Bake the loaves for 15 minutes. Then lower the oven temperature to 375°F and bake for 20 to 30 minutes longer, or until the loaves sound hollow when tapped underneath. Cool on wire racks.

VARIATIONS: PECAN BREAD Use 3 cups (340g) each whole-wheat bread flour (preferably stone-ground) and unbleached white bread flour and prepare the dough as for the Walnut Bread. Replace the walnuts with an equal amount of coarsely chopped, untoasted pecans.

MIXED NUT BREAD Prepare the dough as for the Walnut Bread. Replace the walnuts with 2½ cups (280g) coarsely chopped, toasted mixed nuts, such as walnuts, skinned hazelnuts, pecans, and/or macadamia nuts.

RAISIN BREAD Prepare the dough as for the Walnut Bread, replacing up to 1 cup (110g) of the whole-wheat flour with rye flour, if you wish. Replace the walnuts with 1½cups (225g) raisins.

FRUIT AND NUT BREAD Prepare the dough as for the Walnut Bread. Replace the walnuts with 1½ cups (225g) dark or golden raisins and 1½ cups (170g) coarsely chopped toasted walnuts.

CINDY'S PORTUGUESE SWEET BREADS

INGREDIENTS

Makes 2 loaves
- ⅓ cup (40g) currants
- 1 tablespoon orange juice, rum, Madeira, sherry, or hot water
- 2 0.6-oz cakes fresh yeast (30g), or 2 envelopes active dry yeast (5 teaspoons)
- 1¼ cups (280ml) lukewarm water
- ¾ cup (150g) granulated sugar
- ¼ cup (30g) dry milk powder
- 7–8 cups (795–900g) unbleached white bread flour
- 3 large eggs, beaten
- ½ cup (110g) unsalted butter, softened
- 1 teaspoon salt
- extra flour for dusting
- 1 egg beaten with a pinch of salt for glazing
- Demerara or granulated sugar for sprinkling

a 9-inch round deep cake tin, greased
a large baking sheet

Called pao doce *in Portuguese, this recipe makes two loaves, one with currants and braided, and the other shaped like a small snail, called* caracois.

Cindy Falk (page 52) was given this recipe by a colleague in the Kansas Wheat Commission, and now her eleven-year-old daughter Laura uses it to win baking competitions. Laura makes the neatest braid I have ever seen. To ensure a good shape to your loaf, do not let the shaped dough over-rise or leave it in too warm a place to rise.

Eat this bread sliced and buttered within two days of baking. If you do not plan to eat both loaves, wrap and freeze one loaf for up to two months.

Put the currants in a small bowl. Add the 1 tablespoon of the liquid of your choice and let stand for 1 hour, or until the currants are softened.

Crumble the fresh yeast into the bowl of an electric mixer fitted with a dough hook, or into a large bowl. Mix in 4 tablespoons lukewarm water and 1 teaspoon of the granulated sugar until smooth. Let stand about 5 minutes, or until it starts to become foamy. If using dry yeast, mix the granules and 1 teaspoon of the granulated sugar with 4 tablespoons lukewarm water and let stand until foamy, 5 to 10 minutes (page 18). Add the rest of the water and sugar, the milk powder, and 3 cups (340g) of the flour. Beat on medium speed with a dough hook for 2 minutes, or with your hand or a wooden spoon for 4 minutes, until it is a smooth, thick batter.

With the mixer on low speed, gradually add the eggs, the butter, and the salt and mix until thoroughly combined, or mix in the ingredients with your hand or a wooden spoon. Add enough of the rest of the flour, a handful at a time, to make a soft, but not sticky dough that gathers in a ball around the dough hook or comes together and leaves the sides of the bowl cleanly. Knead the dough on slow speed for 5 minutes until it is smooth and feels "as silky as a baby's behind," as Cindy says. Or, turn out the dough onto a floured work surface and knead for about 10 minutes until smooth and soft.

Wash, dry, and oil the bowl. Return the dough to the bowl, and turn the dough over so the top is oiled. Place the bowl in a large greased plastic bag and tie closed, or cover the bowl with a damp dish towel, and let rise at room temperature, away from drafts, until doubled in size, about 2 hours.

Punch down the dough. Turn it out onto a lightly floured work surface and divide into two equal portions. With lightly floured hands, knead the softened currants and any soaking liquid that has not been absorbed into one portion of the dough. Cover both portions of dough with a damp dish towel and let rest at room temperature, away from drafts, for 20 minutes.

Shape the plain portion of dough into the snail loaf: Roll out the dough with your lightly floured hands into a rope 25 inches long and 1½ inches thick. Coil the rope in the

LET THE BRAIDED LOAF RISE AT ROOM TEMPERATURE, AWAY FROM DRAFTS, UNTIL DOUBLED IN SIZE, ABOUT 1 HOUR.

TO MAKE CINDY'S SPECIAL BRAID, *ARRANGE TWO OF THE DOUGH ROPES IN A CROSS ON THE PREPARED BAKING SHEET.* PLACE THE THIRD ROPE STRAIGHT THROUGH THE MIDDLE, TO *MAKE A STAR SHAPE.* BEGIN BRAIDING, FOLLOWING THE DIRECTIONS IN THE NOTE (BELOW RIGHT).

TOP
A selection of breads baked by Cindy Falk (page 52), including the highly glazed Portuguese Sweet Breads shaped into a long braid and as a snail. Other loaves include her Multi-grain Harvest Bread (page 51), which was baked in a loaf pan, and two round Pioneer Breads (page 52). For this photograph, Cindy slashed the Pioneer Breads with a checkerboard design, rather than the star shape suggested in the recipe.

prepared cake pan, starting in the center and twisting the dough as you coil it around to form a snail shape, and tuck the ends under. Place the pan in a large greased plastic bag and tie closed, or cover with a damp dish towel, and let rise at room temperature, away from drafts, until doubled in size, about 1 hour.

After you've shaped the snail loaf, make the braided loaf. On a lightly floured work surface, divide the currant dough into three equal pieces. Roll out each piece of dough with floured hands into a 16-inch-long rope. Lay the three ropes side-by-side on the prepared baking sheet, then braid the strands together neatly, but not too tightly. (See page 31 and the Note.) Tuck the ends under and pinch to seal. Cover with a damp dish towel and let rise at room temperature, away from drafts, until doubled in size, about 1 hour. During the last 15 minutes of rising, heat the oven to 350°F.

When each loaf has doubled in size, brush with the egg glaze, taking care not to let it dribble down the sides or "glue" the dough to the pan or baking sheet. Sprinkle each with the coarse sugar. The snail loaf will probably be ready to bake before the braid, depending on how warm your kitchen is and how quickly you formed the braid. Slide another baking sheet under the sheet holding the braid to prevent the bottom of the loaf from browning. Put each loaf into the oven when it is ready; the baking times will overlap. Bake each loaf for 30 to 40 minutes, or until it is golden brown and sounds hollow when tapped underneath. Cover the loaves with foil during baking if they appear to be browning too quickly. Transfer to wire racks to cool completely.

NOTE: Another way to braid the loaf is to arrange two of the ropes in a cross shape on the prepared baking sheet. Place the third rope straight through the middle, to make a star shape. Braid the three ropes racing toward you, then turn the baking sheet around and braid the three other ends. This gives a slightly more unusual shape to the loaf. Pinch the ends together and tuck under to give a neat shape.

TIPSY PRUNE FRIENDSHIP CAKE

INGREDIENTS

Makes 1 large loaf

STARTER:

2 cups (280g) unbleached all-purpose flour
1 0.6-oz cake fresh yeast (15g)
2 cups (455ml) water, at room temperature

FOR DAY 1:

1 cup (200g) sugar
1 cup (140g) all-purpose flour
1 cup (230ml) milk, at room temperature

FOR DAY 5:

1 cup (200g) sugar
1 cup (140g) all-purpose flour
1 cup (230ml) milk, at room temperature

FOR DAY 10, FINISHING THE LOAF:

2 cups (250g) roughly chopped prunes
the grated rind and juice of 1 unwaxed orange
1½ tablespoons orange liqueur
1 cup packed (200g) light brown sugar
2 cups (280g) all-purpose flour
½ cup (115ml) vegetable oil
¼ teaspoon salt
2 teaspoons baking powder
2 eggs, beaten

TOPPING:

6 tablespoons (85g) dark brown sugar
2 tablespoons (30g) unsalted butter, at room temperature

a 9- x 13-inch cake pan or roasting pan, greased

NOTE You can use 1 package (¼oz/7g) active dry yeast instead of fresh yeast, dissolving it in warm water.

This is such an odd recipe – a fruit-filled sourdough loaf cake – but one I'm always asked for when I do demonstrations or radio phone-in programs. I believe the recipe originated in Germany, in the days before cakes were made with baking powder. I've eaten it in Amish and German communities in America, and at church suppers in Britain. It is simple to make but takes 13 days for the dough to ferment. However, you will eventually have enough starter to bake your cake plus one to keep for your next cake and two portions to give away. A couple of years ago I gave a portion of starter to Joy Skipper, who assisted on this and The Bread Book, *and she has made a friendship cake every other week since, experimenting with different fillings. This is her favorite.*

To make the starter, put the flour in a large, non-metallic bowl and make a well in the center. Crumble the fresh yeast into the well, then pour in the water and stir using a wooden spoon until the yeast has mixed smoothly with the liquid. Gradually stir in the flour to make a sticky batter. Cover the bowl with a damp dish towel. Leave it on the kitchen table or work surface so the batter can absorb extra yeasts from the air. It's a good idea to make a note of the day or date because it is only too easy to lose your place in the recipe. Stir the batter once a day for each of the next 3 days, and re-dampen the towel each day. At the end of this time, the starter will be ready to use.

To make the dough, stir the starter you have made, or any starter you have been given, and proceed as follows:

DAY 1: Stir the starter and add the sugar, flour, and milk. Stir well to mix, cover with a damp dish towel, and leave overnight at room temperature.

DAY 2: Stir well and re-cover with a damp dish towel.

DAYS 3 and 4: Do nothing but re-dampen the towel each day.

DAY 5: Stir well and add the sugar, flour, and milk. Stir well again, cover with a damp dish towel, and leave overnight at room temperature.

DAY 6: Stir well and re-cover with a damp dish towel.

DAYS 7, 8, and 9: Do nothing but re-dampen the towel each day.

DAY 10: Stir well, then divide the starter dough into four equal portions. Give two portions to friends, with instructions, keep one portion for your next batch (see below), and use one portion to make the loaf.

To make the loaf, put the chopped prunes into a mixing bowl with the grated orange rind and juice and the liqueur. Cover tightly and let soak for several hours or overnight.

Preheat the oven to 350°F.

Add the portion of starter dough to the prunes, together with the sugar, flour, oil, salt, baking powder, and eggs. Using a wooden spoon, mix until thoroughly combined. Spoon into the prepared pan and level the surface. Sprinkle the dark brown sugar over the top and dot with small flakes of the butter. Bake for 30–40 minutes or until a skewer inserted into the center comes out clean. Turn out onto a wire rack to cool.

Serve cut into squares or fingers. The cake is also good eaten warm with custard sauce as a pudding. Eat within 3 days of baking.

NOTE To keep the portion of starter for your next cake, add 1 teaspoon of sugar and stir well, then store in a covered container in the fridge for up to 1 week. To make a fresh cake, begin at Day 1 using this starter.

VARIATION Put the portion of starter into a bowl and mix in 1 cup packed (200g) light brown sugar, ½ cup (85g) golden raisins, 2 cups (280g) all-purpose flour, ½ cup (110ml) vegetable oil, ½ cup (60g) walnut halves, ½ teaspoon salt, 2 teaspoons each ground cinnamon and baking powder, 2 eggs, and 2 apples, peeled, cored, and diced. Put the dough into the prepared pan and add the topping as given. Bake as above.

TEA BREAD

INGREDIENTS

Makes 1 large loaf
2/3 cup (110g) mixed dried fruit and chopped candied peel
2/3 cup (140ml) strong hot tea, strained
about 3/4 cup (170ml) milk, at room temperature
1 0.6-oz cake fresh yeast (15g)
3 3/4 cups (450g) unbleached white bread flour
1 teaspoon salt
1 teaspoon apple-pie spice
2 1/2 tablespoons (30g) sugar
4 tablespoons (60g) butter, chilled and diced
milk for brushing

a large loaf pan, about 9 x 5 x 3 inches, greased

NOTE You can use 1 package (1/4oz/7g) active dry yeast instead of fresh yeast, warming the liquid before dissolving it. For rapid-rise dry yeast, mix it into the flour with the sugar, salt, and spice. Proceed with the recipe, adding the tea and milk liquid to the well in the flour.

This is an old-fashioned recipe where the dried fruit is soaked in strong tea before it is mixed into a sweet and spicy yeasted bread dough. I am very fond of this bread, sliced and buttered, with afternoon tea in summer, and toasted on an open fire in winter. It also makes a jolly good Bread and Butter Pudding (see page 52).

Put the dried fruit and peel into a mixing bowl and pour the hot tea over. Mix well and let soak for 1 hour.

Drain the fruit in a strainer set over a measuring cup. Make the liquid up to 1 1/4 cups (280ml) with the milk. Crumble the yeast into the liquid and stir until smooth and thoroughly mixed.

Mix the flour with the salt, apple-pie spice, and sugar in a large mixing bowl. Add the diced butter and rub in using the tips of your fingers until the mixture looks like fine crumbs. Stir in the drained fruit, then make a well in the center of the mixture. Pour the yeast liquid into this well. Gradually mix the flour into the liquid to make a soft dough.

Turn the dough onto a lightly floured work surface and knead for 10 minutes or until the dough is elastic and not sticky. It does not matter if the fruit bursts open – in fact it will taste better. Return the dough to the bowl, cover with a damp dish towel, and let rise at normal room temperature for about 1 1/2 hours or until doubled in bulk.

Gently punch down the risen dough with your knuckles, then turn onto a lightly floured work surface. Shape into a loaf to fit the pan (see page 76). Put the loaf into the prepared pan, seam-side down, then cover and let rise for about 45 minutes or until doubled in size.

Preheat the oven to 400°F.

Brush the loaf with milk, then bake for 35–40 minutes or until nicely browned and the loaf sounds hollow when carefully tipped out of the pan and tapped on the base. Turn out onto a wire rack and let cool. Eat sliced and buttered or toasted.

VARIATION: STICKY FRUIT ROLLS Prepare the dough and let rise at normal room temperature as above. Punch down the risen dough, then divide into 8 equal pieces. Shape each into a ball and place them, well apart, on two greased baking sheets. Cover and let rise until doubled in size. Bake the rolls for about 20 minutes or until golden brown and puffed up. Remove from the oven and immediately brush with a hot, sticky glaze made by dissolving 3 tablespoons sugar in 3 tablespoons whole milk. Transfer the rolls to a wire rack and let cool completely.

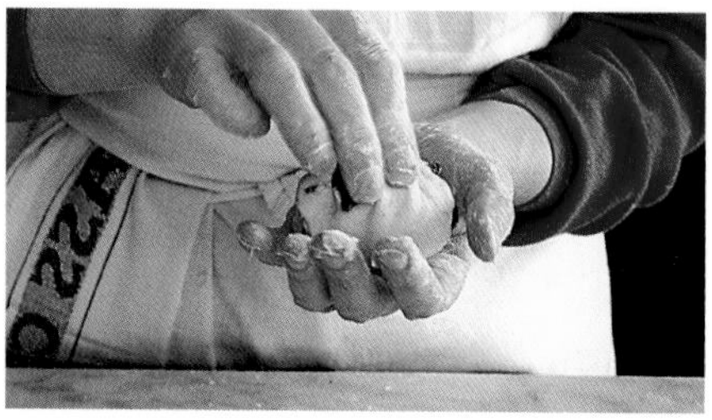

1 TO SHAPE ROLLS, CUP A PIECE OF DOUGH IN ONE HAND AND PULL THE SIDES ONTO THE TOP.

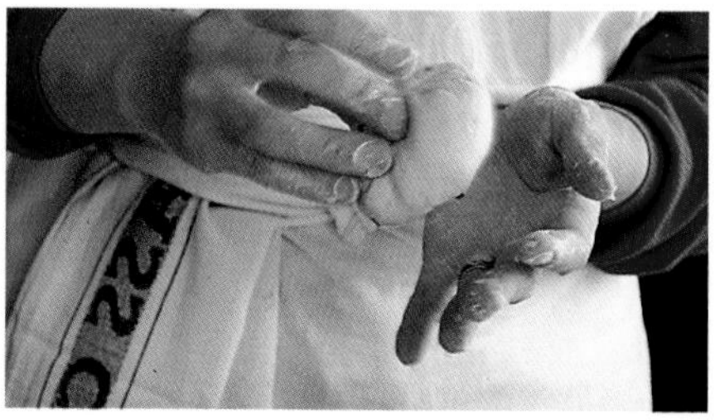

2 PINCH THE TOP TOGETHER. TURN THE ROLL OVER SO THE SMOOTH SIDE IS UPPERMOST.

LEMON DRIZZLE LOAF

INGREDIENTS

Makes 1 large loaf
¾ cup (170g) unsalted butter, at room temperature
1¼ cups (255g) sugar
1¾ cups (255g) self-rising flour
3 eggs, beaten
½ cup (115ml) whole milk
the grated rind of 3 unwaxed lemons

TOPPING:
the juice of 2 lemons
the grated rind of 1 unwaxed lemon
¾ cup (150g) sugar

a large loaf pan, about 9 x 5 x 3 inches, greased and lined on the bottom

ABOVE (left to right): Tea Bread, Sticky Fruit Rolls, and Lemon Drizzle Loaf.

The all-in-one method of making a cake, where all the ingredients – usually flour, butter, eggs, and sugar – are dumped into a mixing bowl and beaten to a smooth, thick batter, is reckoned to be idiot-proof. Indeed, I was able to turn out something edible while only four foot high. I think this method is best reserved for loaf cakes, such as the one here, where taste and moistness are more important than lightness and volume.

If possible, use unwaxed fruit in this plain but intensely flavored loaf. If the fruit has been waxed, be sure to scrub it well with hot soapy water and then rinse thoroughly. Serve with tea or coffee, for a simple dessert with ice cream, or hot out of the oven with custard sauce.

Preheat the oven to 350°F.

Put all the ingredients, except those for the topping, into a large mixing bowl. Using an electric mixer or wooden spoon, beat until thick and fluffy with no sign of lumps or streaks of flour. Spoon into the prepared pan and smooth the surface. Bake in the preheated oven for 50–55 minutes or until a skewer or toothpick inserted into the center comes out clean.

While the loaf is baking, combine all the ingredients for the topping. As soon as the loaf is cooked, remove it from the oven but leave it in the pan. Prick it all over with a toothpick or skewer. Quickly spoon the topping mixture over the surface, then let the loaf cool completely before unmolding. Serve thickly sliced.

NUT AND RAISIN BREAD

INGREDIENTS

Makes 2 medium loaves
3½ cups (450g) stoneground whole-wheat bread flour
1½ cups (230g) unbleached white bread flour
2½ teaspoons salt
1 0.6-oz cake fresh yeast (15g)
1½ cups (340ml) water from the cold tap
1½ tablespoons well-flavored honey
extra flour for dusting
1½ cups (170g) large seedless raisins
1½ cups (170g) toasted and roughly chopped walnuts, hazelnuts, or a mixture

2 baking sheets, greased

NOTE You can use 1 package (¼oz/7g) active dry yeast instead of fresh yeast, dissolving it in warm water. For rapid-rise dry yeast, mix it with the flour and salt. Omit the sponging stage, adding the water all at once. Proceed with the recipe.

VARIATIONS: PECAN BREAD Use 2½ cups (340g) each stoneground whole-wheat bread flour and unbleached white bread flour, and make the dough as above. Replace the raisins and nuts with 2 cups (230g) roughly chopped but untoasted pecans, then proceed with the recipe.

WALNUT OR MIXED NUT BREAD Make the dough, then knead in either 2½ cups (230g) toasted walnut halves or toasted and roughly chopped mixed nuts such as walnuts, hazelnuts, almonds, pecans, cashews, and macadamias. Proceed with the recipe.

Lightly toasting walnuts and hazelnuts in the oven intensifies their rich taste. Combined with the largest, most luscious raisins available, they make a wonderfully flavored loaf that's good simply sliced and buttered or served with cheese.

Mix the flours and salt together in a large mixing bowl and make a well in the center. Crumble the yeast into a small bowl and cream it to a smooth liquid with half of the water and the honey. Pour the yeast liquid into the well in the flour and mix in just enough of the flour to make a thick batter. Let "sponge" for about 15 minutes – it will look bubbly.

Add the remaining cold water to the yeast batter, then gradually work in the rest of the flour to make a soft but not sticky dough. If the dough sticks to your fingers work in a little extra flour a tablespoon at a time. If dry crumbs form and the dough seems stiff and hard to bring together, work in a little extra water a tablespoon at a time.

Turn the dough onto a lightly floured work surface and knead for 10 minutes or until smooth and elastic. Sprinkle the raisins and nuts over the dough and knead them in gently until they are evenly distributed – this will take about 2 minutes.

Shape the dough into a ball and return it to the bowl. Cover with a damp dish towel and let rise at cool to normal room temperature for about 2 hours or until doubled in bulk.

Punch down the risen dough with your knuckles, then turn onto a floured work surface and knead for a minute. Divide the dough in half and shape each portion into a neat ball. Place on the prepared baking sheets, cover as before, and let rise at normal room temperature for about 1½ hours or until doubled in size.

Preheat the oven to 425°F.

Slash the top of each loaf two or three times using a very, very sharp knife. Bake for 15 minutes, then reduce the oven temperature to 375°F and bake for a further 20–25 minutes or until the loaves sound hollow when tipped off the sheets and tapped on the base. Transfer the loaves to a wire rack to cool completely.

Eat the bread within 3 days, or toast, or freeze for up to a month.

GINGERBREAD

INGREDIENTS

Makes 1 large loaf
1½ cups (230g) self-rising flour
½ teaspoon baking soda
1 tablespoon ground ginger
1 teaspoon ground cinnamon
1 teaspoon apple-pie spice
½ cup (110g) unsalted butter, chilled and diced
½ cup (110g) dark molasses
½ cup (110g) golden syrup
½ cup packed (110g) light or dark brown sugar
1 cup (280ml) milk
⅓ cup (45g) grated candied ginger
1 extra large egg, beaten

a large loaf pan, about 9 x 5 x 3 inches, greased and lined on the bottom

A lovely spicy, sticky gingerbread, nicely hot with chopped candied ginger. I like it thickly sliced and buttered, but Anthony prefers it with a slice of moist, slightly sharp cheese.

Preheat the oven to 350°F.

Sift the flour, baking soda, and all the spices into a large mixing bowl. Add the diced butter and rub in with your fingertips until the mixture resembles fine crumbs.

In a small saucepan, melt the molasses with the golden syrup, then let cool to blood heat. Meanwhile, in another small pan, dissolve the sugar in the milk over low heat, stirring occasionally.

Add the candied ginger to the flour mixture. Whisk the milk mixture into the flour mixture, then whisk in the molasses mixture followed by the egg. When thoroughly blended, you should have a thin batter.

Pour the batter into the prepared pan and bake for 45 minutes to 1 hour or until a skewer inserted into the center comes out clean. The gingerbread will rise during baking and then fall and shrink slightly as it cools. Let cool completely in the pan. Turn out and wrap first in wax paper and then in foil. Keep for a couple of days before slicing.

1 GRATE THE CANDIED GINGER INTO THE BOWL WITH THE RUBBED-IN MIXTURE.

2 WHISK IN THE SWEETENED MILK AND THEN THE MOLASSES AND SYRUP MIXTURE.

Just the way I like it: thick slices of Gingerbread spread with unsalted butter.

Jim Friedlander loves to experiment and share recipes. Here are his Apple Almond Cream Pie (see recipe on page 188), Bayberry Bread, and Granny Glyn's Lemon Loaf.

BAYBERRY BREAD

Anthony met Jim and Glynrose Friedlander when he stayed at their Federal-style farmhouse in Freeport, Maine. They describe the Isaac Randall House, built in 1823, as a B and B, "though not as utilitarian as the ones in Britain." And it is quite out of the ordinary: the kitchen-dining room has a hand-painted floor, an old wood stove (now converted to gas) for cooking, and copper pans and utensils everywhere. The eight bedrooms are furnished with lovely old quilts, oriental rugs, working fireplaces, and oil lamps, to give a charming, homey atmosphere.

But the decor is eclipsed by the enormous breakfasts Jim prepares each day. After homemade muesli and fresh fruit salad, he cooks pancakes, french toast (pain perdu), and bacon and eggs to order. To follow there are always a couple of specialty quick breads, and even the odd fruit pie (see Apple Almond Cream Pie on page 188).

As Jim says: "We like to eat, and we like to experiment with recipes we pick up when we travel. Then we like to share them."

Thank you, Jim, and see you soon. Bayberry, by the way, is the local name for cranberry.

INGREDIENTS

Makes 1 medium loaf
1 cup (140g) whole-wheat bread flour
1 cup (140g) all-purpose flour
1 1/2 teaspoons baking powder
1/2 teaspoon baking soda
1/8 teaspoon salt
1/4 teaspoon ground cinnamon
1/8 teaspoon grated nutmeg
1/2 cup (100g) granulated sugar
1/2 cup packed (100g) light brown sugar
4 tablespoons (60g) unsalted butter, chilled and diced
1 1/2 teaspoons grated orange rind
3/4 cup (170ml) freshly squeezed orange juice
1 egg, beaten
1 cup (110g) dried cranberries
1/2 cup (60g) roughly chopped pecans or walnuts
1/3 cup (60g) raisins (optional)

a small loaf pan, about 8 1/2 x 4 1/2 x 2 1/2 inches, or a small roasting pan, greased

Preheat the oven to 350°F.

Put the flours, baking powder, baking soda, salt, spices, and sugars into a large mixing bowl and stir until thoroughly combined. Add the diced butter and rub in with your fingertips to make coarse crumbs. Mix the orange rind with the juice and the egg, and add to the dry mixture. Mix briefly, then fold in the cranberries, nuts, and raisins. As soon as the batter is thoroughly blended, spoon it into the prepared pan.

Bake for 1 hour or until golden and firm. A skewer inserted into the center should come out clean. Turn out onto a wire rack and let cool. Serve thickly sliced, with butter. Best when eaten within 3 days.

NOTE To vary the recipe, Jim uses fresh cranberries, blueberries in season, and dried cherries all year round.

GRANNY GLYN'S LEMON LOAF

INGREDIENTS

Makes 1 large loaf
1 1/3 cups (255g) sugar
1/2 cup + 3 tablespoons (155g) unsalted butter, at room temperature
3 eggs, beaten
the grated rind of 1 1/2 unwaxed lemons
2 cups (280g) all-purpose flour
1/4 teaspoon salt
1 1/2 teaspoons baking powder
2/3 cup (140ml) milk
2/3 cup (60g) ground pecans

TOPPING:
2/3 cup (70g) confectioners' sugar, sifted
the juice of 1 1/2 lemons

a large loaf pan, about 9 x 5 x 3 inches, greased and lined on the bottom

This is another delicious recipe from the Friedlanders of Freeport, Maine. The fresh-tasting lemon loaf cake is easily made by the creaming method. The cake is enriched and flavored with pecans that have been finely ground in a food processor. To preserve the freshness of the nuts, grind them just before making the cake batter.

Preheat the oven to 350°F.

Put the sugar and butter into a mixing bowl and beat until very light and creamy, using a wooden spoon or electric mixer. Gradually beat in the eggs. Using a large metal spoon, gently stir in the lemon rind. Sift the flour with the salt and baking powder and fold in. Gradually stir in the milk followed by the ground nuts. When the batter is thoroughly blended, spoon it into the prepared pan.

Bake for about 1 hour or until risen, golden, and firm. A toothpick inserted into the center should come out clean.

While the loaf is baking, prepare the topping by stirring the confectioners' sugar and lemon juice together until smooth.

Remove the cooked loaf from the oven, and leave it in the pan. Immediately puncture the surface all over with a toothpick or skewer and spoon the topping over the loaf. Let cool completely in the pan. The lemon loaf is best eaten within 3 days of baking.

VARIATION Use freshly ground walnuts instead of pecans.

CELEBRATION BREADS

These elaborate, lightly textured, and richly flavored breads are intended to be a contrast to everyday breads. They often take a special place of pride on tables around the world during Christmas, Easter, the Jewish Sabbath, and Christian harvest celebrations. Made with generous quantities of expensive butter and eggs, these loaves are flavored with spices, honey, candied fruit peels, dried fruits, and nuts. You could be forgiven for thinking the loaves in this chapter are more like cakes than breads.

Yet it is not just the taste that lets you know these breads are out of the ordinary. They look special. Alice's Christmas Loaf (page 158) from Czechoslovakia and the Jewish challahs (page 168) are lovingly braided, using up to nine strands of dough to create intricate patterns. The Alsatian Kugelhopf (page 152), and the Italian Panettone (page 155) are baked in molds that instantly herald a celeb-ration. My husband says my towering Panettone reminds him of a monument. (The Leaning Tower of Pisa, perhaps?) Fluted kugelhopf molds are so attractive that they often double as kitchen decorations in Alsace.

OPPOSITE
A Bulgarian farmer's harvest loaf.
ABOVE *An altar harvest loaf.*

Even the more familiar English Hot Cross Buns (page 160) are finished with a flour and water paste to make them special for Good Friday observances. Loaves shaped to look like sheaves of wheat (page 164) have been made by generations of British country bakers to mark a successful harvest. Served at harvest suppers held in church halls, this decorative loaf came to symbolize the end of hard labor for farm workers and a time of plenty for most farms. This custom is still followed throughout Europe, as you can see from the decorated round loaf proudly displayed by the jovial Bulgarian farmer (opposite). That loaf was made by the local bakery to celebrate a bountiful wine harvest. You can make such a loaf to eat at a Thanksgiving meal; or, bake it for much longer in a very low oven to create an attractive, nonedible decoration (page 165).

Some of the loaves in this chapter can be very time-consuming to make, so if you want to make a celebration bread in a hurry, I suggest you try Bishops Bread (page 160). This is a quick bread as it is not yeast-raised and therefore has no lengthy rising times.

If you do have some free time to spare, however, I hope you will try one of the more elaborately braided loaves, or the Harvest Wheat Sheaf (page 164). These are delicious breads, and not as difficult to make as they look, although they do require time and patience, especially for the first attempt. Anyone who does not feel confident at braiding dough should try Caroll's Twisted Ring (page 170). Strips of the dough are simply braided together, then the loaf is baked in a tube pan so it does not lose its shape.

Like many good bakers, Brigitte prefers the pungency of freshly ground spices. Here she crushes cardamom seeds to add a subtle, yet distinctive, flavor to the stollens.

SPICE MIXTURES

Fragrant spices are important ingredients in these recipes. And if, like me, you have tired of the blandness of commercial ground mixed spices, you will take great pleasure in making your own blends.

Even in 1907, Master Baker John Kirkland (page 65) was writing about the importance of "giving your spice mixture special considerations." His formula was 6 tablespoons (30g) each of ground coriander, ground cinnamon, and ground ginger; 2 tablespoons plus 2 teaspoons (15g) freshly grated nutmeg; and 2 tablespoons (10g) ground white peppercorns or ground allspice.

More recently, Elizabeth David suggested grinding together 1 large nutmeg, 1 tablespoon white peppercorns or whole allspice, 30 whole cloves, a 2-inch piece of dried gingerroot, and a little cumin seed.

You will notice that both these combinations make a small quantity. I suggest you make up a batch when you need it, rather than storing a large amount.

BRESLAU STOLLEN

Breslau, in Silesia, formerly part of Germany but now in Poland, is where my friend Brigitte Friis's mother came from. Brigitte's mother always made these extravagant weihnachtsstollens *several weeks before Christmas. The cardamom is an inspired touch. Liberal applications of melted butter brushed over the stollens after baking are traditional – the stollens absorb the butter, resulting in a moist, ultrarich, cakelike taste and texture.*

INGREDIENTS

Makes 1 large loaf

9 cups (1kg) unbleached white bread flour
2 tablespoons (15g) coarse sea salt, crushed or ground
7 0.6-oz cakes fresh yeast (100g), or 7 envelopes active dry yeast (scant 6 tablespoons)
1 cup (200g) granulated sugar
about ½ cup + 3 tablespoons (155ml) lukewarm milk
1½ cups (230g) whole blanched almonds, chopped finely or roughly
3⅓ cups (500g) raisins
½ cups (250g) chopped mixed candied citrus peel
1 cup (150g) currants
grated rind of 2 large lemons
½ teaspoon ground cardamom
½ teaspoon freshly grated nutmeg
2 cups (1lb/455g) unsalted butter, soft but not melted
4 extra large eggs, beaten
extra flour for dusting
about 3 cups (1½ lb/680g) unsalted butter for brushing
confectioners' sugar for sprinkling

a large baking sheet, greased

Sift the flour and salt into a very large bowl. Make a well in the center of the flour. Crumble the fresh yeast into a medium-size bowl. Stir in 1 tablespoon of the sugar and the lukewarm milk until smooth. If using dry yeast, mix the granules and 1 tablespoon of the sugar with the lukewarm milk and let stand until foamy, 5 to 10 minutes (page 18).

Pour the yeast mixture into the well. Work in a little of the flour into the yeast mixture to make a thick batter. Sprinkle with a little flour to prevent a skin forming. Cover with a dry dish towel and let stand in a warm place (about 75°F) for 15 to 20 minutes until spongy.

In a medium-size bowl, mix the almonds, raisins, candied citrus peel, currants, and the lemon rind. Add 2 tablespoons of the flour from the other bowl and toss to coat. Stir in the spices.

Mix the remaining sugar into the sponge. Add the butter and mix it with the sponge and the flour in the bowl by gently turning the mixture over with your hand until the flour is almost worked in. Gradually add the eggs and work the mixture with your hand until it forms a soft dough that holds its shape. If the dough is too sticky, add flour, 1 tablespoon at a time. If the dough is too dry, add milk, 1 tablespoon at a time.

Turn out the dough onto a well-floured work surface and "knead until it begins to show bubbles," says Brigitte. Large bubbles or blisters should appear after 10 minutes. Re-flour the work surfaces as necessary. The dough will become firmer and more pliable and you should be able to feel the bubbles.

Pat out the dough into a large rectangle about 1-inch thick, with a long side facing you. Spread the fruit and nut mixture along the center of the dough. Fold in the two long edges so they meet in the center. Fold in the short ends. Then, working from the right-hand side, fold the dough over to make a small package. Continue folding the dough over and over on itself, pressing down very lightly with your hand and giving the dough a

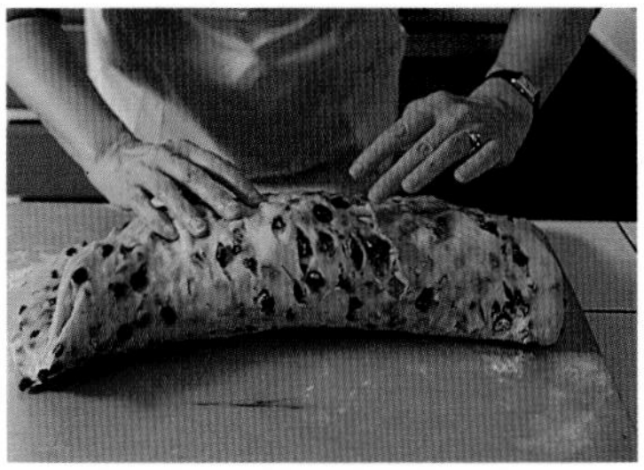

BRIGITTE FOLDS DOWN THE TOP THIRD OF THE DOUGH TO MAKE A THREE-LAYER RECTANGULAR DOUGH SANDWICH.

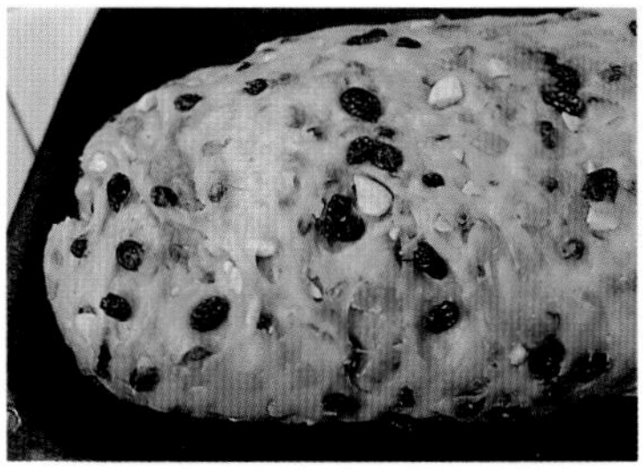

AFTER THE DOUGH HAS RISEN THE SECOND TIME, IT WILL BE DOUBLE IN SIZE AND BE READY TO BAKE.

quarter turn after each folding. Do not worry if the odd piece of fruit escapes; just put it back as make the next fold.

Brigitte incorporates the fruit this way, instead of kneading it into the dough. It takes at least 5 minutes and must be done gently. The dough should not be streaky or sticky, and it will be very soft. Shape the dough into a ball and dust lightly with flour. Return the dough to the bowl if it is large enough, or leave the dough on the floured surface. Cover it with dry dish towels. Let rise at warm room temperature (about 75°F), away from drafts, until doubled in size, about 2 hours.

Turn out the dough onto the floured surface (if it is in the bowl). Punch down the dough. You should hear the air being expelled as you do this. Knead it for 1 minute. Pat out the dough with lightly floured hands to a large rectangle about ½-inch thick, with a long side facing you. Fold the bottom third of the dough up and fold the top third down, to make a long, narrow rectangle with three layers. Pat to round the corners for a neat shape. Slide a second baking sheet under the prepared baking sheet to prevent the stollen from browning too much on the base. Transfer the stollen to the baking sheet. Cover with a dry dish towel and let rise at warm room temperature (75°F), away from drafts, until doubled in size, about 2 hours. During the last 15 minutes of rising, heat the oven to 350°F.

Place the stollen, on the doubled baking sheets, on an oven rack set in the middle position. Bake for 1¾ to 2 hours, or until golden brown and firm, and a skewer inserted into the center comes out clean. If the stollen appears to be browning too quickly during baking, cover with butter wrappers or parchment paper.

Melt 1 cup (230g) of the butter. As soon as the stollen comes out of the oven, brush or smear the butter over the loaf. It should gradually absorb all this butter. Transfer to a wire rack and let cool completely. When cool, wrap in waxed paper and then foil and leave at room temperature.

The next day, heat the oven to 350°F. Unwrap the stollen and place on a baking tray. Warm in the oven for 10 minutes. Melt ¾ cup (170g) of the remaining butter. Remove the stollen from the oven and brush with melted butter until the loaf will not absorb any more. Transfer to a wire rack to cool completely, then wrap in waxed paper and foil again.

Repeat this procedure for the next two days, using the rest of the butter. When the stollen has cooled after the final buttering, sift a thick layer of confectioners' sugar over the top. It is traditionally wrapped in cellophane and tied with a red ribbon, but waxed paper and foil will do. Keep the stollen in a cool place, but not the refrigerator, for at least two weeks and up to six weeks, before serving.

Fruity and spicy, this butter-rich stollen is ideal for holiday entertaining.
For easier mixing and kneading, you can transfer the flour mixture to a stationary mixer fitted with a dough hook before you add the eggs. Add the eggs, then knead on low speed for 5 to 10 minutes, until the dough becomes firm and pliable.

KUGELHOPF

INGREDIENTS

Makes 1 large loaf
about 2 tablespoons (30g) unsalted butter, very soft, for greasing
⅔ cup (60g) sliced almonds
3½ cups (395g) unbleached white bread flour
½ teaspoon salt
1 0.6-oz cake fresh yeast (15g), or 1 envelope active dry yeast (2½ teaspoons)
5 tablespoons (60g) granulated sugar
1 cup (230ml) lukewarm milk
3 large eggs, beaten
grated rind of 1 lemon
6–10 tablespoons (85–140g) unsalted butter, softened, to taste
¾ cup (110g) mixed dark and golden raisins
confectioners' sugar for dusting

a 9- to 10-inch kugelhopf mold

These pretty, almond-topped, fluted loaves can be found in Austria and Germany, as well as in Alsace, France, where the recipe originated. Clarisse Deiss, whose husband Jean-Michel makes the most exquisite wines at Bergheim, in Alsace, became both my culinary guide to the region and wine tutor.

Kugelhopf is the region's traditional celebration cake, baked for weddings, baptisms, wine harvests, and Christmas. The dough is similar to that used for brioche, but the kugelhopf is studded with fruit and sometimes flavored with lemon rind. At Easter, the sweet dough is baked in the shape of a fish or a lamb, and its richness depends on how much butter is included. "If you buy a kugelhopf, always go to a pâtisserie, rather than a boulangerie, because it will contain more butter," Clarisse advised.

The traditional, high-fluted mold is made of earthenware with a hole in the center, which allows the heat to penetrate to the middle of the dough for more even and thorough baking. Molds that are highly decorated on the outside are used for kitchen ornaments when not being used in the oven. Indeed, an elaborate mold was once an essential part of a woman's trousseau. On the wedding day, the bride would be given the family kugelhopf recipe by her mother.

I bought a selection of earthenware molds, some unglazed and plain on the outside, at Ribeauvillé, France, from a shop within sight of the town's famous local attraction – nesting storks. I should add that an equally important event is the town's kugelhopf festival, held each June. Although the earthenware molds are perhaps the prettiest, nonstick, glass, and metal heatproof molds can also be used. But remember, metal molds bake the quickest – a kugelhopf made in an earthenware mold will take about 10 minutes longer to bake than one made in a metal mold. This will keep for up to one week if tightly wrapped in foil, or it can be frozen for one month.

Thickly coat the mold with the 2 tablespoons butter. Evenly line the mold with the almonds by pressing them against the base and sides so they stick. Chill the mold while preparing the dough.

Mix together the flour and salt in a medium-size bowl and make a well in the center. Crumble the fresh yeast into a small bowl. Stir in the sugar and the lukewarm milk until smooth. If using dry yeast, mix the granules and ½ teaspoon of the sugar with half of the lukewarm milk and let stand until foamy, 5 to 10 minutes (page 18). Stir in the

Jugelhopfs are easy t identify with their distinctive shapes.

The best of Alsace – a glass of Jean-Michel Deiss' finest, crisp white wine, a kugelhopf, and a thick, moist pear loaf, another regional specialty. (This one is darker than my recipe for pear loaf on page 132.) The kugelhopf was baked by Clarisse Deiss. She used an old family recipe and baked it in the unglazed, earthenware mold she was given on her wedding day as tradition dictates.

remaining sugar and lukewarm milk.

Pour the yeast mixture into the well in the flour. With your hands, work enough flour from the bowl into the yeast mixture to make a thick batter. Cover with a damp dish towel and let stand at room temperature until spongy, about 30 minutes (page 16).

Add the eggs and lemon rind to the sponge in the well and mix together with a small whisk or your hand. Gradually mix the flour from the bowl into the sponge with your hand to make a very soft and sticky dough. Beat the dough in the bowl with your hand, slapping it up and down, for 5 minutes, or until it becomes firmer, smooth, very elastic, and glossy.

Beat in the butter, beating the dough until the butter is evenly incorporated. Gently mix in the fruit with your hand until evenly incorporated.

Carefully spoon the dough into the chilled mold without dislodging the almonds. The mold should be half full. Cover with a damp dish towel and let rise at warm room temperature (about 75°F), away from drafts, until the dough has almost doubled in size and has risen to about 1 inch below the mold's rim, 40 to 50 minutes. During the last 15 minutes of rising, heat the oven to 400°F.

Bake the kugelhopf for 40 to 50 minutes, or until the loaf is golden brown and a skewer inserted in the center comes out clean. Cover the loaf loosely with butter wrappers or parchment paper if it appears to be browning too quickly during baking. Cool the loaf in the mold for 5 minutes. Then carefully turn it out onto a wire rack to cool completely. To serve, dust with confectioners' sugar by sifting it over the cake. Offer slices of kugelhopf with a glass of Alsatian wine, such as a Tokay Pinot Gris.

SAVORY KUGELHOPF

Clarisse Deiss (opposite) also makes kugelhopfs without the sugar and dried fruit, using bacon or ham instead. The region of Alsace is renowned for cured pork, and one of Alsace's famous dishes, choucroute garni, is rich with smoked or salted pork, bacon, and meaty sausages.

This savory kugelhopf is served in Alsace with an aperitif such as a glass of Riesling or Gewurztraminer before dinner. Eat this loaf within three days of baking.

INGREDIENTS

Makes 1 large loaf

- about 2 tablespoons (30g) unsalted butter, very soft, for greasing
- ⅔ cup (60g) walnut halves
- 3½ cups (395g) unbleached white bread flour
- 1 teaspoon salt
- freshly ground black pepper
- 1 0.6-oz cake fresh yeast (15g), or 1 envelope active dry yeast (2½ teaspoons) plus ½ teaspoon sugar
- 1 cup (230ml) lukewarm milk
- 3 large eggs, beaten
- 6–10 tablespoons (85–140g) unsalted butter, softened, to taste
- 4 oz (110g) thick-sliced bacon or cooked full-flavored ham such as York, Westphalian, or Smithfield, diced

a 9- to 10-inch kugelhopf mold

Thickly coat the mold with the 2 tablespoons butter. Evenly line the inside of the mold with the walnuts, pressing the pieces against the base and sides so they stick. Chill the mold while preparing the dough.

Prepare the dough as for the Kugelhopf (opposite), using the flour, salt, pepper (adding the pepper to the flour), yeast, milk, eggs, and butter.

If using dry yeast, mix the granules and the ½ teaspoon granulated sugar with ½ cup of the lukewarm milk and let stand until foamy, 5 to 10 minutes (page 18). Stir in the remaining lukewarm milk.

Meanwhile, while the dough is "sponging," fry the bacon (if using it) in a medium-size skillet over medium heat until crisp, but not too brown. Remove the bacon pieces with a slotted spoon to paper towels to drain well and cool. Fold in the bacon or ham after beating the butter into the dough.

Carefully spoon the dough into the mold without dislodging the walnuts. Cover with a damp dish towel and let rise at warm room temperature (about 75°F) until the dough has almost doubled in size and has risen to about 1 inch below the mold's rim, 40 to 50 minutes.

During the last 15 minutes or rising, heat the oven to 400°F. Bake as for the Kugelhopf (opposite), but omit the dusting of confectioners' sugar. Cool the loaf in the mold for 5 minutes. Then carefully turn it out onto a wire rack to cool completely.

Twinkling lights and traditional decorations herald the start of the Christmas season in Nuremberg's Christkindelmarkt. Shoppers buy slices of spicy hutzelbrot to nibble as they brows for gifts, or they purchase whole loaves to share with family and friends.

HUTZELBROT

This Bavarian Christmas bread is packed with dried fruits and nuts. It is sold in the traditional Advent markets held in town squares throughout southern Germany.

The oldest of these markets is the Nuremberg Christkindelmarkt. It is held from the Friday before the beginning of Advent until Christmas Eve. The market – with food, toys, and decorations – began about 1639. With row upon row of red-and-white striped stalls, all iced with snow, the market is decorated with tiny white lights, fir tree garlands, and Christmas motifs.

The chilly air is laced with enticing smells – frying sausages, hot spicy gluhwein, caramelized almonds, and roasting chestnuts. Rich and fruity hutzelbrots are sold by the slice, so even their fragrant aroma adds to the atmosphere. Eat this bread sliced and buttered, toasted, or with honey.

Mix together the pears, prunes, figs, dark and golden raisins, dates, kirsch or brandy, and lemon rind in a large bowl. Pour in enough of the boiling water to cover the fruit. Stir well, cover, and let soak overnight.

INGREDIENTS

Makes 2 loaves
1⅔ cups (230g) chopped dried pears
1 cup (200g) chopped pitted prunes
⅔ cup (85g) chopped dried figs
¾ cup (120g) mixed dark and golden raisins
¼ cup (30g) chopped dried pitted dates
2 tablespoons kirsch or brandy
grated rind of ½ lemon
about ¾ cup (170ml) boiling water
about 3½ cups (400g) unbleached white bread flour
1 teaspoon ground cinnamon
½ teaspoon salt
a large pinch each ground cloves and aniseed
1 0.6-oz cake fresh yeast (15g), or 1 envelope active dry yeast (2½ teaspoons)
about 1¼ cups (280ml) lukewarm water
2 tablespoons packed light brown sugar
1 tablespoon honey
extra flour for dusting
6 tablespoons (60g) whole blanched almonds, lightly toasted and chopped
⅓ cup (60g) hazelnuts, lightly toasted, skinned, and chopped
⅔ cup (60g) sliced almonds for decorating (optional)

a large baking sheet, greased

The next day, drain the fruit, reserving any liquid, although most should have been absorbed. Set the fruit aside, covered.

Sift together the flour, cinnamon, salt, cloves, and aniseed in a large bowl. Make a well in the center of the flour mixture. Crumble the fresh yeast into a small bowl. Mix together the fruit soaking liquid, if any, and enough lukewarm water to measure 1¼ cups (280ml). If necessary, heat the fruit liquid mixture in a small saucepan until lukewarm. Stir the brown sugar and the fruit liquid mixture into the yeast until smooth. If using dry yeast, mix the granules and the brown sugar with the lukewarm fruit liquid mixture and let stand until foamy, 5 to 10 minutes (page 18).

Pour the yeast mixture into the well in the flour along with the honey. Mix these ingredients together briefly with a small whisk or your hands. Then mix the flour from the bowl into the yeast mixture with your hand or a wooden spoon to make a soft, but not sticky dough. If the dough is too sticky, work in a little extra flour, 1 tablespoon at a time. If the dough is dry and crumbly, work in a little extra water, 1 tablespoon at a time.

Turn out the dough onto a lightly floured work surface and knead for 10 minutes until smooth and elastic. Return the dough to the bowl (no need to wash or oil the bowl). Cover with a damp dish towel and let rise at room temperature, away from drafts, until doubled in size, about 1½ hours.

Punch down the dough. Turn out the dough onto a lightly floured work surface. Sprinkle the soaked fruit and chopped almonds and hazelnuts over the dough and gently knead for 2 to 3 minutes until they are evenly distributed. Divide the dough into two equal portions and shape each portion into an oval (see The Basic Loaf, page 15–17). Arrange the loaves on the prepared baking sheet. Cover with a damp dish towel and let rise at room temperature, away from drafts, until doubled in size, about 1½ hours. During the last 15 minutes of rising, heat the oven to 400°F.

To decorate the loaves, if you wish, gently press the sliced almonds lightly on the surface. Bake the loaves for 30 to 40 minutes, or until they are golden brown and sound hollow when tapped underneath. Loosely cover the loaves with butter wrappers or parchment paper if they are browning too quickly during baking. Transfer the loaves to wire racks to cool completely. Wrap the cooled loaves in waxed paper and overwrap in foil and keep at room temperature for at least 2 hours, or up to 1 week, before slicing. This helps the flavor to develop. After slicing, it stays fresh for five days.

PANETTONE

You can find panettone – prettily wrapped in cellophane, tied and hung by ribbons – in every Italian delicatessen in England (as well as in the States) as Christmas approaches. It is a specialty of Milan, where bakers vie to make the tallest, lightest, most delicate butter-rich loaf.

Since the classic tall, cylindrical panettone molds are difficult to find, some bakers use large 2-pound coffee cans. I prefer to use a 6-inch-round cake pan that has sides 3 inches high. I extend the pan about 4 inches upward by wrapping it on the outside with a stiff collar made of doubled heavy-duty foil that I secure with a paper clip, and on the inside with a sheet of buttered parchment paper, as if lining a soufflé dish.

For the best results, buy large pieces of candied orange and lemon peel and chop them yourself, as the flavor is much fresher than the ready-chopped variety from supermarkets.

Valentina Harris, the Italian food writer, once served me an excellent festive pudding made with panettone. She sliced off the domed top of the panettone, hollowed out the center slightly, filled it with a warm zabaglione, and replaced the top. You can also eat this loaf simply sliced into wedges like a cake within a week of baking. For the first couple of days after it is baked, this panettone will be moister than those bought from the bakery.

Mix together 2½ cups (280g) flour and the salt in a medium-size bowl and make a well

INGREDIENTS

Makes 1 loaf
about 3 cups (355g) unbleached white bread flour
½ teaspoon salt
1 0.6-oz cake fresh yeast (15g), or 1 envelope active dry yeast (2½ teaspoons)
3 tablespoons lukewarm water
⅓ cup (70g) sugar
2 extra large eggs, beaten
2 extra large egg yolks
grated rind of 1 lemon
a few drops of vanilla extract
¾ cup (170g) unsalted butter, softened
extra flour for dusting
⅔ cup (85g) golden raisins
⅓ cup (60g) finely chopped candied orange and lemon peel
about 3 tablespoons (40g) butter for finishing

a panettone mold, greased, or a 6-inch round, deep cake pan, prepared with foil and parchment paper (see introduction)

in the center of the flour mixture. Crumble the fresh yeast into a small bowl. Stir in the lukewarm water until smooth. If using dry yeast, mix the granules and ½ teaspoon of the granulated sugar with the lukewarm water and let stand until foamy, 5 to 10 minutes (page 18).

Pour the yeast mixture into the well in the flour. Add the sugar and beaten whole eggs to the well. Mix together these ingredients in the well with a small whisk or your hand. Then, with your hand or a wooden spoon, mix enough flour from the bowl into the mixture in the well to make a thick batter. Sprinkle the top with a little of the flour to prevent a skin forming. Let stand at room temperature, away from drafts, until spongy, 45 minutes to 1 hour (page 16).

Add the egg yolks, lemon rind, and vanilla extract to the sponge. Mix together these ingredients in the well. With your hand, gradually beat the remaining flour from the bowl into the sponge to make a soft and very sticky dough. Again using your hand, gradually beat the softened butter into the dough until thoroughly incorporated.

Turn out the dough onto a lightly floured work surface and knead, working in the remaining flour, for 10 minutes, or until soft, satiny, and pliable.

Return the dough to the bowl (no need to wash and oil the bowl). Cover with a damp dish towel and let rise at room temperature, away from drafts, until almost doubled in size, 2 to 2½ hours.

Punch down the dough. Cover with a damp dish towel and let rise again at room temperature, away from drafts, until doubled in size, 1 to 1½ hours.

Punch down the dough. Turn out onto a lightly floured work surface. Toss the golden raisins and chopped candied citrus peel with 1 teaspoon flour in a small bowl to prevent them from sticking together. Sprinkle the raisins and peel over the dough and gently knead in with lightly floured hands until the fruit is evenly distributed, 2 to 3 minutes.

Shape the dough into a ball and drop it into the prepared panettone mold or the lined cake pan. Using the tip of a long, sharp knife, score a cross in the top of the dough.

Cover with a damp dish towel and let rise at room temperature, away from drafts, until doubled in size, about 1 hour.

During the last 15 minutes of rising, heat the oven to 400·F.

Melt 2 tablespoons of the remaining butter in a small saucepan. Brush the top of the panettone with some of the melted butter. Put the third tablespoon of butter in the center of the cross.

Bake the panettone for 10 to 12 minutes, or until it begins to color. Then brush the top again with the rest of the melted butter. Lower the oven temperature to 350°F and bake for 30 to 40 minutes longer, or until the loaf is golden brown and a skewer inserted in the center comes out clean.

Remove the panettone from the oven. It will be fragile, so stand the mold on a wire rack for 5 minutes while the loaf firms up. Gently unmold the loaf and place it on its side on the wire rack to cool completely.

At holiday times, a buttery, fruit-studded panettone makes a lovely gift, especially when wrapped in cellophane and festooned with ribbons.

PLACE REMAINING BUTTER IN THE CENTER OF THE CROSS.

WHEN THE TOP BEGINS TO BROWN, BRUSH AGAIN WITH BUTTER.

I suggest using a mild-flavored olive oil for these decorative Provençal breads, rather than the heavier, fruity extra-virgin oil I more often use in breads. I think it is vital to use good-quality candied orange peel from gourmet shops or by mail order (page 360). It comes in large pieces and has more flavor than the ready-chopped variety from supermarkets. You can chop the peel as finely as you like. To keep it from sticking to the knife, sprinkle the peel with a little flour before you start.

FOUGASSES

INGREDIENTS

Makes 8 small loaves
6 cups (680g) unbleached white bread flour
¾ cup (170g) sugar
1½ teaspoons salt
1 0.6-oz cake fresh yeast (15g), or 1 envelope active dry yeast (2½ teaspoons) plus ½ teaspoon sugar
about 6 tablespoons (85ml) lukewarm water
2 large eggs, beaten
6 tablespoons (85ml) mild olive oil
grated rind and juice of 1 large orange
1 tablespoon orange flower water
¾ cup (85g) chopped candied orange peel
extra flour for dusting
extra oil for brushing

several baking sheets, greased

CUT EIGHT OR NINE SLITS IN EACH TOP, IN A HERRINGBONE DESIGN

This flat-bread recipe comes from Provence, where you find the best candied oranges and orange flower water. Fougasse usually forms the central part of the thirteen desserts (symbolizing the twelve disciples and Christ) that are served for the Christmas Eve meal in Provence. The meal usually begins with fish and vegetable dishes followed by a salad. Then come the thirteen desserts, which include a selection of nougats, raisins, dried figs, glacé fruits, and fresh fruits, such as figs, grapes, apples, clementines, and pears. All these are accompanied by a dessert wine.

Use a mild olive oil in this bread, and good-quality candied orange peel from a gourmet shop (you can buy the orange flower water there, too). Eat the fougasses the day they are baked.

Mix the flour, sugar, and salt in a large bowl and make a well in the center. Crumble the fresh yeast into a small bowl. Stir in the lukewarm water until smooth. If using dry yeast, mix the granules and the ½ teaspoon sugar with the lukewarm water and let stand until foamy, 5 to 10 minutes (page 18). Pour the yeast mixture into the well in the flour. Mix enough flour from the bowl into the liquid with your hand to make a thick batter. Let stand until spongy, about 10 minutes (page 16).

Meanwhile, whisk the eggs, oil, the orange rind and juice, and orange flower water in a medium-size bowl. Add to the sponge in the well and mix together with your hand. Gradually work in the flour from the bowl to make a soft, but not sticky dough. If the dough is dry, add extra water, 1 tablespoon at a time. If the dough sticks to your fingers, add extra flour, 1 tablespoon at a time.

Turn out the dough onto a lightly floured work surface and knead for 10 minutes until smooth and elastic. Wash, dry, and oil the bowl. Return the dough to the bowl, and turn it over to oil the top. Cover with a damp dish towel and let rise at room temperature, away from drafts, until doubled in size, about 1½ to 2 hours.

Punch down the dough. Turn it onto a floured surface and knead in the candied orange peel until distributed, about 5 minutes. Divide the dough into eight equal pieces. Roll out each piece to a ½-inch thick oval that is 9 inches long and about 6 inches wide. Cut eight or nine slits in the top, in a herringbone design. Arrange the fougasses, spaced well apart, on the prepared baking sheets. Lightly cover with a damp dish towel and let rise until almost doubled in size, about 1 hour. During the last 15 minutes of rising, heat the oven to 400°F. Lightly brush the fougasses with olive oil. Place each baking sheet on another sheet to prevent the bottoms from burning. Bake for 15 to 20 minutes, or until the fougasses are golden brown and sound hollow when tapped on the bottom.

Transfer to wire racks to cool completely.

Nine strands of dough are braided together to make this elaborate, almond-studded loaf. Using a freshly ground spice mixture (page 148), instead of pumpkin-pie spice, adds a fresh flavor.

If you don't have time to make the braid, shape the dough into rolls instead. It will make about 25 rolls; follow shaping instructions for Oatmeal Rolls, page 25. Brush the shaped rolls with egg glaze, top each with a halved almond, and let rise, uncovered, at cool room temperature until almost doubled in size, 30–45 minutes. Gently glaze again, then bake at 375°F for about 25 minutes, or until the rolls are golden brown and sound hollow when tapped underneath. Cool on wire racks.

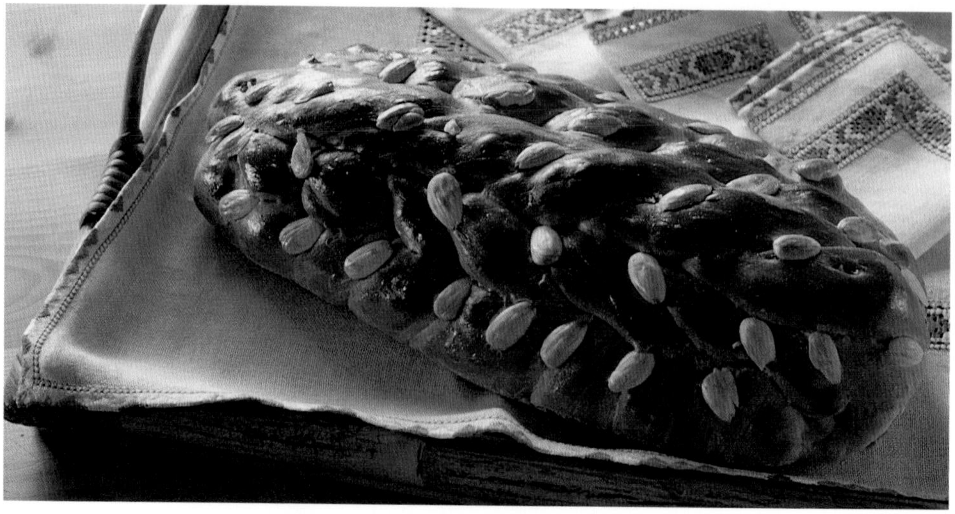

ALICE'S CHRISTMAS LOAF

INGREDIENTS

Makes 1 large loaf

- 2 cups (230g) whole-wheat bread flour, preferably stone-ground
- 1 0.6-oz cake fresh yeast (15g), or 1 envelope active dry yeast (2½ teaspoons)
- 1 tablespoon packed light brown sugar
- 1½ cups (280ml) lukewarm milk or water, or a mixture of the two
- 4 cups (455g) unbleached white bread flour, preferably stone-ground
- ½ cup + 2 tablespoons (110g) granulated sugar
- ½ cup (110g) unsalted butter, diced
- 1 teaspoon each ground cinnamon and pumpkin-pie spice, or to taste
- grated rind of 1 lemon
- 2 large eggs, beaten
- extra flour for dusting
- ¾ cup (110g) mixed dark and golden raisins
- 1 egg beaten with a pinch of salt for glazing
- about ⅔ cup (85g) sliced or halved almonds for decorating
- a baking sheet lined with parchment paper
- thin bamboo skewers

While Anthony Blake and I were visiting Mary Curtis in Ireland (page 88), she took us to meet her friends Gerry and Alice Turner. While Gerry makes wonderful sourdough bread for everyday (page 182), Alice bakes for special occasions with family recipes, including this elaborate Czech loaf with nine strands of dough braided together. Her trick of securing the shape of the braid with bamboo skewers while it rises should be useful to anyone new to shaping dough braids. Look for the skewers in Asian shops. Eat this loaf within four days.

Put the whole-wheat flour into a medium-size bowl and make a well in the center. Crumble the fresh yeast into a small bowl. Stir in the brown sugar and the lukewarm liquid until smooth. If using dry yeast, mix the granules and the brown sugar with half of the lukewarm liquid and let stand until foamy, 5 to 10 minutes (page 18). Stir in the remaining lukewarm liquid. Pour the yeast mixture into the flour. Work the flour from the bowl into the yeast mixture to make a thick batter. Cover with a damp towel and let stand at room temperature, away from drafts, until spongy, about 1 hour.

Mix together the white flour and granulated sugar in a large bowl. Rub in the butter with your fingertips until the mixture looks like fine crumbs. Stir in the cinnamon, pumpkin-pie spice, and the lemon rind. Make a well in the flour mixture. Add the eggs. Then pour in the sponge. Mix the ingredients in the well with a small whisk. Then, with your hand, mix the flour from the bowl into the yeast mixture to make a soft, but not sticky dough. If the dough is dry and crumbly, add milk, 1 tablespoon at a time. If the dough is too sticky, add flour, 1 tablespoon at a time.

Turn out the dough onto a floured surface and knead for 10 minutes until firm, pliable, and smooth. Return to the bowl. Cover with a damp dish towel and let rest at room temperature for 30 minutes.

Turn out the dough onto a floured surface. Roll out the dough, rolling away from you with a floured rolling pin, into a rectangle, about 1½ inches thick, with a short side facing you. Sprinkle one-third of the raisins over the dough, leaving a ½-inch border at the edges. Fold up the bottom third of the dough, then fold down the top third to make a three-layer dough sandwich, as for the Aberdeen Butteries (page 202). Give it a quarter turn to the left so the completely enclosed side is to your left. Roll out to a rectangle again. Sprinkle with another one-third of the raisins, and proceed as above. Repeat the process to incorporate the remaining raisins. Knead the dough just enough to form a ball. Be careful not to overwork the dough. Return the dough to the bowl and cover. Let rise at cool room temperature until doubled in size, 3 to 8 hours.

Punch down the dough. Roll it into a fat rope and cut it into nine pieces. To make the elaborate braid, first make a four-strand braid.

To make a four-strand braid: With floured hands, roll out four pieces of dough into ropes 14 inches long and 1 inch thick. Pinch the ends together firmly at one end. Arrange the four strands side by side and slightly apart, with the unattached ends facing you. Move the strand on the far left under the two strands to its right. Twist the same strand over the last strand it went under, which was originally the third strand from the left. Move the strand on the far right under the twisted two strands in the center. Twist the same strand over the last strand it went under; it then becomes the third strand from the left.

Repeat this process until all the strands are braided. Pinch the ends together. Transfer the braid to the prepared baking sheet and tuck under the ends for a neat finish. Using the edge of your hand, make an indentation lengthwise down the center of the braid.

To make a three-strand braid: Roll out three of the remaining portions of dough into 16-inch-long ropes. Braid the three strands together as for the Braided Loaf (page 31). Carefully place the three-strand braid in the indentation on top of the four-strand braid. Tuck the top ends under the bottom braid for a neat finish. Using the edge of your hand, make an indentation lengthwise down the center of this braid.

Knead the remaining two pieces of dough together with your hands and roll out into a 20-inch-long rope. Place the index finger of your left hand in the center of the rope and press down to hold the rope. Fold the dough over your finger, then wind the two pieces of the strand together to make a twisted rope. Place this in the indentation on top of the assembled braid and tuck the loose ends of the twisted rope under itself.

Pat the loaf to make a neat, high, slim loaf. Insert bamboo skewers near each end and the center. Brush with the egg glaze. Decorate liberally with the almonds, pressing them into the surface. Let rise, uncovered, at cool room temperature until almost doubled in size, 30 minutes to 1 hour. Take care not to over-rise the dough. During the last 15 minutes, heat the oven to 425°F. Brush the loaf with the egg glaze. Bake the loaf for 10 minutes. Lower the temperature to 375°F and bake for 25 to 35 minutes, or until it is firm and golden brown, and sounds hollow when tapped underneath. If the loaf seems to be browning too quickly during baking, cover with butter wrappers or parchment paper. Transfer to a wire rack to cool. Carefully remove the skewers.

TO TOP THE LOAF, ALICE WINDS THE TWO STRANDS OF DOUGH AROUND HER FINGER TO MAKE A TWISTED ROPE.

SHE GENTLY PLACES THE TWIST ON TOP OF THE ASSEMBLED BRAID.

ALICE BRUSHES THE LOAF A SECOND TIME WITH THE EGG GLAZE. THE SKEWERS HELP THE LOAF KEEP ITS SHAPE WHILE BAKING.

SPOON THE BRANDY OVER THE FRESHLY BAKED LOAF

RIGHT
For easy entertaining over the Christmas holidays, make this fruit and nut loaf and serve it with liqueur or brandy.

BISHOPS BREAD

INGREDIENTS

Makes 1 loaf
6 oz (170g) candied pineapple
⅓ cup (60g) candied cherries
⅓ cup (60g) crystallized ginger
1¼ cups (170g) raisins
2 cups (230g) unbleached white bread flour
⅔ cup (60g) walnut halves
⅓ cup (60g) pecan halves
⅓ cup (60g) whole blanched almonds
⅓ cup (60g) Brazil nuts
1 teaspoon baking powder
¼ teaspoon salt
2 extra large eggs
5 tablespoons packed (60g) light brown sugar
¼ cup (60ml) brandy
a jelly-roll pan
a deep 8-inch round cake pan, greased and bottom lined with waxed paper
a 15-oz empty can, label removed and can cleaned, well greased on the outside

A friend in Australia sent me this recipe for a Christmas ring loaf, which seemed most peculiar at first glance. Almost solid with fruit and nuts, the loaf is held together with a little batterlike dough, and after baking is soused in brandy. Because it does not contain yeast and is not decorated or iced, it is a very quick recipe to make – which really is welcome with all the last-minute rush surrounding Christmas.

Heat the oven to 400°F. To prepare the fruit and nuts: Rinse the pineapple, candied cherries, and ginger in a strainer with hot water. Drain, and then dry well on paper towels. If necessary, cut the pineapple and ginger into small chunks. Halve the cherries. Mix the pineapple, cherries, and ginger with the raisins in a medium-size bowl. Then toss with 1 tablespoon of the flour to coat the fruit.

Spread the nuts in an even layer on the jelly-roll pan. Toast in the oven for about 10 minutes, or until very lightly browned, stirring occasionally. Let the nuts cool, but do not chop them. Lower the oven temperature to 300°F.

Stir together the remaining flour, baking powder, and salt in a large bowl. Add the fruit mixture and cooled nuts and mix together well. Put the eggs and sugar in another large bowl and beat with an electric mixer on medium speed until pale and thick. By hand, stir in the flour mixture until well blended. You will have a stiff mixture of fruit and nuts bound together by a little batter. Position the well-greased can in the middle of the prepared cake pan. Spoon the batter into the cake pan around the can and smooth the surface with the back of the spoon.

Bake the bread for 1¼ hours, or until the loaf is firm and golden brown. Remove from the oven and immediately spoon the brandy evenly over the bread. Let the bread cool in the pan on a wire rack. Then turn out the bread. Store at room temperature, wrapped in waxed paper and overwrapped in foil. Eat within a week.

HOT CROSS BUNS

Betty Charlton, who gave me this recipe, lives near Norwich, in Norfolk, England. She is a great baker of yeast doughs and makes the best hot cross buns, according to Joy Skipper, who has assisted Anthony Blake and me with this book. Joy has diligently tasted every bread described in the recipes.

INGREDIENTS

Makes 24

8 cups (900g) unbleached white bread flour

½ cup + 1 tablespoon (110g) sugar, or to taste

2½ teaspoons pumpkin-pie spice, or to taste

1 teaspoon salt

1½ cups (230g) mixed dried fruit, such as dark and golden raisins, currants, and chopped mixed candied citrus peel

2 0.6-oz cakes fresh yeast (30g), or 2 envelopes active dry yeast (5 teaspoons)

2 cups (460ml) lukewarm water

¾ cup (85g) nonfat dry milk powder

½ cup (110g) butter or margarine, softened

2 large eggs, beaten

extra flour for dusting

1 large egg beaten with 1 tablespoon milk for glazing

TOPPING:

¼ cup (35g) all-purpose flour

1 tablespoon sugar

¼ cup (60ml) water

1 or 2 baking sheets, greased

Betty likes to use all unbleached white bread flour from her local mill, Reads. You can, however, replace a portion of the white flour with stone-ground whole-wheat bread flour. These buns are very moist and light, packed with fruit and spice. They are delicious freshly baked on Good Friday, and are equally good for the rest of the Easter weekend when split, toasted, and buttered. If you do not eat all the buns within three days, they will freeze for up to one month. The hot cross buns I tasted in the States were sweeter and less spicy than the British ones, so add more sugar or spice if you prefer.

Heat the oven to its lowest setting. Mix together the flour, sugar (reserving 1 teaspoon if using dry yeast), spice, salt, mixed dried fruit, and candied citrus peel in a large bowl. Make a well in the center of the flour mixture. Put the bowl in the oven for 5 to 8 minutes to warm the ingredients while you prepare the yeast.

Crumble the fresh yeast into a medium-size bowl. Stir in the lukewarm water and nonfat dry milk powder until smooth. If using dry yeast, mix the granules and the reserved 1 teaspoon granulated sugar with ½ cup (110ml) lukewarm water and let stand until foamy, 5 to 10 minutes (page 18). Stir in the milk powder and the remaining lukewarm water. Then stir in the butter or margarine until melted.

Pour the yeast mixture into the well in the warmed flour mixture. Add the eggs to the well and blend together with the yeast mixture with a small whisk or your hands. With your hand or a wooden spoon, gradually work the flour from the bowl into the yeast mixture to make very soft, but not sticky dough. If the dough is dry and crumbly, work in water, 1 tablespoon at a time. If too sticky, work in flour, 1 tablespoon at a time.

Turn out the dough onto a floured surface and knead for 10 minutes, or until smooth and elastic. Return the dough to the bowl. Cover with a damp dish towel and let rise at warm room temperature (about 75°F) until doubled in size, 30 minutes to 1 hour.

Punch down the dough. Turn out onto a lightly floured surface and knead gently for 5 minutes until very smooth and elastic. Weigh the dough and divide it into twenty-four equal portions, or roll it into a fat rope and cut it into twenty-four pieces. Shape each portion into a neat roll (see Oatmeal Rolls, page 25). Arrange fairly close together, but not touching, on the prepared baking sheet. Cover with a damp dish towel and let rise at warm room temperatures until the buns have almost doubled in size and have joined together, 30 to 45 minutes. During the last 15 minutes of rising, heat the oven to 500°F.

While the buns are rising, make the topping: In a small bowl, mix the flour and sugar with enough of the water to make a thick, smooth paste. Spoon the paste into a small pastry bag fitted with a narrow, plain tip. With the back of a table knife, make an indentation about ¼-inch deep in the shape of a cross on the top of each bun. Brush the buns with the egg glaze. Pipe a cross of the flour paste over the indentation on each bun.

Put the buns in the oven, then immediately lower the oven temperature to 400°F and bake for 15 to 20 minutes, or until the buns are nicely golden brown. Transfer the buns to a wire rack to cool. When completely cool, pull the buns apart.

BETTY PIPES THE FLOUR PASTE OVER THE INDENTATION ON TOP OF EACH BUN.

Spicy and fruity hot cross buns are traditionally baked on Good Friday throughout the Christian world.

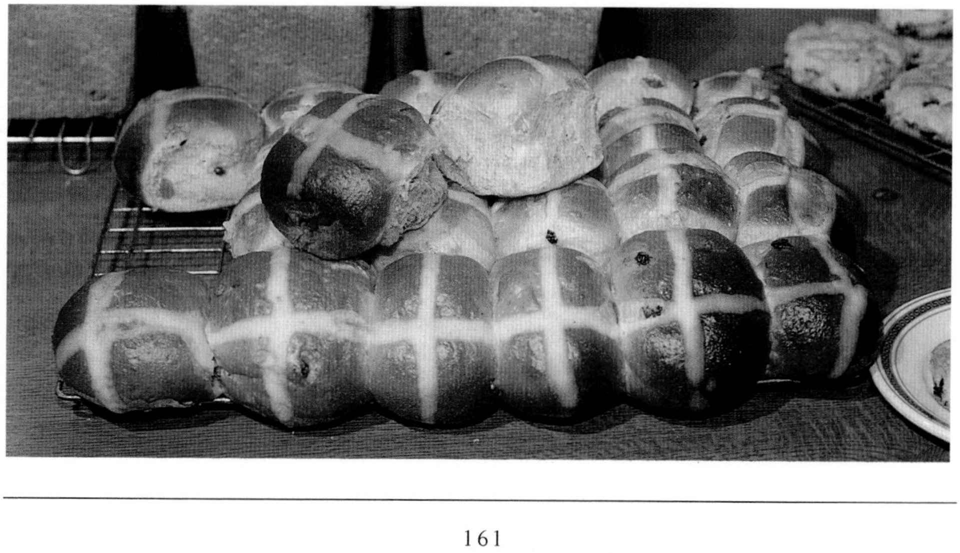

EASTER BRAID

INGREDIENTS

Makes 1 large loaf
5½ cups (680g) unbleached white bread flour
5 tablespoons (60g) sugar
2 teaspoons salt
1 tablespoon apple-pie spice
1 0.6-oz cake fresh yeast (15g)
2 cups (430ml) lukewarm milk
6 tablespoons (85g) unsalted butter, chilled and diced
1 egg, beaten
⅔ cup (110g) currants
3 tablespoons finely chopped mixed candied peel

GLAZE:
beaten egg for brushing
about 3 tablespoons honey, warmed

a large baking sheet, lightly greased

Here the dough traditionally used for Hot Cross Buns – rich with butter, spice, and fruit – is braided into an attractive loaf and glazed with honey. To keep its shape, the dough should not be too soft, and should not be left to rise in a warm spot. Leftover Braid is excellent toasted or used for Bread and Butter Pudding (see page 52).

Put 1⅓ cups (170g) of the flour into a small mixing bowl with the sugar, and make a well in the center. Sift the remaining flour with the salt and spice into a large mixing bowl. Crumble the yeast into the well in the smaller bowl. Pour the lukewarm milk onto the yeast and mix until combined. Work the flour and sugar into the yeast liquid to make a smooth batter. Cover and let "sponge" for about 20 minutes – the batter will become bubbly as the yeast begins to grow.

Add the diced butter to the flour mixture in the larger bowl and rub in, using your fingertips until the mixture looks like coarse crumbs. Stir the egg into the frothy yeast batter and add to the flour. Mix together to form a fairly firm, rather than soft or sticky, dough. Turn the dough onto a lightly floured work surface and knead for 10 minutes or until quite firm, silky smooth, and elastic. Put the dough back into the bowl, cover with a damp dish towel, and let rise at cool to normal room temperature for 1–1½ hours or until doubled in bulk.

Turn the risen dough onto a lightly floured work surface and punch down with your knuckles. Sprinkle over the currants and peel, and gently but thoroughly knead into the dough until evenly distributed. The dough should be quite pliable but not soft, and it should hold its shape well. If not, work in a little more flour. Divide the dough into three equal pieces (ideally, weigh the dough on kitchen scales).

Using your hands, roll each piece into a sausage shape about 16 inches long. Lay the three pieces of dough parallel to each other on the prepared baking sheet, then braid them together neatly but not too tightly. Take care not to stretch the dough unduly. Tuck the ends under. Cover with a damp dish towel and let rise at cool to normal room temperature for about 1 hour or until almost doubled in size.

Preheat the oven to 425°F.

1 ROLL EACH OF THE THREE PIECES OF DOUGH INTO A LONG, EVEN SAUSAGE SHAPE.

2 LAY THE PIECES ON THE BAKING SHEET AND BRAID WITHOUT STRETCHING THEM.

3 TUCK UNDER THE ENDS OF THE FINISHED BRAID, THEN LET RISE BEFORE BAKING.

Carefully brush the loaf with the beaten egg, then bake for 15–20 minutes or until golden. Lower the oven temperature to 400°F and bake for a further 20 minutes or until the loaf sounds hollow when tapped on the base. Transfer to a wire rack, brush with the warm honey, and cool.

NOTE You can use 1 package (1/4oz/7g) active dry yeast instead of fresh yeast. For rapid-rise dry yeast, add it to the 1 1/3 cups (170g) flour and sugar. Pour the measured lukewarm milk into the well in the dry ingredients and proceed with the recipe.

HARVEST WHEAT SHEAF

INGREDIENTS

Makes 1 large loaf

- 12 cups (1.35kg) unbleached white bread flour
- 2½ tablespoons (20g) coarse sea salt, crushed or ground
- 2 teaspoons sugar
- 1 0.6-oz cake fresh yeast (15g), or 1 envelope active dry yeast (2½ teaspoons)
- about 3 cups (690ml) lukewarm water
- extra flour for dusting
- 1 large egg beaten with a pinch of salt for glazing
- a very large baking sheet (see introduction), greased

In autumn, fresh vegetables replace the more traditional flower decorations in Anglican churches throughout Britain to celebrate the harvest festivals. After the service of thanksgiving, many congregations enjoy a meal in the church hall, which can include a decorated loaf of bread, such as this wheat sheaf.

"Toward the end of September or the beginning of October each year, bakers, especially in the southern parts of England, are frequently asked to supply large loaves as ornamental as the baker can make them for harvest festivals in churches," wrote Master Baker John Kirkland in 1907 (page 65). For him, a convenient size was a loaf made of an incredible 26 to 28 pounds of dough. And although he says an ordinary bread dough made a little firmer by adding less liquid will do, this lightly yeasted dough works better. This is a scaled-down version of his recipe to make a wheat sheaf about 17 × 13 inches.

You will need a kitchen scale to make this recipe. If you don't have a scale already, this provides a very good reason to purchase this very useful piece of kitchen equipment.

Mix together the flour, salt, and sugar (if using dry yeast, reserve ½ teaspoon of the sugar) in a very large bowl. Make a well in the center of the flour mixture. Crumble the fresh yeast into a small bowl. Stir in ¾ cup (170ml) of the lukewarm water until smooth. If using dry yeast, mix the granules and the reserved ½ teaspoon sugar with ¾ cup (170ml) of the lukewarm water and let stand until foamy, 5 to 10 minutes (page 18).

Pour the yeast mixture into the well in the flour. Add almost all the remaining lukewarm water and mix well. With your hand or a wooden spoon, work the flour from the bowl into the yeast mixture in the well to make a soft dough. (John Kirkland said it should not be sticky or dry). If the dough is dry and crumbly, work in more of the water, 1 tablespoon at a time. If the dough is too sticky, work in extra flour, 1 tablespoon at a time.

Turn the dough onto a lightly floured work surface and knead for 10 minutes, or until very elastic.

Wash, dry, and oil the bowl. Return the dough to the bowl and turn the dough over so the top is oiled. Cover with a damp dish towel and let rise at room temperature, away from drafts, until doubled in size, about 2 hours.

Punch down the dough. Turn it out onto a floured surface and knead for 2 minutes to work out the air bubbles. Cover with the upturned bowl and let rest for 10 minutes.

To shape the wheat sheaf: Cut off 10 ounces (280g) of the dough. Cover the remaining dough with a damp dish towel (see Note). Roll out the cut-off piece of dough on a lightly floured work surface with a lightly floured rolling pin into a 10 × 6-inch rectangle to form the base for the wheat stalks, patting the dough as necessary to keep the shape. Center a short side of the rectangle on a short side of the prepared baking sheet, so the dough is almost touching one edge of the sheet. (The space should be equal at both long sides, and there should be empty space above the sheaf.)

Roll or pat out 12 ounces (340g) of the remaining dough into a crescent shape with rounded ends, 11 inches wide across the crescent and longer than the rectangle. Position the crescent on top of the rectangle so it looks like a very large mushroom. Prick the dough all over with a fork and brush with water to prevent a crust forming.

To make the wheat stalks: Divide 14 ounces (395g) of the remaining dough into thirty equal pieces, by weight. Roll each piece on a floured surface with your hands into a thin rope about 10 inches long. Twist or braid three ropes together to make the sheaf band. Set this aside. Lay the remaining twenty-seven "stalks" side-by-side along the length of the stalk base, covering it, to create the sheaf. Place the twisted sheaf band across the center of the sheaf, curving it slightly. Do not press the band down onto the sheaf. Tuck the ends under the sheaf.

Set aside 1 ounce (30g) of the remaining dough to make the mouse. Weigh the remaining dough and divide into five equal portions. Divide each fifth into twenty equal pieces by weight, for a total of one hundred pieces. These will form the ears of wheat. Roll each piece with your hand on the floured work surface into a fat, oval-shaped roll. Pinch each roll at one end to make a point and round it at the other end. Using a small

POSITION THE DOUGH CRESCENT OVER THE TOP OF THE STALK BASE AND PRICK THE DOUGH ALL OVER WITH A FORK.

TWIST THREE DOUGH ROPES TOGETHER TO MAKE THE SHEAF BAND.

ARRANGE THE WHEAT STALKS ON THE BASE. PLACE THE TWISTED SHEAF BAND ACROSS THE CENTER OF THE STALKS, CURVING THE BAND SLIGHTLY.

SNIP ANGLED SHALLOW CUTS DOWN THE CENTER OF EACH EAR. THEN SNIP ALONG EACH SIDE, ANGLING THE CUTS IN THE SAME DIRECTION.

ARRANGE THE EARS, A FEW AT A TIME, CLOSE TOGETHER BUT NOT TOUCHING ALONG THE TOP OF THE CRESCENT.

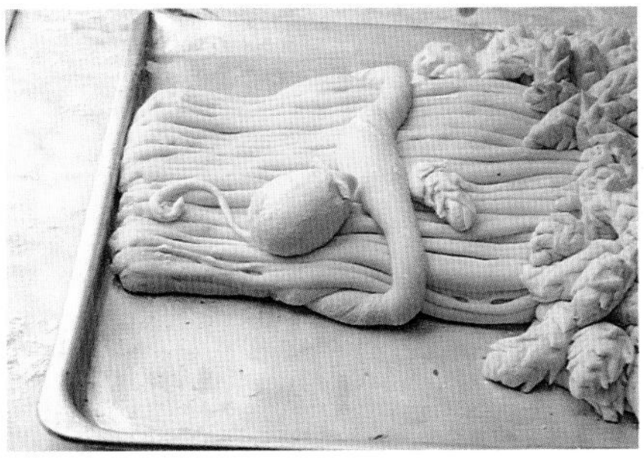

SHAPE THE DOUGH MOUSE, THEN POSITION IT ON THE STALKS AS IF IT IS CLIMBING UP THE SHEAF.

This decorative loaf looks attractive hanging on a kitchen wall, or makes a wonderful housewarming gift for a special friend. If you want to use the wheat sheaf purely for decoration, bake it an extra 6 hours at 250°F.

pair of kitchen scissors, snip angled, shallow cuts down the center of each ear (without cutting all the way through), working from the rounded end to the pointed end. Then make shallow cuts down each side of the first snips, positioning these cuts between the cuts of the center row.

Arrange the ears close together, but not touching, along the edges of the crescent. The next row should be arranged between these ears, leaving about 1½ inches of the first row exposed. Do not arrange the ears too regularly, and leave one or two to droop slightly. Repeat until the crescent center has been filled and all the wheat ears used.

Shape the remaining 1 ounce (30g) dough into an egg-shaped mouse with a pointed nose and a long, thin tail.

Using small scissors, cut two small flaps toward the pointed end, then lift them up and forward to resemble ears. Make two small holes for the eyes.

Brush the underside with water and place it on the stalks as if it is climbing up the sheaf.

Heat the oven to 425°F.

Carefully brush the wheat sheaf with the egg glaze. Then prick "in a good many places," according to Kirkland, with the tip of a pointed knife to prevent the loaf from cracking during baking. The knife holes should be made vertically, following the pattern of the stalks and ears, so there are no visible cuts.

Bake the bread for 15 minutes. Brush with more glaze. Then lower the oven temperature to 325°F and continue baking for 25 minutes longer, or until the loaf is golden brown and very firm.

Let the loaf cool completely on the baking sheet.

NOTE: If your kitchen is warm, it is best to keep the portions of dough you are not using in the refrigerator, tightly covered with plastic wrap. If the dough rises too fast, the sheaf will lose its crisp shape.

HARVEST WREATH

INGREDIENTS

Makes 1 large wreath
$7^1/_4$ cups (900g) unbleached white bread flour, preferably stoneground
$1^1/_2$ tablespoons salt
1 0.6-oz cake fresh yeast (15g)
$2^1/_3$ cups (570ml) water from the cold tap
1 egg, beaten with a large pinch of salt, for glazing

a large baking sheet, greased

As Anthony and I traveled though Europe, we came across many extremely attractive loaves baked to celebrate the harvest. This elaborately decorated loaf was made to eat at a party in a Burgundy vineyard at the end of the vendange, or grape-picking. There is a fair amount of salt in the dough, which enables it to maintain its shape. As with the Easter Braid on page 86, it is important that the dough be smooth but not soft and that it is left to rise in a fairly cool spot.

Put the flour and salt into a large mixing bowl and make a well in the center. Crumble the yeast into a small bowl, add a quarter of the water, and mix to a smooth liquid. Pour into the well in the flour, then add the rest of the water. Gradually mix the flour into the liquid to make a fairly firm dough. Turn the dough onto a lightly floured work surface and knead thoroughly for 10 minutes – the dough must be smooth and pliable. If it is at all sticky, knead in extra flour a tablespoon at a time. Put the dough back into the bowl, cover with a damp dish towel, and let rise at cool to normal room temperature for $1^1/_2$–2 hours or until doubled in bulk.

Punch down the risen dough with your knuckles. Divide the dough into four equal portions. Cover and set aside one portion of the dough to be used for decoration. Using your hands, roll each of the remaining three portions into a sausage shape about 2 feet long. Lay the three sausages parallel to each other on the work surface and hold one end of each together in one hand. With the other hand lift and twist the three strands together. Carefully join both ends of the twisted dough together to make a neat wreath. Transfer to the prepared baking sheet.

1 USE BOTH HANDS TO TWIST THE STRANDS OF DOUGH TOGETHER WITHOUT STRETCHING.

2 JOIN THE ENDS TO MAKE A RING, LIFT IT ONTO THE SHEET, AND NEATEN THE EDGES.

3 ROLL OUT THE REST OF THE DOUGH THINLY AND CUT OUT 9 LEAF SHAPES WITH A KNIFE.

4 TO MAKE THE GRAPES, ROLL THE LEFTOVER DOUGH INTO BALLS OF DIFFERENT SIZES.

Decorating the Harvest Wreath takes time, and a second pair of hands will be welcome. Here Anthony and I present our loaf, ready for baking.

Preheat the oven to 425°F. Turn the reserved piece of dough onto a lightly floured work surface and punch down with your knuckles. Roll it out about 1/4 inch thick. Then, using a very sharp knife and a real vine leaf or a paper pattern as a guide, cut out nine vine leaves. Use the leftover dough to make grapes the size of hazelnuts and small peas.

Attach the vine leaves and grapes in bunches to the wreath, using the egg glaze as a glue. Brush the decorated wreath all over with more egg glaze, then bake immediately in the preheated oven for 30–40 minutes or until the bread sounds hollow when tapped on the base. If the wreath seems to be browning very rapidly, reduce the oven temperature to 400°F. Check the wreath several times during baking to ensure that it is browning evenly, and turn it as necessary. To make sure the decorations remain in place, you may need to stick them back with more egg glaze during baking. Cool the wreath on a wire rack, and eat within 24 hours.

NOTE You can use 1 package (1/4oz/7g)active dry yeast instead of fresh yeast, dissolving it in warm water. For rapid-rise dry yeast, mix it with the flour. Add all the water and proceed with the recipe.

CHALLAH

Challah is the Jewish white egg bread which is often braided into an elaborate loaf. It is regarded as an essential symbol for celebrating the Sabbath on Friday night. The word challah means dough offering in Hebrew. Its meaning dates back from the Temple period, about 380 BC, when a portion of the dough from the Sabbath loaf, generally made with finely-milled flour, rather than the coarse, everyday variety, was given to the temple priests. After the Temple was destroyed in 70 AD, Jews continued this practice symbolically, by throwing a small piece of the challah dough into the fire to burn while a blessing is recited.

Ashkenazi Jews, originally from central and Eastern Europe, often have two symbolic loaves of challah on their Sabbath dinner table. The loaves are covered with a special embroidered cloth, called a challah cover.

The elaborately braided challah, sometimes made with up to twelve strands of dough, was first baked by Central European Jews during the Middle Ages. This special, sweeter loaf was in complete contrast with the coarse, dark, slightly bitter bread eaten during the rest of the week. At the beginning of a Sabbath meal, the challah is blessed. Then, in some traditions, pieces are broken off, dipped in salt, and tossed unceremoniously to the diners, rather than being passed around, to symbolize the gift of bread from God.

Sephardic Jews, originally from Spain, Portugal, North Africa, and the Middle East, do not necessarily bake a special Sabbath loaf. Instead they use two of their everyday breads, such as pitas, or other flat breads. The breads are covered and placed on the Sabbath table to be blessed, and then sometimes broken and dipped in salt.

The symbolic challah made for Rosh Hashana, the Jewish New Year, is circular, or crown-shaped. It signifies peace, unity, and the creation of the Universe. In some communities, for Chanukah, the challah is shaped like a menorah, a seven-branched candle holder. Ukranian Jews may often bake three different shaped challahs: a bird-shaped challah for Yom Kippur, the Jewish day of Atonement; a spiral loaf for Rosh Hashana; and a key-shaped loaf for the Sabbath after Passover.

Some challahs are made with dark or golden raisins, nuts, and saffron, or other spices, depending on the traditions of the community.

The characteristic dark, shiny, reddish-brown color of the commercial varieties is achieved by glazing the loaf with egg yolk tinted with a few drops of red or yellow food coloring.

BRAIDED CHALLAH

This honey-sweetened, saffron-gold, rich dough can be braided into a twist using up to twelve strands, but I am giving only some of the simpler examples in this section. If you are attempting to shape a braid for the first time, you might like to try this tip from Alice Turner (page 158): Insert 10- to 12-inch thin bamboo skewers through the braided strands while the loaf is rising, to help retain the shape.

Traditional challah dough has three risings, but should never be left in too warm a place, or it will become too soft to shape. Glazing the braid twice with egg yolk gives a deeper-colored finish to the loaf. Eat the challah within three days, or freeze for up to one month.

INGREDIENTS

Makes 1 loaf

- *¼ teaspoon saffron strands*
- *1 cup (230ml) boiling water*
- *1 0.6-oz cake fresh yeast (15g), or 1 envelope active dry yeast (2¼ teaspoons)*
- *2 tablespoons honey*
- *about 6 cups (680g) unbleached white bread flour*
- *2 teaspoons salt*
- *3 large eggs, beaten*
- *6 tablespoons (85g) unsalted butter, melted and cooled*
- *extra flour for dusting*
- *1 egg yolk beaten with a pinch of salt for glazing*

2 baking sheets, one of them greased

Crumble the saffron strands into a small bowl. Pour in the boiling water and let stand to infuse until the water cools to lukewarm. Crumble the fresh yeast into a small bowl. Stir in the lukewarm saffron mixture and the honey until smooth. If using dry yeast, mix the granules and the honey with the lukewarm saffron mixture and let stand until foamy, 5 to 10 minutes (page 18).

Stir together the flour and salt in a large bowl and make a well in the center of the flour mixture. Pour the yeast mixture into the well in the flour, followed by the beaten eggs and melted butter. Mix together the ingredients in the well with a small whisk or your hand. Then, with your hand or a wooden spoon, gradually mix the flour from the bowl into the ingredients in the well to form a soft, but not sticky dough. If the dough is too sticky, add a little extra flour, 1 tablespoon at a time. If the dough is dry and crumbly, add a little extra lukewarm water. 1 tablespoon at a time.

TUCK THE ENDS OF THE BRAID UNDER FOR A NEAT FINISH.

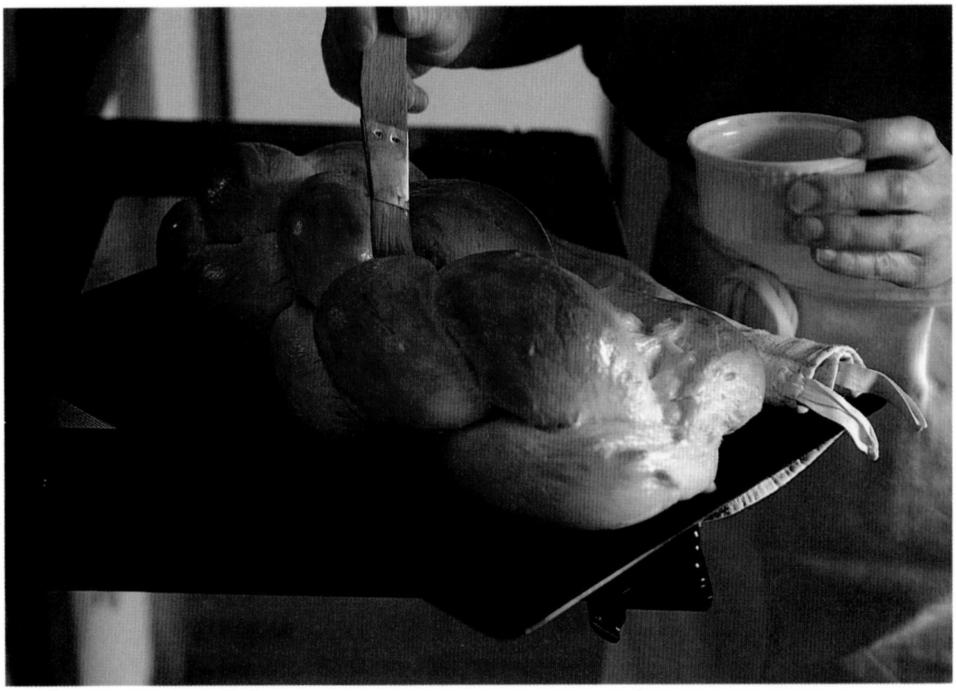

Right
BAKE THE CHALLAH FOR 10 MINUTES. THEN REMOVE IT FROM THE OVEN AND BRUSH A SECOND TIME WITH THE EGG AND SALT GLAZE.

Turn out the dough onto a lightly floured work surface. Knead for 10 minutes until smooth and elastic. Wash, dry, and oil the bowl. Return the dough to the bowl, and turn the dough over so the top is oiled. Cover with a damp dish towel and let rise at room temperature, away from drafts, until doubled in size, about 1½ hours.

Punch down the dough in the bowl. Cover with a damp dish towel and let rise again at room temperature, away from drafts, until doubled in size, about 45 minutes.

Punch down the dough. Turn out the dough onto a very lightly floured work surface. Knead for about 1 minute until the dough is smooth and elastic. Cover the dough with the upturned bowl and let rest for 5 minutes.

To shape a two-strand twist, divide the dough into two equal portions. Using your hands, roll each portion into a 15-inch-long rope about 2 inches thick. Pinch the ropes together firmly at one end. Wind the two ropes together to make a neat twist. Pinch the ends together. Transfer to the prepared baking sheet and tuck the ends under to give a neat shape.

To shape a three-strand braid, see Braided Loaf (page 31).

To shape a four-strand braid, divide the dough into four equal portions. Using your hands, roll each portion into a 13-inch-long rope about 1 inch thick. Pinch the ropes together firmly at one end.

Arrange the four strands side by side and slightly apart, with the unattached ends facing you. Move the strand on the far left under the two strands to its right. Twist the same strand over the last strand it went under, which was originally the third strand from the left. Move the strand on the far right under the twisted two strands in the center. Twist the same strand over the last strand it went under; it then becomes the third strand from the left. Repeat this process until all the strands are braided. Pinch the ends together. Transfer to the prepared baking sheet and tuck under the ends for a neat finish.

To make a double braid, using nine strands, see Alice's Christmas Loaf (page 158).

Cover the shaped challah loosely with a damp dish towel and let rise at room temperature, away from drafts, until doubled in size, 45 minutes to 1 hour. During the last 15 minutes of rising, heat the oven to 425°F.

Slide the second baking sheet under the first to prevent the bottom of the challah from overbrowning. Gently brush the risen challah with the egg glaze. Bake for 10 minutes. Remove from the oven and glaze it again. Return the loaf to the oven, lower the oven temperature to 375°F, and bake for 20 to 35 minutes longer, with the thicker, more complicated braids taking the longer time, until the loaf is a good golden brown and sounds hollow when tapped underneath. If the loaf is browning too quickly, cover loosely with a sheet of foil. Transfer to a wire rack to cool completely.

NOTE: For its second rising, the dough can also be left overnight in the refrigerator.

CAROLL'S TWISTED RING

Caroll Boltin (page 69) uses her challah dough to make a braided ring loaf for family celebrations. But I enjoy this loaf for everyday eating with soup or cheese, especially a mature, runny Milleen from Veronica Steele's dairy in Ireland. Caroll recommends using this rich bread for French toast, or pain perdu. Eat within three days, or use for toast.

INGREDIENTS

Makes 1 loaf

- about 6 cups (680g) unbleached white bread flour
- 2 tablespoons sugar
- 2 teaspoons salt
- 1 0.6-oz cake fresh yeast (15g), or 1 envelope active dry yeast (2½ teaspoons)
- 1 cup (230ml) lukewarm water
- 6 tablespoons (85g) unsalted butter, melted and cooled
- 3 large eggs, beaten
- 1 large egg, separated
- extra flour for dusting
- 1 teaspoon poppy seeds for sprinkling

a 9-inch tube pan, greased

Stir together 1½ cups (170g) flour, the sugar (reserve ½ teaspoon of the sugar if using dry yeast), and the salt in the bowl of a heavy-duty stationary electric mixer fixed with a dough hook. Crumble the fresh yeast into a small bowl. Stir in the lukewarm water until smooth. If using dry yeast, mix the granules and the reserved ½ teaspoon sugar with half of the lukewarm water and let stand until foamy, 5 to 10 minutes (page 18). Stir in the remaining lukewarm water.

Pour the yeast mixture and the melted butter into the flour mixture. Beat on medium speed for 2 minutes. Add the 3 whole eggs and the egg white. Beat on high speed for 2 minutes, or until the dough is very smooth. Gradually add enough of the remaining flour, with the machine on low speed, to make a soft, but not sticky dough that gathers into a ball around the dough hook and leaves the sides of the bowl cleanly. Knead the dough with the dough hook at medium speed for 10 minutes, or until the dough is satiny-smooth and elastic. If the dough is too sticky, add a little extra flour, 1 tablespoon at a time. If the dough is dry and crumbly, add a little extra water, 1 tablespoon at a time.

If you prefer, you can prepare the dough by hand: Mix together 1½ cups (170g) of the flour, the sugar, and the salt in a large bowl. Make a well in the center of the flour. Prepare the yeast mixture as above, using fresh or dry yeast. Pour the yeast mixture and the melted butter into the well in the flour. With your hand or a wooden spoon, gradually work the flour from the bowl into the liquid. Then beat the batter vigorously with your hand for 2 minutes. Add the 3 whole eggs and the egg white and beat with your hand for 4 minutes. Gradually mix in enough of the remaining flour to make a soft, but not sticky dough. Turn out the dough onto a lightly floured work surface and knead for 10 minutes until satiny-smooth and elastic.

CAROLL BRAIDS THE THREE FLAT STRIPS OF DOUGH TOGETHER.

AFTER THE DOUGH IS BRAIDED, CAROLL WILL PUT IT IN THE TUBE PAN.

This ring loaf is easier to shape than more elaborately braided challas, yet it's attractive enough to make any celebration more special. Here Caroll has displayed her loaf with an arrangement of vegetables, a bowl of apples, and an old-fashioned, wooden candelabra.

Put the dough into a lightly oiled bowl, and turn the dough over so the top is oiled. Cover with a damp dish towel and let rise at room temperature, away from drafts, until doubled in size, 1 to 1½ hours.

Punch down the dough. Turn out the dough onto a lightly floured work surface. With lightly floured knuckles, pat the dough out into a 22 × 10-inch rectangle, about 1 inch thick. (You may also roll out the dough with a lightly floured rolling pin.) Cut the rectangle lengthwise into four strips, unequal in width: three strips 3 inches wide, and one strip 1 inch wide.

Pinch the three wide strips together at one end. Braid as for the Braided Loaf (page 31) to make a flat, braided rope 18 to 20 inches long. Arrange the dough in the prepared ring mold, pinching the two ends together. Use the remaining narrow strip of dough to wrap like a strap around the point where the two ends meet and tuck underneath, so the loaf is an even thickness all the way around.

Beat the reserved egg yolk with 1 teaspoon water to make a glaze. Brush over the loaf, making sure not to glue the loaf to the mold. Sprinkle the top of the loaf evenly with the poppy seeds.

Cover with a damp dish towel and let rise at room temperature, away from drafts, until doubled in size, about 1 hour. Check from time to time to make sure the dough is not sticking to the cloth. During the last 15 minutes of rising, heat the oven to 400°F.

Bake the loaf for 10 minutes. Then lower the oven temperature to 350°F and bake 40 minutes longer, or until the loaf is golden brown and a skewer inserted in the center comes out clean.

Let the bread cool in the pan for a couple of minutes. Then carefully turn out onto a wire rack to cool completely.

KULICH

INGREDIENTS

Makes 1 loaf
½ cup (85g) golden raisins
1 tablespoon rum
⅛ teaspoon saffron threads
1 cup (230ml) milk, heated to boiling
⅔ cup (85g) whole blanched almonds
⅓ cup (60g) minced mixed candied orange and lemon peel
1 teaspoon all-purpose flour
½ cup + 2 tablespoons (140g) unsalted butter, at room temperature
1 cup (110g) confectioners' sugar, sifted
6 egg yolks
½ teaspoon salt
2 0.6-oz cakes fresh yeast (30g)
3¾ cups (450g) unbleached white bread flour

a 6-inch round deep cake pan, greased and prepared with foil and wax paper (see recipe)
a baking sheet

This light fruit loaf is made in Russia to celebrate Easter, and contains all the eggs and butter prohibited during Lent. In some parts of Russia, the loaf is covered with a thin, lemony glacé icing and decorated with glacé fruits, but I have left this version plain. Kulich is traditionally eaten with paskha, a sweetened and decorated fruit, nut, and curd cheese dessert made in a similar tall mold. As tall narrow molds are hard to find, some cooks use coffee cans or well-seasoned flowerpots; however, I find these more trouble than they are worth and instead use a small, deep cake pan with a stiff foil collar to extend the depth.

To prepare the pan, wrap a doubled strip of foil around the outside of the greased pan to extend about 4 inches above the rim. Tie on the foil collar securely. Butter a strip of wax paper and use to line the inside of the pan sides and the foil collar.

Preheat the oven to 400°F.

Put the raisins to soak in the rum. Crumble the saffron into a small mixing bowl and pour over the boiling milk. Let infuse for 30 minutes – longer if possible. Put the almonds in a small mixing bowl, add enough hot water to cover, and let soak for 5 minutes. Then drain and cut lengthwise into slivers. Arrange the almonds in a single layer on the baking sheet and toast in the oven for 5–10 minutes or until lightly browned. Let cool. Toss the candied peel with the teaspoon of flour.

Cream the butter with the sugar in a large mixing bowl, using an electric mixer or wooden spoon. When the mixture is light and fluffy, beat in the egg yolks one at a time followed by the salt. If necessary, gently warm the saffron milk until it is just lukewarm, then crumble in the yeast and stir until smooth. Add the flour to the creamed mixture and stir until just combined, then pour in the yeast liquid. Beat with your hand for about 8 minutes or until the mixture comes together to make a very soft, smooth, batter-like dough. Cover the bowl with a damp dish towel and let rise at normal to warm room temperature for about 2 hours or until doubled in bulk.

Punch down the risen dough. Sprinkle it with the soaked raisins, the candied peel, and the toasted almonds. Gently work them into the dough with your hands until evenly distributed. Spoon the dough into the prepared pan; it will be about half full. Cover with a damp dish towel and let rise at normal to warm room temperature for about 1½ hours or until risen almost to the top of the foil and paper collar.

Preheat the oven to 400°F again.

Bake the kulich for 20 minutes or until starting to color, then reduce the oven temperature to 350°F and bake for a further 45–55 minutes or until a skewer inserted into the center comes out clean. If the loaf starts to turn dark brown, cover with a sheet of foil or parchment paper. Put the pan on a wire rack and let cool for 10–15 minutes or until the kulich is firm enough to unmold, then turn it out onto a wire rack to cool completely. Best eaten within 3 days.

NOTE You can use 2 packages (¼oz/7g each) active dry yeast instead of fresh yeast. For rapid-rise dry yeast, mix it with the flour.

1 *AFTER ADDING THE FLOUR TO THE CREAMED MIXTURE, POUR IN THE WARM YEAST LIQUID.*

2 *BEAT THE MIXTURE WITH YOUR HAND, LIFTING IT AND SLAPPING IT DOWN.*

3 *AFTER RISING, ADD THE FRUIT, PEEL, AND NUTS TO THE DOUGH AND WORK IN.*

4 *TRANSFER THE DOUGH TO THE PAN, PREPARED WITH A STIFF FOIL COLLAR.*

SOURDOUGH AND RYE BREADS

One of the joys of baking bread is the miracle of yeast. Yeast is a living thing, needing food, some warmth, and pampering to survive – and to perform its job, which is to make a dough rise. What sets sourdough breads apart from other yeast breads is that much of their rising power comes from the wild yeasts that are naturally present in the air, rather than from commercial yeast.

Sourdoughs are not the types of bread that can be made quickly. A starter can take up to three days to ferment. And once the starter is made, the dough can take as long as ten days to ferment, as in the German Friendship Cake (page 176). The rising times are often lengthy as well. Leaving the doughs for an extra hour or so will not cause them to over-rise, as is the case with most other doughs. This suits me. I like being able to shape a dough that has risen overnight while I boil the kettle for tea at breakfast, knowing that when I finish working in the evening, the dough will be ready for the oven.

OPPOSITE Lionel Poilâne with his sourdough loaves. ABOVE Poilâne bread for sale in Paris.

Rye breads are made with all or part rye flour, a dark gray flour, commonly used in Northern, Middle, and Eastern European baking, which has a distinctly tangy and slightly acidic taste. This taste is enhanced and heightened when the flour is combined with a sour-dough starter.

Unlike wheat flours, rye flour contains very little gluten so doughs made exclusively iwth rye flour are heavy and sticky, and do not rise much. Conse-quently, rye-flour doughs are often lightened, and the gluten boosted by the addition of unbleached white bread flour or stone-ground whole-wheat flour. These combinations make the dough easier to work, but more importantly, I feel the taste is improved. It is worth searching out good, coarse, stone-ground rye flour from local mills, health-food stores, or through mail order (see page 360).

For a basic, heavy rye loaf, combine three parts rye flour to one part wheat flour. A light rye loaf is made with the reverse proportions: one part rye flour to three parts wheat flour. Anthony Blake bakes a loaf of rye bread to perfection every day. He uses equal proportions of rye flour, coarse stone-ground whole-wheat flour, and unbleached white bread flour. Gerry's Sourdough Rye Bread (page 182) also uses this combination of flours, but his recipe begins with a sourdough starter.

Some rye bread recipes, such as Scandinavian Rye Bread (page 187) include buttermilk to provide an extra tang. Molasses is used to impart color and an intense flavor to breads like the Pumpernickel Loaf (page 183).

The flavor of sourdough bread becomes distinctly tangy the longer it is left to rise at a cool temperature. The sourness also depends on the pungency of the starter.

Jeffrey Hamelman, of Hamelman's Bakery, in Brattleboro, Vermont, bakes the best sourdough bread I have tasted outside Europe. He makes 500 loaves of bread each day, and considers delicious, well-flavored sourdough bread to be the highest expression of a baker's skill.

"You learn by your mistakes. There are not any shortcuts to wonderful sourdough," he says. "The important thing to remember is that the dough is alive. The baker performs alchemy, and if he or she is successful the yeast becomes exuberant and more lively. If the baker does not supply the yeast's needs, it will be crippled."

Each afternoon before Jeffrey leaves his bakery, he combines a new batch of dough with a starter and leaves it to ferment for 16 hours. He then adds flour and water at regular intervals until the dough is finally baked 24 hours after it was first mixed. Just like home bakers, Jeffrey has to take account of weather conditions when he prepares his dough. In Vermont, the weather can change dramatically and the winters are very cold; the summers extremely hot.

Sourdough breads are slow to stale, and, as they mature, the flavors mellow and blend. Most sourdough breads will stay fresh for up to a week.

TIPS FOR MAKING SOURDOUGH BREADS

– Flexibility is a key factor when making sourdough breads. The rising times can be variable and unpredictable and, unfortunately, there are times when a dough fails to thrive for no apparent reason. When this happens, you have to accept defeat. Throw away the dough and begin again. Flour and liquid quantities are never precise (as with most yeast breads) because of everyday variations in temperature and humidity and the quality of the flour. Work by feel, and treat the recipes as guides, adding the amounts of ingredients you feel the dough requires.

– There are certain signs that let you know that your starter has "died," is weak, or has gone off. If a starter smells bad, rather than sour, or if it has patches of mold throw it away. Check that it is "alive" by looking for bubbles on the surface and a distinct yeasty, or sour, smell. You will notice that the mixture gradually turns gray as it ferments – this is a good sign. A failed starter will produce a flat, dense loaf. If this happens your starter is not active; you must use a fresh starter for the next loaf.

– Do not use bleached flours. The best starters are made with unbleached, stone-ground flours in which yeasts thrive. The chemical treatment used to bleach flour seems to hinder the development of the starter and – even worse – it may produce a chlorine taste.

– Do not add salt to a starter mixture because it will inhibit the development of the yeast.

– I think a kitchen counter is the best location in the house to leave a starter while it is developing. The kitchen is often warmer than other rooms, and because it is the place where food is prepared, there seem to be more yeasts in the air. The best sourdough breads I have ever made were ones at Anthony Blake's studio, after a week of food photography.

– Do not cover the starter mixture, or the sponge, with plastic wrap, foil, or a lid. Use a damp thin dish towel, to provide a warm, moist environment which will attract the yeasts naturally present in the air and encourage them to multiply.

– When you are leaving a starter to ferment over several days, be sure to re-dampen the towel at least once a day.

– Starters develop at different rates depending on the season and the weather. You will find starters and doughs tend to develop most quickly in hot and humid conditions.

– In my recipes I specify how long you can keep a starter before you have to use it in another loaf. If, however, there is not an instruction in a recipe or you want to keep a portion of the dough to use as a starter for the next loaf for more than three days, you must "feed" it. Add ½ cup (110ml) water from the cold tap and enough flour to make a soft dough every four days. Store the dough in a covered container in the refrigerator or in a cool pantry. Do not keep the starter longer than two weeks.

GERMAN FRIENDSHIP CAKE

I had heard a lot about friendship cakes, a sourdough loaf made from a starter that has been passed from friend to friend, but I had never tasted one until recently. One day, friend and fellow cookery writer Elaine Hallgarten arrived on my doorstep with a container of starter and some instructions that had been given to her. You certainly know who your friends are when you start making this recipe! Coincidentally, a letter from my mother-in-law in America containing a recipe for Amish friendship bread arrived in the next post. It was identical!

This loaf is delicious and simple to make, more like a crumb cake than a bread, but it does take ten days – once you've made the starter. I discovered it is a good idea to write down the date of Day 1, or you might lose your place in the recipe. After ten days, you will have enough starter to give two portions away and keep two portions for yourself: one to bake immediately and one to refrigerate. You cannot use active dry yeast to make this recipe; it simply doesn't work. Eat the bread within three days after baking, or freeze for up to one month.

INGREDIENTS

Makes 1 large loaf

STARTER:

2 cups (280g) unbleached all-purpose flour

1 0.6-oz cake fresh yeast (15g)

2 cups (455ml) water

FOR DAY 1 AND DAY 5:

1 cup (200g) granulated sugar

1 cup (140g) unbleached all-purpose flour

1 cup (230ml) milk

FOR FINISHING LOAF:

2 cups (280g) unbleached all-purpose flour

1 cup (200g) granulated sugar

3 Granny Smith apples, peeled, cored, and diced

½ cup (85g) golden raisins

½ cup (110ml) vegetable oil

2 large eggs, beaten

½ cup (60g) chopped walnuts or pecans

2 teaspoons ground cinnamon

2 teaspoons baking powder

½ teaspoon salt

a few drops of vanilla extract

TOPPING:

½ cup packed (100g) light brown sugar

7 tablespoons (100g) unsalted butter, melted and cooled

a baking pan or roasting pan, about 9 × 13 inches, well greased

The first time I made this fruit-filled sourdough loaf, I gave a portion of the starter to Joy Skipper, who has assisted on this book, and she has made a new loaf every ten days since then. She has also passed on portions of her starter to friends and neighbors in the small Norfolk village where she lives, and the starter is now making its way around Britain.

"Most sourdoughs are too sour to my taste," she says, "but this is delicious."

Joy has also experimented with different flavorings for this loaf, and recommends replacing the golden raisins and apples with finely grated orange rind and prunes.

To make the starter: Put the flour in a large nonmetallic bowl and make a well in the center of the flour. Crumble the fresh yeast into the well in the flour. Then pour the water into the well and stir with a wooden spoon or your hand until the mixture is smooth. Stir the flour from the bowl into the yeast mixture to make a sticky batter.

Cover with a damp dish towel and let stand on the kitchen table or counter, at room temperature, away from drafts, so the batter absorbs the natural yeasts in the air. Stir the batter once a day for each of the next three days and re-dampen the dish towel if it gets dry. The starter is ready to use when it is gray and foamy.

DAY 1	Stir the starter you have made, or the starter you have been given. Add the sugar, flour, and milk to the starter in the bowl. Stir well, cover with a damp dish towel, and let stand overnight at room temperature, away from drafts.
DAY 2	Stir the starter well and re-cover with a damp dish towel.
DAYS 3 and 4	Do nothing. If the dish towel is dry, re-dampen it.
DAY 5	Stir the starter well and add the sugar, flour, and milk. Stir well again, cover with a damp dish towel, and let stand overnight at room temperature, away from drafts.
DAY 6	Stir the starter well and re-cover with a damp dish towel.
DAYS 7, 8 and 9	Do nothing. Re-dampen the dish towel if it is dry.
DAY 10	Stir the starter well and divide the mixture into four equal portions. Give two portions to friends with instructions, keep one portion for your next batch (see below), and use one portion to make the loaf.

To make the dough: Heat the oven to 350°F. Place one reserved portion of the starter in a very large mixing bowl. Add the flour, sugar, apples, golden raisins, oil, eggs, nuts, cinnamon, baking powder, salt, and vanilla to the starter. Mix with your hand or a wooden spoon. When all the ingredients are thoroughly combined, place the dough in the prepared pan and smooth the surface.

For topping: Sprinkle the top of the loaf with the brown sugar, then drizzle with the butter. Bake the loaf for 30 to 40 minutes, or until a wooden skewer inserted in the center comes out clean. Turn out onto a wire rack to cool completely.

TO KEEP A STARTER FOR THE NEXT BATCH: Add 1 teaspoon of granulated sugar to the portion of starter you are going to keep for your next loaf. Stir well, then store in a covered container in the refrigerator for up to one week. To make a fresh cake, begin at Day 1, using this starter.

SIMPLE SOURDOUGH

INGREDIENTS

Makes 1 large loaf

about 12oz (340g) bread dough (use My Favorite Bread, page 73), risen once and kept for at least 24 hours

2 cups (430ml) water from the cold tap

2 tablespoons (15g) sea salt, crushed or ground

2¾ cups (340g) stoneground whole-wheat bread flour

about 2¾ cups (340g) unbleached white bread flour, stoneground if possible

a baking sheet, greased

Sourdough breads are fascinating to make – you never quite know if they will turn out or how they will taste. They are made from a starter dough, which is either made from scratch or is a lump of dough saved from the previous loaf – plus flour, salt, and water.

To make a starter from scratch, you have to make a flour and water batter and let it ferment for several days, during which time it absorbs the yeasts naturally present in the atmosphere. It is this fermentation that produces the appealing sour taste characteristic of this bread. The flavor of the final baked loaf depends on the pungency and quantity of the starter, as well as on the rising time. Because the flavor becomes more pronounced the longer the dough is left, you can tailor the recipe to suit your taste.

When I don't have the time to get a good sourdough starter going – and it can take 5 days – I just cut off a lump of dough from a normal yeast-raised loaf and store it in a covered bowl on the kitchen table (or in the fridge if it's hot) for at least 24 hours. I then use this as my starter. The flavor of the first loaf made this way will be quite mild. If you want to have a sourer loaf, keep the lump of dough for up to 5 days in the fridge.

Sourdough bread is usually left in a cloth-lined basket for its final rising, then inverted onto a sheet for baking; however, this loaf is shaped and then risen and baked on the baking sheet.

Punch down the portion of bread dough, as it will have risen even in the fridge. Put the water into a large mixing bowl, add the salt, and stir until dissolved. Add the bread dough starter and mix using your hands. When the dough has broken down to make a lumpy batter full of strands and small pieces of dough, work in the whole-wheat flour. When thoroughly combined, gradually work in enough white flour to make a soft but not sticky dough.

Turn the dough onto a lightly floured work surface and knead thoroughly for 10 minutes – the dough changes and becomes firmer as you knead it, so it is important not to knead in too much flour at the very beginning. Return the dough to the bowl, cover with a damp dish towel,

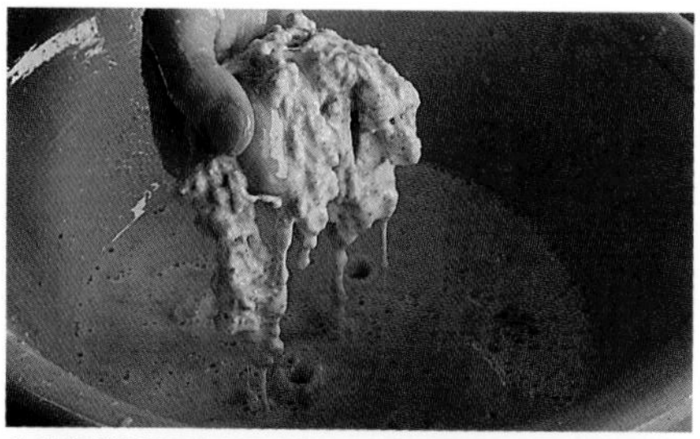

1 USE YOUR HANDS TO SQUEEZE AND MIX THE DOUGH STARTER INTO THE SALT WATER.

2 CONTINUE MIXING VIGOROUSLY TO BREAK DOWN THE DOUGH AND MAKE A LUMPY BATTER.

3 WORK IN THE WHOLE-WHEAT FLOUR. THE DOUGH WILL BE SMOOTH BUT STICKY.

4 ADD ENOUGH WHITE FLOUR TO MAKE A SOFT DOUGH THAT IS NO LONGER STICKY.

and let rise until almost doubled in bulk. In a cool room this will take around 12 hours, or 8 hours at normal room temperature.

Punch down the risen dough with your knuckles. Turn onto a lightly floured work surface and cut off a portion – about 12oz (340g) – to keep as the starter for the next loaf. Cover this starter and store in the fridge for up to 5 days. Shape the rest of the dough into a round or oval loaf (see page 75 or 78). If the dough seems at all sticky or very soft, work in a little more flour, otherwise the loaf won't hold its shape during baking.

Put the loaf onto the prepared baking sheet, then cover and let rise as before until almost doubled in size – 8 hours in a cool room, 4 hours at normal room temperature.

Preheat the oven to 450°F.

Slash the top of the loaf several times, using a very sharp knife. Bake for 20 minutes, then reduce the oven temperature to 400°F and bake for a further 15 minutes or until the loaf sounds hollow when tapped on the base. Transfer to a wire rack to cool.

The loaf will keep well for at least 5 days, and, when no longer at the peak of freshness, makes wonderful toast.

FRENCH SOURDOUGH LOAF

INGREDIENTS

Makes 1 large loaf

STARTER:

- 2 cups (230g) whole-wheat bread flour, preferably stone-ground
- about 1 cup (230ml) lukewarm water

SPONGE:

- ⅔ cup (140ml) lukewarm water
- 2 cups (230g) unbleached white bread flour

DOUGH:

- ¼ cup (55ml) lukewarm water
- 2¼ tablespoons (20g) coarse sea salt, crushed or ground
- about 2 cups (230g) unbleached white bread flour
- extra flour for dusting
- a round wicker basket, about 9 inches wide and 4 inches deep, lined with a heavy floured dry dish towel
- a baking sheet, heavily floured, or a loaf pan, about 10 × 5 × 3 inches, greased

This is my version of the delicious, thick-crusted, chewy loaf made popular by the Poilâne family in Paris. The huge loaves from their bakery in the rue du Cherche-Midi are baked in old, wood-fired ovens, which gives them a delicious, smoky flavor. The sourdough tang in this loaf is quite strong, and may not be to all tastes.

You can vary the flour in this recipe using any combination, including a little rye flour. The loaf is an excellent keeper, tasting better as it matures, and it is best thinly sliced. The first two or three batches will taste good, but will not rise as well as later batches when the starter is established. Eat within one week.

To make the starter: Mix together the flour and enough of the lukewarm water in a small bowl to make a very thick batter. Cover with a damp dish towel and let stand at room temperature, away from drafts, for three days, so it absorbs the yeasts in the air. (Re-dampen the dish towel when necessary.) After three days, the starter should be smelly, gray, and only slightly bubbly.

To make the sponge: Pour the starter into a large bowl. Then add the lukewarm water, stirring to dissolve any lumps in the starter. Add the white bread flour. Beat with your hand or a wooden spoon for about 1 minute to make a thick batter. Cover with a damp dish towel and let stand at room temperature, away from drafts, for 24 to 36 hours, or until it is spongy and slightly bubbly. (Re-dampen the dish towel when necessary.) The longer you leave the sponge, the more pronounced the sour taste will be.

To make the dough: Stir down the sponge. Beat in the lukewarm water and the salt. Then mix in enough white bread flour, about one handful at a time, to make a soft, but not sticky dough.

Turn out the dough onto a lightly floured work surface and knead for 10 minutes until firm, smooth, and elastic, adding more flour as needed. Return the dough to the bowl

OPPOSITE
I like to serve this country-style loaf with cheese and a full-bodied, dry red wine.

(no need to wash and oil the bowl). Cover with a damp dish towel and let rise at room temperature, away from drafts, until almost doubled in size, 8 to 12 hours.

Punch down the dough. Cut off 6 to 8 ounces of the dough (about 1 cup) and set aside for making the next starter (see below). Shape the rest of the dough into a ball and put into the cloth-lined basket, if using, or onto the prepared baking sheet. (The basket gives the loaf a nice round shape.) Or shape into a loaf to fit the prepared pan (see A Plain White Loaf, page 24). Cover with a damp dish towel and let rise at room temperature, away from drafts, until almost doubled in size, about 8 hours. Subsequent batches may take less time to rise.

To bake: Heat the oven to 425°F. If you used the basket, invert the loaf from the basket onto the prepared baking sheet. Using a sharp knife or a razor blade, slash the top of the loaf four times, or make two diagonal slashes across the top if you are baking the loaf in a pan. Sprinkle with a little white flour. Bake the loaf for 20 minutes. Then lower the oven temperature to 375°F and bake for 35 to 55 minutes longer, or until the loaf sounds hollow when tapped underneath. Transfer the loaf to a wire rack and cool completely.

TO KEEP A STARTER FOR THE NEXT BATCH: Put the reserved 6- to 8-ounce (about 1-cup) portion of dough into a greased plastic bag and store in the refrigerator for up to three days. Or place the dough in a small bowl, covered with a damp dish towel, and let stand at room temperature, away from drafts, for up to two days. (To keep the starter longer, see page 176.) To use for making a loaf, start at the sponging stage in the above recipe, and beat in a little extra lukewarm water to make a thick batter. Proceed with the recipe.

TO MAKE THE STARTER: STIR TOGETHER THE WHOLE-WHEAT BREAD FLOUR AND ABOUT 1 CUP LUKEWARM WATER TO MAKE A VERY THICK BATTER.

AFTER THREE DAYS, THE STARTER SHOULD BE SMELLY, GRAY, AND SLIGHTLY BUBBLY.

WHEN THE DOUGH HAS RISEN TO DOUBLE IN SIZE, HAVE READY THE BASKET WITH THE FLOURED CLOTH.

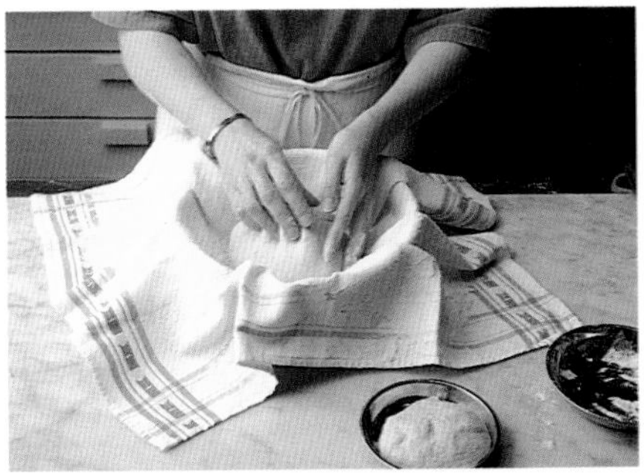

RESERVE 6 TO 8 OUNCES DOUGH FOR THE NEXT STARTER. SHAPE THE REST OF THE DOUGH INTO A BALL AND PUT IT INTO THE CLOTH-LINED BASKET.

AFTER THE DOUGH HAS RISEN AT NORMAL ROOM TEMPERATURE FOR ABOUT 8 HOURS IT WILL HAVE DOUBLED IN SIZE.

SLASH THE TOP OF THE LOAF FOUR TIMES, THEN SPRINKLE WITH FLOUR.

Gerry turns out his dough onto a floured surface for kneading.

GERRY'S SOURDOUGH RYE BREAD

INGREDIENTS

Makes 1 large loaf

STARTER:

2 cups (230g) rye flour

about 1¼ cups (280ml) lukewarm water

SPONGE:

1¼ cups (280ml) lukewarm water

about 2½ cups (280g) rye flour

DOUGH:

1 tablespoon salt

1–2 teaspoons ground caraway seeds, or to taste

2 tablespoons sunflower oil

2 cups (230g) whole-wheat bread flour, preferably stone-ground

2 cups (230g) rye flour

about 2 cups (230g) unbleached white bread flour

extra flour for dusting

a large, oval or round cast-iron casserole with lid, or an ovenproof enamel Dutch oven, greased

"For me, the only bread worth eating is sourdough. Everything else tastes like cake," says Gerry Turner of Bree, County Wexford, in Ireland. Gerry started baking his own bread in 1981, when he moved to Ireland. He had lived in Prague, where he met his charming wife Alice (page 158), and where he developed a liking for rye bread, particularly the sourdough variety.

"I invented a loaf to satisfy our tastes. It was trial and error for many weeks," he says. Part of his technique is to bake the loaf in a covered cast-iron casserole.

Gerry saves a quarter of his prepared dough to use as the starter for the next loaf. His dough is uniquely flavored with ground caraway seeds. A mortar and pestle, a clean coffee grinder, or a spice grinder will do the job nicely.

To make the starter: Mix the flour and water in a large bowl to make a stiff batter. Cover with a damp dish towel and let stand at room temperature, away from drafts, for four days to absorb the natural yeasts in the air. Re-dampen the towel as necessary. After four days, the batter should be very gray and foamy. (Gerry says you need strong nerves, and a good sense of smell is a disadvantage, as the batter will smell dreadful.)

To make the sponge: Stir down the starter in the bowl with a wooden spoon or your hand. Then add the lukewarm water, stirring to dissolve any lumps in the starter. Add enough rye flour to make a very thick, sticky batter – the exact quantity will vary depending on your flour. Sprinkle the surface of the batter with a little more rye flour to prevent a crust from forming. Cover with a damp dish towel and let stand in a cool place, away from drafts, until smelly and bubbly, about 18 hours.

To make the dough: Sprinkle the salt, ground caraway seeds, and sunflower oil evenly onto the sponge. Mix to make a very sloppy batter. Mix in the whole-wheat flour, then the rye flour. Mix in enough of the white bread flour, a handful at a time, to make a soft, but not sticky dough. Turn out the dough onto a floured surface and knead for 10 minutes, or until firm and elastic, adding extra white flour as needed. Cut off one-quarter of the dough and set aside for making the next starter (see below).

Shape the larger piece of dough into an oval or a round to fit the prepared casserole. Put the dough into the casserole and sprinkle with a little rye flour. Cover with the lid and let rise at room temperature, away from drafts, until doubled in size, 1 to 4 hours, depending on the vigor of your dough and the room temperature. When ready to bake, heat the oven to 400°F. Bake the loaf in the casserole, covered, for 50 to 70 minutes, or

OPPOSITE
A loaf just removed from the oven.

until the loaf sounds hollow when unmolded and tapped underneath. Turn the loaf out of the casserole onto a wire rack to cool.

TO KEEP A STARTER FOR THE NEXT BATCH: Grease the inside of a plastic bag. Put the reserved piece of dough in the bag and store in the refrigerator for up to three days to use for the next batch. (To keep the starter longer, see page 176.) To prepare the sponge: Put the reserved dough into a large bowl and pour in enough lukewarm water to cover. Let stand for 5 minutes. Then mix the water and dough together with your hands, squeezing the dough between your fingers. Beat in enough rye flour with your hand to make a very thick batter. Sprinkle the surface of the batter with a little rye flour to prevent a crust from forming. Cover with a damp dish towel and let stand in a cool place, away from drafts, until smelly and bubbly, about 18 hours. Proceed with the recipe.

PUMPERNICKEL LOAF

INGREDIENTS

Makes 2 small loaves
2½ cups (280g) rye flour, preferably coarsely stone-ground
1¼ cups (140g) unbleached white bread flour
1¼ cups (140g) whole-wheat bread flour, preferably stone-ground
2 teaspoons salt
1 0.6-oz cake fresh yeast (15g), or 1 envelope active dry yeast (2½ teaspoons)
1½ cups (340ml) lukewarm water
1 tablespoon packed light brown sugar
¼ cup (85g) unsulfured molasses
1 tablespoon vegetable oil, or 1 tablespoon butter, melted and cooled
extra flour for dusting
1 tablespoon potato starch
2 tablespoons boiling water

2 loaf pans, about 7 × 5 × 3 inches, greased

You cannot buy pumpernickel flour because it does not exist. Pumpernickel bread is actually made of a mixture of several flours, always including a high proportion of rye flour. The dark color of this dense, tasty bread is usually achieved both by tinting the dough with coffee, molasses, cocoa, or even liquid gravy browning and by long, slow baking. The loaf includes only a small amount of molasses, so it is lighter in color than breads made commercially. If you like a tangier-tasting loaf, replace some of the milk with an equal quantity of buttermilk. For a slightly sweeter taste, add ½ cup (85g) raisins to the dough before shaping it into loaves. Across northern Europe, pumpernickel is enjoyed with cured or smoked fish or meats, cheese, and soups.

Mix together the flours and salt in a large bowl and make a well in the center of the flour mixture. Crumble the fresh yeast into a small bowl. Stir in the lukewarm water until smooth. If using dry yeast, mix the granules and the 1 tablespoon brown sugar with half of the lukewarm water and let stand until foamy, 5 to 10 minutes (page 18). Stir in the remaining lukewarm water.

Pour the yeast mixture into the well in the flour. Add the sugar, molasses, and oil or melted butter to the well in the flour and mix these ingredients together with a small whisk or your hand. Mix the flour from the bowl into the liquid in the well with your hand or a wooden spoon to make a soft and slightly sticky dough. It will be difficult to work. Turn out the dough onto a lightly floured work surface and knead for 10 minutes until the dough becomes firm, smooth, and elastic. If necessary, add a little more rye and whole-wheat flours to prevent sticking. The dough will feel heavier than a non-rye dough. Return the dough to the bowl. Cover with a damp dish towel, and let rise at room temperature, away from drafts, until doubled in size, 2 to 3 hours.

Punch down the dough. Turn out the dough onto a lightly floured work surface and knead for 1 minute until it feels elastic. Divide the dough into two equal portions. Shape each into a loaf to fit the prepared pans (see A Plain White Loaf, page 24). Put the shaped dough, seam side down, into the prepared pans. Cover with a damp dish towel and let rise at room temperature, away from drafts, until doubled in size, 1½ to 2 hours. During the last 15 minutes of rising, heat the oven to 400°F.

Whisk together the potato starch and boiling water in a small bowl until smooth. Gently brush the risen loaves with the potato starch glaze. Bake the bread for 35 to 40 minutes, or until it is dark brown and sounds hollow when unmolded and tapped underneath. Turn out onto a wire rack to cool completely. Wrap in waxed paper, overwrap with foil, and keep at room temperature for at least one day or up to one week before slicing thinly.

ORANGE PUMPERNICKEL BREAD

INGREDIENTS

Makes 2 small loaves

2¾ cups (280g) rye flour, preferably coarse stoneground
1⅓ cups (170g) unbleached white bread flour
1 cup (110g) stoneground whole-wheat bread flour
2 teaspoons salt
1 0.6-oz cake fresh yeast (15g)
1½ cups (340ml) lukewarm water
2 tablespoons light brown sugar
¼ cup (85g) molasses
1 tablespoon vegetable oil or melted butter
the grated rind of 1 unwaxed orange
½ cup (85g) raisins

two small loaf pans, about 8½ x 4½ x 2½ inches, greased

NOTE You can use 1 package (¼oz/7g) active dry yeast instead of fresh yeast.

You can't buy pumpernickel flour – pumpernickel bread is made from a blend of several flours and grains. It always contains a fair proportion of rye flour, which accounts for its dense texture and strong flavor. Commercial loaves are often baked for several hours in a slightly steamy oven, which helps develop the dark rich color. This slightly sweet loaf is excellent with creamy cheeses and makes good open sandwiches – we enjoyed something very similar at the Rose Garden tea restaurant in the Huntington Botanical Gardens in Pasadena, California. Pumpernickel bread is also fine toasted and spread with butter and marmalade for breakfast.

Mix the three flours and salt together in a large mixing bowl and make a well in the center. Crumble the yeast into a small bowl and stir it to a smooth liquid with the water. Pour the yeast liquid into the well in the flour, followed by the sugar, molasses, and oil or butter. Mix together all the ingredients in the well, then work in the flour to make a soft and slightly sticky dough – it will be heavy and quite difficult to work.

1 COMBINE THE THREE FLOURS IN A BOWL, MIX TOGETHER, AND MAKE A WELL IN THE CENTER.

2 MIX THE YEAST LIQUID, SUGAR, MOLASSES, AND OIL TOGETHER IN THE WELL.

3 AFTER RISING, ADD THE RAISINS AND GRATED ORANGE RIND TO THE DOUGH AND KNEAD IN.

Turn the dough onto a lightly floured work surface and knead for 10 minutes. The dough will still be heavy but will have become firmer and more elastic. If you find the kneading hard work, cover the dough with the up-turned mixing bowl and take a breather for a few minutes before continuing. Return the kneaded dough to the bowl, cover with a damp dish towel, and let rise until doubled in bulk – about 3 hours at normal room temperature.

Punch down the risen dough with your knuckles, then turn it onto a lightly floured work surface. Sprinkle the orange rind and raisins over the dough and knead for a minute until evenly distributed. Divide the dough in half and shape each piece into a loaf to fit the pans (see page 76). Put into the prepared pans seam-side down. Cover with a damp dish towel and let rise until doubled in size: 1½–2 hours at room temperature.

Preheat the oven to 400°F.

Bake the risen loaves for 35–40 minutes or until they sound hollow when tipped out of the pan and tapped on the base. Turn out onto a wire rack to cool. When cold, wrap in wax paper, then in foil. Keep for a day before slicing.

OPPOSITE
Use slices of Scandinavian Rye Bread to make colorful open-face sandwiches.

ONION AND CARAWAY RYE BREAD

Extremely good with pickled, cured, and smoked fish, this light rye loaf tastes best one or two days after it has been baked. Replace the caraway seeds with toasted cumin seeds for a spicier, more fragrant loaf. This bread is best made with fresh yeast, so I have not given any instructions using dry yeast. Eat within four days of baking.

INGREDIENTS

Makes 1 large loaf

- 2½ cups (230g) rye flour
- about 3 cups (340g) unbleached white bread flour
- 1 tablespoon caraway seeds, or to taste
- 2 teaspoons salt
- 1 0.6-oz cake fresh yeast (15g)
- 1 teaspoon dark brown sugar
- 1½ cups (340ml) mixed lukewarm milk and water
- 1 medium onion, minced
- 2 tablespoons vegetable oil
- extra flour for dusting
- extra caraway seeds for sprinkling

a loaf pan, about 10 × 5 × 3 inches, greased

Mix together the flours, caraway seeds, and salt in a large bowl and make a well in the center. Crumble the fresh yeast into a small bowl. Stir in the brown sugar and the lukewarm milk and water until smooth.

Pour the yeast mixture into the well in the flour. With your hand or a wooden spoon, mix enough of the flour from the bowl into the yeast mixture in the well to make a thick batter. Cover with a damp dish towel and let stand at room temperature, away from drafts, until spongy, about 20 minutes (page 16). Meanwhile, sauté the onion slowly in the oil in a skillet until softened, but not browned, about 10 minutes. Let cool.

Add the cooled onion and any remaining oil in the skillet to the sponge in the well and mix together with your hand or a wooden spoon. Gradually mix the flour from the bowl into the sponge with your hand or a wooden spoon to make a soft, but not sticky dough.

Turn out the dough onto a lightly floured surface and knead for 10 minutes until firm, smooth, and elastic. Return the dough to the bowl. Cover with a damp dish towel and let rise at room temperature, away from drafts, until doubled in size, 2 to 3 hours.

Punch down the dough. Turn it out onto a floured surface and shape into a loaf to fit the prepared pan (see A Plain White Loaf, page 24). Place the dough, seam side down, in the pan. Cover with a damp towel and let rise at room temperature, away from drafts, until doubled in size, 1½ to 2 hours. During the last 15 minutes, heat the oven to 375°F. Gently brush the loaf with water. Sprinkle the top with caraway seeds.

Bake the loaf for 35 to 45 minutes, or until the loaf sounds hollow when unmolded and tapped underneath. Transfer to a wire rack to cool completely.

ADD THE COOLED ONION AND ANY REMAINING OIL TO THE SPONGE.

SPRINKLE THE TOP WITH CARAWAY SEEDS JUST BEFORE BAKING.

SCANDINAVIAN RYE BREAD

INGREDIENTS

Makes 1 loaf

- 1½ cups (170g) unbleached white bread flour
- 3⅓ cups (370g) rye flour, preferably stone-ground
- 2 teaspoons salt
- 2 tablespoons (30g) unsalted butter
- 1 0.6-oz cake fresh yeast (15g), or 1 envelope active dry yeast (2½ teaspoons) plus ½ teaspoon sugar
- ⅔ cup (140ml) lukewarm milk
- ⅔ cup (140ml) buttermilk
- 1 tablespoon barley malt extract
- 1 tablespoon black treacle or unsulfured molasses
- extra flour for dusting

a baking sheet, greased

Buttermilk and a high proportion of rye flour to white bread flour makes this bread the strongest tasting and most densely textured in this chapter. The dough is quite sticky to work and it will feel heavier than even an all-whole-wheat dough – but it is worth the effort. Barley malt extract is found at well-stocked health-food stores.

Wrap the loaf in waxed paper and keep for one day after baking. It will stay fresh for five days, or can be frozen for up to one month.

Mix together the flours and salt in a large bowl. Rub in the butter with your fingertips until the mixture looks like fine crumbs. Make a well in the center of the flour. Crumble the fresh yeast into a small bowl. Stir in the lukewarm milk until smooth. If using dry yeast, mix the granules and the ½ teaspoon sugar with the lukewarm milk and let stand until foamy, 5 to 10 minute (page 18).

Pour the yeast mixture into the well. Add the buttermilk, barley malt extract, and black treacle or molasses and mix these ingredients together. Mix the flour from the bowl into the liquid in the well with your hand or a wooden spoon to make a soft and sticky dough. If the dough is dry and crumbly, add a little more buttermilk, 1 tablespoon at a time. If the dough is too wet, add a little more white flour, 1 tablespoon at a time.

Turn out the dough onto a floured surface and knead for 10 minutes until firm, elastic, and smooth. Return the dough to the bowl. Cover with a damp dish towel and let rise at room temperature, away from drafts, until doubled in size, about 2 hours.

Punch down the dough. Turn out the dough onto a lightly floured work surface and shape into an oval loaf (see The Basic Loaf, page 17). Place the loaf on the prepared baking sheet. Using a sharp knife or a razor blade, slash the loaf down the center. Cover with a damp dish towel and let rise at room temperature, away from drafts, until doubled in size, about 1½ hours. During the last 15 minutes of rising, heat the oven to 400°F. Bake the loaf for 35 to 45 minutes, or until it sounds hollow when tapped underneath. Transfer to a wire rack to cool completely.

LIGHT RYE LOAF

Many rye breads are dark, pungent, and heavy, redolent of Eastern Europe, and ideal for eating with cured fish or smoked and cured meats. They can also be light, milder, more open-textured loaves that make good toast and sandwiches. This loaf, with its high proportion of white flour, is easy to work yet has the distinct taste of rye. And, of course, caraway seeds are the perfect partner to rye.

INGREDIENTS

Makes 1 large loaf

3¾ cups (450g) unbleached white bread flour
2 cups (230g) rye flour, stoneground if possible
1 tablespoon caraway seeds
1 tablespoon (5g) salt
1 0.6-oz cake fresh yeast (15g)
2 cups (430ml) water from the cold tap

a baking sheet, greased

Mix the flours, caraway seeds, and salt in a large mixing bowl and make a well in the center. Crumble the yeast into a small bowl and stir to a smooth liquid with ⅔ cup (140ml) of the water. Pour the yeast liquid and the rest of the water into the well in the flour. Gradually mix in the flour to make a soft but not sticky dough. Turn the dough onto a lightly floured work surface and knead thoroughly for 10 minutes. Return the dough to the bowl, cover with a damp dish towel, and let rise at cool to normal room temperature for about 2 hours or until doubled in bulk.

Punch down the risen dough with your knuckles, then turn it onto a lightly floured work surface. Shape into an oval by kneading it lightly. With the edge of your hand, make a good crease down the center of the dough oval, then roll the dough over to make an oval sausage. Turn the dough over on the work surface so the seam is underneath and the top looks smooth and evenly shaped. Put the shaped loaf, seam-side down, onto the prepared baking sheet. Cover and let rise until doubled in size – about 1 hour at normal room temperature.

Preheat the oven to 425°F.

Uncover the loaf and slash it several times across the top, using a very sharp knife. Bake for 15–20 minutes or until golden, then reduce the oven temperature to 375°F and bake for a further 20 minutes or until the loaf sounds hollow when tapped on the base. Cool on a wire rack. The loaf is best eaten within 4 days, and is also good toasted.

NOTE You can use 1 package (¼oz/7g) active dry yeast instead of fresh yeast, dissolving it in warm water. For rapid-rise dry yeast, mix it with the flours, caraway seeds, and salt. Then add the water and proceed.

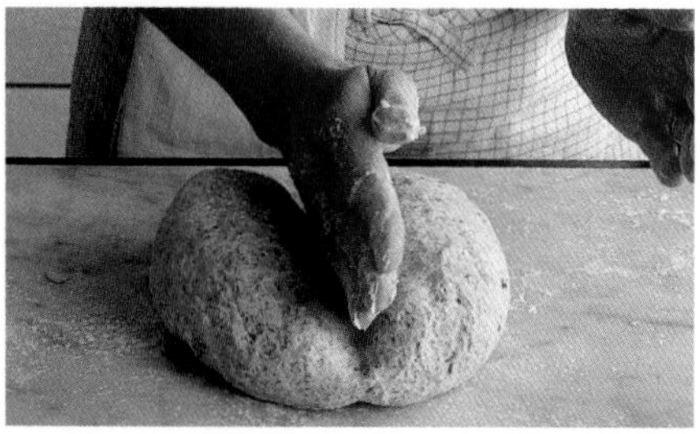

1 MAKE A DEEP CREASE IN THE CENTER OF THE LOAF WITH THE SIDE OF YOUR HAND.

2 ROLL THE LOAF OVER AND PUT ON THE BAKING SHEET, SEAM UNDERNEATH.

Rye breads of all sizes and shapes are baked in Eastern Europe. Here, in Old Plodiv, Bulgaria, a rye dough has been made into a decorative wedding loaf.

DANISH RYE BREAD

INGREDIENTS

Makes 1 large loaf
4½ cups (450g) rye flour
¾ cup (100g) unbleached white bread flour
½ tablespoon sea salt, crushed or ground
1 0.6-oz cake fresh yeast (15g)
⅔ cup (140ml) milk, at room temperature
⅔ cup (140ml) hot water
1 tablespoon molasses
extra flour for dusting

a large loaf pan, about 9 x 5 x 3 inches, greased

David Sharland, of the Savoy Hotel in London, made this loaf for a Scandinavian festival at the hotel when he was pastry chef. He is a big fan of good rye bread, and suggests keeping this well-flavored loaf at least a day before slicing.

Mix the flours and salt together in a large mixing bowl and make a well in the center. Crumble the yeast into a small bowl and mix to a smooth liquid with the milk. Stir the hot water and molasses together until the molasses dissolves. Pour the yeast liquid into the well in the flour, then add the molasses liquid. Quickly mix the flour into the liquids to make a heavy, sticky dough. It will be difficult to work. Because rye flour has far less gluten than wheat flour the loaf will be denser and will not rise as much as one made from all wheat flour.

Turn the dough onto a floured work surface and knead for 5 minutes – it will be hard work at first but the dough should become less sticky and more pliable. (You can always knead for a few minutes, then cover the dough and take a break for 5 minutes.) Shape the dough into a loaf to fit the pan (see page 76). Put the loaf into the prepared pan seam-side down. Using a fork, prick the loaf all the way through in four or five places. Cover the pan with a damp dish towel and let rise at normal to warm room temperature for 2½–3 hours or until almost doubled in size.

Preheat the oven to 450°F.

Bake the loaf for 15 minutes, then lower the oven temperature to 400°F and bake for a further 45–50 minutes or until the loaf sounds hollow when tipped out of the pan and tapped on the base. David recommends turning the loaf out of the pan about 15 minutes before the end of the baking time, and baking the loaf on the oven shelf so it will develop a good crusty finish. Transfer the cooked loaf to a wire rack to cool completely, then wrap in wax paper and foil and keep for a day before eating. The bread keeps well for up to a week.

NOTE You can use 1 package (¼oz/7g) active dry yeast instead of fresh yeast, dissolving it in warm milk. For rapid-rise yeast, mix it with the flours, then add the milk and proceed with the recipe.

ENRICHED DOUGHS

Rich, rich, rich. These are extravagant recipes, where white yeast dough is transformed into luxurious pâtisserie by adding what appear to be extravagant quantities of butter, eggs, or cream. Technique is all-important in working with these doughs – pastry chefs may practice for years before they are satisfied. Equally important are the ingredients. Because of the large amounts of butter, lard, or cream incorporated into these doughs, they must be of the very best quality and really fresh, untainted by "refrigerator smells" or exposure to air. I think firm, pale, and creamy-tasting unsalted butter, or "sweet" butter is best for enriching doughs. Unsalted butter from the French regions of Normandy or Brittany is particularly prized by European pastry chefs. In the States, look for unsalted butter graded AA; it will have the best flavor. Buy butter from a store store with a high turnover. Never try to substitute margarine for butter or coffee lightener for heavy cream, because the results will be disappointing, if not totally inedible. Whole-wheat flour does not lend itself to these recipes either.

As these doughs contain such a high proportion of fat, they have more yeast in proportion to the flour than usual to help them rise. It is wise to let the doughs rise fairly slowly at normal to warm room temperature because, if the room is too hot, the fat will melt and ooze out, and a soggy, heavy dough will be your result. Some soft doughs such as the one for croissants, need to be chilled before shaping, while others, such as brioche dough, are so soft they also need a mold to give them shape. The numerous fairly slow risings in these recipes help to give the breads their fine textures: Aberdeen Butteries (page 202), Michel Roux's Croissants (page 192), and Danish Pastries (page 195) are made like puff pastry, with crisp, flaky layers that should not be damp or doughy; Michel Roux's Brioche (page 203) has an even, fine crumb; Sally Lunns (page 200) have a delicate texture similar to a rich sponge cake, while Rum Babas (page 206) and Savarin (page 207) develop a honeycomb structure, like a bath sponge, ready to absorb plenty of flavored syrup. Lardy Cake (page 199) is a rich, sweet cake with layers of flaky dough.

OPPOSITE Michel Roux and croissants. *ABOVE A basket of freshly baked enriched breads.*

These recipes do take a lot of time and need a bit of practice, but the results are always worth eating and will provide you with a tremendous sense of achievement. You, too, can make croissants like Michel Roux!

MICHEL ROUX'S CROISSANTS

INGREDIENTS

Makes 16–18

3 tablespoons (40g) sugar

1 tablespoon (10g) coarse sea salt, crushed or ground

1 cup + 6 tablespoons (310ml) chilled water

1 0.6-oz cake fresh yeast (15g), or 1 envelope active dry yeast ($2\frac{1}{2}$ teaspoons) plus ½ teaspoon sugar

¼ cup (30g) dry milk powder

$4\frac{1}{2}$ cups (500g) unbleached white bread flour

1 cup + 5 tablespoons (300g) unsalted butter

extra flour for dusting

1 egg yolk beaten with 1 tablespoon milk for glazing

a triangular template, 7 × 7 × 6 inches

2 baking sheets that will fit in your refrigerator, lightly greased

A Meilleur Ouvrier de France, 1976, Pâtissier-Confiseur, Michel Roux is one of France's finest pastry chefs. He is also the owner of a Michelin three-star restaurant in England, the Waterside Inn, at Bray-on-Thames.

As you might suspect, Michel is a perfectionist who cares passionately about his work. He spent many hours developing this exquisite croissant recipe so it can be made at home without specialized pastry training or equipment. Making successful croissants is a challenge for even the most experienced home baker, so remember Michel's warning that "only practice makes perfect," and take it from me that it is worth the effort required to make these. You will not find a better recipe anywhere.

If you want to have freshly baked croissants for breakfast, cover the shaped and glazed dough with plastic wrap and let it rise very slowly overnight in the refrigerator. (The croissants should slowly double in size.) In the morning, let the dough stand at room temperature for about 30 minutes, then glaze again and bake. If the refrigerator is very cold, the croissants may not rise sufficiently overnight. In that case you will have to leave them at room temperature longer, until they are doubled in size.

Croissants are best eaten warm, soon after baking, or at least on the day they are baked. If that is not possible, however, croissants and Petits Pains au Chocolat (page 195) freeze well for up to two weeks. After baking, while they are still warm, place them in freezer bags and freeze immediately. To use, remove them from the bags and place them, still frozen, on a baking sheet. Bake at 500°F for 5 minutes, or until warmed through.

You can also freeze unbaked croissants for up to one week. Place the shaped croissants on a baking sheet as described below. Before glazing them and leaving them to rise, cover the baking sheet well with plastic wrap or a plastic bag and freeze. Then let them thaw in the refrigerator overnight, or at room temperature for 4 to 6 hours. When thawed, glaze and leave to rise until doubled in size. Glaze again and bake as in the recipe.

Dissolve the sugar and salt in ½ cup (110ml) of the cold water. Crumble the fresh yeast into a small bowl. Stir in the remaining water until smooth, then beat in the milk powder. If using dry yeast, heat the remaining water to lukewarm. Mix the yeast granules and the

MICHEL HAS ROLLED OUT THE DOUGH, LEAVING A ROUGH, 5-INCH SQUARE IN THE CENTER.

HE WRAPS THE DOUGH OVER THE BUTTER SO IT IS COMPLETELY ENCLOSED.

TO BEGIN FOLDING, HE TURNS THE DOUGH ON A LONG SIDE. HE THEN FOLDS THE RIGHT THIRD OVER INTO THE CENTER.

MICHEL THEN FOLDS OVER THE LEFT THIRD. THE COMPLETELY ENCLOSED SIDE OF THE DOUGH IS ON HIS LEFT.

AFTER THE THIRD CHILLING, HE ROLLS THE DOUGH INTO A 16 #AA 30-INCH RECTANGLE.

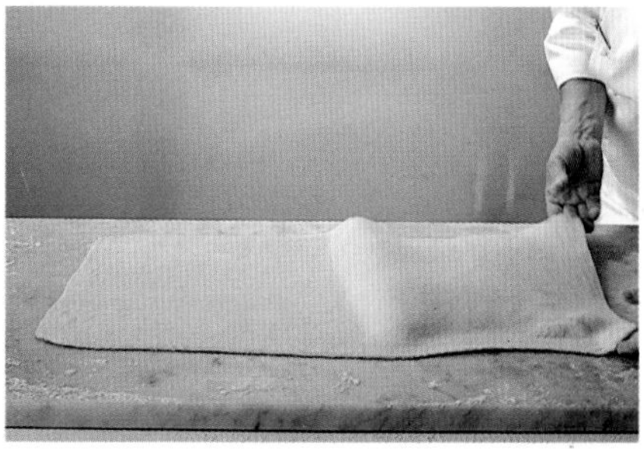

TO AERATE THE DOUGH, HE GENTLY LIFTS AND FLAPS IT AGAINST THE WORK SURFACE.

AFTER TRIMMING THE EDGES, MICHEL CUTS THE DOUGH LENGTHWISE INTO TWO STRIPS.

USING A LIGHTLY FLOURED KNIFE, HE CUTS EACH STRIP INTO EIGHT OR NINE TRIANGLES.

TO SHAPE A CROISSANT, MICHEL GENTLY STRETCHES OUT THE TWO SHORTER POINTS OF THE TRIANGLE.

STARTING FROM THE WIDE EDGE, HE ROLLS THE DOUGH TOWARD THE POINT. HE SHAPES IT INTO A CRESCENT AND PUTS IT ON A BAKING SHEET.

THE CROISSANTS THAT WILL BE CLOSEST TO THE OVEN'S HOT SPOTS ARE ARRANGED SO THE TIPS POINT TO THE CENTER

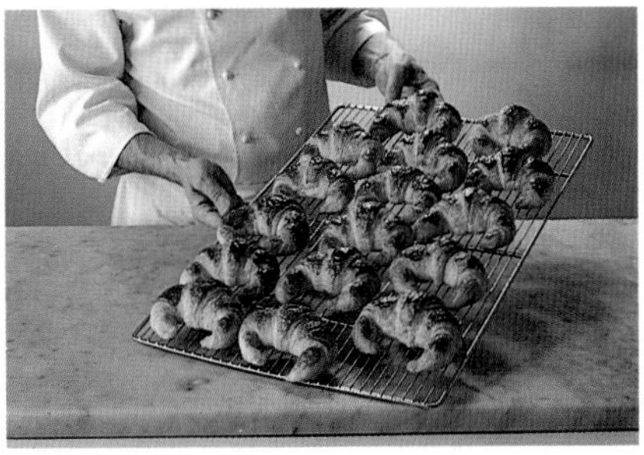

BAKED CROISSANTS WILL BE WELL RISEN AND GOLDEN BROWN. MICHEL COOLS THEM ON A WIRE RACK.

½ teaspoon sugar with the lukewarm water and let stand until foamy, 5 to 10 minutes (page 18). Beat in the milk powder.

Put the flour in the bowl of a heavy-duty stationary electric mixer. Using the dough hook and beating at low speed, beat in the sugar-salt liquid, then beat in the yeast mixture. Stop beating as soon as the ingredients are well mixed and the dough comes away from the sides of the bowl, which should not take longer than 1½ minutes. The dough will be soft and sticky, and it is important not to overwork the dough at this stage. Or, combine the flour, sugar-salt liquid, and the yeast mixture in a large bowl and beat with a wooden spoon until the dough is soft and sticky and comes away from the sides of the bowl, which should not take longer than 3 minutes.

Cover the dough with a damp dish towel and let rise in a warm place (about 75°F, but not more than 86F), away from drafts, until doubled in size, about 30 minutes.

Punch down the dough by quickly flipping it over in the bowl with your fingers to release the carbon-dioxide gases. Do not knead or overwork the dough, or the croissants will be heavy. Cover with plastic wrap and refrigerate for 6 to 8 hours, or until the dough slowly doubles in size. If the dough rises again after an hour, punch it down as above, re-cover, and return to the refrigerator.

If using sticks of butter, shape them into a 5-inch square by cutting the sticks in half lengthwise, arranging the pieces side by side, and mashing them together with your fingertips. Otherwise, using a rolling pin, gently roll and shape the butter into a 5-inch square. The butter must be firm, but still quite pliable, and about the same temperature as the dough when they are combined. If necessary, pound the butter between two sheets of waxed paper with a rolling pin to make it more pliable, or chill until it is firmer.

Punch down the dough. Turn it out onto a lightly floured work surface and shape it into a ball. Using a sharp knife, cut a cross in the top of the dough. Roll out the dough with a lightly floured rolling pin in four places, giving the dough a quarter turn to the left after each roll, making a rough circle with a thick, rough 5-inch square of dough in the center. Brush off any excess flour.

A French-style breakfast of freshly baked croissants and pains au chocolat. In France, butter-rich croissants are sometimes not shaped into crescents, but left straight like these. This custom developed after World War II when butter was in short supply and bakers were forced to make croissants with margarine instead. Shoppers were then able to tell at a glance what they were buying because a crescent shape indicated margarine had been used.

Put the butter on the rough square of dough. Fold the dough over the butter, tucking in the edges and making sure the butter is completely enclosed so it does not ooze out during the following rolling and folding processes.

Roll out the dough, rolling away from you, on a lightly floured surface with a floured rolling pin, into a 16 × 27-inch rectangle. Turn the dough rectangle so a long side faces you. Brush off any excess flour. Fold over the right third of the dough, then fold over the left third on top of the right third to make a three-layer dough sandwich with the completely enclosed side on your left. Use the rolling pin to seal the top, bottom, and right edges by pressing down on them. Wrap the dough in plastic wrap and chill for at least 20 minutes but no more than 45 minutes. Repeat the rolling, folding, and chilling twice more, turning the dough a quarter turn to the left so the enclosed side is on the bottom before each roll. Dust off excess flour.

After the third chilling, roll out the dough with a lightly floured rolling pin into a 16 × 30-inch rectangle, flouring the work surface very lightly as you roll.

Gently lift the dough and flap it against the work surface twice to aerate it and prevent shrinkage during baking, taking care not to spoil the shape of the rectangle. Using a large, lightly floured knife, trim the edges of the dough rectangle to neaten it, then cut the dough lengthwise into two equal strips. You can use a ruler as a guide if you like. Do not re-roll the trimmings – just bake as they are to enjoy as nibbles.

Lay the short side of the triangular template along one long edge of the dough and mark the outline with the back of the knife. Continue this way, using both pieces of dough, until you have marked out a total of sixteen to eighteen triangles. Then cut out the dough triangles. Marking out the triangles first helps prevent mistakes. If you feel confident, cut out the triangles without using the template, as Michel Roux does.

Arrange the triangles on the prepared baking sheets. Cover tightly with plastic wrap and refrigerate for a few moments: If the dough becomes too warm, it may soften and crack while the croissants are being shaped.

Place one dough triangle at a time on the floured work surface with the longest point toward you. (Keep the rest refrigerated.) Gently stretch out the two shorter points. Then, starting from the edge opposite the long point, roll up the triangle toward you; use one hand to roll the dough and the other to gently pull the long point. Make sure that this pointed end is in the center and tucked underneath it, so it will not rise up during baking.

As soon as the croissant is shaped; place it on a lightly greased baking sheet, turning the ends in the same direction in which you rolled the dough to make a curved crescent shape. Space the croissants about 2 inches apart. If your oven has a "hot spot," such as the back, arrange the row of croissants closest to it with the tips pointing towards the center of the sheet or the tips may dry out and burn.

Lightly brush the croissants with the egg glaze, brushing upward from the inside of the crescent, so the layers of dough do not stick together and prevent the croissant from rising properly during baking. Let the croissants rise, uncovered, in a warm (about 75°F), humid place, away from drafts, until doubled in size, 1 to 2 hours. During the last 15 minutes of rising, heat the oven to 450°F.

Very lightly brush the croissants in the same direction again with the egg glaze. Then bake for 15 minutes until golden brown, well risen, and slightly crisp. Lower the oven temperature to 400°F if the croissants are browning too quickly. Transfer them immediately to wire racks to cool, making sure they are not touching.

VARIATION: PETITS PAINS AU CHOCOLATE Croissant dough is also used to make these classic French breakfast rolls, which have a rich, dark chocolate filling. When you are in France, look out for the long, thin bars of couverture chocolate traditionally used for making these. Otherwise, use a good-quality semisweet chocolate.

After the third rolling, folding, and chilling, roll out the dough as for the croissants. Cut the dough into 6 x 4-inch rectangles. Place one or two thin squares of semisweet chocolate on one short end. Fold over the dough loosely to make a small, flattish cylinder. Arrange on a lightly greased baking sheet. Glaze with egg glaze. Let rise, uncovered, then glaze again, and bake as for Michel Roux's Croissants (above). Do not re-roll the trimmings – just bake them as they are to enjoy as nibbles.

DANISH PASTRIES

In Denmark, these crisp and flaky filled sweet pastries are called Vienna bread, or wienerbrot. This is because the method of interleaving yeast-bread dough with butter was brought to Denmark about 150 years ago by Austrian pastry chefs, who, in turn, had learned the technique from Turkish bakers working in Vienna. It was the Danes who added the sweet fillings to the pastries. The three fillings given here are the ones I like best, and you'll need to make all three to fill the four different Danish pastry shapes this recipe makes. If you prefer, you can create your own fillings: Try using a good conserve or jam; sweetened ground walnuts; almond paste; or cottage or farmers' cheese flavored with grated lemon rind and sugar. Vary the fillings and shapes to suit your fancy.

Whatever the filling, the baked pastries should be crisp, light, and flaky, not spongy or cake-like. After the dough has been rolled out, folded, and chilled three times, it can be wrapped well and left in the refrigerator for one day, or frozen for up to two weeks. These are best eaten on the day they are baked.

Golden Danish pastries shaped into twists, windmills, pinwheels, and envelopes.

INGREDIENTS

Makes about 28
- 4 cups (455g) unbleached white bread flour
- 1 teaspoon salt
- 1 0.6-oz cake fresh yeast (15g), or 1 envelope active dry yeast (2½ teaspoons) plus ½ teaspoon sugar
- ¾ cup (170ml) lukewarm water
- 4 tablespoons (60g) lard, vegetable shortening, or unsalted butter, chilled and diced
- 2 large eggs, beaten
- extra flour for dusting
- 1¼ cups (280g) unsalted butter
- Almond Filling (page 176)
- Vanilla Cream Filling (page 176)
- 1 egg, beaten, for glazing
- Apricot Filling (page 176)
- sliced almonds
- Glacé Icing (page 176)
- apricot jam, warmed and strained (optional)

4 baking sheets, greased

Stir together the flour and salt in a large bowl. Crumble the fresh yeast into a small bowl. Stir in the lukewarm water until smooth. If using dry yeast, mix the granules and the ½ teaspoon sugar with the water and let stand until foamy, 5 to 10 minutes (page 18).

Rub the lard, shortening, or butter into the flour with your fingertips until the mixture looks like fine crumbs, lifting your hand well above the bowl to toss and aerate the mixture. Make a well in the center of the flour. Add the yeast mixture to the well. Then mix the eggs into the yeast mixture in the well. Work in the flour from the bowl with your hand or a wooden spoon to make a soft, but not sticky dough. Turn out the dough onto a lightly floured work surface and gently knead for 2 minutes only. Wash and dry the bowl and oil it lightly. Return the dough to the bowl and turn the dough over so the top is oiled. Cover the bowl with a damp dish towel. Let the dough rise at room temperature, away from drafts, until doubled in size, about 1 hour.

Punch down the dough in the bowl. Cover with plastic wrap and chill in the refrigerator for 2 to 4 hours until firmer and chilled, but not hard.

If using sticks of butter, shape them into a 5-inch square by cutting the sticks in half lengthwise, arranging the pieces side by side, and mashing them together with your fingertips. Otherwise, using a rolling pin, roll and shape the butter into a 5-inch square. The butter must be quite firm, but still pliable, and about the same temperature as the dough when they are combined. If necessary, pound the butter between two sheets of waxed paper with a rolling pin to make it more pliable, or chill until it is firmer.

Turn out the dough onto a lightly floured work surface and shape it into a ball. Using a sharp knife, mark four evenly spaced points around the center, stopping about 1½ inches from the center. Roll out the four sections of dough with a lightly floured rolling pin, giving the dough a quarter turn after each roll and leaving a thick, rough 5-inch square of dough in the center. Brush off any excess flour.

Put the butter on top of the rough square of dough. Fold the dough over the butter, tucking in the edges and making sure the butter is completely enclosed so it does not ooze out during the following rolling and folding processes.

Roll out the dough, rolling away from you, on a lightly floured surface with a lightly

FOR THE ENVELOPES, SPOON VANILLA CREAM FILLING IN THE CENTER OF EACH SQUARE.

BRING THE CORNERS UP OVER THE FILLING TO MEET IN THE CENTER. PINCH THE ENDS TOGETHER FIRMLY.

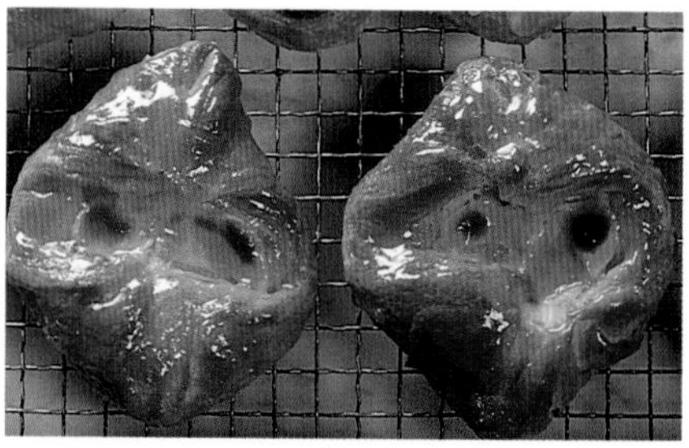

THE BAKED ENVELOPES WILL HAVE A SHINY FINISH IF THEY ARE GLAZED WITH APRICOT JAM.

FOR THE TWISTS, CUT THE FILLED, FOLDED DOUGH INTO NINE STRIPS.

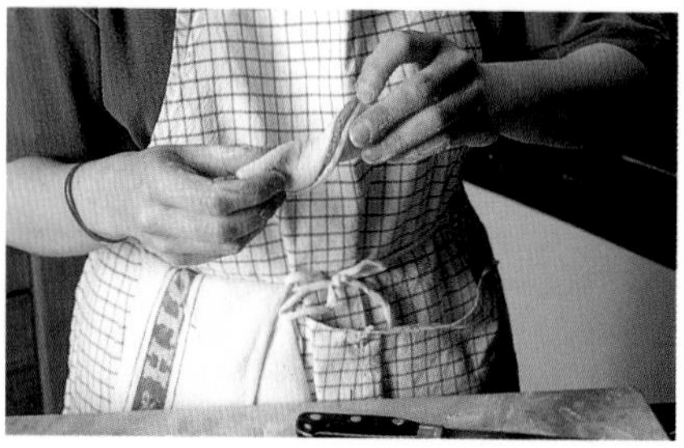

TO SHAPE THEM, TWIST EACH STRIP FIRMLY, TURNING THE ENDS IN OPPOSITE DIRECTIONS.

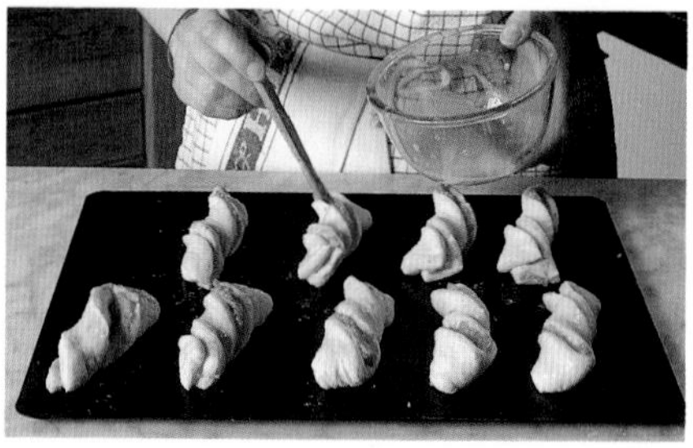

LET THE TWISTS RISE UNTIL ALMOST DOUBLED IN SIZE. THEN BRUSH WITH THE BEATEN EGG GLAZE.

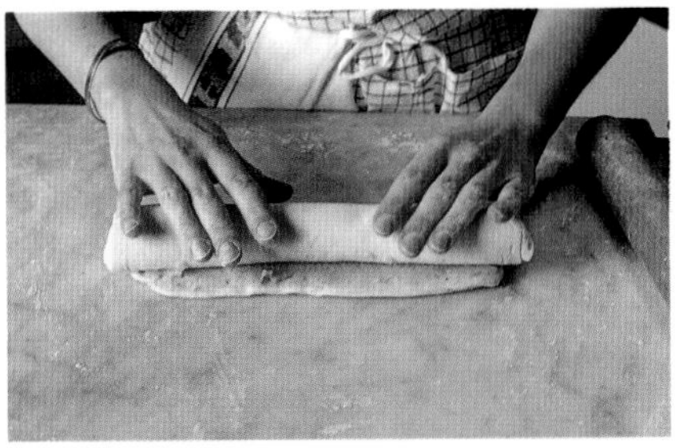

TO SHAPE PINWHEELS, ROLL UP THE FILLED DOUGH FROM A LONG SIDE, LIKE A JELLY ROLL.

USING A LIGHTLY FLOURED KNIFE, CUT THE ROLL INTO ELEVEN EVEN SLICES. ARRANGE ON A BAKING SHEET.

AFTER THE DOUGH HAS RISEN, BRUSH WITH THE EGG GLAZE AND SPRINKLE WITH SLICED ALMONDS.

BRUSH THE EDGES OF THE FILLED WINDMILLS LIGHTLY WITH BEATEN EGG GLAZE.

FOLD EVERY OTHER CORNER INTO THE CENTER. TWIST THE ENDS TOGETHER FIRMLY.

ARRANGE ON A BAKING SHEET, THEN LET THEM RISE UNTIL THEY ARE ALMOST DOUBLED IN SIZE.

floured rolling pin, into an 18 × 6-inch rectangle, with a short edge facing you. Brush off any excess flour from the dough's surface. Fold up the bottom third of the dough, then fold down the top third to make a three-layer dough sandwich that is 6 inches square with the completely enclosed side at the top. Use the rolling pin to seal the side and bottom edges. Wrap in plastic wrap and chill for 15 minutes. Repeat the rolling, folding, and chilling processes twice more. Each time, roll out the dough with the completely enclosed or folded side on your left.

Divide the dough into four equal portions. Then shape and fill the pastries, covering and chilling the portions you are not working with. Here are the shapes and fillings I used for the photographs.

To shape pinwheels, roll out one portion of the dough with a rolling pin to a 9 x 6-inch rectangle, with a long side facing you. Spread evenly with the Almond Filling, leaving a ½-inch border at the edges. Then roll up loosely from the long side, like a jelly roll. Using a lightly floured knife, cut into eleven even slices. Arrange with a cut side up on a greased baking sheet and cover with plastic wrap. Let rise at warm room temperature (about 75°F), away from drafts, until almost doubled in size, 45 minutes to 1 hour.

To shape the envelopes, roll out one portion of the dough with a rolling pin into an 8-inch square. With a lightly floured knife, cut into four equal squares. Put one-quarter of the Vanilla Cream Filling in the center of each square. Brush the corners with a little of the beaten egg glaze, then bring the corners over the filling to meet in the center. Pinch together firmly with your fingers to seal and enclose the filling. Arrange on a greased baking sheet and cover with plastic wrap. Let rise at warm room temperature (about 75°F), away from drafts, until almost doubled in size, 45 minutes to 1 hour.

To shape windmills, roll out one portion of the dough with a rolling pin to an 8-inch square. Cut into four equal squares. Using half the Apricot Filling, put 1 heaping teaspoonful in the center of each square. With a lightly floured knife, make a cut diagonally from each corner to within ½ inch of the center. Brush the edges with a little of the beaten egg glaze. Fold every other corner into the center and twist them together firmly to seal and partially enclose the filling. Arrange on a greased baking sheet and cover with plastic wrap. Let rise at warm room temperature (about 75°F), away from drafts, until almost doubled in size, 45 minutes to 1 hour.

To shape twists, roll out one portion of the dough with a rolling pin to a 9 × 6-inch rectangle. Spread evenly with the other half of the Apricot Filling, leaving a ½-inch border at the edges. Fold the dough in half lengthwise. With a lightly floured knife, cut crosswise into nine equal strips. Twist each strip firmly (some filling may ooze out), then arrange on a greased baking sheet. Cover with plastic wrap. Let rise at warm room temperature (about 75°F), away from drafts, until doubled in size, 45 minutes to 1 hour.

During the last 15 minutes of rising, heat the oven to 425°F. Lightly brush each pastry with the egg glaze, avoiding the cut edges. Sprinkle the pinwheels and twists with sliced almonds. Bake for 10 to 12 minutes, or until well risen and golden. Transfer to a wire rack to cool. You can leave them plain, or brush with a thin layer of strained, warm apricot jam and/or drizzle with Glacé Icing.

Almond Filling

Whisk 1 large egg white in a bowl until stiff peaks form. Fold in 2½ tablespoons (30g) sugar, ½ cup (40g) ground almonds, and 1 tablespoon kirsch or light rum, or a few drops of almond extract. Cover and refrigerate for up to one day until ready to use. Makes enough to fill eleven pinwheels, or four envelopes, or four windmills, or nine twists.

Vanilla Cream Filling

Heat ⅔ cup (140ml) half-and-half with half a split vanilla bean in a small heavy saucepan until scalding (bubbles will appear around the edges). Remove from the heat, cover, and let infuse for 15 minutes. Meanwhile, beat together 1 large egg yolk with 1 tablespoon granulated sugar and 1 tablespoon unbleached all-purpose flour in a small bowl until very thick and almost paste-like. Remove the vanilla bean from the half-and-half, scrape the seeds with the tip of a small knife into the half-and-half, and discard the bean. Whisk the warm half-and-half into the egg mixture. Rinse and dry the saucepan. Return the mixture to the saucepan and simmer over low heat, stirring constantly, until thick enough to coat the back of the spoon. Do not let the mixture boil. Scrape it into a small bowl and cover the surface with plastic wrap to prevent a skin forming. Let cool. Refrigerate for up to one day. Makes enough to fill four windmills or four envelopes; do not use for pinwheels or twists.

After the pastries have cooled, you can drizzle them with Glacé Icing, if you like. Here I am decorating baked pinwheels.

Apricot Filling

Drain a 14-oz can of apricots and purée the fruit in a blender or food processor. Put the purée in a small, heavy saucepan and simmer over medium heat until very thick, stirring frequently to prevent scorching. Let cool. Beat together 2 tablespoons (30g) softened unsalted butter, 2½ tablespoons (30g) sugar, and 1 teaspoon ground cinnamon in a small bowl until soft and smooth. Then beat in the purée. Add a few drops of lemon juice and extra cinnamon to taste, if you wish. Cover and refrigerate for up to one day until ready to use. Makes enough to fill eight windmills or eight envelopes; or eighteen twists; or four windmills and four envelopes and nine twists.

Glacé Icing

Mix 3 tablespoons sifted confectioners' sugar with 1 teaspoon warm water in a small bowl to make a smooth icing that leaves a trail when you lift the spoon. Makes enough to decorate eleven pinwheel Danish pastries.

An old-fashioned, British teatime favorite, yeasted Lardy Cakes are utterly delicious. The outside is crisp, crunchy, and slightly caramelized, while the layered inside is moist and flaky without being too sweet or heavy.

LARDY CAKES

INGREDIENTS

Makes 2 loaves

- 4½ cups (500g) unbleached white bread flour
- 1 tablespoon (10g) coarse sea salt, crushed or ground
- 1 0.6-oz cake fresh yeast (15g), or 1 envelope active dry yeast (2½ teaspoons)
- 1 cup + 3 tablespoons (240g) sugar
- 1 cup (230ml) lukewarm milk
- 1 large egg, beaten
- extra flour for dusting
- 1 cup (230g) lard, or ½ cup (110g) butter and ½ cup (110g) lard, at room temperature and diced
- 1½ cups (230g) mixed golden raisins and currants

2 deep 8-inch round cake pans or springform pans, greased

In the North of England, a good pinch of mixed sweet spice (akin to pumpkin-pie spice in the U.S.) is often added to this dough. In the West Country (the region in southwestern England that includes the counties of Devon, Somerset, and Cornwall), recipes insist on using good pork lard, a holdover from when lardy cake was a luxury saved for feasts, harvest suppers, and farm celebrations. Along with some bakers, I prefer to use half butter and half lard for a lighter texture and richer taste. The calories, however, remain the same.

For many years, I regularly bought lardy cakes from Wreford's, a small, old-fashioned bakery situated right on highway A303 near West Camel in Somerset. Just before their baker Chris Wreford retired, he showed me how to make his especially delicious lardies. This is his recipe, as he learned it from his father.

The cakes should be eaten within two days of baking, but are best warm from the oven, served thickly sliced. Lardy cake is also good toasted, and if you do not eat the second cake right away, it can be frozen, tightly wrapped in plastic wrap or a freezer bag, for up to one month. Thaw at room temperature for 4 to 6 hours, then unwrap, place on a baking sheet, and warm thoroughly in a 350°F oven for 10 minutes.

Mix together the flour and salt in a medium-size bowl. Make a well in the center of the flour. Crumble the fresh yeast into a small bowl. Stir in 1 teaspoon of the sugar and the lukewarm milk until smooth. If using dry yeast, mix the granules and the 1 teaspoon sugar with the lukewarm milk and let stand until foamy, 5 to 10 minutes (page 18). Add the yeast mixture to the well in the flour. Work in just enough of the flour from the bowl with a small whisk or a spoon to make a thin, smooth batter. Sprinkle the batter with a little of the flour to prevent a skin forming. Cover the bowl with a dish towel and let stand at room temperature until the batter becomes spongy and frothy, 20 to 30 minutes.

Add the eggs to the batter. Then gradually work in the remaining flour from the bowl with your hands or a wooden spoon to make a soft, but not sticky dough.

Turn out the dough onto a lightly floured work surface and knead for 10 minutes until smooth and elastic. Wash, dry, and lightly oil the bowl. Put the dough back into the bowl, then turn the dough over so the top is oiled. Cover with a dry dish towel and let rise at room temperature, away from drafts, until doubled in size, 1 to 1½ hours.

Punch down the dough and turn out onto a lightly floured work surface. Divide the dough into two equal pieces; cover one piece and set aside. Divide the lard (or the butter and lard mixture), the remaining sugar, and the dried fruit into two equal batches.

AFTER FOLDING UP THE BOTTOM THIRD OF THE DOUGH OVER HALF THE FILLING, FOLD DOWN THE TOP THIRD TO MAKE A THREE-LAYER DOUGH SANDWICH.

Roll out the uncovered piece of dough on a lightly floured surface with a lightly floured rolling pin into a 10 × 6-inch rectangle, with a short side facing you. Dot the top two-thirds of the dough rectangle with one-third of the first batch of lard, leaving a 1-inch border at the edges of the dough. Sprinkle with one-third of the first batch of sugar and one-third of the first batch of dried fruit. Fold up the uncovered bottom third of the dough over half the filling. Then fold down the top third of the dough to make a three-layer dough sandwich. Use the rolling pin to seal side and bottom edges. Give the dough a quarter turn to the left, so the completely enclosed side is on your left. Then repeat the whole procedure twice more, to make a total of three rollings, fillings, and foldings. Make sure to give the dough a quarter turn to the left each time.

Let the dough rest, uncovered, at room temperature for 5 to 10 minutes. Meanwhile, roll, fill, and fold the second piece of dough the same way, using the remaining batch of lard, sugar, and dried fruit.

Roll out each piece of dough on a lightly floured surface with a lightly floured rolling pin into an 8-inch square. Put a piece of dough into each prepared cake or springform pan, tucking under the corners, so the dough roughly fits the pan. Cover each pan with a damp dish towel and let rise at room temperature, away from drafts, until the dough has almost doubled in size and expanded to fit the pans, 45 minutes to 1 hour. During the last 15 minutes of rising, heat the oven to 425°F.

Just before baking, using the tip of a sharp knife or a razor blade, score the surface of each cake in a criss-cross pattern. Place each cake pan on a jelly-roll pan to catch any fat that may run out of the pans. Bake the cakes for 25 to 30 minutes until golden brown and crisp. Lower the oven temperature to 375°F if the cakes are browning too quickly. Unmold the cakes onto the jelly-roll pans, leaving them upside down. Bake for 5 minutes longer so the fat seeps downward and the bases (which are now on the top) have a chance to get crispy. Turn out onto wire racks to cool.

SALLY LUNNS

INGREDIENTS

Makes 2 cakes

a large pinch of saffron threads
¼ cup (60ml) milk
4½ cups (500g) unbleached white bread flour
2 teaspoons salt
1 0.6-oz cake fresh yeast (15g), or 1 envelope active dry yeast (2½ teaspoons)
1 teaspoon sugar
1 cup (230ml) heavy cream
4 large eggs
3 tablespoons sugar dissolved in 3 tablespoons boiling milk for glazing
clotted cream, lightly whipped cream, or unsalted butter for serving

2 deep 6-inch round cake pans (see Note), or 6-inch copper saucepans, well greased

This very rich, sponge-like cake is similar to the kugelhopf of Alsace (page 152). The dough is so soft it is worked in the bowl and must be baked in a deep pan, as it will not hold a shape.

Who or what was Sally Lunn? All sorts of tales surround the origin of the cake – that Sally Lunn sold cakes along the fashionable streets of Bath, England, in the 18th century; that she was a Bath pastry chef with a shop in Lilliput Alley; or that Sally Lunn is a corruption of "Soleil Lune," the French sun-and-moon cake, a yellow layer cake filled with white clotted cream. There are many versions of the recipe as well, all claiming authenticity. Some enrich the dough with eggs and melted butter, others add milk too, and some use cream. Saffron, the West Country's favorite spice, is often added, and Elizabeth David recommends grated lemon rind or ground mixed sweet spice in her recipe.

This is my favorite recipe for Sally Lunn. In the 18th century, 5-inch cakes were popular, but the larger pans I use in this recipe are easier to come by nowadays. Slices of this are delicious toasted. If you prefer, you may freeze the second cake. Before splitting and filling it, wrap the cooled cake well in plastic wrap and then in foil, or place it in a freezer bag. The cake will keep in the freezer for up to one month. Thaw, wrapped, at room temperature for 4 to 6 hours. Then unwrap, place on a baking sheet, and heat for 5 minutes in a 350°F oven. When the cake is warm, split and fill it as described.

Crumble the saffron into a small bowl. Heat the milk in a small saucepan until scalding (bubbles will appear around the edge). Then pour it onto the saffron, stir, and let stand to infuse until the milk is lukewarm.

Mix together the flour and salt in a large bowl. Crumble the fresh yeast into the saffron liquid. Then stir in the sugar until smooth. If using dry yeast, mix the granules and the sugar with the lukewarm milk mixture and let stand until foamy, 5 to 10 minutes (page

18). Make a well in the center of the flour. Add the yeast mixture to the well. Mix in enough flour from the bowl with your hand or a wooden spoon to make a thick, smooth batter. Sprinkle the batter with a little flour to prevent a skin forming. Cover the bowl with a damp dish towel and let the batter sponge and become frothy, about 15 minutes.

Whisk the cream and eggs together in a medium-size bowl, then add to the well in the flour. With a small whisk or a spoon, blend the cream and egg mixture into the yeast mixture. When thoroughly combined, gradually work in the flour from the bowl to make a very soft, sticky dough. Using your fingers, work the dough in the bowl for 5 minutes, or until it is glossy, smooth, elastic, and no longer sticks to your fingers.

Divide the dough in half. With lightly floured hands, shape each portion into a ball and place one in each of the prepared cake pans or saucepans. Cover them with damp dish towels and let rise at room temperature, away from drafts, until doubled in size, 1½ to 2 hours. During the last 15 minutes of rising, heat the oven to 400°F.

Bake the cakes for about 25 minutes until golden brown and firm. Cover the cakes with a piece of foil or parchment paper if they brown too quickly while baking. When turned out, a completely baked cake will sound hollow if tapped underneath. Turn out the cakes onto a wire rack, and immediately brush with the hot sweet glaze. Let stand until warm, then slice each cake horizontally into three layers. Spread each layer with clotted cream, whipped cream, or good unsalted butter and reassemble. Eat immediately.

NOTE: The 6-inch cake pans called for in this recipe may be purchased at cookware or specialty bakeware stores that sell supplies for making wedding cakes, or by mail order. See List of Suppliers (page 360).

With its rich, sponge-like texture, Sally Lunn can be served plain, or sliced into layers and filled with clotted cream or whipped cream. A more simple presentation would be to spread unsalted butter between the layers.

A delicious Scottish breakfast of warm butteries served with homemade preserves and a pot of tea.

ABERDEEN BUTTERIES

INGREDIENTS

Makes 20

- 6 cups (680g) unbleached white bread flour
- 2 tablespoons (15g) coarse sea salt, crushed or ground
- 1 0.6-oz cake fresh yeast (15g), or 1 envelope active dry yeast (2½ teaspoons) plus ½ teaspoon sugar
- 2 cups (430ml) lukewarm water
- 1 tablespoon sugar
- extra flour for dusting
- ¾ cup (170g) butter, at room temperature
- ¾ cup (170g) lard, at room temperature
- a 3-inch round or oval biscuit or cookie cutter

2-3 baking sheets, lightly floured

These Scottish pastries are delicious served warm for breakfast, with unsalted butter and orange marmalade. All the bakers in Aberdeenshire aim to make pastries that are crisp, flaky, and rich.

Stir together the flour and salt in a large bowl. Crumble the fresh yeast into a small bowl. Stir in the lukewarm water and sugar until smooth. If using dry yeast, mix the granules and the sugar with the lukewarm water and let stand until foamy, 5 to 10 minutes (page 18). Make a well in the center of the flour. Add the yeast mixture to the well. Work in the flour from the bowl and mix to make a soft, but not sticky dough.

Turn out the dough onto a lightly floured work surface and knead for 10 minutes, or so until the dough is smooth and elastic. Wash and dry the bowl. Return the dough to the bowl. Cover the bowl with a damp dish towel and let rise at room temperature, away from drafts, until doubled in size, 1½ hours.

In a small bowl, mash together the butter and lard. Then divide it into three batches. Punch down the dough. Roll out the dough, rolling away from you, on a lightly floured surface with a lightly floured rolling pin, to an 18 x 6-inch rectangle, with a short side facing you. Dot the top two-thirds of the dough rectangle with one batch of the butter and lard mixture, leaving a ½-inch border at the edges. Fold the uncovered bottom third of the rectangle up over half the fat, then fold the top third of the rectangle down to make a three-layer dough sandwich about 6 inches square, with the completely enclosed side at the top. Seal the side and bottom edges by pressing down with a rolling pin. Wrap the dough in plastic wrap and refrigerate for 30 minutes. Repeat the rolling, filling, folding, and chilling processes twice more. Each time, roll out the dough with the completely enclosed side to your left. After the last folding, tightly cover the dough. Then, for easiest handling, chill at least a day, or overnight, before cutting.

Roll out the dough to a circle about ¾ inch thick. Leave to rest, uncovered, for 5 minutes. Brush off the excess flour. Using a floured biscuit or cookie cutter, stamp out about twenty rounds or ovals. Place the cutouts, upside down and apart, on the prepared baking sheets. Cover with plastic wrap. Let stand until slightly risen, about 20 minutes. Meanwhile, heat the oven to 400°F. Bake them for 20 to 25 minutes, or until golden brown and crisp. Transfer to wire racks.

MICHEL ROUX'S BRIOCHE

INGREDIENTS

Makes 1 large brioche
1 0.6-oz cake fresh yeast (15g), or 1 envelope active dry yeast (2½ teaspoons) plus ½ teaspoon sugar
5 tablespoons (70ml) lukewarm milk
2 tablespoons (15g) coarse sea salt, crushed or ground
4½ cups (500g) unbleached white bread flour
6 large eggs, beaten
1½ cups + 1 tablespoon (355g) unsalted butter, softened
2½ tablespoons (30g) sugar
extra flour for dusting
1 egg yolk lightly beaten with 1 tablespoon milk for glazing

a large brioche mold, 9½ inches wide at the top and 4½ inches across the base, greased, or a 7-inch round copper saucepan, greased

"The perfect golden brioche has a delicious rich, buttery flavor, yet it does not leave a trace of butter on your fingers or an aftertaste on the palate," says Michel Roux (page 192).

He likes to use 355g of butter to 500g of flour when he makes brioche; pastry chefs vary the quantity from 110g of butter right up to an extravagant 500g of butter without altering the quantity of flour, but these variations depend on how the brioche is to be used. The most common proportion is half the amount of butter to flour. But remember, the best, freshest unsalted butter is vital for good flavor, whatever quantity of butter you use.

The fine, sponge cake-like crumb of a brioche is achieved through three risings, two at normal room temperature and one in the refrigerator. (If the rising is done at two warm a temperature, the butter will melt and ooze out of the dough.) The soft, rich dough is then chilled before it is shaped, so the dough is firm enough to maintain its distinctive top-heavy shape.

Although brioches are usually eaten warm with butter and preserves for breakfast, firmer, plainer doughs are used for savory dishes such as Alyson Cook's Brie en Brioche (page 115), or for sweeter pastries such as the Fancy Ring Doughnuts (page 97). Richer brioches can be hollowed out and filled with sautéed wild mushrooms or seafood in a spicy or creamy sauce.

Michel Roux says, "For a real treat, cut the brioche into slices, sprinkle with confectioners' sugar, and glaze under a very hot broiler. Serve the slices by themselves for breakfast or, as a monstrous indulgence, warm, with chocolate mousse." He adds that brioche looks very impressive if braided or formed into a crown shape.

Brioche dough can be frozen, wrapped in a freezer bag, after it has risen and been punched down, but before it is shaped. To use, let the dough thaw gradually in the refrigerator for 4 to 5 hours, then proceed with the recipe.

Crumble the fresh yeast into the bowl of a large stationary electric mixer fitter with a dough hook or a large bowl, if mixing by hand. Stir in the lukewarm milk and salt until smooth. If using dry yeast, mix the granules and the ½ teaspoon sugar with the lukewarm milk and let stand until foamy, 5 to 10 minutes (page 18). Stir in the salt.

Add the flour and eggs to the yeast mixture and beat with the dough hook to form a

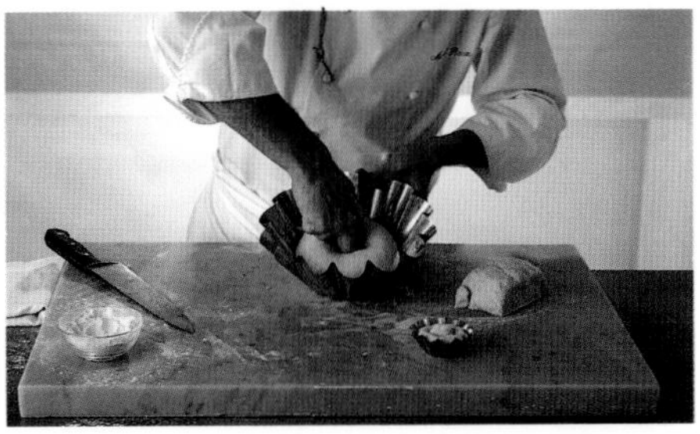

USING HIS FINGERS, MICHEL FORMS A DEEP INDENTATION IN THE LARGE PIECE OF DOUGH IN THE BRIOCHE MOLD.

THE INDENTATION SHOULD EXTEND ALMOST TO THE BOTTOM OF THE MOLD.

HE ROLLS THE SMALLER PIECE OF DOUGH INTO AN ELONGATED PEAR SHAPE.

HE GLAZES THE TOP OF THE RISEN BRIOCHE.

AFTER THE DOUGH HAS RISEN, USING SCISSORS THAT HAVE BEEN DIPPED IN COLD WATER, MICHEL SNIPS ALL AROUND THE EDGE.

WHEN UNMOLDED, BRIOCHES AND MINI BRIOCHE HAVE DISTINCTIVE SHAPES.

soft dough. Then knead the dough with the dough hook until it is smooth and elastic, about 10 minutes. Or, if mixing by hand, stir the flour and eggs into the yeast mixture. With a sturdy wooden spoon or your hand, beat until the dough is smooth and elastic, about 20 minutes.

Beat together the softened butter and sugar in a medium-size bowl until light and fluffy. Beating at low speed, add the butter mixture to the dough, a little at a time, making sure it is completely incorporated after each addition. If you are working by hand, or if the dough feels stiff and it takes a long time to add the butter with the mixer, squeezer the butter mixture into the dough with your hands. Then, continue beating with the dough hook for about 5 minutes, or by hand for 15 minutes, until the dough is perfectly smooth, glossy, shiny, and fairly elastic.

Cover the bowl with a damp dish towel. Let the dough rise at room temperature, away from drafts, until doubled in size, 1¾ to 2 hours.

Punch down the dough by flipping it over quickly with your fingertips not more than two or three times. Return the dough to the bowl. Cover with a damp dish towel and refrigerate for several hours, but not more than 24 hours.

Turn out the dough onto a lightly floured work surface and shape it into a large ball. To make the brioche in a mold, cut off one-third of the dough to make the topknot. Shape the larger piece of dough into a ball and place it in the prepared mold. Form a deep indentation in the center with your fingers, almost down to the bottom of the mold. With your palm held at an angle against the work surface, roll the smaller piece of dough into an elongated pear shape with a narrow neck.

Using lightly floured fingertips, gently press the narrow neck well down into the hole in the center of the large ball.

If you are using the saucepan, line it with a sheet of buttered parchment paper twice the height of the pan. Shape all the dough into a ball, then place in the pan. The brioche will bake into a tall, cylinder shape.

Lightly brush the top of the brioche with egg glaze, working from the outside inward. Take care not to let any glaze run into the crack between the main body of the dough and the topknot, or onto the edges of the mold, because it will prevent the dough from rising properly. Cover with plastic wrap.

Let the dough rise at room temperature, away from drafts, until almost doubled in size, 1½ to 2 hours; it may take an hour or so longer if the dough has been chilled 24 hours. During the last 15 minutes of rising, heat the oven to 425°F.

Glaze the brioche again. Using scissors dipped in cold water, snip all around the edges so the dough doesn't stick to the pan to help it rise properly in the oven. Bake for 40 to 45 minutes, or until the brioche is golden brown and sounds hollow when tapped underneath. If the brioche is browning too quickly, cover loosely with foil. Carefully unmold the brioche and transfer to a wire rack to cool.

VARIATION: MINI BRIOCHES You can use the same dough to make individual, mini brioches. Lightly butter twenty small brioche molds measuring 3¼ inches wide at the top and 1½ inches wide at the base (5 fluid ounce capacity). Weigh the dough and divide it into twenty equal pieces, or roll it into a fat rope and cut it into twenty equal pieces. Shape as for the large brioche, above. Glaze, cover with plastic wrap, and let rise at room temperature, away from drafts, until doubled in size, about 1 hour. Glaze again. Bake in a 425°F oven for about 8 minutes, or until the brioches are golden brown and sound hollow when tapped underneath. Cool on a wire rack.

BABAS AND SAVARINS

A very light, yeasty dough that produces a holey crumb is used to make babas and savarins because it soaks up sugar syrup like a bath sponge. The final result is a thoroughly sodden, cake-like dessert that is, nevertheless, light in texture, never heavy.

Babas are said to have been "invented" in the mid-17th century by Duke Stanislas of Lorraine, who dunked his stale kugelhopf in a rum syrup. He was so taken by his creation, according to the legend, he named it after Ali Baba, his favorite character in A Tale of a Thousand and One Nights. Dome-topped babas are usually baked in individual bucket-shaped baba or dariole molds, then soaked in syrup flavored with rum, although you can use other liqueurs. Kirsch is delicious, especially if you slice strawberries into the reserved syrup to serve with the babas.

Savarins, on the other hand, are ring shaped, large or small. They are made without the currants that are generally included in babas, although the savarin dough is often flavored with other fruit additions, such as grated lemon or orange rind or chopped candied fruit, which are added after the butter is incorporated. The soaking syrup is enhanced with grated lemon or orange rind; spices, such as cinnamon or cardamom; or liqueurs, such as kirsch, rum, Grand Marnier, Cointreau, or Cognac.

A savarin is especially delicious served with a filling in the center of the ring. Try sweetened, vanilla-flavored whipped cream, fruit salad, or poached fruit. Savarins are usually decorated with candied cherries and angelica that has been cut into leaves, but I prefer to do without these ornamental extras.

Correct rising is vital when you make babas and savarins. Not enough time and the dough will be heavy; too much time and the dough will run over the top of the mold during baking. Also, make sure the dough rises in a spot that is warm, but not hot.

Babas and savarins keep well, tightly wrapped, for up to 24 hours. They can also be baked and stored in an airtight container for two or three days, or wrapped and frozen for one month. If frozen, unwrap them, place them still frozen on baking sheets, and reheat in a 350°F oven for 10 to 12 minutes for babas, 15 to 20 minutes for savarins. Baste them with hot syrup shortly before serving.

Saturated with a lemon- or orange-flavored sugar syrup and filled with fresh fruit, a savarin makes a dessert that is as impressive looking as it is delicious. It is ideal to serve for a dinner party. I have filled this one with fresh strawberries and oranges but you can use any fruit.

JUST BEFORE SERVING, SPOON THE RUM OVER EACH BABA.

RUM BABAS

This recipe is adapted from one taught at L'Ecole de Cuisine La Varenne, which is based at the Château du Fey, in France's Burgundy region.

INGREDIENTS

Makes 8
4 cups (230g) unbleached white bread flour
1 teaspoon salt
1½ tablespoons sugar
1 0.6-oz cake fresh yeast (15g), or 1 envelope active dry yeast (2½ teaspoons) plus ½ teaspoon sugar
3 tablespoons lukewarm milk
3 large eggs, beaten
¼ cup (60ml) dark rum
3 tablespoons water
½ cup (70g) currants
½ cup (110g) unsalted butter, softened
SYRUP:
2½ cups (500g) sugar
1 quart (1 liter) water
6 tablespoons dark rum

8 baba molds of 8½ fl oz (245ml) capacity

Stir together the flour, salt, and sugar in a large bowl. Crumble the fresh yeast into a small bowl. Stir in the lukewarm milk until smooth. If using dry yeast, mix the granules and the ½ teaspoon sugar with the lukewarm milk and let stand until foamy, 5 to 10 minutes (page 18). Make a well in the center of the flour. Add the yeast mixture to the well. Then mix the eggs into the yeast mixture. Using your hand, work in the flour from the bowl to make a smooth, very thick batter-like dough.

Knead the dough in the bowl by beating it with your hand. Tilt the bowl slightly and, using your hand like a spoon with fingers together and palm upward, lift the dough and throw it back into the bowl with a slapping motion. Continue kneading for 5 minutes, or until the dough becomes very elastic, smooth, and slightly stiffer.

Cover the bowl with a damp dish towel. Let rise in a warm place (about 75°F), away from drafts, until doubled in size, 45 minutes to 1 hour. Meanwhile, warm the rum and water in a small saucepan. Add the currants and let them soak. Butter the molds and chill them in the freezer for 10 minutes. Butter them again. This double buttering helps prevent the soft, rich dough from sticking; the butter sets and does not get absorbed by the dough as it rises. If the kitchen is very hot and the butter starts to melt, put the molds in the refrigerator; otherwise, leave them at room temperature.

Punch down the risen dough in the bowl. Using your hand as before, gradually beat in the softened butter until the dough, like a very thick batter, is smooth and even, not streaky. Drain the currants and work them into the dough.

Drop the dough from an ungreased metal spoon into the molds, filling each one-third full. Arrange the molds on a baking sheet and cover with a damp dish towel. Let rise at warm room temperature (about 75°F), away from drafts, until the dough rises almost to the top of the molds, 30 to 50 minutes. Check to make sure the dough is not sticking to the cloth. During the last 15 minutes of rising, heat the oven to 400°F.

Bake the babas on the baking sheet for about 20 to 30 minutes, or until they are golden brown and begin to shrink from the sides of the molds. Unmold them onto a wire rack and let cool.

To make the syrup, stir together the sugar and water in a medium-size saucepan over low heat until the sugar is dissolved. Bring to a boil and let boil for 2 to 3 minutes, or until the syrup becomes clear.

Remove the pan from the heat. Add the babas, one or two at a time, to the very hot syrup. Using a large slotted spoon, gently turn them over several times to make sure they absorb as much syrup as possible; they will swell and become very shiny. Using the slotted spoon, carefully lift the babas out of the syrup and onto a plate. Soak the remaining babas. Reserve the remaining syrup. Just before serving, sprinkle the babas with the rum. Add any remaining rum to the reserved syrup and serve separately for spooning over the babas.

VARIATIONS: MINI RUM BABAS Grease about sixteen small baba molds or 4½ fl oz (125ml) capacity, dariole molds, or muffin pans. Make the baba batter as above. Butter and fill the molds as above. Cover with a damp dish towel. Let rise at warm room temperature (about 75°F), away from drafts, until the dough has risen almost to the top of the molds, 20 to 45 minutes. Bake in a 400°F oven for 18 to 20 minutes. Then cool and soak with the syrup and sprinkle with the rum as described above.

GRAND BABA In Alsace and Lorraine, whole giant babas are served at parties or celebration meals. Make the baba batter as above, but let it rise in a well-buttered 9-inch kugelhopf mold and then bake in a 400°F oven for 40 to 45 minutes. Cool and soak with the syrup and sprinkle with the rum as described above.

SAVARIN

Make the Rum Baba batter as opposite, omitting the currants and their rum soak. Butter a large 5-cup (1.15 liter) ring or savarin mold or two smaller 1½-cup (340ml) ring molds, as described in the baba recipe. Fill the mold or molds one-third full with the batter. Let rise at warm room temperature, away from drafts, for 30 to 50 minutes, or until the dough is almost to the top of the mold. Bake in a 400°F oven for 20 to 25 minutes until it is golden and shrinks from the sides of the mold. Unmold it onto a wire rack.

Make the sugar syrup as for Rum Baba (opposite) in a large, shallow pan, adding the finely grated rind and juice of 1 large lemon when the syrup is removed from the heat. If the savarin fits, place it in the very hot syrup in the pan and spoon the syrup over it until it is saturated. If the savarin is too big for the pan, put it on a wire rack set over a jelly-roll pan and spoon the hot syrup over it, reheating any syrup that drips onto the pan and spooning it over the savarin, until all the syrup is absorbed. The savarin will swell and look very shiny.

Just before serving, sprinkle 3 to 4 tablespoons amber or dark rum over the savarin. Fill the center with whipped cream that has been sweetened to taste and flavored with vanilla, or with fresh fruit salad.

THE DOUGH WILL RISE ALMOST TO THE TOP OF THE MOLD.

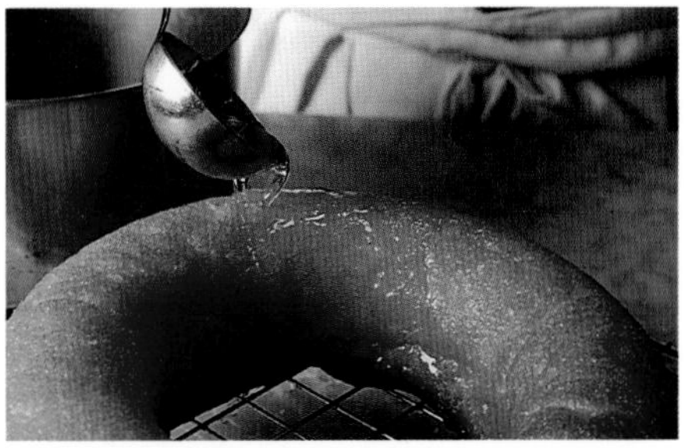

SPOON THE HOT SYRUP OVER THE FRESHLY BAKED SAVARIN.

BRIOCHE

INGREDIENTS

Makes 1 large or 2 medium brioches or 20 small brioches
1 0.6-oz cake fresh yeast (15g)
4 tablespoons lukewarm milk
1½ teaspoons salt
3½ cups (500g) unbleached white bread flour
5 eggs, beaten
1 cup (250g) unsalted butter, at room temperature
2 tablespoons (60g) sugar
⅔ cup (110g) raisins, or good semisweet chocolate, chopped (optional)
1 egg, lightly beaten, for glazing

a large brioche mold, 9½ inches wide at the top, or a large loaf pan, about 9 x 5 x 3 inches, greased (see recipe) OR two medium brioche molds, 6½ inches wide at the top, or small loaf pans, about 8½ x 4½ x 2½ inches, greased OR 20 small brioche molds 3½ inches wide at the top, greased

With its slightly sweet, luxuriously buttery taste and fine sponge-like crumb, the brioche is half-way between bread and cake. It is delicious eaten warm with butter for breakfast or tea. The fine texture of the crumb is achieved by using good fresh unsalted butter and by giving the dough three risings. Two of these should be at normal room temperature – too warm and the butter will melt and ooze out of the dough; the other rising is in the fridge to make the soft, rich dough firm enough to maintain its shape. The dough can be left plain, or flavored with raisins and grated orange rind or with chunks of chocolate.

Here I've adapted the best recipe I know for brioche: it comes from the Michelin Three-Star chef, Michel Roux, and uses an electric mixer to cut out the hard work.

Crumble the yeast into the warm milk and pour into the bowl of an electric mixer fitted with a dough hook. Add the salt, flour, and eggs, and mix to a soft dough. Then knead, still using the dough hook, for about 10 minutes or until the dough is smooth and elastic. Alternatively, you can combine all the ingredients in a large mixing bowl and knead the dough

1 MIX THE YEAST LIQUID, SALT, FLOUR, AND BEATEN EGGS INTO A SOFT DOUGH.

2 AFTER BEATING IN THE BUTTER AND SUGAR, THE DOUGH WILL BE GLOSSY AND ELASTIC.

3 FLOUR YOUR KNUCKLES AND PUNCH THE CENTER OF THE RISEN DOUGH.

4 MAKE A HOLE IN THE CENTER OF THE DOUGH BALL TO HOLD THE SHAPED "TOPKNOT."

5 AFTER THE SECOND RISE, GLAZE THE BRIOCHE WITH BEATEN EGG AND THEN BAKE.

by hand, by beating and slapping the dough up and down in the bowl. This will take 15–20 minutes – the dough is ready when it comes away from the sides of the bowl in one piece.

In another bowl, beat the soft butter and sugar together until light and fluffy. With the electric mixer on low speed, add the butter mixture to the dough a little at a time, making sure each addition is completely amalgamated before adding more. If you are working by hand, squeeze the butter into the dough. Continue to beat for a couple of minutes in the mixer, or 5 minutes by hand, until the dough is smooth, glossy, and elastic. Cover the bowl with a damp dish towel and let rise at normal to warm room temperature (no more than 72°F) for about 2 hours or until doubled in bulk.

Punch down the risen dough in the bowl, using floured knuckles, then cover as before and put into the refrigerator. Let rise in the fridge for several hours but not more than a day.

Turn the dough onto a lightly floured work surface. Sprinkle over the raisins or chopped chocolate, if using, and briefly and gently knead in until evenly distributed. Shape the dough into a large ball.

Prepare the molds or pans: brush with a thin layer of melted butter, then chill until the butter hardens. Brush with a second coat of melted butter and chill briefly. By greasing the mold in this way the butter will not be absorbed by the dough, but it will help to prevent the brioche from sticking during baking.

To make a large brioche in the brioche mold, cut off a quarter of the dough for the top and set aside. Shape the larger piece of dough into a ball and place it in the prepared mold. Make a hole in the center with your fingertips. Roll the small piece of dough into an elongated egg shape with your hand held at an angle against the work surface. Using floured fingertips, gently press the narrow end of the dough "egg" into the hole in the large ball. If you are using a loaf pan, shape the dough following the method on page 76.

If making two medium brioches, divide the dough into two equal portions, then shape each as for the large brioche. For small individual brioches, divide the dough into 20 equal portions and shape each as for the large brioche.

Place the mold(s) or pan(s) in a large plastic bag that has been lightly greased inside, and fasten. Let rise at normal room temperature for 1–1½ hours or until almost doubled in size.

Preheat the oven to 425°F.

Lightly brush the top of the brioche(s) with the egg glaze, working from the outside inward. Take care not to let any glaze run into the crack between the large ball of dough and the top or onto the edges of the mold as this would prevent the dough from rising properly. Bake the brioche(s) in the preheated oven until golden brown and they sound hollow when tipped out of the mold or pan and tapped on the base. The large brioche will take 40–45 minutes; the medium brioches will take 25–30 minutes; and the small brioches 8–10 minutes. Unmold immediately onto a wire rack and let cool.

NOTE You can use 1 package (¼oz/7g) active dry yeast instead of fresh yeast. For rapid-rise dry yeast, add it to the flour and proceed with the recipe, adding the milk with the eggs.

AN INTRODUCTION TO BAKING

Baking combines many pleasures: creative pride in the making, social satisfaction in the sharing, and sensual delight in the eating. However, baking is also a craft and, like other crafts, it has its own unique subtleties and secrets. The recipes in this book have been generously provided by professional bakers and home cooks alike, imparting their specialist knowledge on individual techniques and cooking methods.

Ingredients are a critical element of baking—demand only the best! High quality ingredients will give you high quality results. For cake-making, all the ingredients (including the fat and eggs) must be at room temperature before starting. Unsalted butter has a taste all of its own, and is essential for cakes and pastry-making. Good organic flour is a must, as is fresh yeast, which is cheap and freezes well. When choosing sugars, unrefined cane sugar, including golden caster and golden icing sugar, is the best to use and is available in any good supermarket. Use size 3 (medium) free-range eggs, unless the recipe specifies large eggs—size 2. Nuts should be as fresh as possible; as once exposed to air, the oils in them start to turn rancid, and so are best stored in the freezer. Finally, there is no substitute for real chocolate for depth of flavor and overall finish—never use chocolate-flavoured cake covering or cheap cooking chocolate. See page 288 for more information about chocolate.

Precise measurements are vital for making pastry and cakes, after all it's chemistry! Accurate scales and a good set of measuring spoons are essential. All spoons should be measured level, unless the recipe calls for a rounded or heaped spoon.

You cannot bake well without a good, controllable oven, which should always be preheated. An oven thermometer is essential, as thermostats are often unreliable. The cooking instructions given in each recipe are guidelines; your oven handbook and your experience will teach you which shelf works best. Furthermore, baking times should usually be reduced for fan ovens; again please check your handbook, and for further advice on ovens see the List of Suppliers on pages 360-362.

Electric mixers and food processors can both help make baking more efficient—but take care not to overbeat mixtures, or all your hard work will be for nothing. The machine's handbook will give you information on speeds and times.

If you are intending to do a lot of baking, it is wise to invest in some heavy-duty professional-quality baking tins and trays, which won't buckle or scorch and should last a lifetime.

Lastly, a happy baker is a successful baker—so remember to have fun! Happy baking—and even happier eating!

13.16

COOKIES, SCONES & SMALL CAKES

Chewy, chunky American cookies, thin, crisp European cookies, brownies, muffins, rock cakes, scones – all made by the batch to eat by the dozen. Simple, quick, irresistible.

SHORTBREAD THINS

The traditional recipe for shortbread is three parts flour to two of butter and one of sugar. Most good shortbread bakers, who are usually Scots, like to replace some of the flour with rice flour, ground rice, or cornstarch, to give a lighter, shorter, and sandier texture. The flavor is largely determined by the type and quality of the butter. Good unsalted butter and lactic butter give superb taste as well as texture; whey butter – made by cheese-makers as a by-product – makes a very light, crisp shortbread; while well-salted blended butter tends to make the shortbread heavy and greasy. Several older Scottish bakers told me they mix their local country butter with shortening or margarine to get a lighter, shorter, more delicate cookie. I prefer shortbread thin and crisp; however, the same dough can be rolled out thicker or simply pressed into a lightly greased shortbread mold or shallow cake pan, to make it anything from 1/4 to 1 inch thick. In this case it is best to score the dough into sections before baking, to make it easier to remove afterward.

INGREDIENTS

Makes about 2 dozen

3/4 cup (170g) unsalted butter, at room temperature
7 tablespoons (85g) sugar
1 2/3 cups (230g) all-purpose flour
1/4 cup (30g) rice flour, ground rice, or cornstarch
a little sugar for sprinkling

a 2 5/8-inch fluted round cookie cutter
several baking sheets, lightly greased

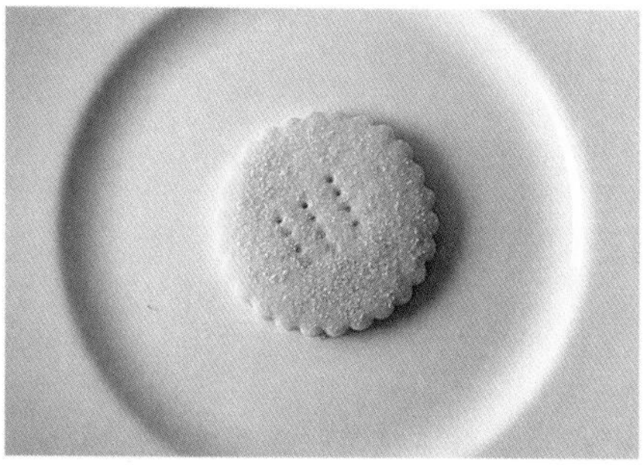

A crisp, buttery Shortbread Thin.

Beat the butter until soft and creamy, using a wooden spoon or electric mixer. Add the sugar and beat until the mixture is pale and fluffy. Sift the all-purpose flour with the rice flour and mix in. When the mixture comes together, turn it onto a lightly floured work surface and knead briefly to make a smooth but not sticky dough. (If it seems sticky, chill until firm.)

Roll out the dough to just under 1/4 inch thick and cut out rounds using the fluted cutter. Gently knead together the trimmings, then re-roll and cut more rounds. Arrange the rounds slightly apart on the prepared baking sheets. Prick the rounds with a fork, and chill for 15 minutes.

Preheat the oven to 350°F.

Bake the cookies in the preheated oven for 12–15 minutes or until just firm and barely colored. Sprinkle with sugar and let cool on the sheets for a minute or two. When firm enough, transfer to a wire rack to cool completely. Store in an airtight tin, and eat within a week.

VARIATION: CHOCOLATE SHORTBREAD Replace 3 1/2 tablespoons (30g) of the all-purpose flour with unsweetened cocoa powder, and sift with the flours. As chocolate shortbread scorches more easily, make it thicker and bake it in a pan.

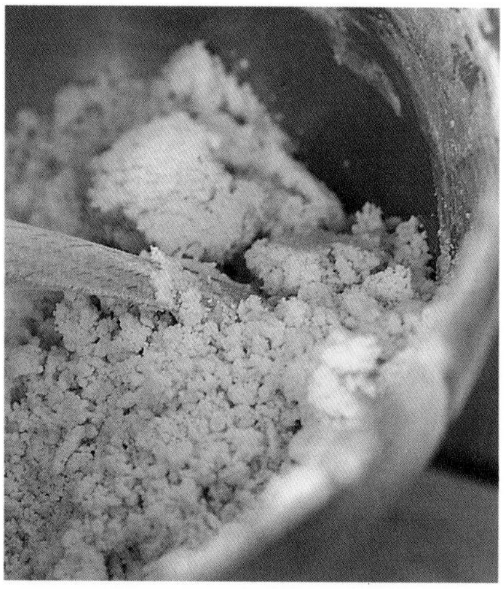

1 *WORK THE ALL-PURPOSE AND RICE FLOURS INTO THE CREAMED BUTTER MIXTURE.*

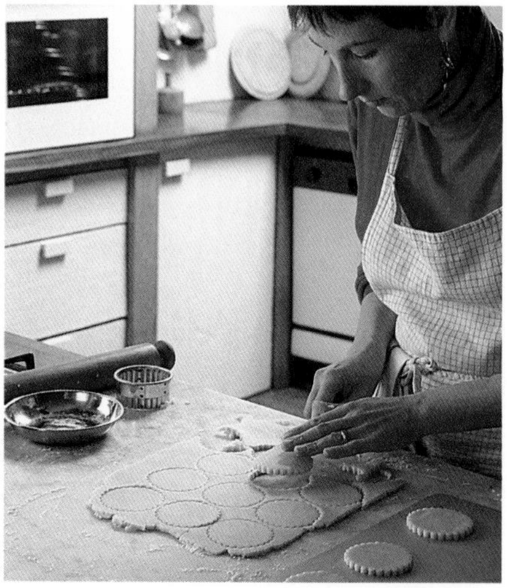

2 *TRANSFER THE ROUNDS TO A GREASED BAKING SHEET WITH A METAL SPATULA.*

PREVIOUS PAGE (left to right) Cranberry Muffins, Brownies, Almond Crescents, Chocolate Chunk Oat Cookies, Tolcarne Ginger Cookies.

MILLIONAIRE'S SHORTBREAD

INGREDIENTS

Makes 2 dozen
FILLING:
a 14-oz (400-g) can condensed milk

BASE:
3/4 cup (170g) unsalted butter, at room temperature
7 tablespoons (85g) sugar
1 2/3 cups (230g) all-purpose flour
1/4 cup (30g) rice flour, ground rice, or cornstarch

TOPPING:
6oz (170g) good semisweet chocolate, chopped
2 tablespoons (30g) butter
about 2oz (60g) white chocolate, for decoration

a 9-inch square cake pan, about 2 inches deep, greased

Super rich – an extravagance of dark chocolate, caramel, and butter shortbread.

WHEN THE LAYER OF CARAMEL IS SET AND FIRM, SPREAD THE CHOCOLATE TOPPING OVER USING A SMALL SPATULA.

To make the caramel filling, put the unopened can of condensed milk in a heavy saucepan and cover with water. Bring to a boil, then simmer, without covering the pan, for 3 1/2 hours, replenishing the water as necessary – the can should always be covered. Let cool before opening the can. The condensed milk will have turned to a fudgy, dark-golden caramel.

Meanwhile, make the shortbread base. Preheat the oven to 350°F. Beat the butter until creamy, using a wooden spoon or electric mixer. Add the sugar and beat until the mixture is light and fluffy. Sift the all-purpose flour with the rice flour, add to the butter mixture, and knead gently for a few seconds until smooth. Press the dough into the prepared pan to make an even layer. Prick all over with a fork, then bake in the preheated oven for 20–30 minutes or until crisp and golden. Cool completely.

When the shortbread base is cold, spread the cooled caramel filling evenly over the top. Chill until firm – about 1 hour.

To finish, gently melt the semisweet chocolate in a heatproof bowl set over a pan of hot but not boiling water. Remove from the heat and stir in the butter until melted and smooth. Spread the mixture evenly over the caramel and let set. Melt the white chocolate in the same way, then use a fork or small spoon to drizzle it over the dark chocolate layer in a zigzag pattern (this can also be done using a paper piping cone). Leave until set and firm before cutting into fingers or squares.

VARIATION To make a quick and even richer caramel, melt 3/4 cup (170g) unsalted butter with 3/4 cup + 2 tablespoons (170g) sugar in a heavy saucepan (non-stick is best). Add the contents of the can of condensed milk – unboiled – and bring the mixture to a boil. Boil, stirring constantly, until the mixture turns a golden caramel color. Pour the hot mixture over the cooled shortbread base, and leave until cold and set before finishing.

GRASMERE SHORTBREAD

INGREDIENTS

Cuts into about 2 dozen pieces

2½ cups (340g) all-purpose flour
1½ teaspoons ground ginger
¾ teaspoon baking soda
¾ cup (170g) slightly salted butter, chilled
¾ cup packed (170g) dark or light brown sugar, sifted

BUTTERCREAM:
½ cup (110g) slightly salted butter, at room temperature
2 cups (230g) confectioners' sugar, sifted
1 teaspoon ground ginger
2 teaspoons minced candied ginger
2 teaspoons syrup from the jar of ginger

a shallow cake pan, 8–8¾ x 12–12½ inches, or a 12- x 7-inch jelly-roll pan that is ¾ inch deep, greased

ABOVE You should not miss the famous Sarah Nelson gingerbread shop on a visit to Grasmere.

RIGHT The view across Lake Windermere to Grasmere, in England's beautiful Lake District.

This recipe comes from our friend and fellow English food writer, Sallie Morris, who describes herself as a Lake District girl, like her mother before her. Sallie says that it was long the tradition in the Grasmere area to give gingerbread, or ginger shortbread, to the children who cut rushes to cover the earthen floor of the local churches. This evolved into an annual rush-bearing ceremony, in August, and those who took part were given a piece of gingerbread stamped with the local Saint's name plus a penny to buy beer. The most famous gingerbread was made by Mrs. Sarah Nelson, and it is still sold in her tiny cottage near the church. The recipe is kept under lock and key in the local bank; indeed, the people who now run the shop had to pay a deposit before they were allowed to see the recipe. There are many theories about the lovely sandy texture of the gingerbread – some claim it contains fine oatmeal, or whole-wheat flour.

This is Sallie's mother's recipe, and was quoted in a book about Sarah Nelson. We think it is more than equal to the original: rich, sandy, and nicely "hot." The shortbread can be served plain, cut into fingers or squares, or sandwiched in pairs with a ginger buttercream filling.

SALLIE PRESSES MOST OF THE SHORTBREAD MIXTURE INTO THE PREPARED PAN (ABOVE RIGHT) AND THEN SCATTERS THE REST EVENLY OVER THE SURFACE (TOP). SHE SANDWICHES PAIRS OF BAKED SHORTBREAD FINGERS WITH GINGER CREAM (ABOVE).

Preheat the oven to 350°F.

Sift the flour, ginger, and baking soda into a mixing bowl. Cut the butter into small pieces, add to the flour, and rub in using the tips of your fingers. When the mixture looks like fine sand, stir in the sugar.

Put three-quarters of the mixture into the prepared pan and press down to make an even layer. Scatter the rest of the mixture evenly over the surface to make a crumbly topping. Use a knife to mark into fingers or squares.

Bake in the preheated oven for 35–40 minutes or until pale golden (if using a jelly-roll pan, increase the cooking time slightly). Cool slightly, then cut into fingers or squares along the marked lines. Leave in the pan until completely cold.

To make the buttercream, beat the butter until creamy using a wooden spoon. Gradually add the confectioners' sugar and ground ginger, beating well, then mix in the minced candied ginger and syrup to make a spreadable cream. Use to sandwich together pairs of shortbread fingers or squares. Once assembled, eat within 3 days.

TOLCARNE GINGER COOKIES

INGREDIENTS

Makes 2½ dozen
2½ cups (340g) self-rising flour
1 cup (200g) sugar
1 tablespoon ground ginger
1 teaspoon baking soda
½ cup (110g) unsalted butter
¼ cup (85g) golden syrup
1 egg, beaten
2 pieces of candied ginger, drained of syrup, minced (optional)

several baking sheets, greased

My favorite cookies – crisp and very gingery. The recipe came from my grandmother, who learned to bake at school a hundred years ago. Sometimes I add a teaspoon or two of chopped candied ginger – the kind preserved in syrup – when I add the egg.

Preheat the oven to 325°F.

Put all the dry ingredients into a mixing bowl and stir until thoroughly combined. Gently melt the butter with the golden syrup. Pour onto the dry ingredients, then add the egg and minced ginger and mix well with a wooden spoon to make a dough.

Using your hands, roll walnut-sized pieces of the dough into balls – you should have about 30. Place well apart on the prepared baking sheets, then slightly flatten each ball with your fingers. Bake in the preheated oven for 15–20 minutes or until crisp and golden. Let cool on the sheets for a minute before lifting onto a wire rack to cool completely. Store in an airtight tin, and eat within a week.

PRESS EACH BALL OF DOUGH TO FLATTEN IT SLIGHTLY; THIS HELPS THE COOKIE SPREAD AND BAKE EVENLY IN THE OVEN.

LEFT *A charming cottage in Devon, England, worthy of a picture postcard.*

A selection of freshly baked treats (clockwise from the top): Tolcarne Ginger Cookies, Shortbread Thins, Chocolate Chunk Oat Cookies, Millionaire's Shortbread.

SWEDISH PEPPER COOKIES

INGREDIENTS

Makes about 5 dozen
1 1/2 cups (300g) sugar
1 cup (230g) unsalted butter, at room temperature
1 tablespoon honey
1 egg, beaten
2 cups (280g) all-purpose flour
1/2 teaspoon salt
1 teaspoon ground ginger
1 teaspoon ground cloves
extra sugar for flattening

several baking sheets, greased

These cookies were baked for us by Rosemary Underdahl, when we visited her in Maine. The recipe comes from her mother-in-law. Although Rosemary's husband was born and raised in Minnesota, his Swedish and Norwegian origins emerge in these, his favorite cookies. Rosemary trained to be a teacher – indeed, she had my little ones under control and eager to please within minutes. She's a natural cook and baker, and is always busy catering for special events and fund-raising galas where her eye-catching and delicate Scandinavian dishes are in demand.

The recipe doesn't actually contain pepper, but the cookies certainly taste spicy. The recipe makes a big batch of cookies – if more convenient, you can bake one of the three portions and keep the other two in the fridge or freezer to bake another time.

Beat the sugar with the butter until pale and fluffy, using a wooden spoon, electric mixer, or food processor. Beat in the honey and the egg. Sift the flour with the salt, ground ginger, and ground cloves, then work into the mixture to make a firm dough.

Divide the dough into three. Shape each portion into a disk and wrap tightly in wax paper. Chill until firm – about 2 hours. The dough can also be frozen for up to a month or kept in the fridge up to 5 days, ready to be shaped for baking.

When ready to bake, preheat the oven to 375°F. Roll marble-size pieces of dough into balls and place them well apart on the prepared baking sheets. Dip the base of a glass in cold water and then into a dish of sugar; press it gently on top of each ball to flatten it into a wafer-thin disk. Re-sugar the glass frequently, when it starts to stick.

Bake for 7–10 minutes or until barely colored and firm. Set each baking sheet on a wire rack to cool for a minute or so, until the cookies are firm enough to lift off onto a cold baking sheet to cool completely. Store in an airtight tin, and eat within 4 days.

1 WORKING QUICKLY, ROSEMARY ROLLS THE WELL-CHILLED DOUGH INTO SMOOTH BALLS THE SIZE OF LARGE MARBLES.

2 SHE FLATTENS THE BALLS USING THE BASE OF A GLASS DIPPED IN SUGAR (THE SUGAR PREVENTS THE DOUGH STICKING).

SWEDISH COCONUT COOKIES

INGREDIENTS

Makes about 6 dozen
1/2 cup (110g) unsalted butter, at room temperature
1/2 cup (110g) shortening
1/2 cup (100g) sugar
1 1/2 cups (230g) all-purpose flour
1/2 teaspoon baking soda
1/2 teaspoon baking powder
1/2 teaspoon pure vanilla extract
1/2 cup (50g) unsweetened shredded coconut

several baking sheets, greased

Right ROSEMARY CUTS THE ROLL OF THOROUGHLY CHILLED DOUGH INTO WAFER-THIN SLICES.

BELOW My nephew Lucas is a big fan of Rosemary's cookies.

This recipe also comes from Rosemary Underdahl's mother-in-law, and is very popular with her daughters, Caitlin and Hannah. Rosemary likes the contrast between American and Scandinavian cookies: the former are large, chewy, and packed with ingredients; the latter are thin, small, and crisp.

Beat the fats together until evenly blended, using a wooden spoon or electric mixer. Add the sugar and beat again until the mixture is light and fluffy. Sift the flour with the baking soda and baking powder, then add to the mixture with the vanilla and coconut. Work the mixture with your hand until it comes together to make a firm dough.

Divide the dough in half and form each portion into a sausage-like roll with your hands – the roll should be about 2 3/8 inches in diameter. Wrap the rolls of dough in wax paper and chill overnight. The dough can be kept in the fridge for up to 5 days or frozen up to a month, so you can bake one portion and keep the other.

When ready to bake, preheat the oven to 350°F. Using a very sharp knife dipped in hot water, cut very thin slices from the roll of dough – no thicker than about 1/16 inch if possible. Rosemary says you shouldn't worry if the slices tear or fall apart; just push them together as you arrange them on the prepared baking sheet, or cut thicker slices.

Bake in the preheated oven for 6–8 minutes or until very pale gold and just lightly brown on the edges – you need to watch the cookies carefully as they can brown very quickly. Set each sheet on a wire rack and let the cookies firm up for a minute or two, then lift the cookies carefully onto a cold baking sheet to cool. Store in an airtight tin, and eat within 5 days.

VARIATION: ALMOND COOKIES
Add 1/4 cup (40g) finely chopped almonds with the coconut.

GERMAN CHRISTMAS SPICE COOKIES

INGREDIENTS

Makes about 2 dozen
1 1/4 cups (170g) all-purpose flour
1 1/2 teaspoons ground ginger
1/2 teaspoon ground cinnamon
1/2 teaspoon apple-pie spice
4 tablespoons (60g) unsalted butter, chilled and diced
7 tablespoons (85g) sugar
2 tablespoons golden syrup
2 tablespoons milk
1 egg yolk

TO DECORATE:
1 1/2 cups (170g) confectioners' sugar, sifted
1 egg white

cookie cutters – star, Christmas tree, bell, Santa, holly leaf, etc.
several baking sheets, greased
a paper piping cone or a small plastic bag
thin ribbon

You can shape these crisp, spicy cookies into stars, Christmas trees, bells, or Santas. Then decorate them and thread them onto thin red ribbon to hang on the Christmas trees or in windows.

Preheat the oven to 375°F.

Sift the flour, ginger, cinnamon, and apple-pie spice into a mixing bowl. Add the diced butter and rub into the dry ingredients using the tips of your fingers, to give fine crumbs. Stir in the sugar. Mix the golden syrup with the milk and egg yolk, add to the bowl, and mix with the dry ingredients to make a soft dough.

Turn the dough onto a floured work surface and knead gently for a few seconds until smooth. Roll out 1/8–1/4 inch thick, then cut out shapes with the cookie cutters. Using a skewer or toothpick, make a hole at the top of each shape large enough to thread a ribbon through. Arrange the cookies on the prepared baking sheets and chill for 10 minutes.

Bake for 10–12 minutes or until golden. Leave on the sheets to cool slightly, then, when the cookies are firm enough, transfer them to a wire rack to cool completely.

To decorate, gradually beat the sifted confectioners' sugar into the egg white to make a smooth icing of piping consistency. Put into the paper piping cone or plastic bag and snip off the point. Pipe a decorative edge on the cookies, or pipe wavy patterns, names, messages, or whatever you fancy. Let set, then thread on ribbons for hanging.

ABOVE The Christmas market in Nürnberg, Germany.

RIGHT During Advent, the Albrecht Dürer stübe restaurant in Nürnberg is lavishly decorated.

OPPOSITE The festive window at the Albrecht Dürer stübe, with decorated spice cookies and traditional ornaments hung on thin ribbons from copper piping.

RIGHT Chocolate Madeleines, made with good semisweet chocolate and cocoa powder.

CHOCOLATE MADELEINES

As Marcel Proust dipped a madeleine into his tilleul, all his memories of childhood flooded back, and he began his search for lost time. If he had been tasting chocolate madeleines instead, the world's longest novel might never have been written – or it might have been even longer, for these are even more of a delight than the traditional lemon-flavored madeleines.

The chocolate version is made by adding melted chocolate and replacing some of the flour with cocoa powder. Madeleines are traditionally baked in shallow shell-shaped molds (look out for the non-stick type), which are sold in specialist kitchenware stores.

INGREDIENTS

Makes 2 1/2 dozen

1/2 cup + 2 tablespoons (140g) unsalted butter
3oz (85g) good semisweet chocolate, chopped
1 cup (140g) all-purpose flour
2 tablespoons unsweetened cocoa powder
a pinch of salt
4 eggs
2/3 cup (140g) sugar
confectioners' sugar for sprinkling

madeleine molds, well buttered (see recipe)

Preheat the oven to 375°F.

With a pastry brush, give the molds a thin coating of melted butter. Chill or freeze until firm, then add a second coat of butter.

To make the madeleines, put the butter and chocolate in a heatproof bowl set over a pan of hot but not boiling water and melt gently. Remove the bowl from the pan and stir until the mixture is smooth. Let cool slightly while preparing the other ingredients. Sift the flour twice with the cocoa powder and salt. Beat the eggs with the sugar using an electric mixer, until the mixture becomes pale and very thick – when the beaters are lifted out, the mixture should make a ribbon-like trail on the surface. Using a large metal spoon, fold the flour mixture into the egg mixture in three batches, then carefully fold in the chocolate mixture until thoroughly combined – the batter will lose a little bulk.

Spoon a heaped teaspoon or so of the batter into each madeleine mold – it should be about two-thirds full. Bake for 10–12 minutes or until just firm to the touch. Cool in the molds for a minute, then gently loosen each madeleine with a round-bladed knife and turn out onto a wire rack to cool completely. Serve dusted with confectioners' sugar. Store in an airtight tin, and eat within a week.

VARIATION: TRADITIONAL LEMON MADELEINES Melt 1/2 cup + 2 tablespoons (140g) unsalted butter and cool slightly. Sift 1 cup + 2 tablespoons (155g) all-purpose flour with a pinch of salt, and beat 4 eggs with 2/3 cup (140g) sugar as above. Fold the flour into the egg mixture, with the grated rind of 1 lemon, then fold in the butter. Bake and cool as above.

BRIGITTE'S ALMOND SQUARES

Brigitte Friis, who comes from Berlin, is a marvelous cook. This is one of her triumphs – a German confection of thin pastry covered with a sticky combination of honey and almonds.

INGREDIENTS

Makes 3 1/2 dozen small squares

PASTRY:

- 1 1/4 cups (170g) all-purpose flour
- 1/2 cup (110g) unsalted butter, chilled and diced
- 2 1/2 tablespoons (30g) sugar
- 1 egg yolk
- a few drops of pure vanilla extract

TOPPING:

- 1 3/4 cups (170g) sliced almonds
- 6 tablespoons (85g) unsalted butter
- 3 tablespoons (40g) sugar
- 2 tablespoons (40g) set honey
- 2 tablespoons cream

a shallow cake pan, 8–8 3/4 x 12–12 1/2 inches, or a 7- x 12-inch jelly-roll pan that is 3/4 inch deep, greased

To make the pastry base, sift the flour into a mixing bowl or food processor bowl. Add the diced butter and rub in using your fingertips, or process, until the mixture looks like bread crumbs. Stir in the sugar. Add the egg yolk and vanilla and work with your hands, or process, to make a smooth, shortbread-like dough.

Press the dough into the prepared pan in an even layer, then prick all over with a fork. Chill for 10–15 minutes or until firm.

Preheat the oven to 375°F.

Bake the pastry base for about 10 minutes or until firm and golden.

For the topping, put the almonds, butter, sugar, and honey into a wide heavy pan – Brigitte uses a non-stick frying pan – and cook over low heat, stirring constantly, until the mixture is a pale straw-gold. Stir in the cream and cook for a few more seconds, then pour over the pastry base and spread in an even layer. Bake for about 10 minutes or until the topping is a deep golden brown.

Let cool in the pan, then cut into small squares. Store in an airtight tin, and eat within 5 days.

CHOCOLATE MACAROONS

INGREDIENTS

Makes 8 filled macaroons

MACAROONS:

3 1/2 oz (100g) good semisweet chocolate, chopped

2 egg whites

1 2/3 cups (140g) very finely ground unblanched almonds

2/3 cup (140g) superfine sugar

FILLING:

4oz (110g) good semisweet chocolate, chopped

1/2 cup (100ml) heavy cream or crème fraîche

a baking sheet, lined with parchment paper

One of my favorite pastry shops is Ladurée in the Rue Royale in Paris. It is the pâtisserie of your dreams: gilt and marble fittings, velvet banquettes, cakes displayed like Cartier necklaces, chic dowagers perched on tiny chairs and attended by pretty young men or immaculate, lace-trimmed grandchildren. Ladurée's cakes are legendary, and best of all are their chocolate macaroons – sheer heaven with chocolat chaud on a cold day.

This is my version of their recipe. It is best made with top-quality semisweet chocolate – one that contains a high proportion of cocoa solids and cocoa butter. Unblanched almonds are the ones that still have the thin papery brown skin. If you can't find them already ground, you can grind them with the sugar in a food processor or blender.

Preheat the oven to 275°F.

Put the chocolate in a heatproof bowl set over a pan of hot but not boiling water and melt very gently; remove from the heat and stir until smooth. Using an electric mixer or whisk, beat the egg whites until they form soft peaks. Gradually beat in the almonds combined with the sugar. Gently fold in the melted chocolate using a metal spoon.

Put a heaped tablespoon of the mixture on the prepared baking sheet and spread to form a round about 3 inches in diameter. Repeat with the rest of the mixture to make 16 rounds. Bake for 1 hour or until firm. Cool slightly on the baking sheet, then transfer to a wire rack to cool completely.

To make the mousse filling, put the chopped chocolate in a small heavy pan with the cream and heat gently, stirring occasionally, until melted. Remove from the heat and let cool, then beat well with a wooden spoon until thick and fluffy. Chill until firm.

Sandwich pairs of macaroons together with the mousse filling, spreading it generously. Leave for about an hour before serving.

I like these macaroons best when they are a couple of days old, and they have become wonderfully sticky.

CHOCOLATE CHUNK OAT COOKIES

Top-quality semisweet chocolate, chopped into large pieces, makes the best chocolate chip cookies – the taste is unrivaled because good chocolate contains far less sugar than commercial chocolate chips. As you bite into a thick chunk of rich chocolate you will realize that bought chocolate chip cookies can never compete with homemade.

INGREDIENTS

Makes about 2 dozen

- 6oz (170g) good semisweet chocolate
- 1/2 cup (110g) unsalted butter, at room temperature
- 6 tablespoons (85g) light brown sugar
- 1 egg, beaten
- 7 tablespoons (60g) self-rising flour
- 1/2 teaspoon baking powder
- 1 1/3 cups (110g) rolled oats
- 1/2 teaspoon pure vanilla extract

several baking sheets, greased

Preheat the oven to 350°F.

Using a large sharp knife, coarsely chop the chocolate; set aside. Beat the butter until creamy using a wooden spoon or electric mixer. Add the sugar and beat until light and fluffy. Gradually beat in the egg and continue beating for 1 minute. Sift the flour with the baking powder and stir into the mixture with the oats and vanilla. When thoroughly combined, add the chocolate and mix well.

Place heaped teaspoons of the mixture, well spaced apart, on the prepared baking sheets. Lightly flatten the mounds, then bake in the preheated oven for 12–15 minutes or until golden and just firm. Let cool on the sheets for a minute, then transfer to a wire rack to cool completely. Store in an airtight tin, and eat within a week.

VARIATION: CHOCOLATE NUT COOKIES Omit the oats, increase the flour by 3 1/2 tablespoons (30g), and add 3/4 cup (90g) chopped hazelnuts.

USE A HEAVY, SHARP KNIFE TO CHOP THE CHOCOLATE INTO LARGE CHUNKS.

HAZELNUT COOKIES

INGREDIENTS

Makes about 2½ dozen
½ cup (70g) hazelnuts
½ cup (110g) unsalted butter, at room temperature
½ teaspoon pure vanilla extract
6 tablespoons (85g) light brown sugar
5 tablespoons (60g) granulated sugar
1 egg, beaten
2 cups (280g) all-purpose flour
1½ teaspoons baking powder
a pinch of salt

several baking sheets

Toasting nuts changes their taste from mild and creamy to an almost caramel, bittersweet richness. These cookies can be made with toasted pecans or untoasted walnuts, but I think hazelnuts give them the best flavor.

Preheat the oven to 350°F.

Spread the hazelnuts on an ungreased baking sheet and toast in the preheated oven for 10–15 minutes or until they turn a rich golden brown and the skin is starting to crack and peel. Gather up the hazelnuts in a clean dish towel so they are held as if in a purse and rub them together to loosen the skins. Chop the skinned nuts coarsely, using a large sharp knife or in a food processor.

Beat the butter with the vanilla until creamy, using a wooden spoon or electric mixer. Add the light brown sugar and the granulated sugar and beat again until the mixture is light and fluffy. Gradually beat in the egg. Sift the flour with the baking powder and salt, and stir into the mixture with the chopped hazelnuts to make a firm dough.

Turn the dough onto a lightly floured work surface and form into a log shape about 8½ x 2¼ inches. Wrap in wax paper or parchment paper and chill until firm – about 2 hours. The dough can be kept in the refrigerator for up to a week.

When ready to bake, preheat the oven to 375°F. Using a large sharp knife, cut the log into slices just under ¼ inch thick. Arrange them slightly apart on greased baking sheets and bake for about 15 minutes or until golden and just firm to the touch. Transfer to wire racks to cool.

Store the cookies in an airtight tin, and eat within 5 days.

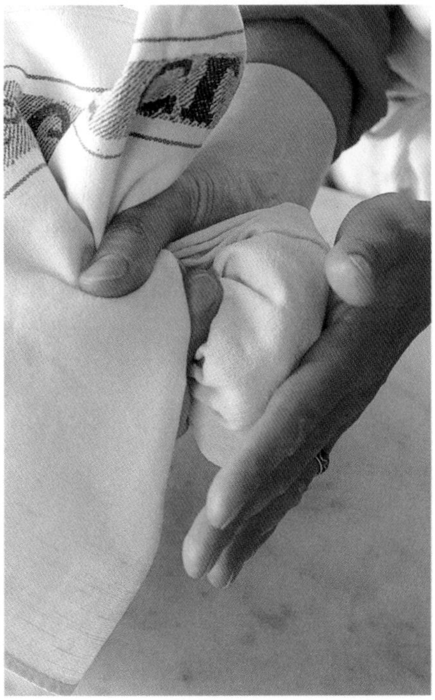

1 GATHER THE TOASTED HAZELNUTS IN A DISH TOWEL AND RUB THEM TOGETHER.

2 THE FRICTION CREATED BY RUBBING THE NUTS WILL LOOSEN THEIR PAPERY SKINS.

LEFT (from left to right): Somerset Easter Cookies, Belgian Spice Cookies, Hazelnut Cookies.

ALMOND CRESCENTS

INGREDIENTS

Makes about 2 dozen
1/2 cup (110g) unsalted butter, at room temperature
2-3 drops of pure almond extract (optional)
1/2 cup (60g) confectioners' sugar, sifted
a pinch of salt
1/2 cup + 2 tablespoons (85g) all-purpose flour, sifted
1 1/3 cups (110g) ground almonds
extra confectioners' sugar for dredging

several baking sheets, greased

ABOVE Almond trees in blossom.

OPPOSITE Sugar-dredged Almond Crescents are well-partnered by a glass of sweet wine.

Every Christmas, a Czech friend used to make a wonderful big box of these snow-white cookies for my mother but wouldn't divulge the recipe. I've since enjoyed them at holiday time in the houses of Polish, German, and Dutch friends, and my American mother-in-law says the recipe is an old Jewish one. From clues dropped here and there I've gradually worked out the proportions – the method is very simple. I like to serve the cookies with fruit desserts such as oranges in caramel, poached pears, or strawberries and cream, as well as with coffee.

Preheat the oven to 325°F.

Using a wooden spoon or electric mixer, beat the butter with the almond extract until very light and creamy. Add the sugar and mix slowly until combined, then beat until fluffy. Add the remaining ingredients and mix thoroughly using a wooden spoon. Knead lightly to bring the dough together – it should be firm.

Take a heaping teaspoon-sized portion of dough and roll it with your hands to make a sausage about 3 inches long, then curve to make a crescent. Place on a prepared baking sheet. Repeat with the rest of the dough, spacing the crescents well apart. Bake in the preheated oven for 15–18 minutes or until firm. The cookies should remain pale with only the tips slightly colored.

Dredge with confectioners' sugar, then let cool on the sheets for a couple of minutes. Transfer to a wire rack to cool completely. Store in an airtight tin, and eat within a week. The flavor develops if the cookies are kept at least a day after baking.

CURVE THE SAUSAGES OF DOUGH INTO NEAT CRESCENT SHAPES USING YOUR FINGERTIPS.

DOUBLE-CHOCOLATE PECAN COOKIES

INGREDIENTS

Makes about 2 1/2 dozen
1 1/4 cups (100g) rolled oats
1 cup (140g) all-purpose flour
a pinch of salt
1/2 teaspoon baking powder
1/2 teaspoon baking soda
7oz (200g) good semisweet chocolate
1/2 cup (110g) unsalted butter, at room temperature
7 tablespoons (85g) granulated sugar
6 tablespoons (85g) light brown sugar
1 egg, beaten
1 cup (110g) coarsely chopped pecans

several baking sheets

Really good chocolate, grated and chopped into large chunks, makes the richest, darkest, most luxurious cookies. I like to add pecans – my favorite nut when cooking with chocolate – but chopped walnuts or a mixture of nuts are also good. To make white-chocolate nut cookies, still use the grated semisweet chocolate, but replace the chopped semisweet chocolate with an equal quantity of good white chocolate.

Preheat the oven to 375°F.

Spread the oats on an ungreased baking sheet and toast in the preheated oven, stirring occasionally, for about 15 minutes or until golden. Let cool, then put into the food processor with the flour, salt, baking powder, and baking soda. Process until the mixture has the texture of sand.

Finely grate 2oz (50g) of the chocolate, and chop the remainder into large chunks using a heavy, sharp knife.

Beat the butter until creamy, using an electric mixer or wooden spoon. Add the sugars and beat again until light and fluffy. Gradually beat in the egg, then continue beating for 1 minute. Stir in the oat mixture, grated and chopped chocolate, and pecans to make a stiff dough – in cold weather, you may need to use your hands to work it together.

Roll walnut-sized pieces of dough into balls with your hands. Place the balls well spaced apart on greased baking sheets and bake for about 12 minutes or until almost firm. Let cool on the sheets for a minute, then transfer the cookies to a wire rack to cool completely. Store in an airtight tin, and eat within 5 days.

Nuts go rancid quite quickly, so when making Double-Chocolate Pecan Cookies use the freshest pecans you can find – just shelled if possible.

SOMERSET EASTER COOKIES

INGREDIENTS

Makes about $1\frac{1}{2}$ dozen
½ cup (110g) unsalted butter, at room temperature
7 tablespoons (85g) sugar
1 egg yolk
1½ cups (200g) all-purpose flour
a pinch of salt
⅛ teaspoon baking powder
⅛ teaspoon grated nutmeg
½ teaspoon apple-pie spice
½ teaspoon ground cinnamon
6 tablespoons (60g) raisins or currants
1 teaspoon minced mixed candied peel

TO FINISH:
1 egg white, lightly beaten
sugar for sprinkling

a 2⅝-inch fluted round cookie cutter
several baking sheets, greased

ABOVE A spicy Somerset Easter Cookie, with its sugary glaze.

TOP RIGHT The River Parrot on Sedgemoor in Somerset, England.

I spent many a happy Easter on a farm in Somerset, so I always associate these short, slightly spicy cookies with England's West Country. My friend Michael Sealey has a passion for afternoon tea, and serves these cookies in stacks of three, tied with yellow ribbon. He likes to use currants, but I prefer raisins. The choice is yours.

Preheat the oven to 400°F.

Beat the butter until creamy, using a wooden spoon or electric mixer. Add the sugar and beat until the mixture is light and fluffy. Add the egg yolk and beat for a further minute. Sift the flour with the salt, baking powder, nutmeg, apple-pie spice, and cinnamon. Add to the butter mixture and stir until thoroughly combined. Add the fruit and peel and mix well with your hands. If the dough seems very stiff or dry and doesn't come together, add a tablespoon of milk.

Turn the dough onto a floured work surface and knead lightly for a few seconds or until smoothly combined. Roll out slightly less than ¼ inch thick. Cut out rounds with the fluted cookie cutter, then re-roll the trimmings and cut out more rounds. Arrange the cookie rounds, spaced a little apart, on the prepared baking sheets.

Bake in the preheated oven for 10 minutes or until pale golden and firm. Remove from the oven. Lightly brush each cookie with egg white, then sprinkle with a little sugar. Return the cookies to the oven and bake for a further 3–5 minutes or until the tops turn golden and crunchy. Transfer to a wire rack to cool.

Store the cookies in an airtight tin, and eat within 5 days.

BELGIAN SPICE COOKIES

INGREDIENTS

Makes about 3 1/2 dozen
1 1/2 cups (200g) all-purpose flour
1/2 teaspoon ground ginger
1/2 teaspoon ground cinnamon
1/2 teaspoon apple-pie spice
1/2 teaspoon baking powder
1/2 cup (110g) unsalted butter, chilled and diced
6 tablespoons (85g) light brown sugar
about 1/3 cup (45g) split (halved) almonds

several baking sheets, lined with parchment paper

These thin, crisp, fragile cookies are of the "ice-box" variety – the dough is shaped into a brick, wrapped, chilled, and then sliced when ready to bake. I like them best with a cup of coffee after dinner, but they are a treat at any time of day.

Sift the flour with the ginger, cinnamon, apple-pie spice, and baking powder. Tip into a food processor, add the diced butter, and process until the mixture looks like fine crumbs. Add the sugar and process until the mixture comes together to make a firm dough – in cold weather you may have to knead the dough a little by hand. The dough can also be made by rubbing the fat into the flour mixture with your fingers, then stirring in the sugar, and finally kneading the dough together.

Turn the dough onto a work surface and form it into a brick shape measuring about 7 x 3 x 1 1/4 inches. Wrap in wax paper and chill until firm at least 2 hours. The dough can be kept in the refrigerator for up to 5 days and then baked when convenient.

When ready to bake, preheat the oven to 400°F. Using a large sharp knife, cut the dough into very thin slices – you should have about 40. Arrange slightly apart on the prepared baking sheets and press an almond half into the middle of each slice. Bake for 5–7 minutes or until golden. Cool on the sheets for a minute, then transfer to a wire rack to cool completely. Store in an airtight tin, and eat within 4 days.

Crisp Belgian Spice Cookies can be freshly baked whenever you want them.

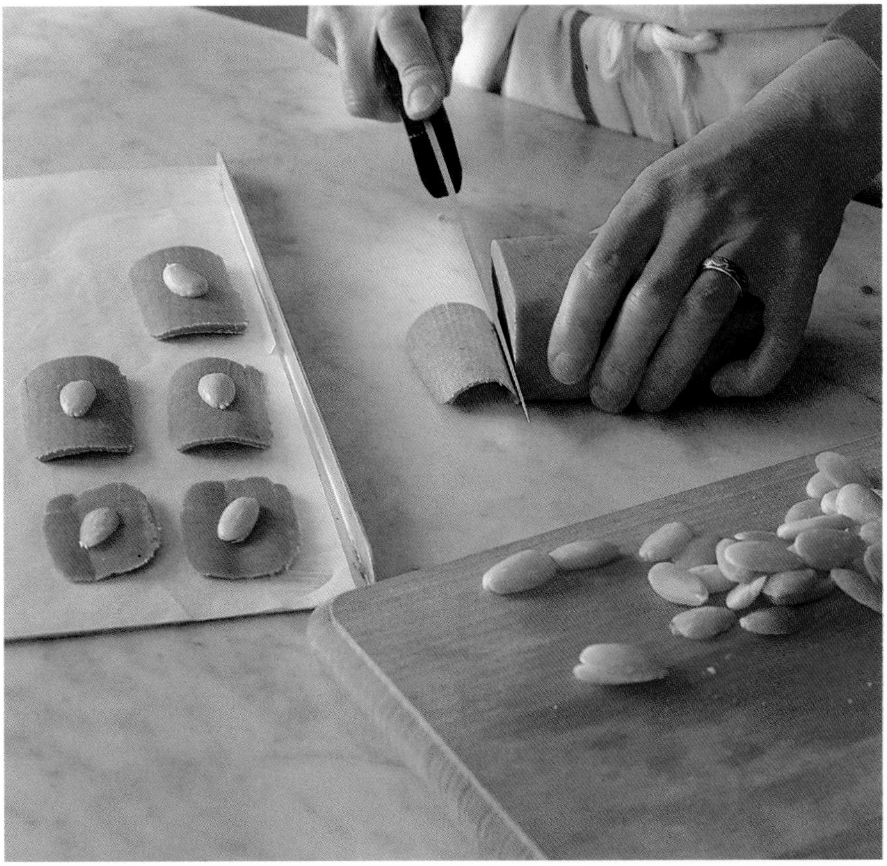

THE DOUGH MUST BE VERY FIRM SO THAT IT CAN BE CUT INTO *WAFER-THIN* SLICES.

PLAIN SCONES

INGREDIENTS

Makes 8
$1^2/_3$ cups (230g) self-rising flour
a pinch of salt
3 tablespoons (40g) sugar
3 tablespoons (40g) unsalted butter, chilled and diced
1 egg, made up to $^2/_3$ cup (140ml) with milk
extra flour for rolling out

a $2^3/_8$-inch fluted round cookie cutter
a baking sheet, greased

I'm quite proud of my scones, if only because they got me my first job. Over the last 20 years I've tried every recipe I've come across – ones using soured milk or buttermilk; risen with various combinations of baking soda and cream of tartar, or baking powder; made with cream, or with golden syrup, with or without eggs. To get a moist, well-flavored scone that is light and well-risen you need a leavening agent or agents – but use too much and you just get a huge scone with a nasty chemical aftertaste. I found it quite difficult to get the proportions to my liking, so I went back to the simplest recipe, using self-rising flour, and got the best results. A light touch is also required here – too much kneading or overworking will develop the gluten in the flour and make the dough elastic, so it becomes tough and hard when baked. Making the dough in the food processor overcomes this to a certain extent – it is also very quick.

I think scones spread thickly with clotted or whipped rich cream and good strawberry preserves make the finest afternoon tea yet invented.

Preheat the oven to 425°F.

Sift the flour and salt into a bowl, then tip into the bowl of a food processor. Add the sugar and run the machine for a few seconds just to combine the ingredients. Add the diced butter and process until there are no lumps and the mixture looks like sand. Beat the egg with the milk just

until mixed. Slowly pour into the processor through the feed tube while the machine is running; stop pouring and turn off the machine as soon as the mixture forms a rather soft but not sticky ball of dough. If the dough seems dry and stiff, add a little extra milk.

Turn the dough onto a well-floured work surface. If the dough feels sticky and is hard to handle, sprinkle it with a little flour and work this in by gentle kneading; however, try not to work the dough more than necessary. Lightly knead the dough until it forms a rough-looking ball, then using your fingers pat it out 3/4 inch thick. Dip the cutter in flour and cut out as many rounds as possible. Gather up the trimmings into a ball, then pat out again and cut more rounds.

Arrange the rounds of dough well apart on the prepared baking sheet and bake immediately. They will take 12–15 minutes and should be a good golden brown, risen, and firm. Transfer from the baking sheet to a wire rack. Eat warm the same day, or split and toast. When completely cold, the scones can be frozen for up to a month.

TO MAKE SCONES WITHOUT A PROCESSOR, sift the flour and salt into a bowl, mix in the sugar, and add the diced butter. Rub the butter into the dry ingredients using the tips of your fingers. When the mixture resembles fine crumbs, add the egg and milk mixture. Stir in using a round-bladed knife to make a soft dough. Finish as above.

1 PROCESS THE BUTTER WITH THE DRY INGREDIENTS TO A SAND-LIKE TEXTURE.

2 ADD ENOUGH EGG AND MILK TO MAKE A SOFT DOUGH THAT IS NOT STICKY.

3 TURN OUT THE DOUGH ONTO A WELL-FLOURED WORK SURFACE.

4 KNEAD THE DOUGH LIGHTLY TO BLEND THE INGREDIENTS, THEN FORM A BALL.

5 PAT OUT THE DOUGH WITH YOUR FINGERS TO A DISK 3/4 INCH THICK.

6 CUT OUT ROUNDS WITH A FLOURED CUTTER AND PLACE ON A BAKING SHEET.

STRAWBERRY SHORTCAKE

INGREDIENTS

Serves 4–5
1lb (450g) ripe strawberries, hulled
1–2 tablespoons sugar, to taste
about 6 tablespoons (85g) unsalted butter, at room temperature, for spreading

SHORTCAKE:
1¾ cups (250g) self-rising flour
½ teaspoon baking powder
⅛ teaspoon salt
6½ tablespoons (80g) sugar
5½ tablespoons (80g) unsalted butter, chilled and diced
about 1 cup (230ml) heavy cream, chilled
a few drops of pure vanilla extract

a 3-inch plain round cookie cutter
a baking sheet, greased

OPPOSITE Strawberry Shortcake, an all-American favorite.

When planning my American father-in-law's 70th birthday dinner, I asked him to name his favorite dessert. "Strawberry Shortcake – but hold the shortcake," was the reply. Will loves strawberries, but finds that too often the shortcake tastes like cardboard. "It should be warm, rich with butter and cream, but also light and flaky," he says. Eventually I came up with this recipe – and it got the smacked lips of approval. The shortcake is similar to British scones (see previous page), but is made with cream instead of egg and milk, giving a texture and taste somewhere between a scone, shortbread, and spongecake. Serve with thick cream.

Preheat the oven to 425°F.

Thickly slice the strawberries and toss with a little sugar. Put aside.

Sift the flour, baking powder, salt, and sugar into a mixing bowl. Add the diced butter and quickly rub into the dry ingredients with the tips of your fingers until the mixture resembles large crumbs. Add the cream and vanilla and mix with a round-bladed knife until the mixture comes together to form a stiff dough.

Turn onto a lightly floured work surface, and pat into a brick. Using a rolling pin, roll out the dough to a rectangle ½ inch thick. Fold the dough into three: fold the bottom third of the rectangle up to cover the center third, then fold the top third down over this, to make three layers. Roll or pat out the dough again until it is 1 inch thick. Cut out rounds using the cookie cutter, then gently knead and re-roll the trimmings to give four or five rounds in all.

Place the dough rounds on the prepared baking sheet and bake in the preheated oven for 10 minutes. Reduce the oven temperature to 350°F, and bake for a further 10–15 minutes or until firm and golden. Leave on the sheet to cool slightly, then carefully transfer the shortcakes to a wire rack to cool completely.

When ready to serve, preheat the oven to 350°F. Split the shortcakes in half horizontally and butter the cut surfaces. Divide two-thirds of the strawberries among the shortcake bases. Cover with the lids and arrange the rest of the berries on top. Put the assembled shortcakes on a baking sheet and heat in the oven for 3–4 minutes or until they are warm and the butter is starting to melt. Eat immediately, with cream.

ARRANGE MOST OF THE STRAWBERRY SLICES ON THE BUTTERED SHORTCAKE BASES.

CRANBERRY MUFFINS

INGREDIENTS

Makes 1 dozen
1 cup (140g) unbleached all-purpose flour
1 cup (140g) stoneground whole-wheat bread flour
1 tablespoon baking powder
1/8 teaspoon salt
1/3 cup (85g) sugar
the grated rind of 1/2 unwaxed orange
1 extra large egg, beaten
1 1/4 cups (280ml) whole milk
2 teaspoons orange juice
1/4 cup (60ml) soybean oil
1 1/4 cups (140g) fresh or frozen cranberries – use straight from freezer

a 12-cup muffin tin, well greased or lined with paper muffin cases (see note)

In New England, white-painted churches like this are a familiar sight. The one shown above is in Mackerel Bay, Maine.

To me, muffins mean New England, and the best ones are made with the tart, juicy fruit of that region – cranberries and wild blueberries, either fresh or frozen. This is my mother-in-law's recipe. The combination of white and stoneground whole-wheat flours gives a good texture and prevents these muffins tasting like cupcakes; the orange contrasts well with the mouth-puckering tartness of the cranberries. Eat warm, preferably on the day of baking.

Preheat the oven to 400°F.

Mix the flours with the baking powder, salt, sugar, and grated orange rind in a mixing bowl. Mix the egg, milk, orange juice, and oil together, then add to the dry ingredients and mix with a wooden spoon until almost evenly blended. Add the fruit and briefly mix again – too much mixing can make the muffins tough.

Spoon the mixture into the prepared tin, dividing equally among the cups. Bake for 20–25 minutes or until a toothpick inserted into the center of a muffin comes out clean. The muffins should be golden and firm, with a distinct cracked peak. Let the muffins cool in the tin for a minute, then turn out onto a wire rack to cool for a further few minutes. Eat while still warm, with or without butter.

VARIATIONS: BLUEBERRY MUFFINS Replace the cranberries with an equal quantity of fresh or frozen blueberries. Omit the orange rind, and replace the orange juice with an equal quantity of lemon juice. You could also use blackberries or raspberries.
CHERRY MUFFINS Replace the cranberries with an equal quantity of pitted fresh cherries. Add 1 teaspoon pure vanilla extract with the orange juice.

NOTE The cups of the muffin tin should be about 2 5/8 inches deep.

BURN O'VAT ROCK CAKES

INGREDIENTS

Makes about 8
$1^2/_3$ cups (230g) self-rising flour
$^1/_4$ teaspoon apple-pie spice
6 tablespoons (85g) unsalted butter, chilled and diced
7 tablespoons (85g) sugar
$^2/_3$ cup (110g) mixed dried fruit and chopped candied peel
1 egg
2 tablespoons milk
1 tablespoon raw brown sugar for sprinkling

2 baking sheets, greased

I'm very fond of good rock cakes, which should be moist, crumbly, slightly spicy, and with a fair amount of dried fruit and candied peel. I got this recipe 20 years ago from a tiny tea shop, now closed, at Burn O'Vat – a beautiful spot near Ballater in Aberdeenshire, Scotland. I always bake a batch for picnics on long car and boat trips.

Preheat the oven to 400°F.

Sift the flour and spice into a mixing bowl. Add the diced butter and rub it into the flour with your fingertips until the mixture resembles fine crumbs. Stir in the sugar and the dried fruit and peel. Mix the egg with the milk, and stir just enough into the fruit mixture to bind to a firm, stiff dough – it is important that the dough holds its shape.

Divide the dough into eight portions and spoon onto the prepared baking sheets in heaped, peaky mounds spaced well apart. Sprinkle with the raw brown sugar. Bake for 12–15 minutes or until golden brown. Transfer to a wire rack to cool completely. Eat the same day or the following day, warmed and spread with butter.

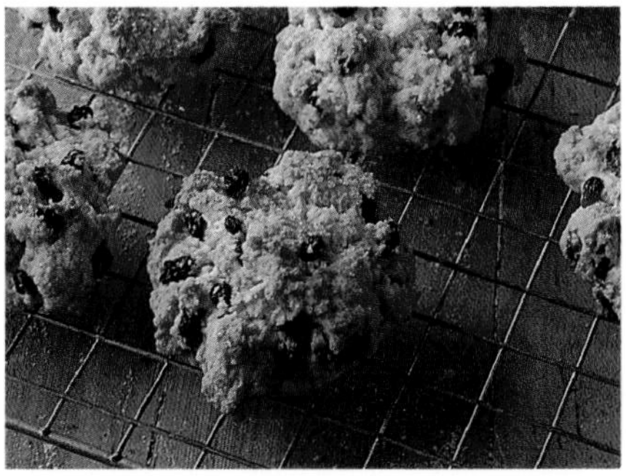

COOL THE ROCK CAKES ON A WIRE RACK.

RIGHT For many years, visitors to the Highlands of Scotland, including Queen Victoria, used to take the steam train from Aberdeen to Ballater.

CAROLL'S BROWNIES

INGREDIENTS

Makes 16 squares
$^{1}/_{2}$ cup + 2 tablespoons (140g) unsalted butter
4 eggs
1$^{2}/_{3}$ cups (340g) sugar
1 teaspoon pure vanilla extract
$^{1}/_{4}$ teaspoon salt
$^{3}/_{4}$ cup (80g) unsweetened cocoa powder
1 cup (140g) all-purpose flour
1 cup (110g) walnut pieces

a 9-inch square cake pan, about 2 inches deep, completely lined with greased foil

After intensive research, Anthony and I have decided that this is the best recipe for brownies we have ever eaten. It is also one of the simplest. It comes from a good friend and good cook, Caroll Boltin, a food historian who lives in the Hudson Valley in New York state.

Making a good brownie – one that is moist and fudgy rather than dry and cakey – requires great self-restraint. The melted butter must be cool when it is added or it will cook the eggs. If you beat the eggs and sugar too vigorously, too much air will be incorporated and the brownies will be more like a cake. The final mixture should be gently stirred rather than beaten, or the brownies will be tough and dry. Most important of all, it is vital to avoid overcooking – Caroll's tip is to test by inserting a skewer halfway between the center and the side of the pan – the center should remain quite moist. It is also a good idea to wrap the cooled cake and keep it overnight before cutting into squares – if you can wait.

Preheat the oven to 325°F.

Very gently melt the butter and let cool. Using a wooden spoon gently beat the eggs with the sugar until well blended and creamy looking. Stir in the cooled butter and the vanilla. Sift the salt, cocoa, and flour together and add to the mixture. Stir until thoroughly blended, then fold in the nuts. Pour the mixture into the prepared pan. Bake for about 40 minutes or until a skewer inserted midway between the center and the side of the pan comes out clean.

Cool in the pan for a few minutes, then lift the cake, still in the foil, out of the pan onto a wire rack. When completely cold, remove the foil and cut into 16 squares. Very good with vanilla ice-cream.

VARIATIONS For children who can't eat nuts I make the same mixture, substituting 4oz (110g) best-quality white chocolate, coarsely chopped, for the walnuts. For parties I double the recipe and bake it in a roasting pan lined with foil.

The best brownies ever – moist and fudgy, with lots of walnuts.

BROWN SUGAR MERINGUES

INGREDIENTS

Makes 4 pairs
2 egg whites
a pinch of cream of tartar (optional)
½ cup packed (110g) light brown sugar, sifted

FILLING:
⅔ cup (140ml) heavy cream, chilled
¼ cup (45g) minced candied ginger

2 baking sheets, lined with parchment paper

1 BEAT THE SUGAR INTO THE EGG WHITES TO MAKE A GLOSSY, FIRM MERINGUE.

2 USE A COUPLE OF LARGE SPOONS TO HEAP THE MERINGUE ON BAKING SHEETS.

The rich caramel flavor of these meringues comes from using light brown sugar rather than white sugar. Although the meringue mixture is made in the usual way, it is important to sift the sugar so that pockets of melted sugar do not form during baking. Use egg whites that are several days old – or add a pinch of cream of tartar if they are very fresh – and have them at room temperature. Pairs of meringues can be sandwiched together with ginger cream, as here, or you can use the chocolate filling for the macaroons on page 226.

Preheat the oven to 250°F.

Put the egg whites and cream of tartar into a spotlessly clean, grease-free bowl (avoid plastic if possible as it is difficult to keep really clean). Beat, slowly at first and then gradually increasing the speed, until the whites form a smooth foam that will stand in soft peaks. Take care not to overbeat the meringue to stiff peaks or it will collapse during baking. Beat in the sugar a tablespoon at a time. The final meringue should form firm peaks when the beaters are lifted out.

Spoon onto the prepared baking sheets to form 8 even-sized heaps. Bake in the preheated oven for 3–4 hours or until firm, dry, and crisp. Let cool completely, then store in an airtight tin until ready to assemble – they can be kept for a week at this stage.

To finish, whip the cream until stiff and stir in the ginger. Use to sandwich pairs of meringues together. Eat immediately if you like crisp meringues – after a couple of hours they become slightly and deliciously gooey, which is how I like them.

PUDDINGS & DESSERTS

Although taken to be synonymous, there is a difference between a pudding and a dessert. Traditionally, puddings are made with flour, eggs, and milk or cream, while desserts are based on fruit. The word dessert comes from the French desservir*, meaning to clear the table of plates and sweep the crumbs from the cloth ready for the last, most decorative course.*

QUEEN OF PUDDINGS

INGREDIENTS

Serves 4
2 cups (85g) fresh white bread crumbs or spongecake crumbs
1/2 cup (100g) sugar
the grated rind of 1 large unwaxed lemon
2 cups (430ml) whole milk
3 tablespoons (45g) unsalted butter
3 extra large eggs, separated
1/4 cup strawberry preserves

4 ramekins of 1 1/4-cup capacity, greased

The best English puddings are the old-fashioned nursery favorites. I am not sure where this recipe comes from, but along with chocolate Castle Puddings (see opposite), it was one of my childhood treats. You can use any good jam or preserves, or even lemon curd.

Preheat the oven to 325°F.

Put the crumbs and 1 tablespoon of the sugar into a mixing bowl and stir in the lemon rind. Heat the milk with the butter in a saucepan until the butter just melts, then pour the mixture over the crumbs and stir well. Let soak for 15 minutes. Stir in the egg yolks.

Divide the custard mixture among the prepared ramekins and bake in the preheated oven for 15–20 minutes or until the custards are just set and firm to the touch. Remove from the oven and spoon the jam onto the surface of the custards.

Beat the egg whites in a spotlessly clean, grease-free bowl until they form stiff peaks. Gradually beat in the remaining sugar to make a stiff, glossy meringue. Spoon the meringue on top of the jam. Return the ramekins to the oven and bake for about 10 minutes or until the meringue topping is lightly browned.

Serve warm or at room temperature, with cream or crème fraîche.

BAKE QUEEN OF PUDDINGS JUST UNTIL THE MERINGUE TOPPING IS LIGHTLY BROWNED.

PREVIOUS PAGE *At the end of an afternoon of baking, Dee Dee Meyer finishes icing a raspberry torte.*

CASTLE PUDDINGS

INGREDIENTS

Makes 8

SPONGE PUDDINGS:

½ cup (110g) unsalted butter, at room temperature
½ cup + 1 tablespoon (110g) sugar
2 eggs, beaten
½ cup + 2 tablespoons (85g) self-rising flour
½ teaspoon baking powder
⅓ cup (30g) ground almonds
3 tablespoons (15g) unsweetened cocoa powder
1 tablespoon milk

SAUCE:

2 cups (430ml) whole milk
¼ cup (20g) unsweetened cocoa powder
5 tablespoons (60g) sugar
2 tablespoons (15g) cornstarch
2 egg yolks

8 dariole molds of about 3-fl oz capacity, greased

These are chocolate and almond sponge puddings, baked in dariole molds, then turned out and served with chocolate custard sauce. When I was small, I pretended they were Saracen castles surrounded by moats; like any good Crusader I demolished them completely.

Preheat the oven to 350°F.

To make the puddings, beat the butter until creamy, using a wooden spoon or electric mixer. Gradually beat in the sugar. When the mixture is very light and fluffy, beat in the eggs a tablespoon at a time, beating well after each addition. Sift the flour with the baking powder, ground almonds, and cocoa powder, then fold into the beaten mixture with the milk, using a large metal spoon.

Spoon the mixture into the prepared molds, which should be two-thirds full. Stand the molds in a bain-marie – a roasting pan half-filled with very hot water. Cover the whole thing with foil, then bake in the preheated oven for about 30 minutes or until firm.

Meanwhile, make the sauce. Heat the milk in a heavy saucepan until scalding hot. Sift the cocoa, sugar, and cornstarch into a mixing bowl. Stir in the egg yolks to make a smooth, thick paste, then stir in the hot milk. When thoroughly blended, pour the mixture into the saucepan and stir over low heat until thickened – do not let the sauce boil.

To serve, carefully loosen the puddings with a small metal spatula or round-bladed knife, and unmold onto a deep dish or individual plates. Spoon the sauce around the base of the puddings and eat immediately. Allow two puddings per adult, one for a child.

LITTLE HONEY-NUT PUDDINGS

INGREDIENTS

Makes about 12
4 tablespoons (60g) unsalted butter, at room temperature
3 tablespoons (60g) honey
2 eggs, beaten
2/3 cup (110g) chopped dried figs
1 cup (110g) chopped blanched almonds
1/2 cup (60g) pine nuts
1/2 heaped cup (60g) currants
2/3 cup (110g) raisins
1/2 heaped cup (60g) golden raisins
1 small apple, such as a McIntosh, peeled, cored, and grated
1/2 teaspoon apple-pie spice
1/4 cup packed (60g) dark brown sugar
2 1/2 cups (110g) fresh white bread crumbs
1/3 cup (60g) minced mixed candied peel
a pinch of salt
the grated rind and juice of 1 small, or 1/2 large, unwaxed lemon

12 dariole molds of about 3-fl oz capacity, greased

As I discovered, by accident, these individual honey-nut puddings can be baked rather than steamed. The recipe is wonderfully odd: it contains no flour, just bread crumbs, and has no suet, just butter. It also contains plenty of nuts, almonds, and pine nuts, honey as well as dark brown sugar, and figs along with the other dried fruits. It is so good that I now make this at Christmas rather than the traditional sticky-rich plum pudding. Once the ingredients are assembled, the pudding is quick and simple enough to make for a winter Sunday lunch. Serve with brandy butter, cream, or ice-cream.

Preheat the oven to 325°F.

Put the butter into a large mixing bowl and beat until creamy, using a wooden spoon or electric mixer. Beat in the honey. Gradually beat in the eggs, a tablespoon at a time. The mixture will resemble scrambled eggs at this point. Put all the other ingredients into another bowl and mix well. Stir into the butter mixture. When thoroughly blended, spoon into the prepared dariole molds – they should be seven-eighths full. Cover each mold with a piece of greased parchment paper, pleated in the middle, then tie it on with string.

Set the molds in a bain-marie – a roasting pan half-filled with very hot water. Cover the whole thing with foil and bake in the preheated oven for about 1 hour or until the puddings are firm to the touch and have shrunk slightly from the sides of the molds.

Carefully loosen the puddings using a small metal spatula, then unmold onto individual serving plates and serve hot.

BEAT THE EGGS WITH A FORK UNTIL WELL MIXED, THEN BEAT INTO THE HONEY MIXTURE.

LEFT Serve Little Honey-Nut Puddings hot, dusted with confectioners' sugar.

DOTTY'S BAKED OATMEAL

INGREDIENTS

Serves 6
½ cup (115ml) soybean or sunflower oil
2 eggs, beaten
1 cup (170g) sugar
3½ cups (280g) quick-cooking oats
2 teaspoons baking powder
½ teaspoon salt
1 cup (230ml) whole milk

TO SERVE:
chopped fresh peaches or strawberries
cream

a deep baking dish or soufflé dish, about 8 inches in diameter, greased

RIGHT *Dottie and Andy Hess serve their guests a hearty farmhouse breakfast, which usually includes Baked Oatmeal with a fresh fruit compote.*

Dotty and Andy Hess have a 170-acre family farm, mainly cattle, pigs, and corn, in Mount Joy, in Lancaster County, Pennsylvania. Since their seven children have now left home, Dotty has converted the bedrooms of their pretty farmhouse to take in bed-and-breakfast guests.

Staying with the Hess family was a real treat for us: the rooms are charmingly decorated and exquisitely comfortable, with a candlelight in each window in the local Mennonite style. The highlight of each day was a hearty farmhouse breakfast made almost entirely with home-grown ingredients. One morning Dotty greeted us with glee – she had just cut the first asparagus spears of the season and was about to cook them with the breakfast eggs.

To whet our appetite – as if she needed to – she gave us baked oatmeal. It is nothing like porridge, but rather resembles an oatmeal muffin. It was accompanied by a compote of peaches that had been grown in the back garden. The dish was so good that Dotty made it for us again the next morning, this time with her strawberries. This is her recipe, which I like to make for family lunches – it has become a favorite.

Preheat the oven to 350°F.

Mix the oil with the eggs and sugar. When thoroughly blended, stir in the oats, baking powder, and salt followed by the milk. Mix well, then pour into the prepared baking dish.

Bake for 35–40 minutes or until golden and firm to the touch. Serve warm, with the fresh fruit and cream.

VARIATION Dotty sometimes adds grated raw apples, ground cinnamon, and chopped walnuts or pecans to the mixture before pouring it into the baking dish.

CHERRY CLAFOUTIS

INGREDIENTS

Makes an 8-inch tart, to serve 4–6

PASTRY:

- 1¼ cups (170g) self-rising flour
- a pinch of salt
- 2 tablespoons sugar
- 6 tablespoons (85g) unsalted butter, chilled and diced
- 1 egg yolk, mixed with 2 tablespoons ice water

FILLING:

- 1lb (450g) ripe cherries, pitted, or a 14-oz (411-g) can pitted black cherries, drained
- 6 tablespoons (85ml) cream
- 2 extra large eggs, beaten
- 3 tablespoons ground almonds
- 1 tablespoon kirsch or brandy
- 1½ tablespoons (20g) unsalted butter, melted

- an 8-inch loose-based tart pan
- a baking sheet

Above CAREFULLY POUR THE RICH EGG CUSTARD MIXTURE OVER THE FRUIT IN THE BAKED PASTRY SHELL.

The classic French clafoutis is a cross between an egg custard and a popover, studded with fruit. This is a version of French chef Roger Vergé's very rich, very light clafoutis with a pastry base. Fresh cherries work best, but frozen or canned cherries are good too, as are fresh or plump dried apricots, or juicy prunes.

To make the pastry, put the flour, salt, and sugar into the bowl of a food processor and briefly mix. Add the diced butter and process until the mixture resembles fine crumbs. With the machine running, add the yolk mixture through the feed tube. As soon as the dough comes together, stop the machine – the dough should be soft but not sticky. Alternatively, the dough can be made by hand (see page 302). Wrap and chill for 10 minutes.

Preheat the oven to 400°F. Put a baking sheet in the oven to heat up.

Roll out the pastry dough on a lightly floured work surface to a round about 10 inches in diameter. Using the rolling pin as a support, lift the dough and drape it over the tart pan. Gently press the dough into the pan to line the sides and bottom. Trim off any excess dough, and prick the bottom all over with a fork. Chill for 10 minutes.

Line the pastry shell with a piece of wax paper and fill with pie weights. Set the tart pan on the preheated baking sheet and bake the pastry shell for 10 minutes. Carefully remove the paper and weights – the pastry will still be soft. Return the tart shell to the oven and bake for a further 5 minutes or until firm and lightly golden. Remove the pan from the oven, leaving the baking sheet inside. Do not unmold the tart shell.

Make sure the cherries – both fresh and canned – are thoroughly drained. Put the cream, eggs, ground almonds, and kirsch or brandy in a bowl and mix thoroughly, then mix in the melted butter. Arrange the cherries in the tart shell, then slowly pour the custard mixture over them. Set the tart pan on the hot baking sheet again and bake for 15–20 minutes or until the filling is golden and set. Carefully remove the clafoutis from the tart pan and serve warm, with whipped cream.

DEE DEE'S RASPBERRY TORTE

INGREDIENTS

Serves 8

BASE:

$1^1/_3$ cups (200g) all-purpose flour
1 teaspoon baking powder
$^1/_3$ cup (60g) sugar
$^1/_2$ cup (110g) butter, at room temperature
1 egg, beaten
$^1/_4$ cup (85g) raspberry jam

FILLING:

$^2/_3$ cup (110g) sugar
$^1/_2$ cup (110g) butter, at room temperature
$^1/_2$ teaspoon pure almond extract
2 eggs, beaten
2–3 tablespoons sliced almonds for sprinkling

TOPPING:

$^1/_4$ cup (85g) raspberry jam
$^1/_2$ cup (60g) confectioners' sugar, sifted
about 2 teaspoons lemon juice

a 10- to 11-inch springform cake pan, greased

While staying with Dotty and Andy Hess we were invited to dine with a family who belong to the Old Order River Brethren. Dee Dee and Jack Meyer and their six children live near Manheim, in a house built with the help of their Amish friends. The Old Order communities – the Amish, the Mennonites, and the Brethren – came to Pennsylvania from the German part of Switzerland in the early 18th century. Jack explained that all stemmed from the Anabaptists – rebaptizers – who believe in making a conscious choice to accept God and only baptize adults.

So-called "Pennsylvania Dutch" cooking has a strong German influence. It is an oral tradition, taught from one generation to the next, and each nutritious meal is prepared from scratch. The dishes are hearty and simple – most farming families eat three full meals a day. The ingredients are those easily obtainable from local farms: beef, chicken, and pork; potatoes, corn, and cucumbers; milk and eggs; grains and beans; apples and soft fruits. Fruit and vegetables are preserved by canning and pickling.

Dinner at the Meyers was memorable. Dee Dee and a friend spent most of the afternoon cooking for the eight members of the family and fourteen guests. As the children arrived home from school, even the smallest were given tasks. We all dined at one long table, lit by oil lamps, and Jack explained that they enjoyed the opportunity to entertain paying guests: "It is good for other people to see how we live, to share a meal with us, to ask questions." To go hungry is to ignore the bounty of the earth, and the Old Order Communities take advantage of every occasion – weddings, barn raisings, Sabbath dinners – to enjoy a delicious meal together.

To make the base, put the flour, baking powder, and sugar into a mixing bowl, and stir to combine. Add the butter and egg and work the ingredients together, using a round-bladed knife, a fork, or wooden spoon, until the mixture resembles coarse crumbs. Using your hands, press the crumbs together, then gently knead to make a shortbread-like dough.

With the heel of your hand, press the dough into the bottom of the prepared pan to make an even layer. Spread the jam over the base, then chill for 10 minutes. Meanwhile, preheat the oven to 350°F.

To make the filling, put the sugar, butter, almond extract, and eggs into a mixing bowl. Using an electric mixer, beat until very light and fluffy.

BELOW Dee Dee's children – even the youngest – help her prepare dinner for her guests.

Spoon the mixture onto the jam-covered base and spread evenly. Sprinkle with the sliced almonds.

Bake for about 40 minutes or until firm and golden. Let cool until the torte is firm enough to handle, then unclip the side of the pan and carefully remove it.

Beat the jam to soften it a little, then gently spread over the top of the torte. Mix the confectioners' sugar with enough lemon juice to make a smooth and pourable icing. Using a small spoon, drizzle the icing over the torte. Serve warm or at room temperature, within 24 hours of baking.

ABOVE The farmhouse the Meyers built near Manheim, Pennsylvania.

RIGHT Dee Dee Meyer.

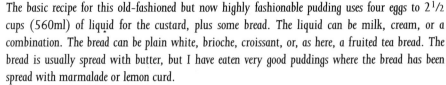

BREAD AND BUTTER PUDDING

INGREDIENTS

Serves 4–6
1 1/4 cups (280ml) whole milk
1 1/4 cups (280ml) light cream
1 vanilla bean, split
a pinch of salt
4 eggs
1/2 cup + 1 tablespoon (110g) sugar or vanilla-flavored sugar
5 thin slices, about 6oz (170g), tea bread (page 96), white bread, or brioche (page 90)
about 3 tablespoons (45g) unsalted butter, at room temperature
confectioners' sugar for sprinkling

a shallow baking dish of about 1-quart capacity, buttered

The basic recipe for this old-fashioned but now highly fashionable pudding uses four eggs to 2 1/2 cups (560ml) of liquid for the custard, plus some bread. The liquid can be milk, cream, or a combination. The bread can be plain white, brioche, croissant, or, as here, a fruited tea bread. The bread is usually spread with butter, but I have eaten very good puddings where the bread has been spread with marmalade or lemon curd.

Put the milk, cream, vanilla bean, and salt into a saucepan and heat slowly until scalding hot. Remove from the heat, cover, and set aside to infuse for 20 minutes.

Put the eggs and sugar into a large wide-mouthed measure or mixing bowl and lightly whisk together. Remove the vanilla bean from the milk mixture, then whisk into the egg mixture.

Butter the bread. Cut each slice in half diagonally, and cut off the crusts if desired. Arrange in the prepared baking dish so the top edges of each piece of bread are above the rim. Carefully pour the custard down the sides of the dish. Let stand for 2 hours.

When ready to cook, preheat the oven to 325°F. Stand the baking dish in a bain-marie – a roasting pan half-filled with lukewarm water – and bake for about 40 minutes or until just firm to the touch. If the custard is overcooked, it will separate and become watery.

Heat the broiler. Remove the baking dish from the bain-marie and sprinkle the top of the pudding with sifted confectioners' sugar. Put the dish under the hot broiler for a few seconds, until the sugar is golden and caramelized. Serve warm or at room temperature, with cream or ice-cream.

Above AS YOU POUR THE CUSTARD INTO THE DISH, CAREFULLY LIFT THE BREAD SO THE CUSTARD CAN MOISTEN ALL THE SLICES.

Right THE PUDDING IS COOKED WHEN IT IS JUST FIRM TO THE TOUCH IN THE CENTER.

CHOCOLATE BREAD PUDDING

INGREDIENTS

Serves 4–6
6oz (170g) plain or chocolate brioche (page 90), challah, or milk bread
3 cups (710ml) whole milk
1/4 cup (50g) sugar
3 extra large eggs, beaten
2/3 cup (110g) raisins
1/3 cup (40g) finely chopped toasted hazelnuts
a few drops of pure vanilla extract
4oz (110g) good semisweet chocolate, finely grated or melted
2 teaspoons baking powder
1 teaspoon ground cinnamon
1/4 teaspoon freshly grated nutmeg
4 tablespoons (60g) unsalted butter

a baking dish of about 1-quart capacity, buttered

Above USE A LARGE KNIFE TO CUT THE BRIOCHE INTO NEAT, SMALL CUBES.

Above right TO ENSURE THAT THE PUDDING IS MOIST, TAKE IT OUT OF THE OVEN AS SOON AS IT IS DONE.

Kenny's restaurant serves the best Cajun and Creole food in London. It is owned and run by a Scot who's proud to be an honorary citizen of New Orleans – as a mere non-resident alien spouse of an American, I'm jealous. Kenny's puddings are served in magnificently large portions, and this is my favorite. He serves it with ice-cream or egg custard sauce flavored with bourbon.

Dice the brioche, challah, or bread, discarding the crusts. Mix the milk with the sugar and eggs in a mixing bowl. Stir in the cubes of bread and let soak for 30 minutes.

Meanwhile, preheat the oven to 325°F.

Stir the raisins, hazelnuts, vanilla, and chocolate into the bread mixture. Sift the baking powder with the spices and stir in. Spoon or pour into the prepared baking dish and dot the top with the butter.

Bake for 1–1 1/4 hours or until just firm to the touch. Serve hot or warm, on its own or with ice-cream or custard sauce.

PARIS·BISTRO

TURKISH LEMON PUDDING

INGREDIENTS

Serves 6–8
2 cups (300g) all-purpose flour
1½ cups (340g) sugar
3 extra large eggs
1 cup (230ml) plain yogurt, preferably thick strained Turkish or Greek yogurt
1½ teaspoons baking soda
the juice of ½ lemon
½ cup (115ml) boiling water
clotted or whipped cream for serving

SYRUP:
2 cups (455ml) water
2 cups (450g) sugar
the juice of 1½ lemons

a baking dish, about 8 x 12 inches, greased

This recipe comes from my friend, Zeynep Conker Stromfelt, whose mother is pastry chef at a top Istanbul restaurant. Zeynep is a living cookbook of classic Turkish recipes, but she is especially fond of this typical family pudding: "It comes from my grandmother; it is quick and simple to prepare; and my children adore it." The unusual batter bakes to a very light sponge which is then soaked, like a baba or savarin, in a sweet, very lemony syrup. I thought it would be made with honey, but Zeynep explained that honey is not used in Turkish cooking.

Preheat the oven to 325°F.

Put the flour into a mixing bowl and stir in the sugar, then the eggs. Add the yogurt, baking soda, and lemon juice. Mix thoroughly to make a very thick, lump-free batter. Pour into the prepared baking dish and bake for 45 minutes to 1 hour or until a skewer inserted into the center comes out clean. The sponge will peak in the center.

While the sponge is baking, make the syrup. Boil the water in a medium-sized saucepan, then add the sugar and stir over low heat until dissolved. Bring back to a boil and boil for 1 minute, then remove from the heat and add the lemon juice. For an even more intense flavor you can add grated lemon rind to taste, but this is less popular with children. Keep the syrup hot.

As soon as the sponge comes out of the oven, loosen the edges and prick it all over with a skewer. Pour the boiling water over. Cover the sponge with foil and let stand for about 10 minutes or until the water has been completely absorbed.

Prick the sponge again, then slowly spoon the very hot syrup over – it will gradually be absorbed and the sponge will swell. Serve at room temperature, with clotted or whipped cream.

This pudding is best when quickly made and immediately baked, so Zeynep assembles all the ingredients before she starts work. The mixture is unusual in that it contains yogurt.

MOTHER-IN-LAW'S APPLE CRISP

INGREDIENTS

Serves 4–6
6 large tart apples, such as Granny Smiths
$1\frac{1}{2}$ cups (230g) blueberries – fresh or frozen (don't thaw)
the grated rind and juice of 1 small unwaxed lemon
sugar (optional)

TOPPING:
1 cup (140g) all-purpose flour
$\frac{1}{2}$ cup (100g) light brown sugar
110g (4oz) unsalted butter, diced
$1\frac{1}{2}$–2 cups (170–230g) walnut pieces

a large shallow baking dish, lightly greased

When we visit my husband's family in Yarmouth, Maine, everyone gathers together for our first dinner at home. Each member of the family cooks something, and dessert is always the same – my mother-in-law's apple and blueberry crisp. Annette got this recipe from her mother-in-law, so by giving it to me she establishes a family tradition. I prefer this fruit crisp to its English cousin, the apple crumble, because the topping is lighter and crunchier. As with a crumble, you can vary the fruit filling to suit the season – peach and raspberry, blackberry and apple or pear, pear and prune, plum and orange, apricot and banana, rhubarb and red currant. The blueberries that grow wild up on the Maine coast are a delicacy – small but very juicy with a distinct tartness, which is enhanced by a little lemon rind and juice.

Preheat the oven to 375°F.

Peel, core, and dice the apples. Put into a bowl with the blueberries and the grated lemon rind and juice. Toss gently until thoroughly mixed. Add a little sugar (light brown or granulated) to taste if using sour or very tart fruit – Granny Smith apples usually don't need sugar. Put the fruit into the prepared baking dish in an even layer.

To make the topping, combine the flour and sugar in a mixing bowl. Add the butter and rub and squeeze into the flour mixture – it should not look like bread crumbs but rather form flakes or pea-sized lumps of dough. Stir in the nuts. Sprinkle the topping evenly over the fruit.

Bake for about 30 minutes or until the fruit is tender but not mushy, and the topping is crisp and golden. The fruit juices will probably bubble up through the topping in places, which looks very appetizing. Eat warm or at room temperature, within 24 hours of baking, with ice-cream, yogurt, crème fraîche, or whipped cream.

ABOVE Yarmouth, Maine, where my husband's family lives.

OPPOSITE My mother-in-law Annette lends me her kitchen as well as her best recipes.

FRUIT BASKETS

INGREDIENTS

Serves 6

COOKIES:

1 extra large egg white
5 tablespoons (60g) superfine sugar
2 tablespoons (30g) unsalted butter, melted and cooled
3½ tablespoons (30g) all-purpose flour, sifted
the grated rind of ½ unwaxed orange
2oz (60g) good semisweet chocolate, chopped

CREME ANGLAISE:

⅔ cup (140ml) very creamy milk or cream
3 extra large egg yolks
2½ tablespoons (30g) sugar, or to taste
the grated rind of ½ unwaxed orange
1 tablespoon orange liqueur

FRUIT FILLING:

about ¾lb (340g) prepared fresh fruit, such as a mixture of raspberries, strawberries, grapes, apples, currants, mango, plums, peaches – whatever is available
3 tablespoons orange juice or orange liqueur

several baking sheets, greased
small individual brioche molds, squat tumblers, or oranges, lightly greased

These delicate, crisp cookie baskets are made with a basic tuile mixture. They are dipped in chocolate, just to coat the rim, and are filled with fresh fruit salad and served with crème anglaise. The baskets are shaped by draping the just-baked cookies over an oiled brioche mold, though a small tumbler or cup, or even an orange, could be substituted. The recipe will make more cookies than you need, to allow for failures or breakages.

Preheat the oven to 350°F.

To make the cookie baskets, put the egg white into a spotlessly clean, grease-free, non-plastic bowl. Beat until stiff, then gradually beat in the sugar, followed by the cooled melted butter and, finally, the sifted flour. If using an electric mixer, do this on low speed. Gently stir in the grated orange rind.

Spoon a teaspoon of the batter onto a prepared baking sheet and spread into a thin disk about 4 inches in diameter. Bake for about 5 minutes or until a pale gold color. Remove from the oven. Using a metal spatula, immediately loosen the cookie from the baking sheet and quickly drape it

over a mold or orange – it will harden very rapidly. Let cool before removing from the mold or orange. Once you have the knack of this process you can bake the cookies two at a time.

To finish the baskets, melt the chocolate on a heatproof plate set over a pan of hot but not boiling water. Turn each basket upside-down and dip the rim into the melted chocolate. Turn the right way up and let set. You will need 6 baskets.

To make the crème anglaise, heat the milk in a heavy saucepan until scalding hot. Cream the egg yolks with the sugar until thick and pale, then gradually stir in the hot milk. Stir thoroughly, then pour into the rinsed-out milk pan. Cook over very low heat, stirring constantly with a wooden spoon, until the custard thickens enough to coat the back of the spoon. This can take as much as 5 minutes. Do not be tempted to hurry the process; if the custard boils it will curdle and cannot be used. Strain the thickened custard into a measure and stir in the orange rind and liqueur. Sprinkle the surface of the custard with a little sugar to prevent a skin from forming. Let cool, then cover and chill.

When ready to serve, set a basket on each dessert plate. Toss the prepared fruit with the juice or liqueur, then spoon into the baskets. Spoon a little crème anglaise around the base of each basket. Eat immediately.

RICH CHOCOLATE SOUFFLÉ

INGREDIENTS

Serves 4

6oz (170g) good semisweet chocolate, chopped

$^2/_3$ cup (140ml) heavy cream

3 eggs, separated

2 tablespoons brandy

2 egg whites

3 tablespoons superfine sugar

confectioners' sugar for sprinkling

4 ramekins of $1^1/_4$-cup capacity, buttered and sugared (see recipe)

This exceedingly rich, classic French soufflé is like a hot chocolate mousse. It is made without flour, and has a light, meltingly soft texture. For the best taste you should use the finest semisweet chocolate you can find – with a high proportion of chocolate liquor. The method is quick and straightforward – if you can make meringue, you can make this soufflé.

Preheat the oven to 425°F.

Brush the ramekins with melted butter, then sprinkle with sugar to make an even coating on the bottom and sides. This will help the soufflé mixture to rise well and evenly, as well as giving a nice crunchy, thin crust. Stand the prepared ramekins on a baking sheet or in a roasting pan.

Put the chocolate into a heavy-based pan with the cream. Set over very low heat and stir occasionally until melted. Remove from the heat and stir until smooth. Gently stir in the egg yolks, one at a time, and then the brandy. Set aside.

Put the 5 egg whites into a spotlessly clean, grease-free bowl and beat until stiff peaks form. Sprinkle with the sugar and briefly beat again to make a smooth, stiff meringue. If you overbeat the meringue at this stage (it will start to look grainy), it will do more harm than good, and the end result will be less smooth.

The chocolate mixture should be just warm, so gently reheat it if necessary. Using a large metal spoon, add a little of the meringue to the chocolate mixture and mix until thoroughly combined. This "softens" the chocolate – loosens the consistency – to make it easier to combine with the meringue. Pour the chocolate mixture on top of the remaining meringue in the bowl and gently fold the two mixtures together until thoroughly combined but not over-mixed.

Spoon or pour into the prepared ramekins: the soufflé mixture should come to just below the rim. Bake at once, for 8–10 minutes. Remove from the oven when they are barely set: the centers should be soft and wobble when gently shaken. Sprinkle with confectioners' sugar and eat immediately.

1 COMBINE THE HEAVY CREAM AND PIECES OF CHOCOLATE IN A SAUCEPAN.

2 HEAT GENTLY UNTIL MELTED. REMOVE FROM THE HEAT AND STIR UNTIL SMOOTH.

3 ADD THE EGG YOLKS TO THE CHOCOLATE MIXTURE, ONE AT A TIME, STIRRING.

4 ADD THE BRANDY AND STIR UNTIL IT HAS BEEN COMPLETELY BLENDED IN.

5 THE CHOCOLATE MIXTURE SHOULD BE VERY SMOOTH AND GLOSSY. SET IT ASIDE.

6 BEAT THE EGG WHITES UNTIL STIFF, THEN ADD THE SUGAR AND BEAT BRIEFLY.

7 ADD A SPOONFUL OF THE MERINGUE TO THE WARM CHOCOLATE MIXTURE.

8 POUR THE CHOCOLATE MIXTURE ONTO THE REMAINING MERINGUE IN THE BOWL.

9 GENTLY FOLD THE TWO MIXTURES TOGETHER UNTIL EVENLY COMBINED.

10 DIVIDE THE SOUFFLÉ MIXTURE AMONG THE RAMEKIN DISHES AND BAKE AT ONCE.

ALMOND AND APPLE SLICE

INGREDIENTS

Cuts into 8 slices

PASTRY:

- 3/4 cup (110g) all-purpose flour
- a pinch of salt
- 5 tablespoons (60g) sugar
- 4 tablespoons (60g) unsalted butter, chilled and diced
- 2 egg yolks

FILLING:

- 6 tablespoons (60g) golden raisins
- 3 tablespoons rum or fruit juice
- 1 1/2lb (680g) apples – Pippins or McIntosh
- 1 teaspoon ground cinnamon
- 2 tablespoons (30g) unsalted butter
- 1/2 cup (60g) roughly chopped blanched almonds
- 1 teaspoon apple-pie spice

TOPPING:

- 1 egg white
- 1 tablespoon all-purpose flour
- 12oz (340g) white marzipan

TO FINISH:

- 2–3 tablespoons strained apricot jam, warmed, for glazing
- about 1/3 cup (30g) toasted sliced almonds for sprinkling

a baking sheet, greased
a pastry bag fitted with a 3/8-inch plain tip

In this Swiss recipe, rich, crisp sweet pastry is covered with fried almonds, topped with a mound of apples, and finished with a marzipan lattice. It is substantial but not too rich, and can be made several hours before serving.

To make the pastry, put the flour, salt, and sugar into the bowl of a food processor and mix briefly. Add the butter and process until the mixture resembles coarse crumbs. With the machine running, add the egg yolks through the feed tube, and process until the mixture forms large clumps. Do not overprocess or the dough will be greasy and heavy. Turn the dough onto the work surface and gather into a ball. Wrap and chill until firm – about 45 minutes. Meanwhile, heat the oven to 375°F.

Roll out the pastry dough on a lightly floured work surface to a 4 1/2- x 12-inch rectangle that is about 1/4 inch thick. Roll the rectangle around the rolling pin and transfer it to the prepared baking sheet. If necessary neaten the edges, either by trimming with a large sharp knife or by gently shaping with your hands. Flute the edges with your fingers, and prick the pastry rectangle well all over with a fork. Chill for about 15 minutes or until firm.

Bake for 10–12 minutes or until golden and firm. Cool for a minute, then loosen the underside with a large spatula. Let cool on the baking sheet. Increase the oven temperature to 425°F.

While the pastry base is cooling, make the filling. Mix the golden raisins with the rum and set aside to soak. Peel, core, and thickly slice the apples. Mix with the raisins and any soaking liquid left. Add the cinnamon. Toss well, then tip into a baking dish or roasting pan. Bake for 15 minutes or until the apples are barely tender. Let cool in the dish.

Melt the butter in a small heavy pan. Add the chopped almonds and apple-pie spice and cook gently, stirring frequently, for 5 minutes or until golden. Let cool.

To make the topping, put the egg white and flour in a food processor.

DECORATE THE EDGE OF THE PASTRY RECTANGLE BY FLUTING WITH YOUR FINGERS.

OPEN OUT THE PASTRY BAG AND STAND IT UPRIGHT IN A MEASURE FOR SUPPORT, THEN SPOON IN THE MARZIPAN MIXTURE.

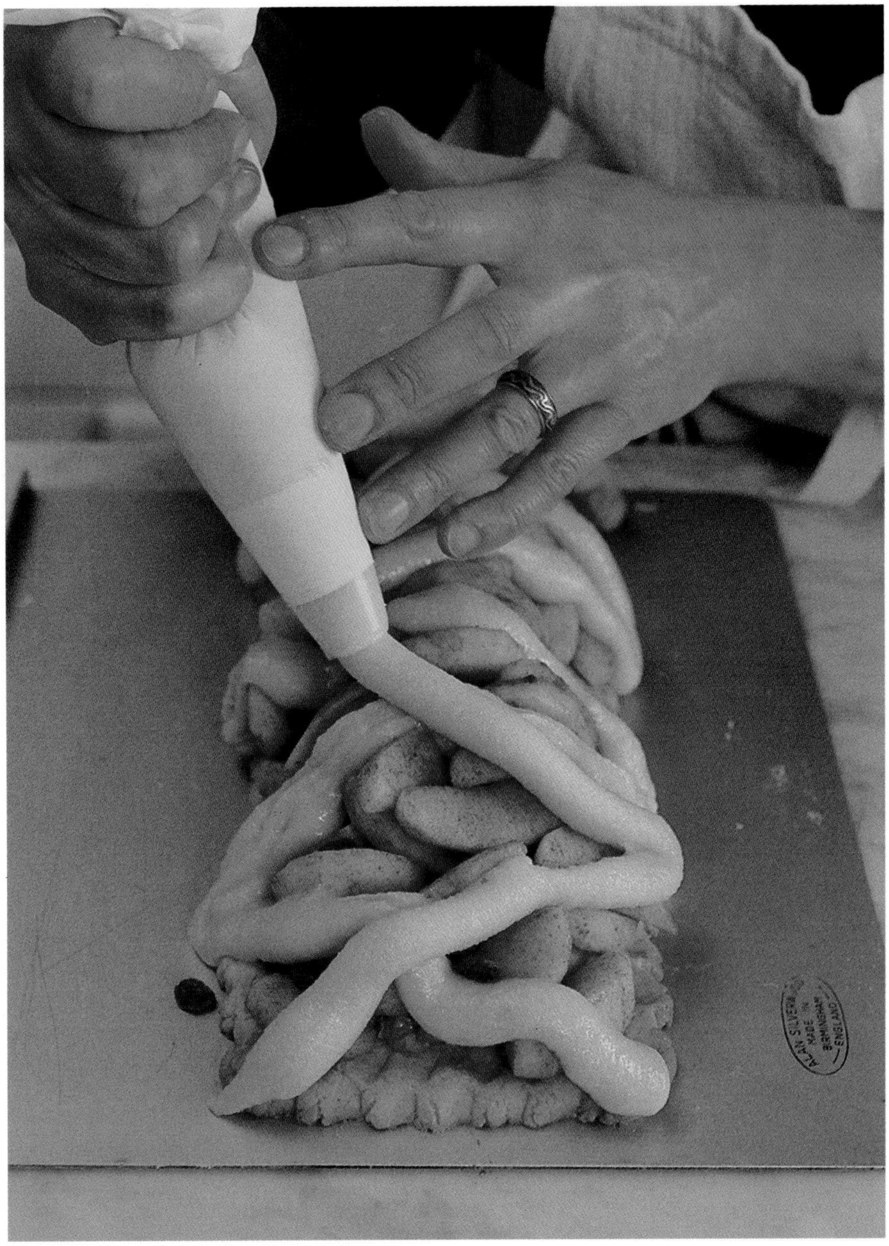

PIPE THE MARZIPAN MIXTURE OVER THE APPLE TOPPING TO MAKE A ZIGZAG LATTICE PATTERN.

Break up the marzipan with your hands and add to the processor. Process until smooth. If it is a very hot day and the mixture seems too difficult and runny to pipe, put it in the fridge to chill for 30 minutes. Spoon the mixture into the pastry bag fitted with the plain tip.

To finish the slice, preheat the oven to 450°F. Spoon the nut mixture onto the pastry base on the baking sheet. Leave a narrow border of pastry showing. Spoon the apple mixture on top, mounding it neatly and evenly with your hands. Finally, pipe on the marzipan mixture in a zigzag lattice pattern. Let stand for about 10 minutes.

Bake for 5–8 minutes or until barely golden. Let cool for 15 minutes, then brush the top with the warmed apricot jam and sprinkle with the toasted sliced almonds.

Serve at room temperature, within 24 hours of baking. Delicious with vanilla ice-cream, cream, crème anglaise (see page 260), or crème fraîche.

STRAWBERRY BABAS

INGREDIENTS

Makes 12

DOUGH:

$1^3/_4$ cups (230g) unbleached white bread flour
1 teaspoon salt
$1^1/_2$ tablespoons (15g) sugar
1 0.6-oz cake fresh yeast (15g)
3 tablespoons milk, lukewarm
3 eggs, beaten
the grated rind of 1 unwaxed lemon
$^1/_2$ cup (110g) unsalted butter, at room temperature

SYRUP:

$2^1/_2$ cups (500g) sugar
1 quart (1 liter) water
the grated rind and juice of 1 large unwaxed lemon, or to taste

FILLING:

1 cup (250g) mascarpone or ricotta cheese
$^1/_2$lb (250g) strawberries, washed and hulled
fine shreds of lemon rind for decorating (optional)

12 dariole molds of about $^1/_2$-cup capacity, buttered (see recipe)
a baking sheet

Babas are like very light sponge cakes soaked in a flavored syrup. But, in fact, they are made from a yeast dough enriched with eggs and butter, rather than a cake batter leavened with baking powder. Popular rum babas contain rum-soaked currants, and more rum is poured over after baking. The babas here are flavored with lemon, and are filled before serving with mascarpone or ricotta and sliced strawberries. You could also sprinkle over a little brandy or kirsch.

To make the dough, mix the flour, salt, and sugar in a mixing bowl, and make a well in the center. Crumble the yeast into a small bowl and cream it to a smooth paste with the lukewarm milk. Pour into the well in the flour, then mix in the eggs. Work the flour into the liquids with your hand, to make a smooth, very thick, batter-like dough. Knead the dough, in the bowl, by beating it with your hand: tilt the bowl slightly and, using your hand like a spoon, lift the dough and throw it back into the bowl with a slapping motion. Continue for 5 minutes or until the dough becomes very elastic, smooth, and slightly stiff. Cover the bowl with a damp dish towel and let rise in a warm place for 45 minutes to 1 hour or until the dough has doubled in bulk.

Butter the molds thoroughly. Chill them in the freezer for 10 minutes and then butter them again – this double buttering helps prevent the delicate dough from sticking to the molds and makes unmolding the soft-crusted babas very easy. The butter sets, so it will not be absorbed by the dough as it rises.

Punch down the risen dough with your knuckles, then using your hand as before, beat in the grated lemon rind and the soft butter. When the mixture is very smooth, with no streaks, use two spoons to divide it among the prepared molds. They should be just under half full. Arrange the molds on the baking sheet, cover with a damp dish towel, and let rise at normal to warm room temperature until the dough reaches almost to the top of the molds. This will take about 45 minutes – check to make sure the dough is not sticking to the dish towel.

1 WHEN THOROUGHLY BEATEN, THE DOUGH WILL BE ELASTIC.

2 USE A PASTRY BRUSH TO COAT THE INSIDES OF THE MOLDS WITH SOFT BUTTER. CHILL AND BUTTER AGAIN.

RIGHT The babas can be split horizontally or vertically before filling generously with creamy mascarpone and fruit.

Preheat the oven to 400°F.

Bake the babas for 15–20 minutes or until golden brown and beginning to shrink away from the sides of the molds. Turn out very carefully onto a wire rack and let cool.

To make the syrup, stir the sugar and water in a saucepan over low heat until dissolved. Then bring to a boil and boil, without stirring, for 2–3 minutes or until the syrup clears. Stir in the lemon rind and juice.

Remove the pan from the heat. Add the babas, a couple at a time, to the hot syrup and let them soak for a minute or so, turning them over. Lift them out with a slotted spoon onto a serving plate. When cool, keep covered until ready to serve.

To make the filling, beat the mascarpone or ricotta until fluffy. Slice the strawberries and sweeten with a little sugar if necessary.

Slice off the top of each baba at an angle. Spoon a little mascarpone or ricotta onto the cut surface of each baba, then top with strawberries and replace the cut-off top. Sprinkle with liqueur, if using, and shreds of lemon rind and serve as soon as possible.

NOTE You can use 1 package (¼oz/7g) active dry yeast instead of fresh yeast. For rapid-rise dry yeast, add it to the flour, salt, and sugar. Proceed with the recipe, adding the lukewarm milk with the eggs.

APRICOT ALMOND BRAID

INGREDIENTS

Cuts into about 8 slices

DOUGH:

1¾ cups (230g) unbleached white bread flour
½ teaspoon salt
3 tablespoons (40g) unsalted butter, chilled and diced
⅔ 0.6-oz cake fresh yeast (10g)
5 tablespoons (70ml) milk, at room temperature
1 egg, beaten

FILLING:

¾ cup (110g) roughly chopped dried apricots
⅔ cup (140ml) orange juice
6 tablespoons (85g) unsalted butter, at room temperature
½ cup (60g) light brown sugar
⅓ cup (30g) ground almonds
6 tablespoons (60g) golden raisins
¼ cup (60g) toasted and roughly chopped blanched almonds
the grated rind of 1 unwaxed orange

TO FINISH:

⅓ cup (30g) toasted sliced almonds for sprinkling

a large baking sheet, greased

NOTE You can use 2 teaspoons active dry yeast instead of fresh yeast, dissolving it in warm milk. For rapid-rise dry yeast mix it with the flour and salt, then proceed with the recipe.

Ideal for picnics and alfresco meals, this is a moist and fruity, well-flavored cake made from sweet yeast dough. It is filled with chopped dried apricots and ground and chopped almonds.

To make the filling, put the apricots and orange juice into a small pan. Bring to a boil, then remove from the heat and let soak while making and rising the sweet yeast dough.

Mix the flour and salt in a large mixing bowl. Rub in the butter to make fine crumbs. Make a well in the center. Crumble the yeast into a small bowl and cream it to a smooth liquid with the milk. Stir in the egg. Pour the yeast mixture into the well in the flour. Gradually work the flour into the liquid to make a soft but not sticky dough. Turn the dough onto a lightly floured work surface and knead for 10 minutes or until very smooth and elastic. Return the dough to the bowl, cover with a damp dish towel, and let rise at normal room temperature for about 1 hour or until the dough has doubled in bulk.

Meanwhile, prepare the filling. Drain the soaked apricots, reserving the liquid to glaze the baked braid. Beat the butter with the sugar until fluffy, then work in the ground almonds followed by the drained apricots, golden raisins, chopped almonds, and orange rind.

Punch down the risen dough with your knuckles, then turn onto a lightly floured work surface. Roll out to a rectangle about 10 x 12 inches. Spread the filling evenly over the dough, then roll up fairly tightly from one long side, like a jelly roll. Using your hands, gently roll the cylinder on the work surface to make it longer and thinner – it should be about 18 inches long. Lift it onto the prepared baking sheet.

Using a large, very sharp knife, cut the roll lengthwise into three equal strips, leaving them joined at one end. Working with the cut sides facing upward as much as possible, braid the three strips together. Pinch the ends together and tuck under neatly. Cover loosely with a damp dish towel and let rise at normal room temperature for about 1 hour or until the braid has doubled in size.

Preheat the oven to 400°F.

Bake the risen braid for about 25 minutes or until golden brown and firm. Remove from the oven. Heat the reserved orange juice and brush over the hot braid. Sprinkle with the sliced almonds and transfer to a wire rack to cool. Serve warm, with cream. Eat within 2 days. To reheat the braid, wrap in foil and heat for about 10 minutes at 350°F.

1 AFTER SPREADING WITH THE APRICOT FILLING, ROLL UP THE DOUGH QUITE TIGHTLY.

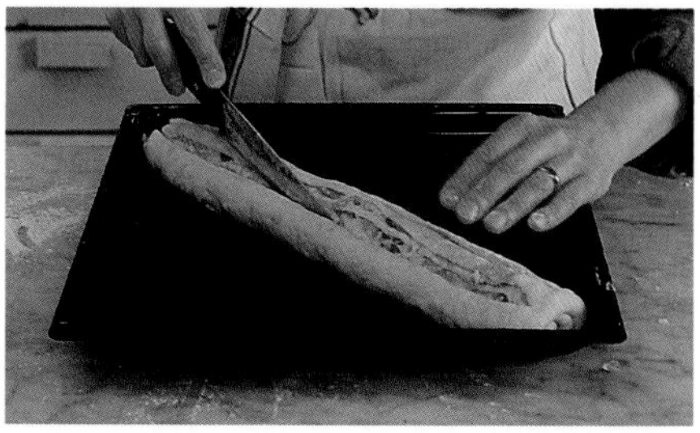

2 CUT THE ROLL DOWN ITS LENGTH INTO THREE STRIPS, THEN BRAID THESE TOGETHER.

RED FRUIT SLUMP

INGREDIENTS

Serves 4
1-1¼lb (500g) fresh or frozen red fruits
3–4 tablespoons sugar, to taste
2 tablespoons water or crème de cassis

DUMPLINGS:
7 tablespoons (60g) self-rising flour
2 tablespoons (30g) unsalted butter, chilled and diced
1½ tablespoons (15g) sugar
a pinch of ground cinnamon
2 tablespoons milk

a baking dish of about 1-quart capacity

This is another German dessert from Brigitte Friis (see her divine Almond Squares on page 225). A mixture of red fruits is cooked until the juices just start to run, then tiny pastry dumplings are added, and the dessert is baked until the fruit is just tender and the dumplings are cooked and feather-light. Brigitte freezes fruit from her garden – cherries, raspberries, blackberries, loganberries, strawberries, and currants – to make this dessert, but frozen mixed red fruits, sold in bags, and fresh fruit both work just as well.

Preheat the oven to 375°F.

Put the fruit (there is no need to thaw frozen fruit) in the baking dish and sprinkle over the sugar and the water or cassis. Cover with a lid or foil and bake in the preheated oven for 10–12 minutes or until the juices start to run – the time will depend on the type and ripeness of the fruit, and whether it is fresh or frozen.

Meanwhile, make the pastry dumplings. Sift the flour into a small mixing bowl, add the diced butter, and rub in using the tips of your fingers until the mixture resembles fine crumbs. Stir in the sugar and cinnamon, and bind to a soft but not sticky dough with the milk. Using your hands, roll the mixture into 12 small balls.

Remove the baking dish from the oven, uncover, and stir the fruit gently. Arrange the pastry balls in the dish so they are nestling in the hot fruit juices. Cover again and bake for about 15 minutes or until the dumplings are firm to the touch. Serve hot, warm, or at room temperature, with ice-cream, cream, or crème fraîche.

CARROLL'S FUDGE PIE

INGREDIENTS

Serves 6–8
1 cup (200g) sugar
½ cup (110g) unsalted butter, at room temperature
2 eggs, separated
2½oz (70g) good semisweet chocolate, chopped
⅓ cup (50g) all-purpose flour
a few drops of pure vanilla extract
a pinch of salt

CHOCOLATE CREAM:
3 tablespoons unsweetened cocoa powder
⅓ cup (40g) confectioners' sugar
⅔ cup (140ml) heavy cream, chilled
a few drops of pure vanilla extract

a 9-inch pie pan, about 1½ inches deep, or a tart pan (not loose-based), greased

Caroll Boltin, who makes the best brownies in the world (see the recipe on page 242), prefers this very rich chocolate pudding to Mississippi Mud Pie or Death By Chocolate. She adds that it is embarrassingly easy and quick to make for something that tastes so good. Serve in very thin slices with whipped cream, chocolate cream (recipe below), or ice-cream.

Preheat the oven to 325°F.

Beat the sugar and butter together until creamy, then beat in the egg yolks one at a time. Melt the chocolate in a heatproof bowl set over a pan of hot but not boiling water, then remove from the heat and let cool, stirring occasionally. Beat the cooled chocolate into the yolk mixture. Add the flour, vanilla, and salt and fold into the mixture, using a large metal spoon, until thoroughly combined.

In a spotlessly clean and grease-free bowl, beat the egg whites until stiff peaks form. Fold into the chocolate mixture in three batches.

Spoon into the prepared pie or tart pan and spread evenly. Bake for 30 minutes. Let cool and then chill.

To make the chocolate cream, sift the cocoa powder and sugar into the cream. Stir gently until combined, then cover and chill for 2 hours. The mixture should be quite stiff. Stir in the vanilla. If the cream isn't stiff, whip it until it holds its shape. The chocolate cream can also be used to sandwich chocolate macaroons or meringues (pages 226 and 243).

Decorate the fudge pie, if desired, with piped chocolate cream, or serve the cream separately.

FAMILY & CELEBRATION CAKES

From the seemingly plain but luxurious Quatre-quarts to the richest, most seductive of chocolate cakes, here are recipes for coffee time and afternoon tea as well as dessert.

QUATRE-QUARTS OR POUND CAKE

INGREDIENTS

Makes 1 large loaf-shaped cake
4 eggs
about 1 cup (250g) unsalted butter, at room temperature
about 1¼ cups (250g) sugar
a pinch of salt
½ teaspoon pure vanilla extract
about 1¾ cups (250g) self-rising flour
6 tablespoons (60g) chopped crystallized fruit, soaked in 2 tablespoons rum overnight

a large loaf pan, about 9 x 5 x 3 inches, lined with a double thickness of greased parchment paper

PREVIOUS PAGE Royal Scotsman Fruit Cake (left), Walnut Cake.

Quatre-quarts was just a rich sponge cake to me until we visited la Maison Bernachon in Lyons, France. Called the best little chocolate shop in the world, it owes its reputation to father and son perfectionist chocolatiers and pâtissiers, Maurice and Jean-Jacques Bernachon. Beside the divine chocolate, made by hand from scratch, are heavenly cakes and pastries. There is also a salon de thé where you can try in miniature the miracles available in the boutique. Here Jean-Jacques prepared for us a breakfast of coffee and large slices of moist, very rich, angelically light, vanilla quatre-quarts studded with fruits confits macerated in rum. Of all their superlative creations this, the simplest, was my favorite. Jean-Jacques showed us the kitchens where trays of freshly picked local fruits were being prepared for the long process of cooking in sugar syrup, which turns them into the luscious fruits confits. A large dish of cherries was being steeped in brandy. The attention to detail is fanatical; there are no short cuts to perfection.

Jean-Jacques explained the intricacies of the seemingly simple quatre-quarts: the eggs must be weighed first and then the same quantity weighed in flour, the finest butter, and sugar. The cake can be made in two ways. In the first, the butter is beaten until very creamy; the sugar is gradually beaten in to make a very light and fluffy mixture; the eggs are added a tablespoon at a time while beating vigorously; and, finally, the flour is gently folded in. In the second, the egg yolks and sugar are beaten to a thick foam; the butter is melted and cooled, then folded in, followed by the flour and, finally, the beaten egg whites. This latter method, favored by the French, makes a lighter, more tender cake, but it tends to be dry, while the former can be heavy and tough if not well made. I tried both ways, following Jean-Jacques' instructions, and preferred the creaming method. Before you begin, be sure that all the ingredients are at room temperature or it will be difficult to incorporate air into the mixture.

Preheat the oven to 400°F.

Weigh the 4 eggs together – the total weight should be 8¾–9¼oz (250–260g). Use exactly the same weight of butter, sugar, and flour.

Put the soft butter in the bowl of an electric mixer and beat at low speed until very creamy. Gradually beat in the sugar, then beat the mixture at high speed until it becomes very white and light in texture. Lightly beat the eggs with the salt, then beat into the creamed mixture a tablespoon at a time, beating well after each addition. This will take at least 7 minutes.

1 BEAT THE BUTTER AND SUGAR TOGETHER UNTIL VERY WHITE AND LIGHT.

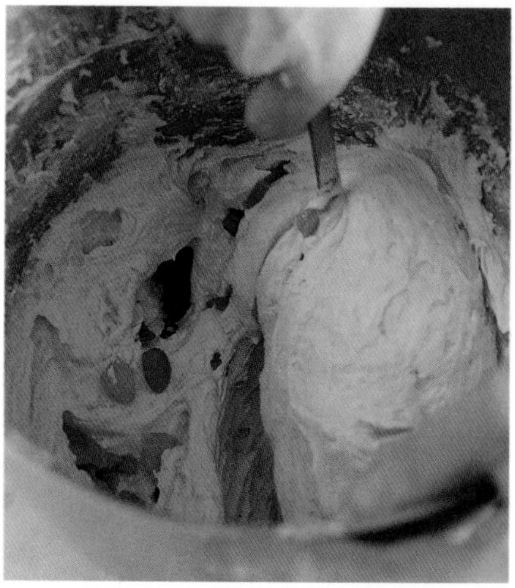

2 ADD THE FLOUR, THEN GENTLY FOLD IN THE RUM-SOAKED FRUIT.

Quatre-quarts is made with equal weights of eggs, butter, sugar, and flour. The recipe here is flavored with vanilla and includes some luscious rum-soaked crystallized fruit. Alternatively, you can bake a chocolate-flavored cake and add rum-soaked golden raisins.

Beat in the vanilla. If the mixture starts to separate or split and slide around in the bowl, add a tablespoon of the flour with the last portions of egg. Sift the flour into the bowl and gently fold into the mixture using a large metal spoon. Try to avoid stirring or beating: cut downward through the mixture with the edge of the spoon and then fold over; give the bowl a quarter turn and repeat the cutting and folding; continue until there are no more streaks of flour. Add the fruit – it should have absorbed all the rum – and fold it in in the same way.

Spoon the batter into the prepared pan – it should be three-quarters full. Smooth the surface until level. Bake for 40–50 minutes or until a toothpick inserted into the center comes out clean. Cool in the pan for a minute, then lift the cake out of the pan, peel off the paper, and let cool completely on a wire rack. Store in an airtight tin, and eat within 5 days. The fruit will tend to settle toward the bottom during cooking, but don't worry – this is quite normal.

VARIATION: CHOCOLATE QUATRE-QUARTS Replace 1/3 cup (50g) of the weighed flour with the same amount of unsweetened cocoa powder and sift into the bowl with the flour and 1/2 teaspoon baking powder. Use 1/3 cup (60g) golden raisins soaked in 2 tablespoons rum instead of the crystallized fruits.

SEVILLE ORANGE CAKE

Dessert oranges often lack sharpness and intense flavor, so it is hard to make a really orangey sponge cake that is not oversweet or cloying. However, good-quality Seville orange marmalade, preferably homemade with plenty of chunky peel and a slightly sharp taste, transforms a sponge batter.

INGREDIENTS

Makes an 8-inch round cake

- $\frac{3}{4}$ cup (170g) unsalted butter, at room temperature
- $\frac{3}{4}$ cup + 2 tablespoons (170g) sugar
- 3 extra large eggs, beaten
- $1\frac{1}{4}$ cups (170g) self-rising flour
- $\frac{1}{2}$ teaspoon baking powder
- 7 tablespoons (140g) Seville orange marmalade, gently warmed
- 2 tablespoons milk

ICING:

- 1 cup (110g) confectioners' sugar, sifted
- 2 tablespoons warm water

an 8-inch round deep cake pan, greased and lined on the bottom (see pages 282-3)

Preheat the oven to 350°F.

Beat the butter until creamy, using an electric mixer or wooden spoon. Add the sugar and beat until light and fluffy. Gradually beat in the eggs, beating well after each addition. Sift the flour with the baking powder and gently fold into the mixture using a large metal spoon. When thoroughly blended, add half of the marmalade and the milk and carefully fold in.

Spoon the sponge batter into the prepared pan and spread to level the surface. Bake in the preheated oven for 45–50 minutes or until golden and firm to the touch. Turn out onto a wire rack and immediately brush with the remaining warm marmalade. Let cool completely.

To make the icing, use a wooden spoon to mix the confectioners' sugar and the warm water until smooth and lump-free; the icing should be fairly runny. Spoon over the top of the cake and let it run down the sides. Let set – about 1 hour. Store in an airtight tin, and eat within 4 days.

OPPOSITE (from top to bottom) Seville Orange Cake, Cinnamon Apricot Cake, February Cake (see recipe on page 280).

1 BEAT IN THE EGGS LITTLE BY LITTLE.

2 CUT AND FOLD IN THE SIFTED FLOUR.

CINNAMON APRICOT CAKE

This lovely moist cake contains plenty of juicy apricots and isn't oversweet.

INGREDIENTS

Makes an 8-inch round cake

- $\frac{1}{2}$ cup + 1 tablespoon (130g) unsalted butter, at room temperature
- $\frac{2}{3}$ cup packed (130g) light brown sugar, sifted if lumpy
- $1\frac{1}{4}$ cups (170g) self-rising flour
- 1 teaspoon ground cinnamon
- $\frac{1}{3}$ cup (30g) ground almonds
- 3 extra large eggs, beaten
- 1 cup (140g) chopped dried apricots
- $\frac{1}{4}$ cup (20g) sliced almonds

an 8-inch round deep cake pan, greased and lined on the bottom (see pages 282-3)

Preheat the oven to 325°F.

Beat the butter until creamy, using a wooden spoon or electric mixer. Add the sugar and beat until light and fluffy. Sift the flour with the cinnamon and ground almonds. Very slowly beat the eggs into the creamed mixture, beating well after each addition and adding a little of the flour mixture with the last batch. Using a metal spoon, carefully fold in the rest of the flour mixture and the apricots. When thoroughly combined, spoon into the prepared pan and level the surface. Sprinkle evenly with the sliced almonds.

Bake in the preheated oven for about 1 hour or until a skewer inserted into the center comes out clean. Let cool in the pan. Store in an airtight tin, and eat within 4 days.

WALNUT CAKE

INGREDIENTS

Makes a 7-inch layer cake

- 3/4 cup (170g)) unsalted butter, at room temperature
- 2/3 cup (140g) sugar
- 1 tablespoon golden syrup
- 2 extra large eggs, beaten
- 1/2 cup (60g) roughly chopped walnuts
- 1 1/4 cups (170g) self-rising flour, sifted

FILLING:

- 1/2 cup (110g) unsalted butter, at room temperature
- 1 1/2 cups (170g) confectioners' sugar, sifted
- a few drops of pure vanilla extract
- 2 tablespoons hot milk
- 1/4 cup (30g) very finely chopped walnuts

ICING:

- 2 cups (230g) confectioners' sugar, sifted
- 2–3 tablespoons hot water
- walnut halves for decoration

two 7-inch round shallow cake pans, greased and lined on the bottom (see pages 282-3)

I am very fond of the old-fashioned walnut cakes I remember from childhood, but finding a good recipe has been difficult. The American-style cakes made with oil tasted fine, but the texture seemed too rubbery, while the whisked egg-and-sugar recipes popular in Europe were too tough and dry. The traditional British method of creaming the butter and sugar and then beating in the eggs made a moist but slightly heavy cake. This recipe, with golden syrup, makes a very light but moist and well-flavored cake that keeps well. The layers of nut sponge have a filling of walnut buttercream and the cake is finished with a thick glacé icing.

Preheat the oven to 350°F.

Using an electric mixer or a wooden spoon, cream the butter until light, then gradually beat in the sugar. Beat well until the mixture becomes light and fluffy, then beat in the syrup. Gradually beat in the eggs, beating well after each addition. Fold in the walnuts and the sifted flour using a large metal spoon.

Divide the batter between the prepared pans and smooth the surface. Bake in the preheated oven for 25–30 minutes or until the cakes are springy to the touch. Turn the cakes out of the pans onto a wire rack and let them cool.

To make the filling, cream the butter until soft, using an electric mixer or wooden spoon, then beat in the confectioners' sugar at slow speed to make a fluffy, smooth mixture. Beat in the vanilla, milk, and walnuts.

To make the icing, put the sifted confectioners' sugar into a mixing bowl and work in the hot water using a wooden spoon to make a very smooth, thick, spreadable icing. Cover tightly until ready to use.

To assemble, split each cake in half horizontally using a long sharp knife – the nuts will cause the crumb to tear slightly, so if possible cut the day after baking. Spread a third of the filling on half of one cake, then cover with the other piece. Spread with half the remaining filling. Put the base of the second cake on top and spread with the remaining filling. Cover with the last piece of cake. Spread the glacé icing over the top of the cake and ease it down the sides. Use as few movements as possible to avoid a lot of crumbs in the icing. Leave for an hour or so before serving, to let the icing set. Store in an airtight tin, and eat within 5 days.

1 WITH THE MACHINE RUNNING, ADD THE GOLDEN SYRUP TO THE MIXTURE.

2 THE CAKES MUST BE COMPLETELY COLD BEFORE YOU SPLIT THEM IN HALF.

This magnificent walnut tree (right), reputed to be one of the largest walnut trees in Britain, is planted in the grounds of Marble Hill House, Twickenham, Surrey (top).

FEBRUARY CAKE

INGREDIENTS

Makes an 8-inch round cake

- ½ cup (110g) unsalted butter, at room temperature
- 6 tablespoons (85g) dark brown sugar, sifted if lumpy
- 2 extra large eggs, beaten
- 1 cup (230g) good mincemeat
- 1 tablespoon orange juice
- 1¼ cups (170g) self-rising flour
- a little raw brown sugar for sprinkling

an 8-inch round deep cake pan, greased and lined on the bottom (see pages 282-3)

I like to save a jar of homemade Christmas mincemeat (see page 307) to make this cake in February. It is usually such a dreary, wet month, and a good cake cheers us all up. This is a very quick and simple cake to make and has all the rich, spicy flavors of the well-matured mincemeat.

Preheat the oven to 325°F.

Using an electric mixer or wooden spoon, beat the butter until creamy. Add the sugar and beat until light and fluffy. Gradually beat in the eggs, beating well after each addition. Stir in the mincemeat, orange juice, and flour using a large metal spoon. When thoroughly blended, spoon the batter into the prepared pan and level the surface. Sprinkle evenly with a little raw brown sugar.

Bake in the preheated oven for 1–1¼ hours or until a skewer inserted into the center comes out clean. The cake will have slight cracks. Loosen the cake and turn it out onto a wire rack to cool completely. Wrap in wax paper, put into an airtight tin, and keep for a day before cutting. Eat the cake within a week of baking.

1 AFTER THE EGGS HAVE BEEN MIXED IN, ADD THE RICH, MOIST MINCEMEAT.

2 ADD THE ORANGE JUICE FOLLOWED BY THE FLOUR AND COMBINE THOROUGHLY.

3 THE MIXTURE WILL BE QUITE STIFF. SPOON IT INTO THE CAKE PAN.

4 SMOOTH THE SURFACE, THEN SPRINKLE WITH SOME RAW BROWN SUGAR.

ROYAL SCOTSMAN FRUIT CAKE

INGREDIENTS

Makes an 8-inch round cake
1⅔ cups (230g) all-purpose flour
1½ teaspoons baking powder
a pinch of salt
¾ cup (170g) unsalted butter, at room temperature
¾ cup packed (170g) light brown sugar
4 eggs, beaten
⅔ cup (60g) ground almonds
2 cups (340g) mixed dried fruit and chopped candied peel
⅔ cup (110g) candied cherries, rinsed, dried, and halved
1–2 tablespoons milk
8oz (230g) white marzipan
½ cup (45g)) sliced almonds

an 8-inch round deep cake pan, greased and lined with greased parchment paper (see pages 282-3)

ABOVE RIGHT Glen Nevis, Fort William, Scotland.

Years ago I was lucky enough to have a very short trip on the famous steam train, the Royal Scotsman. Traveling around Scotland on this train is true luxury – enjoying the glorious scenery of God's Own Country in wonderful comfort and with excellent Scottish food. This rich, moist fruit cake, with its hidden layer of marzipan, was served at tea with pistachio shortbreads. It has become a firm favorite with my family.

The baked Royal Scotsman Fruit Cake, straight from the oven.

Preheat the oven to 350°F.

Sift the flour with the baking powder and salt, and set aside. Using an electric mixer, beat the butter until creamy, then gradually beat in the sugar. Beat until very light and fluffy. Gradually beat in the eggs, beating well after each addition. Add a tablespoon of the flour with the last two additions of egg. Using a large metal spoon, fold in the rest of the flour and the ground almonds. When thoroughly blended, fold in the fruit mixture and the cherries. Add enough milk to make a batter that just falls from the spoon when tapped.

Spoon half the batter into the prepared pan and smooth the surface. Roll out the marzipan into a disk to fit the pan and place it gently on top of the cake batter. Spoon the rest of the batter on top. Smooth the surface, then make a slight hollow in the center so the cake will rise evenly. Sprinkle with the sliced almonds.

Bake in the preheated oven for 30 minutes, then reduce the oven temperature to 325°F and bake for a further 1¼–1½ hours or until a skewer inserted into the center of the cake, just down to the marzipan layer, comes out clean. (The marzipan will be soft and sticky, so if you push the skewer into it it will be hard to tell if the cake itself is cooked.) Let cool completely in the pan before turning out.

Remove the parchment paper, then wrap in wax paper and keep in an airtight tin for about 3 days before cutting.

KATIE STEWART'S DUNDEE CAKE

INGREDIENTS

Makes an 8-inch round cake
$1\frac{1}{4}$ cups (170g) all-purpose flour
$\frac{3}{4}$ cup (110g) self-rising flour
$\frac{1}{2}$ teaspoon salt
$\frac{2}{3}$ cup (60g) ground almonds
$\frac{3}{4}$ cup (170g) butter, at room temperature
$\frac{1}{4}$ cup (60g) shortening
1 cup packed (230g) light brown sugar, sifted if lumpy
4 extra large eggs, at room temperature
the finely grated rind of 1 unwaxed lemon
2 cups (340g) golden raisins
$1\frac{1}{3}$ cups (230g) currants
$\frac{2}{3}$ cup (110g) chopped mixed candied peel
about 18 blanched almond halves

an 8-inch round deep cake pan, greased and lined with greased parchment paper (see below)
a baking sheet and plenty of newspaper

1 KATIE ALWAYS USES HER HAND TO CREAM THE FAT WITH THE SUGAR.

2 SHE WRAPS THICK NEWSPAPER AROUND THE PAN TO PREVENT SCORCHING.

The Scots have a long tradition of baking, and Dundee has a reputation for the richest, most luxurious fruit cakes. Spices, sugar, and citrus and dried fruits arrived at the port from overseas, and fine white wheat flour was imported from England. This cake dates from the 17th century when it was a favorite at the court of Mary Queen of Scots – the royal bakers indulged the Queen's sweet tooth, her love of ostentation, and her dislike of cherries, with a cake that was packed with expensive and uncommon ingredients.

Katie Stewart has long been a heroine of mine, ever since I spent a school holiday cooking every single recipe in her Times Cookery Book. *Katie, who comes from Aberdeen, has had an illustrious career. Like her mother she trained at the Domestic Science School in Aberdeen before moving down to London and Westminster College. After even more training – at the Cordon Bleu in Paris – Katie worked as a home economist for Nestlé in White Plains, New York. Back in Britain, she started writing for* Woman's Mirror *in 1959, then moved on to* The Times *and* Woman's Journal, *where she has been Cookery Editor for 26 years.*

Katie's fruit cakes, baked to recipes handed down from her mother, are superb, and it was a great treat to watch her make them at her home in Sussex, England.

Preheat the oven to 350°F.

Sift the flours with the salt and almonds, and set aside.

In a large mixing bowl cream the fats and sugar together until soft and light, using your hand, a wooden spoon, or an electric mixer. Katie uses her hand for this – she says it is messy but quick. Mix the eggs with the grated lemon rind. Beat the egg mixture into the creamed mixture a little at a time – at least five batches – beating well after each addition. If the mixture starts to curdle or slide around in the bowl, add some of the sifted flour mixture with the last few additions of the egg mixture.

Mix a tablespoon of the flour with the fruit and peel. Using a metal spoon, lightly fold half of the remaining flour into the creamed mixture, then add the fruit mixture and, finally, the rest of the flour. Gently mix to make a medium soft consistency: the batter should drop off the spoon when it is given a gentle shake.

Spoon the batter into the prepared pan and spread level with a spoon, gently pressing the batter down. Lightly moisten the top of the cake with wet knuckles; this will prevent a hard, dry crust from forming before the cake has set. Place the almond halves on top in a neat circle. Tie newspaper, folded into four thicknesses, around the pan to prevent scorched or dry sides. Put a tray of water on the floor of the oven – this helps to keep the cake moist.

Set the cake pan on a thick pad of newspaper on a baking sheet and bake in the center of the preheated oven for 45 minutes. Lower the oven temperature to 325°F and bake for a further $1\frac{3}{4}$ hours – giving a total cooking time of $2\frac{1}{2}$ hours. Let the cake cool in the pan overnight before turning out. When the cake is quite cold – 24 hours after baking – wrap it in wax paper and store in an airtight tin for a week before cutting.

LINING A ROUND CAKE PAN

Many cakes need only to have the bottom of the pan lined, but when baking a fruit-rich cake, all pans – even non-stick ones – should be lined

Katie in her kitchen with Charlie, the dog. On the table are freshly baked Queen Mary Tartlets (see recipe on page 310) and Dundee Cake.

on the bottom and around the sides, using heavy wax paper or non-stick parchment paper. The lining prevents the cake from sticking to the pan. For fruit cakes with a long baking period, the lining on the bottom and sides also helps prevent the cake from scorching and drying out.

First, brush the inside of the pan with melted butter so the paper will adhere – for good smooth sides it is important the paper does not become wrinkled. Cut out a disk of parchment paper to fit the bottom of the pan: set the pan on a sheet of paper and draw around the base. If only lining the bottom of the pan, put the disk of paper in place. If lining the sides as well, first measure the circumference and depth of the pan; cut a strip of paper the same length as the circumference and three times as wide as the depth of the pan. Fold the paper strip in half lengthwise. Turn up the folded edge 1 inch and snip this, up to the turned-up fold, at 1-inch intervals. Brush the paper above the snipped edge with melted butter, then fit the paper strip inside the pan so the snipped edge lies flat on the bottom and the rest smoothly lines the side. Put the disk into the pan to cover the bottom and the snipped paper edge.

Gâteau Noir (left) and Stout Cake.

STOUT CAKE

INGREDIENTS

Makes an 8-inch round cake

- 1¼ cups (170g) best-quality large seedless raisins
- 1¼ cups (170g) best-quality golden raisins
- 7 tablespoons stout or dark beer
- ¾ cup (170g) unsalted butter, at room temperature
- ¾ cup packed (170g) dark brown sugar, sifted
- 3 eggs, beaten
- 1⅔ cups (230g) all-purpose flour
- 1½ teaspoons apple-spice spice
- ⅓ cup (60g) chopped mixed candied peel
- ¾ cup (85g) walnut pieces

an 8-inch round deep cake pan, greased and lined with greased parchment paper (see pages 282-3)

This is a dark, spiced fruit cake made with lots of raisins soaked in stout, plus walnuts for extra crunch. Made with the best fruit, it will be a good keeper, and can be covered with marzipan and royal icing, for a traditional finish.

Put all the raisins in a bowl and pour over the stout. Mix well, then cover tightly and let soak overnight.

Next day, preheat the oven to 325°F.

Beat the butter until light, using an electric mixer or wooden spoon. Gradually beat in the sifted sugar, then continue beating until the mixture becomes lighter and fluffy in texture. Gradually beat in the eggs, beating well after each addition. Sift the flour and the apple-pie spice into the bowl, and carefully fold in using a large metal spoon. Add the soaked fruit and any liquid left in the bowl, followed by the mixed peel and the walnuts. When thoroughly blended, spoon into the prepared pan and smooth the surface level.

Bake in the preheated oven for 1½ hours or until a skewer inserted into the center comes out clean. If the top of the cake looks as if it is becoming too brown, cover with a double sheet of parchment paper. Let cool in the pan, then turn out. Remove the lining paper and wrap in wax paper. Store in an airtight tin for 3–5 days before cutting.

GÂTEAU NOIR

INGREDIENTS

Makes 1 very large cake

2/3 cup (140ml) each rum, port, brandy, cherry brandy, and water
2 teaspoons Angostura bitters
1 teaspoon ground cinnamon
1 cinnamon stick
1 teaspoon freshly grated nutmeg
1/2 teaspoon ground cloves
1/2 teaspoon ground allspice
1/2 teaspoon salt
2 tablespoons dark brown sugar
4 1/2lb (2kg) mixed dried and candied fruit and peel (about 12 cups)
2 cups (450g) unsalted butter, at room temperature
3 cups (450g) raw brown sugar
8 extra large eggs, beaten
3 cups (450g) self-rising flour, sifted
1 cup (110g) chopped mixed nuts – pecans and almonds for choice
2 teaspoons pure vanilla extract

a roasting pan, about 13 1/2 x 11 1/2 inches, lined with greased foil

The legendary Creole Christmas cake, heavy – in every sense – with dried fruits and liquor, is not for the faint-hearted. It is very rich, and moist enough to be eaten as a dessert. I enjoy it with strong coffee. The recipe calls for a lot of ingredients, but the method is simple. I use the "luxury fruit" mixture available in 500g packets at my local supermarket, although you can use your own mixture of raisins, golden raisins, currants, mixed candied peel, chopped dried apricots and prunes, candied pineapple and cherries. The fruits are simmered with the spices and alcohols to plump them up. Then, after a few days of soaking, they are mixed with the rest of the ingredients and baked in a large roasting pan. Having tried this cake, I no longer make the traditional British Christmas cake, and my family is very happy with the change.

Put the rum, port, brandy, cherry brandy, water, bitters, ground and stick cinnamon, nutmeg, cloves, allspice, salt, brown sugar, and the fruit mixture into a large non-aluminum saucepan. Bring slowly to a boil, then simmer gently for 10 minutes, stirring frequently. The mixture will be moist, but most of the liquid will have been absorbed. Tip into a large heatproof glass or china bowl and let cool completely. Then cover and leave for 3–5 days to mature, stirring every day.

When ready to bake the cake, preheat the oven to 275°F.

Put the butter into a very large mixing bowl with the raw brown sugar and beat until fairly light, using a wooden spoon. Gradually beat in the eggs – this is quite hard work but the mixture does not need to beaten as thoroughly as a sponge cake (see Quatre-quarts, page 274). Some of the flour can be added with the last few portions of egg to prevent the mixture from curdling or splitting. Stir in the rest of the flour using a large metal spoon, then work in the fruit mixture, with any liquid left in the bowl, the nuts, and the vanilla extract. When thoroughly blended, spoon into the prepared pan and level the surface.

Cover the pan quite loosely with a double layer of parchment paper, then bake for about 3 1/2 hours or until just cooked in the center; test with a skewer – the cake should be quite moist. Let cool completely in the pan, then turn out and peel off the foil. Wrap in wax paper and store in an airtight container for several days before cutting.

1 AFTER 3–5 DAYS OF MARINATING IN LIQUOR AND SPICES, THE FRUIT MIXTURE IS VERY MOIST AND SOFT.

2 WHEN WELL MIXED, SPOON THE HEAVY, FRUIT-DENSE CAKE BATTER INTO THE FOIL-LINED ROASTING PAN.

RHUBARB CHEESECAKE

INGREDIENTS

Makes a 10-inch cake, to serve 10–12

CRUST:
1 cup (110g) graham-cracker crumbs
½ teaspoon ground ginger
2½ tablespoons (30g) sugar
4 tablespoons (60g) unsalted butter, melted

FILLING:
2lb (900g) cream cheese
the grated rind of 1 unwaxed lemon
1 teaspoon pure vanilla extract
1 cup (200g) sugar
4 extra large eggs, beaten
2 cups (455ml) sour cream

TOPPING:
½lb (250g) trimmed young rhubarb, rinsed
3 tablespoons red-currant or raspberry jelly

a 10-inch springform cake pan, greased
a baking sheet

My ideal cheesecake is deep and rich, yet light and fluffy, with plenty of flavor. My husband, who is from New York, likes the heavy, middle-European kind of cheesecake that sticks briefly to the top of your mouth and then lingers around the hips. Both types are baked rather than set with gelatin, and can be left plain or topped with fresh or poached fruit and then a glaze. This recipe is my favorite – sorry Alan – and is covered with the tender young forced rhubarb available in the spring. As this delicate fruit breaks up very readily, it is cooked slowly in the oven in red-currant or raspberry jelly and the juices are used for the glaze. Other fruit toppings could be raspberries or strawberries, poached or fresh apricots or peaches, large sweet blackberries, mixed fresh red, black, and white currants, figs, or cherries. As a glaze choose a jelly or strained jam to suit the fruit. For some reason the Philadelphia brand of cream cheese works best in this recipe – I have had disappointing results with other cream cheeses.

Preheat the oven to 300°F.

To make the crust, mix the graham-cracker crumbs with the ground ginger, sugar, and melted butter. Tip the mixture into the prepared pan, then press onto the bottom, using the back of a spoon, to make an even layer. Chill for 30 minutes while making the filling.

Put the cream cheese, grated lemon rind, vanilla, and sugar into the bowl of an electric mixer (the mixture can also be beaten by hand using a wooden spoon, but it is hard work). Beat at low speed until the mixture is very smooth, then increase the speed and gradually beat in the eggs, scraping down the sides of the bowl from time to time. When well mixed, pour in the sour cream and stir with a wooden spoon until the mixture is thoroughly combined.

1 PRESS THE CRUMB MIXTURE FIRMLY INTO THE BOTTOM OF THE SPRINGFORM PAN.

2 THOROUGHLY WASH THE LEMON, THEN GRATE THE RIND INTO THE BOWL.

3 WHEN THE CHEESE AND CREAM MIXTURE IS SMOOTH, POUR IT INTO THE PAN.

4 CUT THE RHUBARB NEATLY, THEN COOK IN A BAKING DISH WITH THE JELLY.

BRUSH THE RHUBARB WITH THE HOT, SYRUPY COOKING JUICES TO GLAZE.

Pour the filling into the pan – it should be seven-eighths full – and set the pan on a baking sheet. Bake in the preheated oven for 1 3/4–2 hours or until just firm. The cheesecake will puff up, but it will sink on cooling and then usually cracks across the middle.

When the cheesecake is cooked, turn off the oven and open the door a few inches – wedge it, if necessary. Leave the cheesecake inside to cool slowly for 1 hour. Then remove from the oven, set the pan on a wire rack, and leave until completely cold. Cover and chill overnight before unmolding and decorating.

To make the topping, preheat the oven to 350°F. Cut the rhubarb into pieces about 1 1/4 inches long. Spread the jelly on the bottom of a baking dish and arrange the rhubarb in a single layer on top. Cover and cook in the preheated oven for about 20 minutes or until just tender, stirring very gently from time to time. Let cool.

When ready to decorate the cheesecake, remove the rhubarb from the liquid, draining well. Spoon the rhubarb cooking juices into a small pan and bring to a boil. Simmer until syrupy. Arrange the fruit on top of the unmolded cheesecake, then brush with the hot syrup. Chill until set – about 30 minutes – before serving. Store in a covered container in the fridge, and eat within 3 days.

CHOCOLATE, THE FOOD OF THE GODS

RIGHT Sacks of cocoa beans waiting to be mixed and roasted at the Bernachon maison du chocolat in Lyons, France.

BELOW After roasting for 20 minutes the cocoa beans have to be cooled before shelling.

BOTTOM Noël Sevre can tell whether or not the beans have been properly roasted by their smell.

Until I went to Lyons, France, the nearest I had come to the principal ingredient of chocolate was the *Theobroma cacao* in the Princess of Wales Conservatory in Britain's Kew Gardens. This "food of the gods" tree, which grows to almost 65 feet in the wild and around 13 feet on plantations, is found in tropical America and Africa. The large, yellow-green fruits of the tree contain white juicy pulp and hard bitter seeds, and it is these seeds from which chocolate and cocoa are made.

After the fruits are harvested and the seeds removed, they are left to ferment for 4–6 days – the heat of this fermentation kills the seed's embryo and starts chemical reactions that change the initial inedibly bitter taste. Next, the seeds – now beans – are dried in the sun, and then they are put into sacks for sale.

It was a hot, sticky day when I visited the Bernachon *maison du chocolat* in Lyons. I expected to be greeted by a cloying smell, which would put me off all sweets for weeks. Instead there was merely a slightly heady, bitter aroma. The factory is, in fact, a chocolate-making *atelier* – one room containing all that is required. In one corner the ingredients are neatly arranged: sacks of beans, bags of crystal sugar, a shoe box of glossy vanilla beans, and a bowl of melted cocoa butter.

Unlike coffee, chocolate cannot be made with just one type of bean, and it is the blend of beans – up to 12 varieties here – that gives the final product its special flavor. Jean-Jacques Bernachon only buys the finest and most costly beans: chuao from Venezuela, para from Brazil, the santa-fe, sambirand, and guayaquil from Trinidad and Ecuador. He compares the beans to the *premiers grands crus* wines of Bordeaux – each variety has an individual character and adds a different quality to the blend: aroma, bitterness, depth of flavor, or richness.

The chocolate-maker, Noël Sevre, explained the process *chez* Bernachon. The almond-shaped beans are first picked over by hand to check for damage: each variety is a different color, ranging from pale coffee to a rich mahogany-brown. They are then roasted – like coffee – for 20 minutes at

ABOVE After a day and a half of conchage, the finished chocolate is poured into trays and left to set into blocks.

RIGHT Jean-Jacques Bernachon and his pride and joy – the gâteau president.

350°F, which cracks the shells and releases a pleasant toasty smell. Once cooled the beans are lightly crushed to remove the shells without damaging the precious kernels. These are then ground to make a paste, and are mixed in small batches with melted cocoa butter from Holland, a little sugar – the quantity depends on how the chocolate will be used – and real vanilla from Madagascar. The resulting dryish, clay-like "dough" is mixed and put through a giant mangle three times, a process called *broyage*. The final key step is *conchage*, or conching, a long, slow operation – around 36 hours here – which gently melts and stirs or grinds the ingredients until smooth and mellow. The resulting chocolate is then set as blocks.

Cocoa beans contain roughly 50% fat and 50% meat or solids. Pressing

ABOVE Hand-made chocolates are given the gold-leaf treatment before they are dispatched to Paul Bocuse's restaurant.

the cocoa paste releases some of the fat from the ground kernels – this is the cocoa butter. If the pressed paste is then further ground up and dried it becomes cocoa powder. Cocoa butter is added to the chocolate mixture to increase the fat content, to make it smoother, and to make it melt in the mouth as it has a low melting point. The quantity of cocoa solids – the dry cocoa paste plus the added cocoa butter – determines the quality and depth of flavor of the chocolate. *Couverture*, used for fillings and icings, is around 55%; *amer* or bitter is 65%; *super amer* or extra bitter (best for eating and making desserts and fine cakes) is around 70%; and *sans sucre* or unsweetened (used in many recipes for cakes and cookies and for sauces by the catering trade) is 100%.

Great care must be taken when melting chocolate because if it is overheated it easily scorches and becomes a hard, solid mass. The best way to melt it is to put the chopped chocolate into a heatproof bowl set over a pan of hot but not boiling water (or in a double boiler). The water should not touch the base of the bowl, nor should the chocolate come into contact with steam from the water. Stir the chocolate gently until smooth, then remove the bowl from the heat.

Sadly, the production of chocolate at Maison Bernachon is small, and Jean-Jacques will not allow it to be sold anywhere else. So a trip to Lyons or a visit to Paul Bocuse's restaurant nearby is the only way to taste chocolate perfection. Jean-Jacques is married to the great chef's daughter, Jeanne, who runs the Bernachon Passion tea shop/restaurant. Bocuse serves their hand-made chocolates, flecked with real gold leaf, and the *president gâteau*, created by Maurice, Jean-Jacques' father. This triumph of the *chocolatier* and the *pâtissier* resembles one of the British Queen Mother's Ascot hats with its ruffles and frills, except that she never wears brown.

BELOW Maison Bernachon sells incomparable pâtisserie and gâteaux, as well as the famous chocolates. If you cannot wait until you reach home, you can taste everything in the tea shop/restaurant next door.

DEVIL'S FOOD CAKE

INGREDIENTS

Makes an 8-inch layer cake
3oz (85g) good semisweet chocolate, chopped
1/2 cup (110g) unsalted butter
6 tablespoons (85g) dark brown sugar
1 tablespoon golden syrup
1 1/3 cups (170g) cake flour
1/3 cup (30g) unsweetened cocoa powder
1/2 teaspoon baking soda
2 extra large eggs, beaten
6 tablespoons milk

FILLING AND FROSTING:
3 tablespoons (40g) unsalted butter, at room temperature
1/2 cup (40g) unsweetened cocoa powder
2 1/2 cups (280g) confectioners' sugar
6 tablespoons milk
2 teaspoons strong black coffee

two 7-inch round shallow cake pans, greased and lined on the bottom (see pages 282-3)

Above right SPREAD THE SOFT FROSTING THICKLY OVER THE ASSEMBLED CAKE, THEN LEAVE OVERNIGHT BEFORE CUTTING.

It has taken me a long time to find a really good recipe for this popular cake. Most devil's food cakes look impressive but taste of little except sugar. This unorthodox recipe makes a light cake that is not too deep but has plenty of flavor. The rich chocolate fudge frosting contrasts well with the slightly bitter, double chocolate sponge. Like most chocolate cakes it is best left overnight before cutting.

Preheat the oven to 325°F.

To make the cake, put the chocolate, butter, sugar, and golden syrup in a saucepan set over low heat and melt, stirring frequently. Remove from the heat and let cool.

Sift the flour, cocoa powder, and baking soda into a mixing bowl. Make a well in the center and pour in the cooled melted chocolate mixture. Stir with the flour until well mixed, then add the eggs and milk and beat gently until the batter is thoroughly combined.

Spoon the batter into the prepared pans and spread evenly. Bake for 20–25 minutes or until firm to the touch. Let cool completely before turning out of the pans.

To make the filling and frosting mixture, beat the butter until creamy, using a wooden spoon or electric mixer. Sift the cocoa and confectioners' sugar into the bowl, and add the milk and coffee. Mix on low speed until combined, then beat vigorously until smooth and creamy. Taste and add a little more cocoa or coffee if necessary.

Spread a third of this mixture on one of the cakes and set the second cake on top. Spread the rest of the mixture evenly over the top and down the sides. Cover and leave in a cool place – but not the fridge – overnight so that the frosting can become firm and the cake can mature. The cake is best eaten within 3 days.

PECAN FUDGE CAKE

INGREDIENTS

Makes a $9\frac{1}{2}$-inch round cake
12oz (340g) good semisweet chocolate
$\frac{3}{4}$ cup (170g) unsalted butter
$\frac{1}{2}$ cup (60g) unsweetened cocoa powder, sifted
5 extra large eggs
$1\frac{1}{4}$ cups (255g) sugar
1 cup (100g) roughly chopped pecans
confectioners' sugar for dusting

a $9\frac{1}{2}$-inch springform cake pan, greased and lined on the bottom (see pages 282-3)

This is a wonderfully rich and moist cake, more like a heavy mousse than a sponge because it contains no flour. The rich but not sweet taste comes from a combination of semisweet chocolate (which should have a high proportion of cocoa solids and cocoa butter) and cocoa powder. It can be served as a dessert with vanilla ice-cream or crème anglaise (see page 260).

Preheat the oven to 350°F.

Put the chocolate and butter in a heavy saucepan, or in a heatproof bowl set over a pan of hot but not boiling water, and melt very gently, stirring frequently. Remove from the heat and stir in the cocoa. Let cool

1 BEAT THE EGGS WITH THE SUGAR UNTIL THE MIXTURE IS THICK ENOUGH TO MAKE A RIBBON-LIKE TRAIL.

2 REMOVE THE BOWL FROM THE HEAT AND GENTLY FOLD IN THE COOL CHOCOLATE MIXTURE WITH A LARGE SPOON.

3 FINALLY, MIX IN THE CHOPPED PECANS. SPOON INTO THE PREPARED CAKE PAN AND BAKE IMMEDIATELY.

while beating the eggs: put the eggs into a large heatproof bowl and beat briefly. Add the sugar and set the bowl over a pan of simmering water; the water should not touch the base of the bowl. Beat, using a portable electric mixer, until the mixture is very light and fluffy and has tripled in bulk. When the beaters are lifted out of the mixture it should leave a very visible ribbon-like trail on the surface. Remove the bowl from the heat and carefully fold in the chocolate mixture, followed by the pecans. Spoon into the prepared pan and smooth the the surface.

Bake for 30–35 minutes. The top of the cake will be firm but the inside should still be moist – if this cake is overcooked it will be too dry and crumbly to slice. Let cool completely in the pan, then unmold and dust with confectioners' sugar. Store in an airtight pan, and eat within 4 days.

BELOW Devil's Food Cake (see recipe on page 291), Pecan Fudge Cake.

THE BEST CHOCOLATE CAKE

INGREDIENTS

Makes 1 heart-shaped cake
4oz (110g) good semisweet chocolate, chopped
½ cup (110g) unsalted butter, at room temperature
7 tablespoons (85g) sugar
4 extra large eggs, separated
1⅓ cups (110g) ground almonds
a pinch of salt

GANACHE FROSTING:
½ cup (115 ml) heavy cream
4 oz (110g) good semisweet chocolate, chopped

a heart-shaped pan, about 8 inches long from tip and just under 8 inches across the center, greased and lined on the bottom

I have yet to find a cake to better this one. It is rich and very chocolatey but not sweet or cloying; it is moist but not heavy. But however carefully it is prepared it will only be as good as the chocolate used. Top-quality semisweet chocolate. containing a lot of cocoa butter, has less sugar than lesser quality chocolate, which usually has flavorings and other additives as well.

The recipe originally came from Jean-Pierre St Martin, the chef-patron of the Viscos restaurant in the tiny village of St Savin, perched high up in the Pyrenees in southwestern France. For his cake, he used 8 eggs and 250 grams of everything else – butter, sugar, chocolate, and ground almonds – but gradually, through experimentation, I have reduced the sugar. There is no flour in the recipe, nor any leavening agent – the lightness comes from the beaten egg whites. The cake is covered with a ganache made from equal quantities of chocolate and cream. For a softer, more fudgy frosting use a little more cream than chocolate; for a harder, darker, and more intense coating use a little more chocolate than cream.

Although I suggest a heart-shaped pan, you can also use an 8-inch round cake pan. Double quantity cake batter will fill a 9-inch round deep cake pan – ideal for a birthday cake.

Preheat the oven to 400°F.

Very gently melt the chocolate in a heatproof bowl set over a pan of hot but not boiling water. Stir until smooth, then remove from the heat and let cool while preparing the rest of the mixture. Using an electric mixer or wooden spoon, cream the butter until light in a mixing bowl. Add the

Jean-Pierre St Martin outside his restaurant, Les Viscos, in southwestern France.

sugar and beat until fluffy, then beat in the egg yolks one at a time, beating well after each addition. Beat in the cooled chocolate, then stir in the almonds using a large metal spoon.

In a spotlessly clean, grease-free bowl, beat the egg whites with the pinch of salt until they form soft peaks. Gently fold them into the chocolate mixture in three batches using a large metal spoon.

Spoon into the prepared pan and level the surface. Bake in the preheated oven for 15 minutes, then reduce the oven temperature to 350°F and bake for about 10 minutes longer or until just cooked in the center (test with a skewer). It is important not to overcook this cake or it will not be moist. Run a round-bladed knife around the side of the pan to loosen the cake, but do not turn it out. Set the pan on a wet dish towel and let cool. When cold, unmold the cake, wrap in wax paper, and store in an airtight tin to mature for a day before icing.

To make the ganache icing, heat the cream until scalding hot but not boiling. Remove from the heat and add the chopped chocolate. Leave until completely melted and smooth, stirring occasionally. When cool and thick enough to spread, use to cover the sides and top of the cake. Let set in a cool spot – not the fridge (chilling will make the cake hard and the icing will have beads of condensation when it is served). Eat within 4 days.

1 BE SURE THE MELTED CHOCOLATE IS COMPLETELY COOLED BEFORE BEATING IT INTO THE CAKE MIXTURE.

2 ONCE THE CHOCOLATE HAS BEEN INCORPORATED, USE A LARGE SPOON TO FOLD IN THE GROUND ALMONDS.

3 IN A SPOTLESSLY CLEAN BOWL, USING CLEAN BEATERS, BEAT THE EGG WHITES JUST UNTIL SOFT PEAKS FORM.

4 TO KEEP ALL THE AIR THAT HAS BEEN BEATEN IN, FOLD THE WHITES INTO THE BATTER IN THREE BATCHES.

HAZELNUT MERINGUE CAKE

INGREDIENTS

Makes an 8-inch cake, to serve 8–10

CAKE:

1 1/3 cups (185g) skinned hazelnuts
1 cup (200g) superfine sugar
6 extra large egg whites
a pinch of salt

FILLING AND FROSTING:

2 cups (500ml) heavy cream
12oz (350g) good semisweet chocolate, chopped
unsweetened cocoa powder for sprinkling

2 baking sheets, lined with parchment paper (see recipe)
a pastry bag fitted with a 3/4-inch plain tip

This is a slightly simplifed version of one of Maison Bernachon's most famous gâteaux. It is not very difficult to make, yet tastes wonderful and looks very French and glamorous. The cake part is made from a meringue flavored with toasted and ground hazelnuts, and the filling and frosting are a thick ganache of heavy cream and dark, rich chocolate. (Be sure to use a top-quality chocolate.) The assembled cake should be chilled overnight before cutting.

Preheat the oven to 325°F.

Draw an 8-inch circle on two sheets of non-stick parchment paper. Use to line the baking sheets, turning the paper over so the drawn circle is on the underside.

Put the hazelnuts into a roasting pan or baking dish and toast in the preheated oven until a good, even brown. Cool, then work in a food processor to make a coarse powder. Mix the hazelnuts with all but 2 tablespoons of the sugar and set aside.

Put the egg whites and pinch of salt into a spotlessly clean, grease-free, non-plastic bowl – a stainless steel mixer bowl is fine. Beat the whites, starting slowly and then gradually increasing the speed, until soft peaks form. Beat in the reserved 2 tablespoons of sugar at high speed, then continue beating until the whites form stiff peaks. Using a large metal spoon, gently fold in the hazelnut and sugar mixture.

1 GENTLY COMBINE THE POWDERED HAZELNUT MIXTURE AND THE MERINGUE.

2 PIPE THE HAZELNUT MERINGUE MIXTURE IN A SPIRAL TO MAKE A NEAT DISK.

Spoon half the meringue mixture into the pastry bag fitted with the plain tip. Pipe onto one of the baking sheets in a disk inside the drawn circle: start at the center and pipe around and around in circles outward. Use the remaining mixture to pipe a second disk in the same way. Bake the disks in the preheated oven for 1–1½ hours or until golden, firm, and crisp, turning and rotating the sheets so the disks cook evenly. Let cool completely, then peel off the paper.

Meanwhile, prepare the chocolate filling. Heat the cream in a heavy saucepan until scalding hot but not boiling. Remove from the heat and gradually stir in the chocolate. Stir gently until completely melted and smooth, then let cool, stirring occasionally, until the mixture is thick enough to spread. You can hasten the process by chilling the cooled mixture. If it becomes too cold and hard to spread, warm it gently.

To assemble the cake, put one disk of hazelnut meringue on a serving platter and spread with about a third of the chocolate cream mixture, using a metal spatula. Spread gently and try not to press down on the meringue as this could crush it. Put the second meringue disk on top. Quickly spread the rest of the chocolate mixture over the top and down the sides to cover completely. It does not matter if the frosting is not completely smooth. If the chocolate becomes hard to spread it may help to dip the spatula in hot water. Wipe the excess frosting off the plate, then chill the cake overnight.

Remove from the fridge about 30 minutes before serving, unless the weather is very hot, and dust liberally with cocoa powder. Keep in the fridge in a covered container, and eat within 2 days.

A SIMPLE WEDDING CAKE

INGREDIENTS

Makes a 10-inch round cake
2 cups (450g) unsalted butter, at room temperature
the finely grated rind and juice of 3 large unwaxed lemons
2 1/4 cups (450g) sugar
8 eggs, beaten
2 cups (170g) ground almonds
1 2/3 cups (230g) self-rising flour
5 tablespoons (40g) cornstarch
3/4 teaspoon baking powder
2–3 tablespoons milk, if necessary

TO COVER WITH MARZIPAN:
about 1/3 cup lemon curd (see recipe opposite)
confectioners' sugar for dusting
2lb (900g) marzipan

TO COVER WITH ICING:
a little sherry or brandy for brushing
2 1/2lb (1.1 kg) icing fondant, prepared according to package directions

a 10-inch round deep cake pan, greased and lined with greased parchment paper (see pages 282-3)
a large round cake board, about 13 inches in diameter
flowers for decoration

1 MAKE A SOFT, DROPPING CONSISTENCY.

2 TEST THE CAKE WITH A FINE SKEWER.

I like this cake so much I made it for my own wedding two years ago. It is a lovely rich sponge, flavored with ground almonds and lemon, and is fairly quick and simple to make. Even though I covered the cake with marzipan and white icing like a traditional British wedding cake, I was anticipating a few raised eyebrows. However, most guests asked for a second piece – and the recipe. I made the cake on the Wednesday before my Saturday wedding, and it took only about two hours from start to finish. The next day I covered it in marzipan, commercially made, and left it to dry for 24 hours before covering in icing fondant. Just before the wedding party, I decorated the top and the base of the cake with roses and flowering herbs to match my bouquet.

A half quantity of the cake batter can be baked in an 8-inch round deep pan, then covered with 1 3/4lb (800g) marzipan and 2lb (900g) icing fondant. Because of the long baking time it is important to prepare the pan well – use three layers of parchment paper for lining, and cover the cake during baking if necessary.

Preheat the oven to 350°F.

Beat the butter with the lemon rind until soft and creamy, using an electric mixer. Gradually beat in the sugar, then beat until the mixture becomes very pale and fluffy. Beat in the eggs a tablespoon at a time, beating well after each addition. Add the ground almonds with the last few additions of egg, to prevent the mixture from separating. Sift the flour with the cornstarch and baking powder. Using a large metal spoon, fold into the creamed mixture in batches alternately with the lemon juice. If necessary, add a little milk to make a soft consistency that will drop from the spoon. Spoon into the prepared pan and smooth the surface.

Bake in the preheated oven for 30 minutes, then reduce the oven temperature to 325°F and bake for a further 1–1 1/4 hours or until well risen and springy to the touch. A skewer inserted into the center should come out clean. (If baking a smaller cake, reduce the oven temperature to 300°F and bake for a further 1–1 1/4 hours.) If the cake seems to be browning too much, cover with a double sheet of parchment paper. Leave in the pan until completely cold before turning out. The cooled cake can now be covered in marzipan, or wrapped in wax paper and foil and kept up to 5 days before covering.

To cover the cake in marzipan, first remove all your rings and bangles to prevent making marks and dents. Turn the cake upside-down and place it in the center of the cake board. Check that the top surface is level. Brush the cake all over with lemon curd. Lightly dust the work surface with sifted confectioners' sugar, then knead the marzipan until smooth. Roll it out into a round large enough to cover the top and sides of the cake (use a piece of string to measure the distance up one side of the cake, across the top and then down the other side). As you roll, move the marzipan around to prevent it from sticking, but do not turn it over. Carefully wrap the marzipan around the rolling pin, then lift it over the cake. Gently unroll the marzipan so the edge just touches the board on the far side. Then continue unrolling the marzipan over the cake so it covers the cake evenly and touches the board all around. Using the palm of your hand, smooth the marzipan on the top surface, and down against the sides of the cake to make sure it is well fixed. Trim excess marzipan. Let dry for 1–2 days.

To cover the cake with icing, first remove all your rings and bangles.

Brush the marzipanned cake with a little sherry or brandy so the icing will stick. Knead the icing fondant until smooth, then roll it out and cover the cake as for the marzipan. If air bubbles form, prick them at one side with a pin, then gently rub the bubble to expel the air. With your palm, spotlessy clean and dry, smooth and polish the surface of the icing. Do not press too hard with your fingers or there will be dents in the icing. Set the iced cake aside in a cool, dry place to dry for up to 3 days.

To finish the cake, decorate with fresh, silk, or sugar flowers. If using fresh flowers, arrange on top or use a special holder or ring available from specialist cake decorating suppliers and some kitchenware stores; the flowers will wilt rapidly if pushed into the icing. Decorate the base of the cake where it meets the cake board with foliage, ribbons, or piped icing. The cake will cut into 45 pieces, and is best eaten within a week of baking.

LEMON CURD

Lemon curd is used here to stick the marzipan to the lemon-flavored cake, but it can also be used to fill layer cakes, to spread on scones (see page 236), or mixed with whipped cream as a filling for cakes and pastries such as mille-feuilles (page 316) or profiteroles (page 319).

INGREDIENTS

Makes about 1lb (450g)

½ cup (110g) unsalted butter, diced

1 cup + 2 tablespoons (230g) sugar

the grated rind and juice of 2 large or 3 small unwaxed lemons

3 extra large eggs, beaten

spotlessly clean, sterilized jars

Put the butter, sugar, and lemon rind and juice into the top of a non-aluminum double boiler or into a saucepan set in a bain-marie – a roasting pan of boiling water. Cook, stirring constantly with a wooden spoon, until smooth and melted. Add the eggs and stir until very thick and opaque. If the mixture boils it will scramble, so avoid short cuts.

Spoon into prepared jars and leave until cold, then cover and store in the fridge until ready to use – up to 2 weeks

PASTRIES

Pastry is not just the container for a wonderful filling, its taste and texture should enhance the whole dish. With the help of a food processor, superb pastry is easy to achieve.

MAKING PASTRY SUCCESSFULLY

Rich, short pastry is easy to roll and cut if it is chilled first.

PREVIOUS PAGE A selection of mincemeat pies.

Making pastry is the exact opposite of bread making – you don't want to develop the gluten in the flour, as this makes the dough elastic, so heavy-duty kneading and man-handling are to be avoided. Also, to prevent the finished pastry from being greasy or heavy, it is important that the fats do not begin to turn oily or melt as you work the mixture; so use them cold and firm straight from the fridge where possible, and work rapidly, handling the mixture as little as possible.

For years I thought of my perpetually cold hands as a nuisance until other cooks told me I was lucky – their hot hands, the bane of their lives, hindered pastry-making. Many now make pastry in the food processor as it cuts down on handling, though it is important to run the machine only until the dough just comes together: if over-processed, the dough will become oily and sticky.

To make basic short pastry by hand, first lightly toss the flour and any other dry ingredients with the fat so the pieces of fat are coated in flour. Then cut the fat into smaller pieces about the size of your little fingernail, using one or two round-bladed knives or a wire pastry cutter. Finally, gently rub the fat and flour between the fingertips (not the palm of your hand), a small quantity at a time, until there are no visible lumps of fat and the mixture resembles fine crumbs. As you work, lift your hands up to the rim of the bowl so the mixture will become aerated as it falls back down into the bowl. (If using shortening, omit the rubbing-in stage.)

Bind the mixture together with icy cold water, or another liquid, using only just enough to make a soft dough. If the dough is dry and hard it will be difficult to roll out and use, but if it is too wet and sticky it will be tough and heavy when baked. Once the dough comes together, turn it onto a lightly floured work surface and very gently and briefly knead the dough to make it smooth and even.

To make pastry in a food processor, combine the flour and any other dry. ingredients in the food processor bowl. Add the pieces of fat and process for about a minute or just until the mixture forms fine crumbs. Then, with the motor running, pour in the water or other liquid through the feed tube. The mixture should clump together within a minute. As soon as the mixture clumps together, stop the machine to prevent over-working. If the mixture doesn't come together, add more water a teaspoon at a time. Turn the dough onto a lightly floured work surface and gently knead for a few seconds to form a smooth ball.

Richer pastry doughs, such as rich short pastry and almond pastry, need to be chilled before rolling out. Basic piecrust doesn't normally need chilling, unless the kitchen is hot or the pastry dough shows signs of becoming oily. Wrap in wax paper and chill for 15–20 minutes or until firm enough to roll out. Chilling helps the dough to relax, but it is not the antidote to over-working.

Puff pastry, the richest of all the pastries, remains the biggest challenge. The only short cut is to use a food processor to make the initial dough – the *détrempe*. The tricky part, incorporating as much butter as flour, has to be achieved by rolling and folding the dough by hand in a very precise fashion. But be reassured – success comes with practice.

SHORT or PIE PASTRY

INGREDIENTS

Makes about 12oz (340g)
$1^2/_3$ cups (230g) all-purpose flour
$^1/_8$–$^1/_4$ teaspoon salt
4 tablespoons (60g) unsalted butter, chilled and diced
$^1/_4$ cup (60g) lard, chilled and diced, or shortening
about 3 tablespoons icy water to bind

This pastry, with its short and light, crumbly texture, is the simplest to make and the most versatile to use. In its most basic form, pie pastry is a dough made from all-purpose flour, fat, a little salt, and some cold water. The shortness of the pastry depends on the type of fat used and the way it is incorporated into the flour. Firm unsalted butter gives the best flavor, but a mixture of lard or shortening, and butter gives the best texture – that important melt-in-the-mouth quality. Many recipes give one part fat to two of flour, by weight, that is 1oz (30g) fat to 2oz (60g) flour, the fat being made up of equal amounts of butter and lard or shortening.

To make the pastry dough by hand, sift the flour and salt into a mixing bowl. Add the diced fats and toss lightly until well coated in flour. Using a round-bladed knife, two knives, or a wire pastry cutter, cut the fats into small pieces, then rub the fats into the flour with the very tips of your fingers. (Omit the rubbing-in if using shortening.)

When the whole mixture looks like fine crumbs, with no clumps of fat, gradually pour in the water while stirring with a round-bladed knife. Keep stirring until the dough comes together – this can take a couple of minutes. If any dry crumbs still remain at the bottom of the bowl, add

1 *ADD THE FATS TO THE FLOUR AND USE A ROUND-BLADED KNIFE TO CUT THE FATS INTO QUITE SMALL PIECES.*

2 *RUB THE FLOUR AND PIECES OF FAT TOGETHER USING YOUR FINGERTIPS, LIFTING THE MIXTURE AS YOU RUB.*

3 *WHEN THE MIXTURE RESEMBLES FINE CRUMBS, SLOWLY ADD JUST ENOUGH COLD WATER TO BIND TO A DOUGH.*

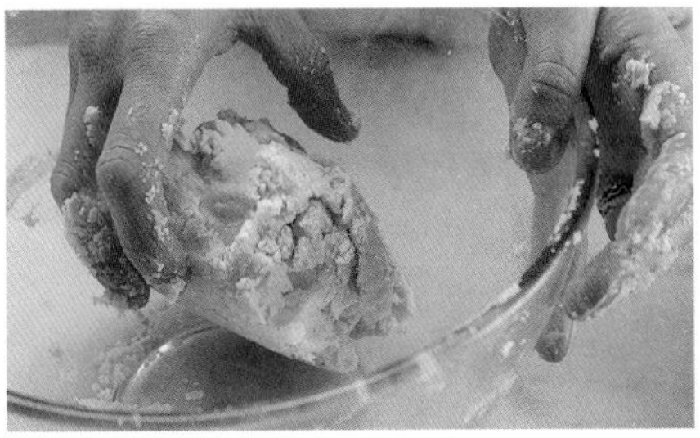

4 *GATHER THE DOUGH TOGETHER IN YOUR HANDS AND FINISH BY MIXING BRIEFLY ON A FLOURED WORK SURFACE.*

more water a few drops at a time. The dough should hold together and be on the firm side of soft. If the dough is sticky or wet, stir in extra flour a little at a time. Turn onto a floured work surface and use your hand to bring the dough together to form a ball – try not to handle or work the dough too much because you don't want the fats to begin to melt and make the pastry oily. If you find that this does happen, and the dough begins to feel soft, wrap it in wax paper and chill it in the refrigerator for 15–20 minutes or until it is firm but not hard.

Alternatively, make the dough in a food processor (see page 302).

Roll out the dough on a lightly floured work surface, using a lightly floured rolling pin. Carefully lift and move the dough from time to time during rolling to check it is not sticking to the work surface; dust with extra flour as necessary.

1 PROCESS THE FATS AND FLOUR TOGETHER TO A CRUMB-LIKE TEXTURE.

2 ONCE WATER IS ADDED, THE DOUGH WILL COME TOGETHER IN A CLUMP.

RICH SHORT PASTRY

Increasing the proportion of fat to flour – from half fat to flour to three-quarters fat to flour, by weight – makes the pastry taste richer. It also makes it slightly more difficult to work, so here the food processor is a blessing. Sugar, added before or after the fat is rubbed in, makes the pastry crisper as well as sweeter, but it also increases the risk of scorching during baking. Instead of water an egg yolk binds the dough and adds additional richness and color – just the yolk is used as egg white tends to make pastry tough. Rich short pastry is made in the same way as short pastry but needs to be chilled before rolling out.

INGREDIENTS

Makes about 1lb (450g)

1⅔ cups (230g) all-purpose flour

⅛–¼ teaspoon salt

5-6 tablespoons (60g) granulated or confectioners' sugar

¾ cup (170g) unsalted butter, chilled and diced

1 extra large egg yolk

a little ice water to bind as necessary

To make the pastry dough by hand, sift the flour, salt, and sugar into a mixing bowl. Add the diced butter and rub in with your fingertips until the mixture resembles fine crumbs. Stir in the egg yolk using a round-bladed knife; if necessary add a little ice water to bind the mixture and make a dough that is not too soft and neither sticky nor hard and dry. Wrap the dough in wax paper and chill for 15–20 minutes or until firm but not hard.

Alternatively, make the dough in a food processor.

To use, roll out as for short pastry.

1 TAKE THE BUTTER STRAIGHT FROM THE FRIDGE AND DICE IT QUICKLY BEFORE ADDING TO THE FLOUR AND SUGAR.

2 AFTER MIXING IN THE EGG YOLK AND WATER, STOP THE MACHINE AS SOON AS THE DOUGH COMES TOGETHER.

ALMOND PASTRY

The addition of ground almonds gives rich short pastry an even richer flavor, and a good crumbly, light texture. I like to use this pastry for fruit tarts as well as for mincemeat pies. The sugar can be either confectioners' sugar – which gives the pastry a fine, crisp texture – or granulated, which makes it slightly more crumbly. Again, I prefer to make the dough in the food processor.

INGREDIENTS

Makes about 1lb 3oz (530g)

- $1^2/_3$ cups (230g) all-purpose flour
- $^1/_8$–$^1/_4$ teaspoon salt
- $^1/_2$ cup (40g) ground almonds
- 7–8 tablespoons (85g) granulated or confectioners' sugar
- $^3/_4$ cup (170g) unsalted butter, chilled and diced
- 1 extra large egg yolk

To make the pastry by hand, sift the flour, salt, ground almonds, and sugar into a mixing bowl. Add the diced butter and cut into the flour mixture using a round-bladed knife. When the butter has been reduced to small flakes, use your fingertips to rub it into the flour. When the mixture looks like fine crumbs, stir in the egg yolk using a round-bladed knife to make a soft but not sticky dough. If there are dry crumbs left at the bottom of the bowl, add ice water a few drops at a time. Wrap the dough in wax paper and chill for 15–20 minutes or until firm but not hard.

Alternatively, make the dough in a food processor.

To use, roll out as for short pastry.

FOR THE BEST TEXTURE, SIFT THE GROUND ALMONDS WITH THE FLOUR, SUGAR, AND SALT TO REMOVE ANY LUMPS.

MINCEMEAT PIES

INGREDIENTS

Makes 12

1 batch short, rich short, or almond pastry dough (pages 303-305)

3/4–1lb (340–450g) mincemeat (see recipe opposite)

granulated or confectioners' sugar for sprinkling

two plain or fluted round pastry or cookie cutters, one 4-inch and one 3-inch

a small star, leaf, or tree-shaped cutter (optional)

3-inch tartlet molds

Just as locally grown asparagus is even more of a treat because it is only in season for a few weeks in May, so the first mincemeat pies taste best because I know it is Christmas Eve. To fill me with seasonal cheer, just shut me in the kitchen with a batch of pastry, jars of homemade mincemeat, and the Festival of Nine Carols and Lessons from King's College, Cambridge, on BBC radio.

Mincemeat pies can be made with short, rich short, or, my absolute favorite, almond pastry – I find puff pastry a bit too rich. Or you can use commercially made sheets of phyllo.

Preheat the oven to 350°F.

Roll out the pastry dough on a floured work surface to about 1/16 inch thick. Cut out 12 rounds using the larger cutter and 12 rounds using the smaller cutter, re-rolling the trimmings as necessary. Line the tartlet molds with the larger rounds, gently pressing the dough against the sides of the molds with your thumb to remove any air bubbles. Put 1 1/2–2 teaspoons of mincemeat in the center of each pastry shell.

Dampen the edges of the pastry shells using a pastry brush dipped in cold water. Cover with the smaller rounds and seal the edges by gently pressing down with an upside-down round cutter or small glass that just fits inside the rim of the mold. Make a small steam hole in the center of each top crust using a skewer.

If you like, cut a star, leaf, or Christmas tree shape out of the center of the smaller rounds before using to cover the pies. Alternatively, the pies can be decorated with shapes cut from the pastry trimmings – stick these onto the crust by dampening the undersides.

Bake the pies for 25–30 minutes or until firm and just golden – the richer pastries tend to brown very quickly so keep an eye on them. Let cool in the molds for several minutes. When the pastry firms up enough to allow the pies to be unmolded, transfer them to a wire rack. Serve warm or at room temperature, dusted with granulated or confectioners' sugar, with brandy butter (hard sauce), cream, or ice-cream. When completely cold, store in an airtight tin and eat within 5 days, or freeze.

NOTE Tartlet molds with the same diameter can vary in depth, so the size of cutter needed for the dough rounds to line the molds will depend on the depth of those you use.

1 LIGHTLY MOISTEN THE RIMS OF THE PASTRY SHELLS WITH COLD WATER BEFORE COVERING WITH THE TOP CRUST.

2 TO SEAL THE PIES, GENTLY PRESS DOWN WITH AN UPTURNED CUTTER THAT IS SLIGHTLY SMALLER THAN THE MOLD.

LUXURIOUS MINCEMEAT

INGREDIENTS

Makes about 3lb (1.35kg)
$1\frac{1}{3}$ cups (230g) currants
$1\frac{1}{2}$ cups (230g) large raisins
$\frac{1}{2}$ cup (85g) finely chopped mixed candied peel
$\frac{1}{3}$ cup (60g) chopped candied ginger
1 cup (110g) grated tart apple
$\frac{1}{2}$ cup (110g) shredded beef suet or vegetarian suet
$\frac{1}{4}$ cup (30g) chopped blanched almonds
$\frac{1}{4}$ cup (30g) chopped walnuts
the grated rind and juice of $\frac{1}{2}$ unwaxed orange
the grated rind and juice of $\frac{1}{2}$ unwaxed lemon
$\frac{3}{4}$ cup packed (170g) dark brown sugar
$\frac{1}{2}$ teaspoon each ground cinnamon, grated nutmeg, and apple-pie spice
$\frac{2}{3}$ cup (140ml) brandy or ginger wine

sterilized jars and lids

I like mincemeat to be fruity and moist but not too sweet, and nicely steeped in brandy. The nuts add a crunchy texture as well as improving the balance of flavors. Mincemeat can also be used to make an easy fruit cake (see page 280) or to fill a large double-crust pie or Jalousie (page 312).

Put all the ingredients into a large mixing bowl and mix thoroughly. Cover tightly and let stand in a cool spot for a day to allow the flavors to infuse and blend. Stir from time to time.

Give the mincemeat a good mix, then spoon into the prepared jars. Cover and leave in the fridge or a cold place for several weeks to allow the mincemeat to mature. Before using, stir well. Always store opened jars of mincemeat in the refrigerator.

Christmas Eve – mincemeat pies, mulled wine, and an aromatic log fire.

RIGHT *A snow-covered church in Bavaria.*

SHORTBREAD-TOPPED MINCE PIES

INGREDIENTS

Makes 20
1 batch short, rich short, or almond pastry dough (pages 303-305)
about 1lb (450g) mincemeat (page 307)

TOPPING:
3/4 cup (170g) unsalted butter, at room temperature
5 tablespoons (60g) sugar
1 1/4 cups (170g) all-purpose flour
1 1/3 cups (110g) ground almonds

a 4-inch plain or fluted round pastry or cookie cutter
3-inch tartlet molds
a pastry bag fitted with a large star tip

These mincemeat pies are lighter than they appear, and disappear even faster than ordinary mincemeat pies. Although the bases can be made from short or rich short pastry, almond pastry is the most delicious when combined with good mincemeat and this rich, but not sweet, almond shortbread mixture piped on top.

Preheat the oven to 350°F.

Roll out the pastry dough fairly thinly and cut out 20 rounds using the pastry cutter (use a large cutter, according to the depth of your molds), re-rolling the trimmings as necessary. Use to line the molds. Put 1 1/2–2 teaspoons of mincemeat into each pastry shell.

To make the topping, beat the butter with the sugar until light and fluffy, then mix in the flour and the almonds. Use your hands to bring the mixture together, kneading gently until smooth; it should be just soft enough to pipe. Spoon the mixture into the pastry bag fitted with the star tip and pipe a swirl on the top of each mincemeat-filled pastry shell. Chill for 5 minutes.

Bake for 25–30 minutes or until a light golden brown. Let cool slightly in the molds. When the pastry is firm enough to unmold, transfer the pies carefully to a wire rack. Eat warm or at room temperature, plain or with cream or ice-cream. When completely cold, store in an airtight tin and eat within 5 days, or freeze.

PHYLLO MINCEMEAT PIES

INGREDIENTS

Makes about 16
$4^1/_2$oz (125g) phyllo pastry, about 8 sheets
$^1/_2$ cup (110g) unsalted butter, melted
$^3/_4$–1lb (340–450g) mincemeat (page 137)
confectioners' sugar for dusting

3-inch tartlet molds

I first discovered these on a visit to The Walnut Tree Inn, near Abergavenny in South Wales. Watching the chef and proprietor, Franco Taruschio, make petit-four mincemeat pies to serve with coffee at Christmas was a revelation – the quickest, lightest, crunchiest mincemeat pies can be made from phyllo pastry. The pastry is simply cut into squares, brushed with melted butter, and then used to line the molds and to cover the mincemeat filling.

Preheat the oven to 350°F.

If the pastry is frozen, thaw according to the package directions. Once unwrapped, keep the pastry covered with plastic wrap or a damp dish towel to prevent it from drying out. Lay one sheet of pastry on the work surface. Cut the sheet into $3^1/_2$- to 4-inch squares using a large sharp knife or kitchen scissors (if your molds are deep, cut slightly larger squares) and brush them with melted butter. Use three squares, arranged at different angles, to line each mold, and lightly press into the bottom. The pastry should hang over the rim of the mold.

Put $1^1/_2$–2 teaspoons of mincemeat in the center of each pastry shell. Cover with another two squares of pastry, crumpled lightly like a scarf.

Bake for 8–10 minutes or until a good golden brown and crisp. Remove from the molds and cool on a wire rack. Serve warm or at room temperature, dusted with sifted confectioners' sugar. Store the mincemeat pies in an airtight tin, and eat them within 2 days.

1 USING A PASTRY BRUSH, COAT THE CUT SQUARES OF PHYLLO WITH A THIN LAYER OF MELTED BUTTER.

2 LINE EACH MOLD WITH THREE SQUARES OF BUTTERED PHYLLO, ARRANGING THEM AT SLIGHTLY DIFFERENT ANGLES.

3 SPOON A LITTLE MINCEMEAT INTO THE CENTER OF EACH PHYLLO-LINED MOLD, WITHOUT OVERFILLING.

4 COVER EACH PIE WITH TWO MORE SQUARES OF BUTTERED PASTRY, CRUMPLED UP LIKE A CHIFFON SCARF.

LEFT Franco Taruschio making phyllo mincemeat pies in his kitchen at The Walnut Tree Inn.

QUEEN MARY TARTLETS

INGREDIENTS

Makes 12

PASTRY:

¾ cup (110g) all-purpose flour

a pinch of salt

5 tablespoons (70g) margarine, butter, or a mix of fats, chilled and diced

½ teaspoon sugar

1 egg yolk

2 teaspoons ice water

FILLING:

4 tablespoons (60g) margarine or butter, at room temperature

5 tablespoons (60g) sugar

1 extra large egg

⅔ cup (110g) golden raisins

3 tablespoons (30g) finely chopped mixed candied peel

a 4-inch plain or fluted round pastry cutter

3-inch tartlet molds

Another Scottish recipe from Katie Stewart (see page 282) – simple, sweet, fruit-filled tartlets dating back to the court of Mary Queen of Scots. The pastry can be made with margarine, butter, or a mixture of either with lard or shortening.

Preheat the oven to 375°F.

Make the pastry: sift the flour and salt into a mixing bowl, add the fat, and cut and rub in with your fingertips until the mixture looks like fine crumbs (do not rub in shortening). Stir in the sugar. Mix together the egg yolk and water, then stir into the mixture to make a firm dough.

Roll out the dough fairly thinly on a lightly floured work surface. Cut out 12 rounds using the pastry cutter, re-rolling the trimmings as necessary. Use the rounds to line the tartlet molds, pressing the dough gently against the bottom and sides of the molds to eliminate any air bubbles. Try not to stretch the dough as you do this.

For the filling, beat the margarine or butter with the sugar until light and fluffy, then beat in the egg. When thoroughly blended, stir in the raisins and the chopped candied peel. Divide the filling equally among the tartlet shells and smooth the surface.

Bake for 15–20 minutes or until the pastry under the filling is cooked – to test, carefully loosen and lift out the filling from one tartlet using a small round-bladed knife.

Remove the tartlets from the molds and let cool on a baking sheet. Eat warm or at room temperature, within 24 hours of baking.

ROUGH or QUICK PUFF PASTRY

INGREDIENTS

Makes about 12oz (340g)
$1^2/_3$ cups (230g) all-purpose flour
$^1/_4$ teaspoon salt
4 tablespoons (60g) butter, chilled and finely diced
4 tablespoons (60g) lard, chilled and finely diced, or shortening
about 4 tablespoons ice water to bind

Rough puff is quicker, simpler, and less rich than puff pastry, but it still has plenty of layers of crisp, light pastry, and it is ideal for deep-dish fruit pies as well as tarts. Although you can use all butter for a richer taste, I find a combination of butter and lard or shortening helps the dough to rise more during baking and makes a lighter pastry. To make rough puff, flakes of fat are combined with flour and water to make a soft, lumpy dough, which is then rolled out and folded six times, just as with puff pastry. This incorporates the fat into the dough in hundreds of layers.

Sift the flour and salt into a mixing bowl. Add the fats and stir gently with a round-bladed knife until the pieces are thoroughly coated in flour. Stir in enough ice water to bind the dough, adding it a tablespoon at a time. The dough should be lumpy, soft, and moist, but not sticky or wet.

Turn the dough onto a lightly floured work surface and form it into a brick shape by gently patting with floured fingers. Using a floured rolling pin, roll out the dough away from you into a rectangle 18 x 6 inches. Fold the dough in three like a business letter: fold the bottom third of the dough up to cover the center third, then fold the top third down to cover the other two layers. Gently but firmly seal the edges by pressing down with the rolling pin. This is the first "turn."

Lift up the piece of dough and give it a quarter turn counterclockwise, so that the folded edges are now at the sides. Roll out and fold in three again, then give the dough a quarter turn counterclockwise; repeat. After this third "turn," wrap the dough and chill for 20 minutes, then do three more "turns," to make a total of six. Chill for 20 minutes before using.

1 THE DOUGH SHOULD LOOK LUMPY, SOFT, AND MOIST BUT NOT WET OR STICKY.

2 SHAPE THE DOUGH INTO A BRICK, THEN ROLL IT OUT TO MAKE A RECTANGLE.

3 FOLD THE RECTANGLE OF DOUGH IN THREE LIKE A BUSINESS LETTER.

4 PRESS THE EDGES OF THE FOLDED DOUGH WITH THE ROLLING PIN TO SEAL THEM.

CARAMELIZED MANGO JALOUSIE

INGREDIENTS

Serves 4

1 batch rough puff pastry dough (page 314)
2 medium to large, ripe mangoes
2 tablespoons sugar
2 pieces of candied ginger, minced (optional)

GLAZE:
a little egg white, lightly beaten, for brushing
1 tablespoon sugar for sprinkling

a baking sheet, lightly greased

Instead of mangoes, you can use lightly poached, forced spring rhubarb for this delicious pastry. Other possible fillings include ripe cherries, pitted and tossed with sugar; quartered apricots; apple slices mixed with mincemeat; or some very good preserves.

Heat the broiler.

Wrap the prepared pastry dough and let rest in the fridge while making the filling (this will help the gluten in the flour to relax).

Peel the mangoes and cut the fruit away from the central pit, taking two pieces from each mango. Slice each piece lengthwise like a fan so the slices remain attached at one end. Arrange the four mango "fans" on the prepared baking sheet and sprinkle with the sugar. Broil for a few minutes or until the tops of the fruit become golden and caramelized. Remove and let cool completely.

Preheat the oven to 425°F.

On a lightly floured work surface, roll out the pastry dough to a rectangle 12 x 10 inches. Using a large sharp knife, trim the edges to make them straight, then cut the rectangle in half lengthwise to make two long

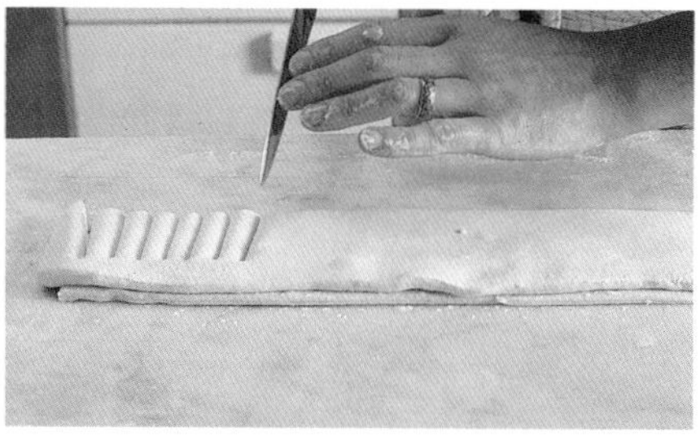

1 FOLD THE PASTRY STRIP IN HALF AND CUT SLITS ACROSS THE FOLD.

2 MOISTEN THE PASTRY EDGES USING A PASTRY BRUSH DIPPED IN COLD WATER.

3 SCORE THE SIDE SO THE PASTRY WILL RISE EVENLY DURING BAKING.

narrow strips. Cut cleanly without dragging the dough. Put one strip on the clean, greased baking sheet. Lightly dust the other strip of dough with flour and fold it in half lengthwise. Cut slits across the fold, about 3/8 inch apart, leaving an uncut border about 3/4 inch wide along the top, bottom, and sides. When opened the strip should look like a Venetian blind.

Arrange the cold caramelized mango fans in a line down the center of the strip of dough on the baking sheet. Scatter the ginger over, if using. Dampen the edges of the strip with a brush dipped in cold water. Lay the cut strip of dough on top and carefully unfold to cover the base and filling. Gently press the edges to seal, then trim to neaten. Using a small knife, score the sides: hold the knife parallel to the assembled pastry and gently knock the blade against the pastry sides to make a series of horizontal marks – the pastry sides will look like the closed pages of a book. Using two fingers and the small knife, flute the edges all around by gently pressing the fingertips down and drawing the knife up between them to form small scallops.

Chill the pastry for 5 minutes, then bake for 20 minutes or until golden and crisp. Remove the baking sheet from the oven. Brush the jalousie lightly with egg white, then sprinkle with sugar. Return to the oven and bake for a further 5 minutes.

Serve warm, with cream, ice-cream, or crème fraîche.

PUFF PASTRY

INGREDIENTS

Makes about 1lb 5oz (600g)
1¾ cups (250g) all-purpose flour
½ teaspoon salt
1 cup (250g) unsalted butter, cold
1 teaspoon lemon juice
about ½ cup (125ml) ice water

A selection of puff pastry confections and other tea-time treats at Betty's of Harrogate, in northern England.

This, the lightest, richest, flakiest, and most delicious of all pastries, is time-consuming to make and tricky to master. Oh, but the taste is worth it! Nothing can compare to its butteriness, for this pastry contains as much butter as flour, incorporated into the dough by rolling and folding six times, to form seemingly hundreds of airy layers. It makes a fine mille-feuilles *layered with cream and fruit, or it can be used for* chaussons *(fruit turnovers) or a* Pithiviers *– a pastry filled with a rich almond frangipane.*

As with all pastry it is important to avoid developing the gluten in the flour (this is only desirable when making bread dough, where the resulting elasticity is essential). With puff pastry, over-working and stretching the dough would result in it shrinking alarmingly and becoming tough. Although lemon juice helps to prevent this, I prefer to make the détrempe *– the initial dough – in the food processor, to cut down on handling, and I stick religiously to the chilling times.*

The butter is most easily incorporated if it is cold – the same temperature as the détrempe *– but pliable rather than hard. So I use it straight from the fridge and beat it with a rolling pin to get the right consistency. It is vital not to let the butter get warm and start to ooze out of the dough or the pastry will not rise during baking and will be end up greasy and heavy.*

For convenience, the dough can be stored in the fridge for 4 days, or frozen, after you have given it four "turns." Then the last two "turns" can be completed when you want to use the dough.

Sift the flour and salt and tip into the bowl of a food processor. Add 2 tablespoons (30g) of the butter, cut into dice, and process until the mixture resembles fine crumbs. Mix the lemon juice and water. With the machine running, pour the liquid in via the feed tube in a steady stream, to make a ball of soft dough that is fairly moist but not sticky or wet. If the dough seems dry or there are crumbs left in the bottom of the bowl, add a little extra water a teaspoon at a time. Turn the dough onto a lightly floured work surface and shape into a ball, then cut a deep cross in the top (this helps reduce the elasticity). Wrap and chill for 15 minutes.

Dust the remaining slab of butter with a little flour, then place it between two pieces of plastic wrap. Pound with a rolling pin until the butter is half as thick as it was. Remove the plastic. Fold the butter in two, then place between the plastic and pound again. Keep pounding and folding in this way until the butter is pliable but not soft, then fold and beat the butter to make a square with 5-inch-long sides.

Set the ball of dough on a lightly floured work surface. Using a floured rolling pin, roll out the dough to make four flaps with a thick square of dough – the size of the square of butter – in the center. Lift the dough and give it a quarter turn after rolling each flap. Put the square of butter, dusted with flour, on the central square of dough and fold the four flaps over the butter so it is completely enclosed. Gently press the seams to seal. Turn the piece of dough upside down, then lightly press with the rolling pin several times to flatten the dough – do this gently because the fat must not be forced out of its dough wrapping.

Lightly roll out the dough into a rectangle 18 x 6 inches, rolling away from your body in short, brisk movements. Fold the dough in three like a business letter: fold the bottom third up to cover the center third, then fold the top third down to cover the other two layers, making a neat square of dough. Lightly press the edges with the rolling pin to seal. This completes the first "turn."

Lift up the piece of dough and give it a quarter turn counterclockwise, so that the folded edges are now at the sides. Roll out the dough into a rectangle and fold it in three again, just as before. Use two fingers to mark the dough with a couple of dents, to indicate that it has had two "turns," then wrap the dough and chill for 15 minutes.

Give the dough two more "turns," and mark with four little indentations. Wrap and chill the dough as before. At this point the pastry can be stored in the fridge for 4 days or frozen. Before using, give the dough two more "turns," to make a total of six.

1 DUST THE SLAB OF CHILLED BUTTER WITH FLOUR, THEN POUND WITH THE ROLLING PIN UNTIL PLIABLE BUT FIRM.

2 ROLL OUT THE BALL OF DOUGH IN FOUR DIRECTIONS TO MAKE FOUR FLAPS WITH A THICK SQUARE IN THE CENTER.

3 SET THE FLOURED BUTTER SQUARE IN THE CENTER AND FOLD THE FLAPS OF DOUGH OVER TO ENCLOSE IT.

4 LIGHTLY PRESS THE SQUARE OF DOUGH WITH THE ROLLING PIN TO FLATTEN IT, THEN ROLL OUT INTO A RECTANGLE.

5 FOLD THE RECTANGLE IN THREE – THE BOTTOM THIRD UP, THEN THE TOP THIRD DOWN – TO MAKE A SQUARE SHAPE.

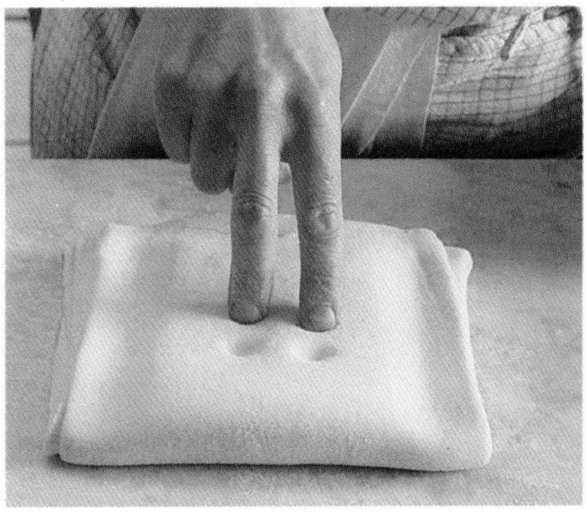

6 MAKE DENTS IN THE PASTRY WITH YOUR FINGERS AS A REMINDER OF HOW MANY "TURNS" YOU'VE COMPLETED.

MILLE FEUILLES

INGREDIENTS

Serves 6–8
½ batch puff pastry dough (page 314), about 10½oz (300g)
3–4 tablespoons good raspberry preserves
⅔ cup (140ml) heavy cream, chilled and whipped
1¼ cups (150g) raspberries
confectioners' sugar for dusting

a large baking sheet, lightly greased

This recipe shows off puff pastry to its best advantage – it is simply baked in a sheet, then sliced into three, and layered with cream and fruit. You can use a variety of fillings to suit the season: pastry cream (see recipe page 336) instead of whipped fresh cream, strawberries, fresh sliced peaches or apricots, pitted cherries, fresh currants, or lightly poached and well-drained fruit like rhubarb or pears. Once assembled, eat as soon as possible because the pastry quickly becomes soggy.

Preheat the oven to 425°F.

Roll out the pastry dough to a square with 12-inch sides, then trim the edges to straighten them using a large sharp knife. Avoid dragging the knife or pulling the dough as this will distort the shape. Put the square of dough upside down on the prepared baking sheet and prick the dough all over with a fork.

Bake for 10 minutes or until well risen, golden, and crisp. Remove from the oven and cool on a wire rack.

Cut the cold pastry into three equal rectangles, each measuring 4 x 12 inches. If necessary, trim the sides to neaten them. Put one pastry rectangle on a serving plate and spread with the jam, then cover with half of the whipped cream. Spread the rest of the whipped cream on a second pastry rectangle and place this on top. Arrange the fruit on the cream very gently, then cover with the third rectangle of pastry. Dust with sifted confectioners' sugar, and serve.

CHOUX PASTRY

INGREDIENTS

Makes a 3-egg quantity
3/4 cup (110g) all-purpose flour
3/4 cup + 1 tablespoon (185ml) water from the cold tap
1/8 teaspoon salt
5 tablespoons (75g) unsalted butter, diced
3 eggs, beaten

Unlike short pastry and other rubbed-in pastries, choux is cooked in a saucepan before it is baked in the oven. The soft dough – made from butter, water, flour, salt, and egg – is piped or dropped in spoonfuls onto a baking sheet. In the oven it rises and puffs up to make a crisp, hollow container. Choux pastry is used for éclairs and profiteroles (cream puffs) to be filled with pastry cream (crème pâtissière), whipped cream, or ice-cream, or beignets, which are deep-fried fritters served with a fruit sauce.

To make successful choux pastry it is important to measure the ingredients very carefully and accurately. In addition, the water must not boil and begin to evaporate before the butter in it has melted. The eggs should be added gradually because if too little is beaten into the dough it will be hard and flat; if too much is added the dough will be too soft to pipe and will not hold a shape.

Sift the flour onto a piece of paper. Put the water, salt, and butter into a medium-sized saucepan and heat gently until the butter has completely melted. Rapidly bring the mixture to a boil, then immediately remove from the heat and tip in all the flour. Beat vigorously with a wooden spoon – the mixture will look a complete mess and a failure at the start but will come together to make a smooth, heavy clump of dough. Return the pan to a low heat and beat the dough for half a minute to dry it slightly. It should come away from the sides of the pan to form a smooth ball.

Turn the dough into a large mixing bowl and let cool until tepid. Then, using an electric mixer – you can use a wooden spoon if you prefer, but it is hard work – gradually beat in the eggs, beating well after each addition. Beat in just enough egg to make a smooth and shiny, paste-like dough that falls from the spoon when lightly shaken. Keep covered until ready to use.

1 DO NOT LET THE *WATER* BOIL BEFORE THE BUTTER HAS COMPLETELY MELTED.

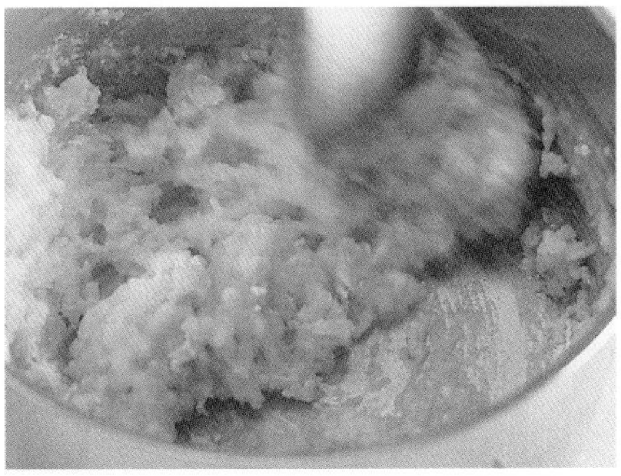

2 OFF THE HEAT, BEAT IN THE FLOUR VIGOROUSLY USING A WOODEN SPOON.

3 RETURN TO A LOW HEAT AND BEAT THE DOUGH TO DRY IT SLIGHTLY.

4 BEAT IN JUST ENOUGH EGG TO MAKE A FAIRLY STIFF, PASTE-LIKE DOUGH.

TINY ÉCLAIRS

INGREDIENTS

Makes about 24

1 batch choux pastry (page 317), with a pinch of sugar added with the salt

COFFEE PASTRY CREAM:

3 egg yolks
5 tablespoons (60g) sugar
2 heaped tablespoons (20g) all-purpose flour
2 tablespoons (15g) cornstarch
1¼ cups (280ml) whole milk
2 teaspoons instant coffee or to taste
a small piece of butter

GLACÉ ICING:

1½ cups (170g) confectioners' sugar, sifted
2 teaspoons instant coffee dissolved in 2 tablespoons boiling water

a pastry bag fitted with a ⅝-inch plain tip
2 baking sheets, greased and dampened

Clare Cave, a friend who caters parties for the Duke of Westminster and up, cooked the most heavenly food for my wedding party, but I can only remember eating the miniature, lighter than air, utterly delicious éclairs. The finger-size choux pastry cases must be well-cooked and crisp before they are filled, otherwise they quickly become soggy. Whipped cream, chocolate mousse (see the Chocolate Macaroons on page 226), or pastry cream can be used to fill them – here I've used coffee pastry cream, and coated the tops with a coffee glacé icing. Eat as soon as possible after assembling.

Preheat the oven to 375°F.

For éclairs, choux paste should hold its own shape and be stiff enough to pipe, so add the last spoonfuls of egg very slowly. Spoon the choux paste into the pastry bag fitted with the plain tip and pipe éclairs the size of your little finger on the prepared baking sheets. Space the éclairs well apart to allow for rising and spreading.

Bake for 20 minutes or until crisp and golden. Remove from the oven, and make a small hole in one end of each éclair, using a skewer or toothpick, to let out the steam. Return the éclairs to the oven and bake for a further 3–4 minutes. Cool on a wire rack.

To make the pastry cream, beat the egg yolks with the sugar in a heatproof mixing bowl until light and creamy. (To avoid spills set the bowl on a damp cloth.) Sift in the flour and cornstarch and mix until smooth. Heat the milk in a heavy saucepan until scalding hot, then add the coffee and stir until dissolved. Pour onto the egg mixture, stirring briskly to make a smooth, creamy liquid. Tip into the rinsed-out saucepan and cook, stirring constantly, until the mixture boils, then beat vigorously until smooth. Turn into a bowl and rub the surface with a little butter to prevent a skin from forming, then let cool.

Spoon the cold pastry cream into the clean, dry pastry bag fitted with the plain tip. Pipe into the éclairs through the steam hole (if necessary, enlarge the steam hole slightly so you can insert the tip).

For the coffee glacé icing, put the sifted sugar into a small mixing bowl and stir in the hot coffee to make a smooth icing. Dip the top of each filled éclair in the icing and let set. Eat within 4 hours.

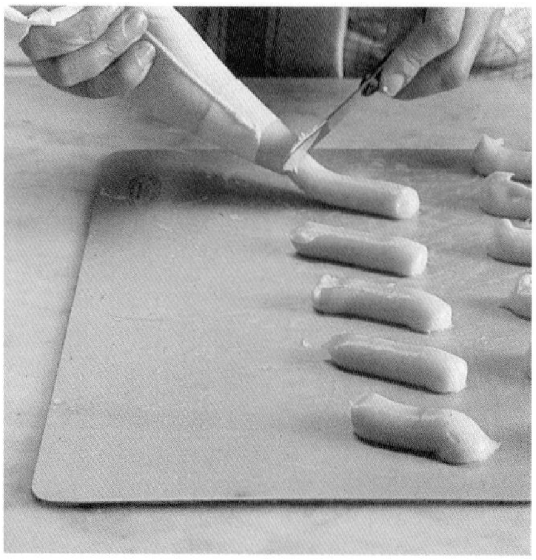

1 PIPE THE ÉCLAIRS, CUTTING THE DOUGH OFF NEATLY WITH A SMALL KNIFE.

2 TO ENSURE CRISP PASTRY, MAKE A SMALL STEAM-HOLE IN EACH BAKED ÉCLAIR.

VARIATIONS: CHOCOLATE ÉCLAIRS Omit the coffee in the pastry cream. Melt 4oz (110g) good semisweet chocolate and add to the cooked pastry cream, off the heat, before transferring it to the bowl. Replace the coffee powder in the icing with 1 tablespoon unsweetened cocoa powder.

PROFITEROLES Put the choux pastry into the pastry bag fitted with the plain tip and pipe rounded mounds about 1 inch wide and 1/2 inch high onto the prepared baking sheets. Lightly brush with beaten egg, making sure that it does not drip down and glue the pastry to the sheet. Bake as above. When cold, fill with coffee, vanilla, or chocolate pastry cream, whipped cream, or, my favorite, vanilla ice-cream. Serve with a sauce – chocolate, caramel, or fruit, depending on the filling.

LEFT Rena Salaman works rapidly to assemble her baklava.

ABOVE The finished baklava (see recipe on next page).

PHYLLO PASTRY

These wafer-thin sheets of pastry, spelled phyllo or filo, are now used for all kinds of sweet and savory dishes. Traditional Greek baklava (see page 322) and mincemeat pies (page 309) are just two delicious examples. Strudel, pastis, and brik doughs are similar to phyllo, though slightly thicker; all become crisp, light, and flaky when baked.

While you can make strudel and pastis doughs at home – kneading, stretching, rolling, and pulling a soft and very pliable dough of flour, egg, and water to make a sheet so thin you can read the newspaper through it – phyllo is always bought commercially made. Supermarkets and specialty gourmet stores sell frozen brands. The quality of frozen phyllo varies from the abysmal to the wonderful, and I have been disappointed many times, but it is only through trial and error that you will find a good brand.

When using frozen phyllo, it is important to follow the directions on the package. Thawing should be at room temperature, and once thawed and unwrapped the pastry sheets must be kept covered with a damp dish towel or plastic wrap while you are working on the recipe. This is vital, because if the pastry dries out, it hardens, cracks, and crumbles and becomes almost impossible to fold.

RENA'S BAKLAVA

INGREDIENTS

Cuts into about 24 pieces
1lb 2oz (500g) phyllo pastry
$3^1/_4$ cups (380g) coarsely chopped walnuts (see recipe)
2 tablespoons sugar
1 teaspoon ground cinnamon
$^3/_4$ cup + 1 tablespoon (185g) unsalted butter, melted
2 tablespoons water from the cold tap

SYRUP:
$1^2/_3$ cups (330g) sugar
$1^1/_4$ cups (300ml) water
1–2 cinnamon sticks, depending on their size and your taste
2 teaspoons lemon juice
3 tablespoons clear honey, preferably Greek and thyme-scented

a roasting pan, about 12 inches in diameter if round or $14^1/_2$ x $9^3/_4$ inches if rectangular (see recipe)

This is a real mouth-opener, and nothing like commercial baklava. The recipe comes from the distinguished Greek cook and food writer, Rena Salaman. It is made with commercial phyllo pastry, plenty of walnuts, and some cinnamon. Other cooks use pistachios or almonds, but Rena prefers walnuts because they have a greater depth of flavor and a little sharpness to counterbalance the sugar syrup. No special equipment is needed as Rena bakes the baklava in a roasting pan.

If the pastry is frozen, thaw according to package directions. Once unwrapped, keep it covered with plastic wrap or a damp dish towel to prevent it from drying out.

Preheat the oven to 350°F.

The walnuts should be chopped to the consistency of coarse bread crumbs. Mix them with the sugar and cinnamon in a bowl. Set aside.

Unfold the phyllo sheets and choose a roasting pan that best fits their shape: round or rectangular. The sizes of pans suggested usually fit almost perfectly, but you can use other size pans and then just fold in the edges of the phyllo sheets a little. Using a pastry brush, grease the pan liberally with melted butter to prevent sticking.

Cover the bottom of the pan neatly with a sheet of phyllo and brush it with butter. Continue adding sheets, buttering each one. When you have layered about six sheets of phyllo, spread with about a third of the walnut

1 BRUSH THE PHYLLO SHEETS WITH BUTTER BEFORE OR AFTER ARRANGING THEM IN THE PAN, AS YOU WISH.

2 WHEN THERE ARE SIX SHEETS IN THE PAN, SPRINKLE IN A THIRD OF THE WALNUT FILLING AND SPREAD EVENLY.

3 COVER WITH TWO MORE BUTTERED PHYLLO SHEETS BEFORE ADDING MORE OF THE WALNUT FILLING.

4 AFTER ADDING THE FINAL LAYER OF FILLING, FOLD IN THE EDGES OF THE PHYLLO SHEETS OVER THE SURFACE.

filling. Cover with two more sheets of buttered phyllo and spread with half of the remaining filling. Place two sheets of buttered phyllo on top and spread evenly with the rest of the filling. Fold in the edges of the phyllo sheets all around to enclose the filling, rather like a parcel. Place the remaining phyllo on top, buttering each sheet before lifting it. Trim the excess pastry around the edges using a small knife or a pair of scissors – remember that phyllo pastry tends to shrink so do not trim too much.

Now comes the tricky part. Phyllo pastry is too brittle to be cut neatly after it has been baked, so the pieces have to be cut before it goes into the oven. Using a sharp knife cut the baklava carefully into oblong pieces. Ideally the pieces should be the same size, but if not, it is not the end of the world. Sprinkle the cold water all over the surface with your fingertips: the moisture will prevent the pastry edges curling up in the oven.

Bake in the preheated oven for 15 minutes, then turn up the temperature to 375°F and bake for a further 15–20 minutes or until the surface is crisp and light golden. Remove from the oven and let cool while you make the syrup.

Put the sugar and water in a saucepan and heat, stirring, until the sugar dissolves, then bring to a boil. Add the remaining ingredients, cover, and simmer for about 10 minutes to make a light, syrupy consistency. Remove from the heat and let the syrup stand for 10 minutes.

Pour the syrup slowly through a fine strainer over all of the warm baklava. Leave it to absorb all the syrup. The baklava is delicious freshly made, but it will also keep well for 3–4 days, covered with plastic wrap.

5 *AFTER COVERING WITH THE REST OF THE PASTRY, TRIM OFF THE EXCESS AT THE EDGE WITH A SHARP KNIFE.*

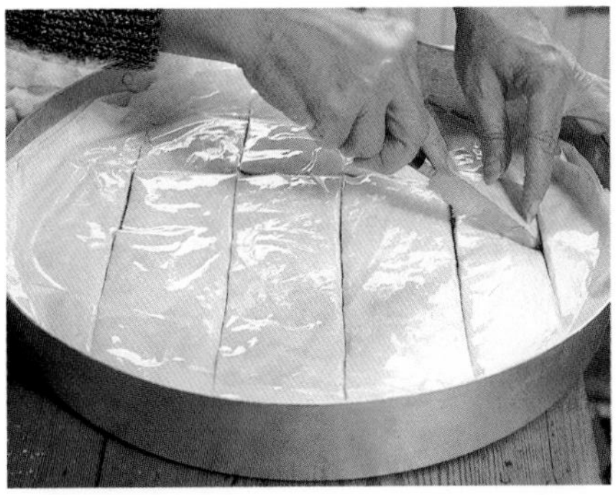

6 *CUT THROUGH THE BAKLAVA TO MARK OUT SMALL SQUARES OR OBLONGS, THEN SPRINKLE WITH WATER AND BAKE.*

7 *ONCE THE SUGAR HAS DISSOLVED, BRING THE SYRUP TO A BOIL AND ADD THE CINNAMON, JUICE, AND HONEY.*

8 *LET THE SYRUP COOL SLIGHTLY BEFORE POURING IT, THROUGH A STRAINER, EVENLY OVER THE WARM BAKLAVA.*

PIES & TARTS

Making a clear distinction between a pie and a tart isn't easy: both have a pastry base and a filling, but both may also have a pastry crust or other topping. Whatever you call them, the case and its contents should not merely share a plate – they ought to make a good marriage.

LEMON MERINGUE PIE

INGREDIENTS

Makes an 8-inch pie, to serve 6

PASTRY:
- 1 1/4 cups (170g) all-purpose flour
- a pinch of salt
- 1 1/2 tablespoons (20g) sugar
- 1/2 cup (110g) unsalted butter, chilled and diced
- 1 egg yolk, mixed with 2 teaspoons ice water

FILLING:
- the grated rind and juice of 3 large unwaxed lemons
- 5 tablespoons (40g) cornstarch
- 1 1/4 cups (280ml) water
- 2 egg yolks
- 7 tablespoons (85g) sugar
- 3 tablespoons (45g) unsalted butter, diced

MERINGUE TOPPING:
- 3 egg whites
- 2/3 cup (140g) superfine sugar

an 8-inch loose-based tart pan

PREVIOUS PAGE Summer Fruit Tart.

It may be corny, but this is my favorite dessert. The lemon filling is nicely sharp and well-flavored, and unlike most recipes it is made rich and creamy with butter. To keep the pastry base from going soggy, bake it thoroughly before adding the filling. If you cannot find unwaxed lemons, give the fruit a good scrub with hot, soapy water before grating the rind.

Note that the recipe uses three eggs: one yolk for the pastry, the other two yolks for the filling, and the three whites for the meringue topping.

Make the pastry: sift the flour and salt into a mixing bowl and stir in the sugar. Add the diced butter and rub into the dry ingredients, using the tips of your fingers, until the mixture resembles fine crumbs. Using a round-bladed knife, stir in the egg yolk mixture to make a slightly firm dough – it should not be dry and crumbly nor soft and sticky. The dough can also be made in a food processor (see page 302). Chill the dough until firm – about 15 minutes.

Turn the dough onto a lightly floured work surface and knead for a couple of seconds or until smooth. Roll out to a round about 10 1/2 inches in diameter. Roll the dough up around the rolling pin and lift it over the tart pan. Gently unroll the dough so it drapes over the pan. Carefully press the dough onto the bottom of the pan and up the sides so there are no pockets of air. Roll the rolling pin over the top of the tart pan to cut off the excess dough.

The sides of the pastry shell should stand slightly above the rim of the tart pan, just in case the pastry shrinks during baking. So use your thumbs to press and ease the pastry sides upward to make a neat rim that is about 1/4 inch higher than the pan. Curve your forefinger inside this rim and gently press the pastry over your finger so the rim curves inward rather

1 ROLL THE DOUGH AROUND THE ROLLING PIN AND LIFT IT OVER THE TART PAN.

2 CUT OFF THE EXCESS DOUGH BY ROLLING THE PIN OVER THE TOP OF THE PAN.

3 POUR THE HOT FILLING INTO THE BAKED PASTRY SHELL AND SPREAD EVENLY.

4 SPOON THE MERINGUE ON TOP AND SPREAD GENTLY WITH A KNIFE.

than over-hanging the rim of the pan. (This makes unmolding easier.) The pastry rim can be fluted with your fingers to match the fluting of the pan sides. Prick the bottom of the pastry shell all over with a fork to prevent the pastry from bubbling up during baking. Chill for 10–15 minutes or until the pastry is firm.

Preheat the oven to 400°F.

Bake the pastry shell (see page 328). Remove from the oven and let cool slightly while you make the filling. Leave the oven on at 350°F.

Put the grated lemon rind and juice into a small heatproof bowl with the cornstarch. Add 2 tablespoons of the water and stir well. Bring the rest of the water to a boil in a medium-sized saucepan. Pour the boiling water onto the cornstarch mixture, stirring constantly, then tip the contents of the bowl into the saucepan. Cook, stirring constantly, until the mixture boils. Reduce the heat and simmer for 2 minutes, stirring frequently, to make smooth, thick paste.

Remove from the heat and beat in the egg yolks and sugar, and then the butter. When thoroughly combined and there are no streaks in the mixture, spoon it into the baked pastry shell and spread evenly.

To make the meringue topping, put the egg whites into a non-plastic, spotlessly clean, grease-free bowl and beat until soft peaks form. Gradually beat in the sugar, then beat well to make a stiff, shiny meringue. Spoon the meringue over the lemon filling to cover completely, spreading it out gently with a knife or metal spatula.

Bake for 15–20 minutes or until the meringue is just firm and a good golden brown. Serve at room temperature, within 24 hours of baking.

HOW TO BAKE PASTRY SHELLS

FILL THE PAPER-LINED PASTRY SHELL WITH A LAYER OF PIE WEIGHTS OR DRIED BEANS.

Cut a round of non-stick parchment paper about the same size as the round of pastry dough used to line the pan. Crumple up the paper, then open it out and gently press it into the pastry shell to cover the bottom and sides – this is easy if the pastry is chilled and firm. It is important to press the paper into the angle where the sides meet the bottom. Fill the paper-lined shell with enough pie weights, dried beans, uncooked rice, or dry bread crusts to weigh it down. Bake the pastry shell in a preheated 400°F oven for 15 minutes or until lightly golden and just firm. Carefully remove the paper and beans, lower the oven temperature to 350°F, and bake the pastry shell empty for a further 5–7 minutes or until the bottom is crisp and lightly golden.

TREACLE TART

INGREDIENTS

Makes an 8-inch tart, to serve 6
ROUGH PUFF PASTRY:
1 cup (140g) all-purpose flour
1/8 teaspoon salt
2 1/2 tablespoons (35g) butter, chilled and diced
2 1/2 tablespoons (35g) lard, chilled and diced, or shortening
2–3 tablespoons ice water to bind

FILLING:
about 6 rounded tablespoons golden syrup (see recipe)
about 2 1/2 cups (110g) fresh white bread crumbs
the grated rind and juice of 1 large unwaxed lemon, or to taste

an 8-inch loose-based tart pan

ARRANGE THE PASTRY STRIPS ON THE FILLING TO MAKE A NEAT WOVEN LATTICE.

This is an old-fashioned English dessert. The recipe here has plenty of lemon to flavor the filling of golden syrup (which has replaced the original treacle) and bread crumbs. I like to use rough puff pastry for the tart shell, but you can also use a simple short pastry (see page 303) or a slightly sweet rich short pastry (see the recipe for Lemon Meringue Pie on page 326).

To make the rough puff pastry, sift the flour and salt into a mixing bowl. Add the fats and stir gently with a round-bladed knife until the pieces are coated with flour. Stir in just enough icy water to bind the dough – it should be very lumpy and soft but not sticky or wet.

Turn the dough onto a lightly floured work surface and form it quickly into a rough brick shape. Using a floured rolling pin, roll out the dough away from you into a rectangle about 3/8 inch thick. Fold the dough in three like a business letter: fold the bottom third of the dough up to cover the center third, then fold the top third down to cover the other two layers. Gently but firmly seal the edges by pressing down with the rolling pin. This completes the first "turn."

Lift up the piece of dough and give it a quarter turn counterclockwise, so that the folded edges are now at the sides. Roll out and fold in three again, just as before, then give the dough a quarter turn counterclockwise; repeat. After this third "turn," wrap the dough and chill for 20 minutes, then complete three more "turns" – to make a total of six. Chill the dough for 20 minutes.

Roll out the dough to a round about 10 inches in diameter and use to line the pan. Roll the pin over the top of the pan to cut off the excess dough. Reserve the trimmings to make the lattice. Chill the pastry shell and trimmings while you make the filling.

Preheat the oven to 400°F.

Gently heat the syrup until it becomes runny, then remove from the heat and stir in the bread crumbs and lemon rind and juice. Let stand for 10 minutes. If the mixture seems very sloppy, add another spoonful of crumbs; if the mixture seems stiff and dry, add another spoonful of syrup.

Treacle Tart (left), Croustade aux Pommes (see recipe on page 346).

NOTE Golden syrup, in jars or cans, is found in most gourmet shops or better supermarkets.

Taste the mixture and add more lemon juice if necessary.

Spoon the filling into the pastry shell; don't press down to level the surface. Roll out the dough trimmings 1/4 inch thick and cut into thin strips. Lay the strips across the filling to make a lattice pattern, sticking the ends to the rim of the pastry shell with a little cold water. The pastry strips can be twisted before sticking the ends down if you want to make the tart look fancier.

Bake for 15 minutes, then reduce the oven temperature to 375°F and bake for a further 10 minutes or until golden. Serve warm.

LEMON TART

INGREDIENTS

Makes a 9-inch tart, to serve 6

PASTRY:

1 cup (140g) all-purpose flour
a pinch of salt
6 tablespoons (85g) unsalted butter, chilled and diced
$2\frac{1}{2}$ tablespoons (30g) sugar
1 egg yolk
1–2 tablespoons ice water
a little egg white, lightly beaten, for brushing

FILLING:

3 eggs
1 egg yolk
$\frac{2}{3}$ cup (140ml) heavy cream
$\frac{1}{2}$ cup + 1 tablespoon (110g) sugar
the grated rind of 2 unwaxed lemons
the juice of 3 lemons

a 9-inch loose-based tart pan
a baking sheet

In a weekend newspaper, I once read a review of fashionable restaurants rated according to the quality of the lemon tarts they served! It is hard to get the balance right when making this dessert – the pastry must be crisp, and the filling should be lemony, creamy, fresh-tasting, and fairly light. In the simple recipe here, the filling is like a light lemon curd made with cream rather than butter. Serve the tart with fresh strawberries or raspberries, and crème fraîche. Use unwaxed lemons if possible; otherwise scrub the fruit well with hot, soapy water before grating the rind.

To make the pastry dough, sift the flour and salt into a bowl, add the diced butter, and rub into the flour, using the tips of your fingers, until the mixture resembles fine crumbs. Stir in the sugar. Add the egg yolk and 1 tablespoon of water and stir into the flour mixture to bind, using a round-bladed knife; add more water if necessary. Quickly bring the mixture together with your hands, without kneading, to make a firm but not sticky ball of dough. Alternatively, you can make the dough in a food processor (see page 302). Wrap the dough and chill for about 30 minutes.

Roll out the dough on a lightly floured work surface to a round about 11 inches in diameter and use to line the tart pan. Trim off the excess dough by rolling the rolling pin across the top of the pan, then neaten the rim with your fingers. Prick the bottom of the pastry shell all over with a fork, then chill for 15 minutes.

Preheat the oven to 375°F.

Bake the pastry shell (see page 328). It is important to cook the pastry thoroughly or the base of the finished tart will be soggy. Remove from the oven but do not unmold. Immediately brush the bottom of the pastry shell with a little egg white, and let cool. (The egg white helps to keep the pastry from turning soggy once the filling is added.) Reduce the oven temperature to 325°F and put a baking sheet in the oven to heat up.

To make the filling, put all the ingredients into a large measure and whisk, by hand, just until thoroughly combined.

Set the pastry shell, still in the pan, on the hot baking sheet and pour in three-fourths of the filling. Put into the oven, then carefully pour in the rest of the filling – this way you avoid spilling the filling as you put the tart into the oven. Bake for 25–30 minutes or until the filling is firm when the tart is gently shaken. Let cool before unmolding. Serve the tart at room temperature or chilled.

RIGHT The display of luscious tarts at La Boite à Dessert in Lyons, France.

STRAWBERRY CHEESE TART

INGREDIENTS

Makes a 25.5cm (10in) tart, to serve 8

PASTRY:

210g (7½oz) plain flour
1 tablespoon caster sugar
a pinch of salt
110g (4oz) unsalted butter, chilled and diced
2–3 tablespoons orange juice to bind

FILLING:

340g (12oz) cream cheese – Philadelphia brand seems to work best
100g (3½oz) caster sugar
2 eggs, size 2, beaten
1 tablespoon grated orange rind
150g (about 5oz) strawberries, thinly sliced

GLAZE:

3 tablespoons apricot or strawberry conserve
1 tablespoon lemon juice

a 25.5cm (10in) loose-based flan tin

This light summery dessert, a cross between a cheesecake and a creamy fruit flan, comes from Rosemary Underdahl of Yarmouth, Maine (see pages 220 for her wonderful cookie recipes). She says that out of season the strawberries can be replaced with pears lightly poached in – leftover – sparkling wine or champagne, rosé for choice, or with sliced nectarines. The pastry for the tart is very rich so it is best rolled out between sheets of cling film or baking parchment.

To make the pastry, mix the flour with the sugar and salt, then rub in the butter, using your fingertips, until the mixture resembles fine crumbs. Add 2 tablespoons orange juice and stir into the flour mixture to bind, using a round-bladed knife; add more orange juice if necessary. Quickly bring the mixture together with your hands, without kneading, to make a fairly firm dough that is not dry or crumbly. Alternatively, you can make the dough in a food processor (see page 302). Shape the dough into a flat disc, then wrap and chill for 10 minutes.

Roll out the dough between two sheets of cling film or non-stick baking parchment to a round about 30.5cm (12in) in diameter. Peel off the top sheet of film or paper, turn the round of dough over and lay it over the tin. Gently press the dough into the tin to line the bottom and sides evenly, then peel off the remaining cling film or paper. Do not cut off the excess pastry dough, but instead fold it back into the tin and press gently, to make the sides twice as thick. Prick the bottom of the pastry case all over with a fork, then cover and chill in the freezer for 30 minutes.

Strawberries in the market in Lyons, France.

Preheat the oven to 400°F.

Line the chilled pastry shell with non-stick parchment paper and fill with pie weights (see the instructions for baking pastry shells on page 328). Bake for about 10 minutes or until just firm, then remove the paper and weights and bake for a further 8–10 minutes or until lightly browned. Let the pastry shell cool completely.

Lower the oven temperature to 350°F.

To make the filling, beat the cream cheese with the sugar until smooth and creamy, then gradually beat in the eggs followed by the orange rind.

Pour the filling into the cold pastry shell. Bake for 30 minutes or until set. Let cool on a wire rack before unmolding.

Arrange the sliced strawberries on top. To make the glaze, heat the preserves with the lemon juice until runny, then strain into a clean pan. Warm gently and then brush over the fruit to glaze it lightly. Chill for about 1 hour before serving.

STRAWBERRY MARZIPAN TART

I am very fond of the combination of strawberries and almonds, which makes this a favorite dessert. It is quite a substantial tart – the pastry case is filled with an almond sponge flavored with orange and then topped with sliced fruit. For a glossy finish the arranged strawberries can be brushed with a glaze of hot red-currant jelly, but if the fruit is loaded with flavor I prefer to leave it plain. As with most almond desserts, this tart improves on keeping a day or so before the fruit is added.

INGREDIENTS

Makes a 9-inch tart, to serve 6–8

PASTRY:
- 1¼ cups (170g) all-purpose flour
- 7 tablespoons (100g) unsalted butter, chilled and diced
- 2½ tablespoons (30g) sugar
- 1 egg yolk
- about 1 tablespoon ice water

FILLING:
- 1 cup (230g) unsalted butter, at room temperature
- 7 tablespoons (85g) sugar
- 2 eggs, beaten
- the grated rind and juice of 1 unwaxed orange
- 2⅔ cups (230g) ground almonds

TOPPING:
- ½lb (230g) ripe strawberries, hulled and sliced

a 9-inch loose-based tart pan

To make the pastry dough, sift the flour into a bowl, add the diced butter, and rub into the flour, using the tips of your fingers, until the mixture resembles fine crumbs. Stir in the sugar. Add the egg yolk and water and stir into the flour mixture to bind, using a round-bladed knife; add more water if necessary. Quickly bring the mixture together with your hands, without kneading, to make a soft but not sticky ball of dough. Alternatively, you can make the dough in a food processor (see page 302). Wrap the dough and chill for 20 minutes.

Preheat the oven to 350°F.

Roll out the pastry dough on a lightly floured work surface to a round about 11 inches in diameter and use to line the tart pan. Chill while preparing the filling.

Beat the butter until creamy, then beat in the sugar and continue beating until light and fluffy. Gradually beat in the eggs, beating well after each addition. Beat in the orange rind and juice, then fold in the ground almonds using a large metal spoon. Spoon the filling into the pastry shell and level the surface.

Bake in the preheated oven for 45 minutes to 1 hour or until golden and firm to the touch. Let cool before unmolding. If possible, wrap the tart and store in an airtight tin overnight before finishing.

Arrange the sliced strawberries in overlapping circles on top of the tart just before serving. Serve at room temperature.

TARTE TATIN

INGREDIENTS

Makes a 12-inch tart, to serve 8–10

PASTRY:

- $1\frac{1}{2}$ cups (200g) all-purpose flour
- a pinch of salt
- $2\frac{1}{2}$ tablespoons (30g) sugar
- 7 tablespoons (100g) unsalted butter, chilled and diced
- 1 egg yolk
- 2 tablespoons ice water

FILLING:

- $\frac{1}{2}$ cup (110g) unsalted butter
- 1 cup (200g) sugar
- about $4\frac{1}{2}$lb (2kg) apples, such as Granny Smith, Golden Delicious, McIntosh, Pippins

a 12-inch heavy frying pan or skillet with an ovenproof handle, or a tarte tatin mold

This upside-down apple tart, traditionally cooked in a heavy cast-iron frying pan, can be made with puff pastry or a sweet short pastry. I find the classic French recipe slightly too rich, heavy, and sweet to enjoy at the end of a meal, so mine uses less butter and sugar. Here you can really taste the fruit as well as the caramel. It is best to use tart, crisp apples for the filling and to pack them together tightly. Do not put the pastry on top of the apples until they are sitting in a good brown caramel or the tart will be soggy and insipid-tasting.

Make the pastry dough by hand (see page 302) or in a food processor: put the flour, salt, and sugar in the bowl of the processor and process until mixed. Add the diced butter and process until the mixture resembles fine crumbs. With the machine running, add the egg yolk and ice water through the feed tube, and process until the mixture binds together to form a firm but not dry dough. If there are dry crumbs, gradually add a little more water. Wrap and chill while preparing the apples.

1 COOK THE APPLE HALVES IN THE FRYING PAN WITH THE BUTTER AND SUGAR UNTIL A RICH CARAMEL IS FORMED AND MOISTURE FROM THE APPLES HAS EVAPORATED.

2 COVER THE CARAMELIZED APPLES WITH THE PASTRY CRUST, GENTLY UNROLLING IT FROM THE ROLLING PIN, THEN TUCK THE EDGES DOWN INSIDE THE PAN.

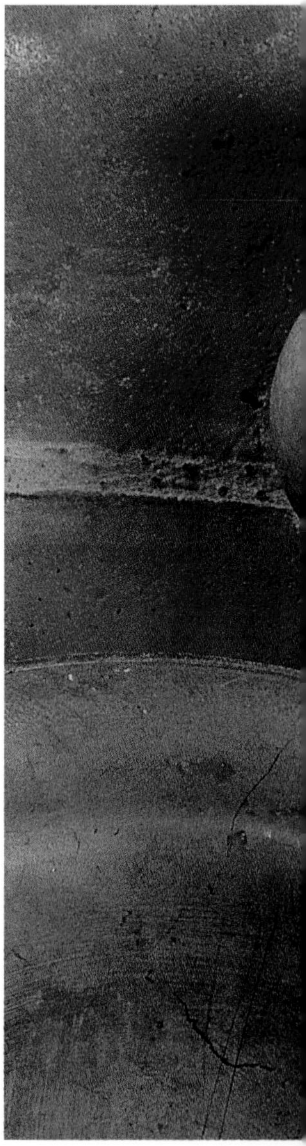

Cut the butter into thin slices and arrange on the bottom of the frying pan to cover completely. Sprinkle over the sugar to make an even layer. Peel, halve, and core the apples. Arrange in the pan, on top of the butter and sugar, so the apple halves stand up vertically. Pack the apples tightly together so the tart will not collapse in the oven.

Put the pan over a medium heat on top of the stove and cook for 20–30 minutes or until the butter and sugar have formed a richly colored caramel, and all the moisture from the apples has evaporated. Remove from the heat.

While the apples are cooking, preheat the oven to 425°F.

Roll out the dough on a lightly floured surface to a round to fit the top of the pan. Roll up the dough around the rolling pin and lift over the pan. Gently unroll the dough so it covers the apples completely. Quickly tuck the edges of the crust down inside the pan, then prick the crust all over with a fork. Bake for 20–30 minutes or until golden brown and crisp.

Cool slightly, then loosen the edges of the crust and turn out the tart upside down so the pastry is under the caramelized apples. Eat warm or at room temperature, with ice-cream or crème fraîche.

SUMMER FRUIT TART

INGREDIENTS

Makes a 9- to 10-inch tart, to serve 8

- ½ batch puff pastry dough (page 314), about 10½oz (300g)
- 2 tablespoons liqueur de noisette, eau de vie, or kirsch
- 2–3 large, ripe peaches
- about 12 ripe apricots
- 2 cups (230g) ripe, sweet cherries
- 3 tablespoons red-currant jelly
- 1 tablespoon toasted sliced almonds
- black-currant leaves for decoration (optional)

PASTRY CREAM:

- 1¼ cups (280ml) rich creamy milk
- 1 vanilla bean, split, or 1 teaspoon pure vanilla extract
- 4 extra large egg yolks
- 5 tablespoons (60g) sugar, plain or vanilla-flavored
- 2 tablespoons all-purpose flour

a 9- to 10-inch loose-based tart pan

ABOVE Katie Barber proudly shows off her Summer Fruit Tart.

OPPOSITE Juicy, aromatic summer fruits being prepared for sale in the market in Lyons, France.

This pretty, fresh fruit tart comes from Katie Barber, who moved from England, where she ran a successful restaurant, to central France. There she has opened her house to bed-and-breakfast guests, and has gained a reputation among the local population for cooking very good dinners.

Preheat the oven to 400°F.

On a floured work surface, roll out the pastry dough to a round about 2½ inches larger than your tart pan. Use the dough to line the pan, letting the excess dough drape over the rim. Chill for 15 minutes, then cut off the excess dough with a very sharp knife, taking care not to stretch it. Prick the bottom of the pastry shell all over with a fork, then bake (see page 328). Leave until completely cold. (It is important to cook the pastry shell well or the tart will become soggy soon after assembling.)

To make the pastry cream, put the milk and the split vanilla bean (but not the extract) into a heavy saucepan and heat slowly until scalding hot. Remove from the heat, cover the pan, and let infuse for 20 minutes. Whisk the egg yolks with the sugar until very light and thick, then whisk in the flour until there are no lumps. Remove the vanilla bean, then whisk the milk into the egg mixture. Tip the mixture into the saucepan and cook over medium heat, whisking constantly, until the mixture boils and thickens to a smooth, creamy consistency. Cook gently, whisking, for a couple of minutes or until there is no raw flour taste. Remove from the heat and stir in the vanilla extract, if using. Sprinkle the top of the pastry cream with a little sugar or melted butter to prevent a skin from forming, then let cool.

Add half the liqueur to the cold pastry cream and beat until completely smooth. Spread over the bottom of the cold pastry shell.

Prepare the fruit: slice the peaches; halve or quarter the apricots; pit the cherries, leaving a few whole and joined by the stems in pairs for decoration. Arrange the fruit attractively over the pastry cream.

Heat the red-currant jelly with the rest of the liqueur and stir vigorously until smooth, then brush over the fruit to glaze it. Scatter the almonds over and serve as soon as possible, decorated with black-currant leaves and the reserved cherries.

NOTE To make a lighter pastry cream, you can stir in ⅔ cup (140ml) heavy cream which has been lightly whipped just before it is to be used.

VARIATIONS: MIXED FRUIT TART Make the pastry shell and pastry cream as above, but omitting the liqueur. Decorate with small whole fruits, such as tiny apricots and figs, grapes, cherries, strawberries, red currants, raspberries, and blackberries, plus tiny vine leaves and wild roses. Let your imagination run riot.

APRICOT TART Make the pastry shell and pastry cream as above, but omitting the liqueur. Add 1 tablespoon each of ground almonds, almond or apricot liqueur, and whipped cream to the pastry cream. Decorate with poached apricot halves and sliced almonds, and glaze with the apricot poaching liquid, well reduced, or apricot jelly.

TARTE À LA CRÈME

INGREDIENTS

Makes a 10½- to 11-inch tart, to serve 8–10

½ batch puff pastry dough (page 314), about 10½oz (300g)

1 quart (1 liter) UHT French cream (see note)

7 tablespoons (80g) sugar

a 10½-11-inch loose-based tart pan

NOTE: The only cream that works is UHT (Ultra Heat-Treated) long-life French cream. It is available from some gourmet food shops.

This recipe comes from restaurateurs Max Renzland and his twin brother, the late Marc Renzland, whose friendliness and skills as a chef are sadly missed. Their first restaurant, in Kew in Surrey, England, quickly gained a reputation for some of the best, and most scrupulously French, food in London. Their hospitality overwhelmed their customers...and eventually their restaurant because portions were more than generous, extra courses were added at no extra charge, and wine was used in sauces by the magnum rather than by the ladle. The restaurant closed, but a while later they turned up farther down the Thames, cooking at a café restaurant, Le Petit Max, in Hampton Wick. There is now also a larger place in London, called Chez Max. This tart has been on every one of their menus since they first opened. A combination of light, buttery pastry and pure cream, it is wonderful.

Roll out the pastry dough to a large, thin round about 13¾ inches in diameter and use to line the tart pan. Let the excess dough hang over the edge of the pan – do not cut it off. Chill for 25 minutes.

Preheat the oven to 400°F.

Prick the bottom of the pastry shell all over with a fork, then bake until crisp and golden, about 15 minutes. Let cool in the pan.

Put the cream and sugar in a heavy-based saucepan and slowly bring to a boil. Simmer until reduced by 60% – about 1 hour – stirring frequently. Pour into the baked tart shell and carefully slide into the oven (at the same temperature). Bake for about 15 minutes or until golden.

Let cool, then use a sharp knife to trim off the excess pastry around the edge. Serve the tart at room temperature.

CAREFULLY POUR THE HOT, THICKENED CREAM INTO THE BAKED PASTRY CASE.

RIGHT Marc Renzland with a Tarte à la Crème – the pastry edges are trimmed after baking and cooling.

DANISH STRAWBERRY SHORTBREAD

INGREDIENTS

Serves 6–8

SHORTBREAD BASE:

1 2/3 cups (230g) all-purpose flour
a pinch of salt
1/2 cup + 1 tablespoon (70g) confectioners' sugar
3/4 cup (170g) unsalted butter, chilled and diced
2 extra large egg yolks
a few drops of pure vanilla extract

TOPPING:

1lb (450g) ripe strawberries, hulled
about 2/3 cup (230g) raspberry or red-currant jelly
1–2 tablespoons water

a large baking sheet, greased

This gorgeous summer dessert, of rich, crisp shortbread topped with whole strawberries under a shiny glaze, is adapted from a Cordon Bleu recipe. With a food processor the base is so simple to make, and you can use any soft fruit in season – raspberries, large sweet blackberries, peaches, apricots – with a suitable jelly or strained jam to glaze.

Above SHAPE, FLUTE, AND PRICK THE PASTRY BASE, THEN CHILL IT WELL BEFORE BAKING.

Top right BRUSH THE JELLY GLAZE OVER THE STRAWBERRIES. FOR AN EVEN, THIN COVERING THE JELLY GLAZE MUST BE BOILING HOT.

To make the shortbread, sift the flour, salt, and confectioners' sugar into the bowl of the food processor. Add the diced butter and process until the mixture resembles fine crumbs. With the machine running, add the yolks and vanilla extract through the feed tube. When the mixture has come together, remove it, shape into a ball, and wrap. Chill until the dough is firm enough to roll out – about 30 minutes.

Roll out the dough on the prepared baking sheet to a round about 10 inches in diameter and about 1/4 inch thick. Flute the edge by pinching the dough between your fingers, then prick the base all over with a fork. Chill for about 10 minutes.

Preheat the oven to 350°F.

Bake the shortbread base for 20–25 minutes or until just firm and lightly golden. Leave on the baking sheet until cool and quite firm before attempting to transfer to a wire rack. When the shortbread base is cold, place it on a serving platter or bread board.

To prepare the topping, check the strawberries for blemishes, then wipe gently to clean them – wash only if the berries look gritty or muddy or you are dubious about them. Put the jelly into a small saucepan with 1 tablespoon of water. Heat gently, stirring frequently as the jelly melts, then beat vigorously with a wooden spoon to make a smooth, thick syrup.

Brush a little hot jelly over the shortbread base. Arrange the strawberries upright on the base with the pointed ends upward – I find it easiest to start at the edge. The berries should cover the shortbread base completely. Brush the berries with the boiling hot jelly glaze to coat them thoroughly. If the glaze becomes thick and difficult to use, reheat it and add a little extra water. Let set – about 20 minutes – then serve with cream or ice-cream. Eat within about 4 hours of assembling.

PLUM TART

INGREDIENTS

Makes an 8-inch tart, to serve 6

PASTRY:

5 tablespoons (70g) unsalted butter, at room temperature

1/3 cup (40g) confectioners' sugar, sifted

the grated rind of 1/2 unwaxed lemon

1 egg yolk

1 cup (140g) all-purpose flour

FILLING:

10 ripe plums, about 1lb 2oz (500g)

2 tablespoons ground almonds

2 tablespoons (30g) unsalted butter, cut into small pieces

2 tablespoons granulated or raw brown sugar, or to taste, for sprinkling

1/4 cup (30g) slivered almonds

an 8-inch cast-iron frying pan or skillet or a loose-based tart pan

This recipe is based on a tart I enjoyed in Düsseldorf. It arrived at the table in a small cast-iron pan, and tasted as wonderful as it looked. Fully ripe purple plums that are juicy and sweet are the best to use; you can also use yellow or green plums, although you may have to add extra sugar. The tart can also be made in a loose-based tart pan.

To make the pastry, beat the butter until creamy, then beat in the sugar and lemon rind. When the mixture is light and fluffy, beat in the egg yolk. Work in the flour, first stirring and then gently kneading to bring the dough together. It should be soft but not sticky. Wrap and chill until firm – about 1 hour.

Roll out the dough on a lightly floured surface to a round about 10 inches in diameter and use to line the pan or tart pan. (If using a pan, it is easiest to cut out a neat round of dough for lining.) Prick the bottom of the pastry shell all over with a fork, then chill for 20 minutes.

Meanwhile, rinse and quarter the plums, discarding the pits. Preheat the oven to 375°F.

Sprinkle the ground almonds over the bottom of the pastry shell. Arrange the plum quarters on top so the fleshy side is uppermost. Dot with the butter and sprinkle with the sugar. Bake for 30 minutes or until the fruit is almost tender. Scatter the almonds over the plums and bake for a few more minutes or until the almonds are golden. Serve the tart warm or at room temperature.

1 PUT THE ROUND OF DOUGH IN THE PAN AND PRESS ONTO THE BOTTOM AND SIDES TO REMOVE ANY AIR BUBBLES.

2 SPRINKLE IN THE GROUND ALMONDS. THEY WILL ABSORB THE PLUM JUICE AND PREVENT THE PASTRY BECOMING SOGGY.

3 ARRANGE THE PLUM QUARTERS ON THE LAYER OF GROUND ALMONDS, WITH THE SKIN-SIDE UNDERNEATH.

4 DOT THE PLUMS WITH SMALL PIECES OF BUTTER AND SPRINKLE WITH SUGAR TO GIVE A MOIST TOPPING.

ENGLISH DEEP-DISH FRUIT PIE

INGREDIENTS

Makes a medium pie, to serve 6

PASTRY:

$1\frac{1}{4}$ cups (170g) all-purpose flour
$\frac{1}{2}$ cup (110g) unsalted butter, chilled and diced
about 4 tablespoons ice water

FILLING:

about $2\frac{1}{2}$lb (1.1kg) apples (see right)
about 3 tablespoons light brown sugar, to taste
2 tablespoons water or orange or lemon juice
sugar for sprinkling

an oval deep pie dish, about $8\frac{3}{4}$ x $6\frac{1}{4}$ inches, or a casserole

The traditional English fruit pie is made in a special oval china or ovenproof glass dish, deep enough for plenty of filling. Apples, preferably those that are crisp and tart, make the most popular filling (often tossed with grated orange or lemon rind and juice). For variety, they can be flavored with cinnamon and dark brown sugar, or mixed with raisins or toasted nuts. Other fruits can be mixed with the apples: blackberries, of course, but also cranberries – fresh, frozen, or dried – or fresh or frozen blueberries. Another excellent combination is pear and raspberry. I also like rhubarb (or gooseberries) with sliced oranges, or rhubarb and red currants. The pastry, a top crust only, is usually short pastry, though rough puff makes an excellent covering for cherry or rhubarb pies.

Preheat the oven to 400°F.

Make the pastry dough by hand (see page 302) or in a food processor: put the flour and butter into the bowl of the processor and process until the mixture looks like fine crumbs. With the machine running, gradually add the water through the feed tube, to make a soft but not sticky dough. Wrap and chill while preparing the fruit.

Peel, core, and thickly slice the apples. Toss them with the sugar and water or juice. Add spices, grated orange or lemon rind, or dried fruit to taste and mix well.

Pile the fruit into the pie dish, mounding it slightly in the center. Some cooks like to use a china pie bird, putting it in the center of the dish so the top sticks up above the fruit filling. A pie bird is good if you are short of filling because it prevents the crust sagging in the middle. Also, if the filling is likely to become very juicy during cooking, the pie bird will prevent the crust becoming soggy.

Roll out the dough on a floured work surface to an oval about 3 inches larger all around than the dish. Cut off a strip of dough about $\frac{3}{8}$ inch wide and long enough to fit around the rim of the dish. Dampen the rim of the dish and press the strip of dough onto the rim, joining the ends neatly. Dampen this pastry rim.

Lay the remaining piece of dough over the dish, centering it so it completely covers the pie. Press the dough onto the strip on the rim to seal the top crust to the pie dish. Trim off the excess dough with a sharp knife – the trimmings can be kept for decorations.

The sides of the crust can be scored to give a good-looking edge as well as sealing them: use the back of a small knife held horizontally to make small knocks, or cuts, into the side of the crust all around. The edge can

1 PRESS A STRIP OF PASTRY ONTO THE DAMPENED RIM OF THE DISH TO HELP THE CRUST STAY IN PLACE.

2 TO AVOID STRETCHING THE DOUGH, USE THE ROLLING PIN TO SUPPORT IT AS YOU LIFT IT OVER THE PIE.

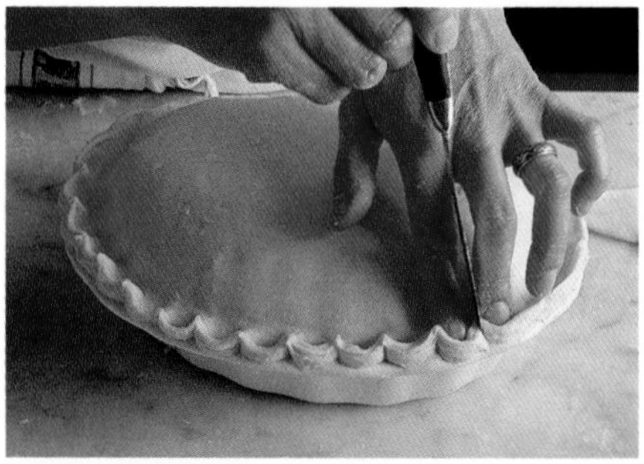

3 AFTER SCORING THE SIDE OF THE CRUST, GIVE THE EDGE AN ATTRACTIVE SCALLOPED FINISH WITH A SMALL KNIFE.

Apple and Raspberry Pie.

then be fluted by placing two fingertips on the pastry rim and gently drawing a small knife between them to give a scalloped look. If decorating the crust with dough trimmings, cut out the shapes and stick them on with a little water.

Make a steam hole in the center of the pie with the tip of a knife or a skewer (directly over the pie bird, if using), then bake for about 30 minutes or until the pastry is golden and crisp. Sprinkle with sugar, and serve hot, warm, or at room temperature.

VARIATIONS If you would rather use rough puff pastry, follow the recipe given on page 141, using $1\frac{1}{4}$ cups (170g) all-purpose flour and 3 tablespoons (40g) each butter and lard or shortening.

If using another fruit with the apples (or pears), use about 2lb (900g) apples plus about $\frac{1}{2}$lb (230g) blackberries, blueberries, cranberries, or raspberries, and toss with the water and sugar to taste.

MRS. BUSH'S PRIZE-WINNING PIE

INGREDIENTS

Makes a 9-inch pie, to serve 6
FILLING:
2 large Bramley apples, about 1lb (450g)
1 tablespoon water
sugar to taste

PASTRY:
$1^2/_3$ cups (230g) all-purpose flour
4 tablespoons (60g) hard lard, chilled and diced
4 tablespoons (60g) salted butter, chilled and diced
8 teaspoons ice water
1 egg, beaten with a pinch of salt, for glazing
1 tablespoon sugar for sprinkling

a shallow 9-inch pie pan, about $^3/_4$ inch deep

RIGHT Mrs. Jean Bush with her prize-winning apple pie. As she says, this pie served with fresh cream is the true taste of Nottinghamshire, England.

In the 1994 Open Apple Pie Competition, organized by the Women's Institute in Nottinghamshire, England, Jean Bush won first prize with this recipe. The competition was held near where the first Bramley apple tree was grown. Hundreds of pies, all made with Bramley apples, were entered.

Mrs. Bush gave me some sound advice about baking apple pie. She cooks the apples first and then leaves them to cool before putting them into the pie. Bramleys make a good pie filling because they have three times more malic acid than Golden Delicious. It is this, and a lower sugar content, that gives them their tangy flavor, which isn't lost during cooking. The unique texture of the Bramley is caused by air trapped in the cells of the apples; this helps the flesh turn wonderfully fluffy as the cells expand with heat. American varieties such as Gravenstein and Greening can be substituted for Bramleys.

JEAN BUSH USES A CARDBOARD PATTERN TO CUT PERFECT PASTRY DECORATIONS FOR HER PIE.

AFTER PUTTING THEM IN PLACE, SHE BRUSHES THE PIE VERY EVENLY AND LIGHTLY WITH EGG BEFORE BAKING

Peel, core, and slice the apples. Put into a microwave-proof dish with the tablespoon of water and cook in the microwave on high setting for 2 minutes. Let cool, then add sugar to taste.

While the apples are cooling, make the pastry dough. Sift the flour into a large mixing bowl, add the fats, and cut into very small pieces, then rub into the flour, using your fingertips, until the mixture resembles fine crumbs. Add the water and toss with a round-bladed knife to bind the ingredients. Knead lightly to make a soft but not sticky dough, then wrap and chill for 20 minutes, if necessary.

Preheat the oven to 425°F.

Roll out half of the pastry dough on a cold, floured work surface to a round about 12 inches in diameter. Use to line the pie pan, leaving the excess dough hanging over the edge. Spoon in the apple filling. Roll out the rest of the pastry dough to a round as before. Brush the rim of the bottom crust with water, then cover the pie with the top crust. Press the edges together to seal, then trim off the excess dough and flute the edges with a fork. This makes the pie look attractive as well as helping to seal together the top and bottom crusts.

Gather up the dough trimmings, knead them together lightly, and then roll out thinly. Cut out decorations such as leaves, apples, or an apple tree. Stick the decorations to the pie with a little water, then brush the top crust all over with the beaten egg. Cut a slit in the middle of the crust.

Bake in the preheated oven for 30 minutes or until golden and crisp. Sprinkle with sugar, and serve hot, warm, or at room temperature.

BELOW Judges Wendy Whittaker and Olympic swimmer Duncan Goodhew examine the entries in the 1994 Open Apple Pie Competition. The judging took several hours.

BELOW RIGHT Judge Margaret Foss takes a closer look at one of the entries.

CROUSTADE AUX POMMES

INGREDIENTS

Makes a 12-inch pie, to serve 8
½lb (250g) phyllo pastry (see recipe)
½ cup + 2 tablespoons (140g) unsalted butter
4 Bramley, Gravenstein, Greening, or other baking apples, about 2lb (900g)
½ cup (100g) sugar
1–2 tablespoons Calvados (optional)
confectioners' sugar for sprinkling

a 12-inch springform cake pan, greased and sprinkled with sugar

The beauty of this apple pie, from the southwest of France, is its simplicity: there is no pastry to make, just sheets of phyllo to butter and arrange in the pan. The filling is simply apples cooked in butter and sugar until golden and slightly caramelized. The best pan to use is a springform, although you could also use a deep tart pan, taking care not to let the pastry stick to the rim.

If the pastry is frozen, thaw according to the package directions. Once unwrapped, keep the pastry covered with plastic wrap or a damp dish towel to prevent it from drying out.

Melt 4 tablespoons (60g) of the butter in a large heavy pan. Peel, core, and thickly slice the apples, then put into the hot butter and cook until almost tender. The slices should keep their shape as much as possible, so don't stir, but shake the pan from time to time to prevent them from sticking. Sprinkle over about half of the sugar and cook, tossing and shaking the pan, until the sugar starts to caramelize the apples. Remove from the heat, sprinkle with the Calvados, and let cool.

Preheat the oven to 425°F.

1 LINE THE PAN WITH OVERLAPPING SHEETS OF PHYLLO, BRUSHING THEM WITH BUTTER AND SPRINKLING WITH SUGAR.

2 SPOON THE COOLED CARAMELIZED APPLE AND CALVADOS FILLING INTO THE PHYLLO-LINED PAN.

3 FOLD IN THE EDGES OF THE PASTRY TO COVER THE FILLING, THEN BRUSH WITH BUTTER AND SPRINKLE WITH SUGAR.

4 GENTLY ARRANGE THE CRUMPLED SHEETS OF PHYLLO PASTRY ON THE TOP, PILING THEM UP.

DUST THE WARM CROUSTADE WITH CONFECTIONERS' SUGAR BEFORE SERVING.

Melt the rest of the butter in a small pan. Line the bottom of the prepared pan with two or three sheets of phyllo pastry, overlapping them where necessary and letting the edges flop over the rim of the pan. Brush the layered pastry with a little melted butter and sprinkle with some of the remaining sugar. Add another two or three sheets of phyllo; brush with butter and sprinkle with sugar. Repeat once more so that about half the phyllo has been used. Spoon in the apple filling, then fold the edges of the phyllo in over the filling as if wrapping a parcel. Brush the folded-in pieces of phyllo with butter and sprinkle with sugar. Lightly brush the remaining sheets of phyllo with butter, then cut or tear them in half, across or diagonally. Crumple up each piece, rather like a chiffon scarf, and gently arrange in a pile on top of the apples – the whole thing should resemble a big, silly, frilly hat.

Sprinkle with any remaining butter, then bake for about 20 minutes or until golden and crisp. Carefully unmold and dust liberally with sifted confectioners' sugar. Serve warm, with ice-cream or crème fraîche, or an apple and Calvados sorbet.

DOUBLE-CRUST FRUIT PIES

YOU CAN SEAL THE PASTRY RIM BY CRIMPING WITH THE BACK OF A FORK.

As in the English Deep-Dish Fruit Pie on page 342, the fruit and pastry in the double-crust fruit pies here can be varied to suit the season and your fancy. A metal pie pan will give the crispest pastry base because it conducts heat the best, although ovenproof glass and china pie pans can also be used. It is best to bake these pies on a baking sheet to catch any juices that bubble out. Some cooks like to toss very juicy fruit – peaches and cherries, for example – with a little cornstarch so the filling will hold together instead of running out when the pie is cut. You can make a plain closed top crust or a lattice top (see below). For a plain top crust, roll out the larger portion of dough into a round 1 inch larger than the diameter of the pie pan and use to cover the pie. Firmly press the top crust onto the dampened border of the bottom crust to seal, then cut off the excess dough with a sharp knife. Score the sides (see page 342), then finish the edge by crimping – pressing down with the back of a fork – or fluting with your fingers. Make a steam hole in the center of the top crust and decorate, if desired, with leaves cut from the dough trimmings.

RHUBARB AND ORANGE PIE

INGREDIENTS

Makes a 9-inch pie, to serve 6

PASTRY:

2 cups (280g) all-purpose flour
a pinch of salt
5 tablespoons (70g) unsalted butter, chilled and diced
5 tablespoons (70g) lard, chilled and diced, or shortening
1 tablespoon sugar plus more for sprinkling
about 4 tablespoons ice water to bind

FILLING:

$1\frac{1}{2}$lb (680g) trimmed young rhubarb
1 unwaxed orange
about 4 tablespoons sugar, to taste

a shallow 9-inch pie pan, about 3/4 inch deep
a baking sheet

OPPOSITE Rhubarb and Orange Pie. The lattice topping on this pie was made using a lattice cutter.

Both short and rough puff pastry are suitable for this irresistible pie. When red currants are in season, use them instead of orange, as an unusual companion for the rhubarb.

Preheat the oven to 400°F.

To make the pastry dough, sift the flour and salt into a bowl, add the fat, and cut and rub into the flour, using the tips of your fingers, until the mixture resembles fine crumbs. Stir in the sugar. Add 3 tablespoons of water and stir into the flour mixture to bind, using a round-bladed knife; add more water if necessary. Quickly bring the mixture together with your hands, without kneading, to make a soft but not sticky ball of dough. Alternatively, you can make the dough in a food processor (see page 342). Wrap the dough and chill while you make the filling.

Wash the rhubarb, then cut into pieces about 3/4 inch long. Grate the rind from the orange and reserve. Cut off all the peel and white pith, then either slice the orange thinly or cut out sections, depending on the quality of the flesh. Mix the rhubarb with the grated orange rind, orange slices or sections, and the sugar.

Divide the dough into two portions, one slightly smaller than the other. Roll out the smaller portion on a lightly floured work surface to a round about 11 inches in diameter and use to line the pie pan, letting the excess dough drape over the rim of the pan. Spoon in the filling, leaving the border around the rim of the pan clear and mounding the fruit neatly in the center. Brush the pastry border with cold water. Roll out the rest of the dough to a round about 10 inches in diameter and stamp out a lattice with a special cutter. Put the lattice crust in place and press the edges to seal. (Alternatively, cut strips and arrange them in a lattice pattern as in the

Blueberry Pie on page 350.) Finish by scoring and then crimping or fluting the edge (see opposite).

Set the pie pan on a baking sheet and bake for 20 minutes. Reduce the oven temperature to 350°F and bake for a further 10–15 minutes or until the pastry is golden. Sprinkle with sugar, and serve warm.

BLUEBERRY PIE

INGREDIENTS

Makes a 9-inch pie, to serve 6

PASTRY:

2 cups (280g) all-purpose flour
1/4 teaspoon salt
1 3/4 tablespoons sugar
3/4 cup + 1 tablespoon (185g) unsalted butter, chilled and diced
3 tablespoons cold milk plus more for glazing

FILLING:

3 cups (450g) fresh or frozen blueberries
1/2 teaspoon ground cinnamon
7 tablespoons (60g) all-purpose flour
1 cup + 2 tablespoons (230g) sugar, or to taste
1 tablespoon (15g) butter

a shallow 9-inch pie pan, about 3/4 inch deep
a baking sheet

Wild blueberries taste better than cultivated ones, so look out for them for this luscious pie, even frozen wild berries. The rich pastry, bound with milk rather than the more usual water, is best rolled out between sheets of plastic wrap or parchment paper.

Make the pastry in a food processor: sift the flour, salt, and sugar into the processor bowl, add the butter, and process until the mixture resembles fine crumbs. With the machine running, add enough milk through the feed tube to make a soft but not sticky dough. Wrap the dough in plastic wrap and chill for 30 minutes.

Divide the dough into two portions, one slightly larger than the other. Roll out each portion between two sheets of plastic wrap or non-stick parchment paper to a thin round; the round from the larger portion should be about 11 inches in diameter and that from the smaller portion should be about 9 1/2 inches. Chill the smaller round, and use the other to line the pie pan: peel off the top sheet of plastic or paper, turn the round of dough over, and lay it over the pie pan. Gently press the dough into the pan to line the bottom and sides evenly, then peel off the remaining plastic wrap or paper. Do not cut off the excess pastry dough.

To make the filling, mix together all the ingredients except for the butter. Spoon into the bottom crust and dot with the butter, cut into small pieces. Brush the pastry rim with a little water. Peel the plastic or paper from the remaining dough round. Cut into strips about 3/8 inch wide and

arrange over the filling to make a lattice, sticking the ends of the strips to the bottom crust with a little water. (Alternatively, you can leave the top crust plain – see page 348 – but don't make a steam hole in the center. Trim and seal the edges together firmly, then score the sides (see page 342) and flute or crimp the edges neatly.) Chill the pie for 30 minutes.

Preheat the oven to 425°F.

Brush the pastry lattice or top crust with milk to glaze. If the crust is plain, use a small sharp knife to make eight or nine slits, evenly spaced. Set the pie pan on a baking sheet and bake for 25–30 minutes or until the pastry is golden and the filling is bubbling through the lattice or slits. Serve warm, with ice-cream.

SHEILA'S PEACH PIE

INGREDIENTS

Makes a 9-inch pie, to serve 8

PASTRY:
- 1 1/2 cups (200g) all-purpose flour
- 1/2 cup + 2 tablespoons (140g) unsalted butter, chilled and diced
- 1/2 cup (40g) ground almonds
- 1/3 cup (40g) confectioners' sugar, sifted
- 1 egg yolk
- 2 tablespoons cold milk

FILLING:
- 2lb (900g) peaches
- 5 tablespoons (60g) sugar
- 1/2 teaspoon ground cinnamon
- 3 tablespoons cornstarch
- 3 tablespoons (15g) ground almonds

TO FINISH:
- 1 egg white, beaten, for brushing
- sugar for sprinkling

- a 9-inch pie pan, about 1 1/2 inches deep, or loose-based tart pan
- a baking sheet

This recipe comes from an American friend, Dr. Sheila Rossan, whom I met every day for years at the local swimming pool. We used to swap recipes, and bring in samples to aid recovery from our exertions. This is her masterpiece – the best peach pie you are ever likely to eat. It has a very rich and delicate pastry that is quite hard to handle and which is best made in a food processor. The filling needs good ripe peaches, and the cornstarch helps to thicken the juices released during baking. You can make this in a pie pan or a loose-based tart pan.

Make the pastry dough in a food processor: put the flour and the diced butter into the bowl and process just until the mixture resembles coarse crumbs. Add the ground almonds and sugar and process or pulse briefly just to mix. With the machine running, add the egg yolk and milk through the feed tube and process until the mixture comes together to make a soft but not sticky dough. Wrap and chill for 30 minutes.

Roll out the dough between two pieces of plastic wrap or non-stick parchment paper to a thin round about 12 inches in diameter. Peel off the top sheet of plastic or paper, turn the round of dough over, and lay it over the pie pan. Gently press the dough into the pan to line the bottom and sides evenly, then peel off the remaining plastic wrap or paper. If any cracks or tears appear, push the dough together to seal the hole. Trim off the excess dough and keep to make the lattice, then chill the pie shell and trimmings while you make the filling.

Preheat the oven to 375°F.

Peel the peaches, then slice thickly into a bowl to catch all the juices. Sprinkle over the sugar, cinnamon, and cornstarch and toss gently to combine. Sprinkle the ground almonds over the bottom of the pie shell and spoon the peach mixture on top. Gently knead together the dough trimmings, then roll out thinly and cut into strips about 3/8 inch wide. Arrange over the top of the pie to make a lattice, sticking the ends of the strips to the rim of the bottom crust with a little cold water.

Bake the pie for 25 minutes, then brush the pastry lattice with egg white and sprinkle with the sugar. Return to the oven and bake for a further 20–25 minutes or until the pastry is golden and the filling is bubbling. Serve warm, with vanilla ice-cream.

BETTY'S SHOO FLY PIE

INGREDIENTS

Makes a 9-inch pie, to serve 8–10

PASTRY:
1⅓ cups (185g) all-purpose flour
¼ teaspoon salt
¼ cup (60g) lard, chilled and diced, or shortening
2 tablespoons (30g) butter, chilled and diced
2–3 tablespoons icy water

CRUMB TOPPING:
1 cup (140g) all-purpose flour
¼ cup (60g) lard or butter, chilled and diced, or shortening
½ cup packed (100g) light brown sugar

FILLING:
¼ teaspoon salt
1 teaspoon baking soda
1 cup (230ml) boiling water
1 cup (340g) light or unsulfured molasses

a 9-inch pie pan, about 1½ inches deep

Betty Groff and her favorite Shoo Fly Pie.

While we were in the United States, we were told several times that we had to meet Betty Groff, "the Julia Child of the Pennsylvania Dutch." Encouraged by James Beard, she has done more than any other food writer to modernize and publicize the food of her community: "I cook old family dishes with a lighter touch: less cream, butter, and stodge. What with central heating, cars, and office work, few people want to eat as our grandparents did." Cooking is in her blood – her grandmother had a butcher's shop; her father cured hams and air-dried beef; her mother made the pies. It was a strict Mennonite upbringing – Betty had to keep to the dress code – "but every meal was a party." The family farmhouse is now a restaurant – called Groff's Farm – and Betty still serves meals family-style.

Preheat the oven to 375°F.

To make the pastry dough, put the flour into a mixing bowl and add the salt and fats. Rub the fat into the flour with the tips of your fingers, or cut it in with a wire pastry cutter, until the mixture resembles crumbs. Gradually add enough water just to bind the crumbs together (it will need less on a damp day), tossing the mixture gently with your hand. Press lumps of the dough gently against the sides of the bowl so it comes together. The less the dough is handled, the lighter it will be. Alternatively, you can make the dough in a food processor.

Turn the dough onto a generously floured work surface. Gently pat it into a ball, then flatten it lightly and pat the edges to smooth out the rough sides. Roll out the dough into a round about 12 inches in diameter and use to line the pie pan. Crimp the edges with your fingers. Put the pastry shell into the oven, just as it is, to part-bake for 6–10 minutes; it will just be starting to puff up. (This part-baking helps prevent the pastry from becoming soggy when the filling is added.) Let cool while preparing the crumbs and filling.

To make the crumb topping, put all the ingredients into a mixing bowl and rub the fat into the flour and sugar, using your fingertips, until the mixture looks like fine crumbs.

To make the filling, dissolve the salt and baking soda in the boiling water in a small saucepan. Then add the light molasses and mix thoroughly. Bring back to a boil, then remove from the heat and set aside to cool slightly.

Pour the filling into the pie shell – it should not be more than two-thirds full or the filling will boil over. Sprinkle evenly with the crumb topping. Bake for 10 minutes, then reduce the oven temperature to 350°F and bake for a further 30 minutes or until the center of the filling doesn't wobble when the pie is shaken.

Let cool completely, and serve at room temperature.

1 BETTY CRIMPS THE PIE EDGE USING THE THUMB AND FOREFINGER OF ONE HAND AND THE FOREFINGER OF THE OTHER.

2 SHE SPRINKLES THE CRUMB TOPPING EVENLY OVER THE SYRUP FILLING AND BAKES THE PIE IMMEDIATELY.

BETTY'S AMISH VANILLA PIE

INGREDIENTS

Makes a 9-inch pie, to serve 8–10

PASTRY:
1 1/3 cups (185g) all-purpose flour
1/4 teaspoon salt
1/4 cup (60g) lard, chilled and diced, or shortening
2 tablespoons (30g) butter, chilled and diced
2–3 tablespoons ice water

FILLING:
2 cups (455ml) water
1/2 cup (100g) sugar
2 tablespoons all-purpose flour
1 cup (340g) light unsulfured molasses
1 egg, beaten
1 teaspoon pure vanilla extract

CRUMB TOPPING:
1 cup (140g) all-purpose flour
1/2 cup (100g) sugar
4 tablespoons (60g) butter, chilled and diced
1/4 teaspoon baking soda
1/4 teaspoon cream of tartar

a 9-inch pie pan, about 1 1/2 inches deep

An Amish horse and buggy in Lancaster County, Pennsylvania.

RIGHT Shoo Fly Pie and an uncut Amish Vanilla Pie.

Preheat the oven to 375°F.

Make the pastry dough, line the pie pan, and part-bake the shell as for Shoo Fly Pie (see page 353). Let cool.

To make the filling, heat the water in a saucepan over medium heat until it is fairly hot but nowhere near boiling. Mix the sugar with the flour and whisk into the hot water. Whisk in the molasses. As soon as it has melted and the mixture is smooth, whisk in the egg. Continue whisking until the mixture thickens – it should barely come to a simmer and must not boil. Remove from the heat and let cool before stirring in the vanilla.

To make the crumb topping, put all the ingredients into a mixing bowl and rub between your fingertips until the mixture resembles fine crumbs.

Pour the filling into the cooled pie shell, and sprinkle the surface evenly with the crumb topping. Bake for 10 minutes, then reduce the oven temperature to 350°F and bake for a further 30 minutes or until the center of the filling is firm when the pie pan is gently shaken. Serve at room temperature.

STEPHEN BULL'S PECAN BUTTER TART

INGREDIENTS

Makes a 10-inch tart, to serve up to 16

PASTRY:
1⅔ cups (230g) all-purpose flour
a pinch of salt
2½ tablespoons (30g) sugar
½ cup + 3 tablespoons (155g) unsalted butter, chilled and diced
1 extra large egg yolk, mixed with 1 tablespoon ice water

FILLING:
1¼ cups packed (280g) dark brown sugar
1 cup (230g) unsalted butter
½ cup (170g) maple syrup
½ cup (170g) golden syrup
5 extra large eggs
1 teaspoon pure vanilla extract
1 cup (170g) raisins
4½ cups (500g) roughly chopped pecans

a 10-inch springform cake pan

I first tasted this most wonderful of traditional butter-rich pecan pies at Vivian's, our local gourmet shop. Vivian is an old friend of the chef and restaurateur, Stephen Bull, who once had a restaurant nearby and now has three in London – Fulham Road, the restaurant in Blandford Street, and The Bistro in St. John Street. I decided to take the bull by the horns, as it were, and ask for the recipe. It requires a lot of nuts, but the pie is very large and cuts into 16 slices.

ABOVE A piece of wonderful Pecan Butter Tart.

TOP RIGHT Stephen Bull and his Pecan Butter Tart in the Fulham Road restaurant.

Make the pastry dough by hand (see page 302) or in a food processor: sift the flour, salt, and sugar into the processor bowl, add the diced butter, and process until the mixture resembles fine crumbs. With the machine running, add the egg and water mixture through the feed tube. Run the machine until the dough comes together in a ball. It should be soft but not sticky. If this has not happened after a minute and there are dry crumbs, add more water, a teaspoon at a time. Wrap and chill for 15 minutes.

Preheat the oven to 400°F.

On a floured work surface, roll out the dough to a round about 13 inches in diameter and use to line the pan. Prick the bottom of the pastry shell all over with a fork, then chill for 10 minutes. Bake the pastry shell (see page 328), then let cool while making the filling. Reduce the oven temperature to 300°F.

Put the sugar, butter, and both syrups into a large saucepan and bring to a boil. Cook over medium heat for 5 minutes, stirring frequently to prevent sticking, then remove from the heat and set aside. Put the eggs into a large bowl and beat well, then stir in the vanilla extract, the raisins, and, finally, the nuts. When thoroughly blended, add the syrup mixture and mix well.

Pour the filling into the baked pastry shell and bake for 1 hour or until the filling is fairly firm to the touch.

Let cool completely, and serve with cream or vanilla ice-cream.

DIANE'S CHOCOLATE PECAN PIE

INGREDIENTS

Makes a 9-inch pie, to serve 8

PASTRY:

1 cup (140g) all-purpose flour

1/2 teaspoon salt

6 tablespoons (85g) fat (see recipe), chilled and diced if using butter or lard

2-3 tablespoons icy water

FILLING:

1/2 cup (110g) margarine or butter, melted

1/4 cup (35g) all-purpose flour

1/4 cup (30g) unsweetened cocoa powder

1 cup (200g) sugar

1/4 teaspoon pure vanilla extract

2 eggs, beaten

1 cup (100g) pecan halves

TO FINISH:

1/2 heaped cup (60g) pecan halves

a 9-inch pie pan, about 1 1/2 inches deep

Diane Dorsey makes light, melt-in-the-mouth pastry for her pecan pie.

James Swink of Young's Pecans in North Carolina recommended that we visit the best pecan pie baker he knew – Diane Dorsey. Diane was very matter of fact about her unusual pecan pie, the recipe for which is much sought after locally. Diane said she made it up by combining her favorite fudge and traditional pecan pie recipes. The result is like a very nutty brownie in a pastry shell. Diane makes her pastry with shortening, but you can use butter, lard, or margarine, or a combinations of fats instead.

In South Carolina, much of the pecan crop comes from yard trees rather than commercial orchards.

Preheat the oven to 350°F.

To make the pastry dough, put the flour and salt into a mixing bowl and add the fat. If using shortening, mix it into the flour with a spoon or round-bladed knife; hard fats should be rubbed in with your fingertips until the mixture resembles fine crumbs. Then add the water and mix, using your hands or a round-bladed knife, to make a soft but not sticky dough. Knead very gently until the dough just comes together.

Turn the dough onto a lightly floured work surface. Roll out fairly thinly into a round about 12 inches in diameter. Rather than roll up the dough around the rolling pin, Diane uses this method: fold the dough in half and in half again, into quarters, and lift it into the pie pan. Unfold the dough and press it gently onto the bottom and sides to line the pan completely. Decorate the rim of the pie shell by pressing down all around with the back of a fork, then cut off any excess dough. Leave in a cool place – not the fridge – while preparing the filling.

Mix the melted fat with the flour using a metal or wooden spoon; don't worry if the mixture looks slightly lumpy. Add the cocoa and mix well. Stir in the sugar, then the vanilla, and, finally, the eggs. When thoroughly blended, stir in the pecans.

Pour the filling into the pastry case. Decorate with the extra nuts. Bake for 25 minutes or until the filling feels just firm to the touch. Let cool completely, and serve at room temperature.

ABOVE At Young's Pecans, the nuts are graded for size and then checked for damage before shelling.

RIGHT Chocolate Pecan Pie, combining the best of traditional pecan pies with chocolate fudge.

APPLE ALMOND CREAM PIE

INGREDIENTS

Makes a 9-inch pie, to serve 8

PASTRY:

1 2/3 cups (230g) all-purpose flour
a pinch of salt
4 tablespoons (60g) unsalted butter, chilled and diced
1/4 cup (60g) lard, chilled and diced, or shortening
2–3 tablespoons ice water to bind

ALMOND CREAM:

8oz (230g) almond paste (marzipan), crumbled
1/2 cup (110g) unsalted butter, at room temperature, diced
2 tablespoons all-purpose flour
2 eggs, beaten

TOPPING:

4 large, tart apples
1 tablespoon lemon juice
2 tablespoons sugar

a 9-inch metal pie pan, about 1 1/2 inches deep

ABOVE The Isaac Randall House in Freeport, Maine, home of the Friedlanders.

TOP RIGHT (from left to right): Apple Almond Cream Pie, Bayberry Bread, Granny Glyn's Lemon Loaf.

OPPOSITE Jim Friedlander takes a freshly baked Apple Almond Cream Pie from the oven.

This is one of the best apple pies I have ever tasted. The recipe comes from Jim Friedlander of Freeport, Maine (also see the two quickbread recipes on pages 100-101). The pie is much easier to make than it first appears, though a food processor is essential. You also need good, tart apples, such as Granny Smiths or Pippins.

Preheat the oven to 450°F.

Make the pastry dough by hand (see page 302) or in the food processor: put the flour, salt, and fats into the processor bowl and process until the mixture looks like fine crumbs. With the motor running, slowly pour in 2 tablespoons of the water through the feed tube. If the dough has not come together to form a ball within a minute, gradually add more water, to make a soft but not sticky dough.

Turn the dough onto a lightly floured work surface. Cut off a third of the dough; wrap and chill the larger portion. Roll out the smaller piece to a round about 12 inches in diameter and use to line the pie pan. Let the excess dough hang over the rim. Put on one side.

Now prepare the almond cream. Put the almond paste and butter into the bowl of the food processor and process until smooth. Add the flour and the eggs and process once more, until the mixture is smooth, creamy, and thoroughly blended.

Peel, halve, and core the apples, then cut into slices 3/8 inch thick. Cut each slice crosswise into three. Put the apples in a bowl and toss with the lemon juice and sugar.

Spoon the almond cream mixture into the bottom of the pastry shell, then cover with the apples, mounding them slightly in the center. Roll out the remaining dough to a round about 11 inches in diameter to make the lid. Dampen the rim of the pie shell, then cover the pie with the top crust. Press the edges together to seal firmly. Using a sharp knife, cut off the excess dough, then cut 6 slits in the top crust.

Put the pie in the preheated oven, then immediately reduce the oven temperature to 375°F. Bake for 45–50 minutes or until golden brown. Sprinkle with a little sugar and let cool.

Serve the pie warm or at room temperature.

PARIS-BISTRO

EQUIPMENT

BRIDGE KITCHENWARE
214 E. 52nd Street
New York, NY 10022
800-274-3435
Professional bakeware, cookware, tools.
Catalog available.

BROADWAY PANHANDLER
520 Broadway
New York, NY 10012
212-966-3434
Bakeware, cookware, tools.

DEAN & DELUCCA, INC.
MAIL ORDER DEPARTMENT
560 Broadway
New York, NY 10012
800-221-7714
Specialty bakeware, including brioche pans, cookware, tools.
Catalog avaliable.

KING ARTHUR® FLOUR
BAKER'S CATALOG
P.O. Box 876
Norwich, Vermont 05055
800-827-6836
Specialty bakeware and tools.
Catalog available.

KITCHEN KRAFTS
P.O. Box 805
Mount Laurel, NJ 08054
800-776-0575
Specialty bakeware.
Catalog available.

LA CUISINE
323 Cameron Street
Alexandria, VA 22314
800-521-1176
Cookware and bakeware; baking ingredients.
Catalog available.

MAID OF SCANDINAVIA
3244 Raleigh Avenue
Minneapolis, MN 55416
800-328-6722
Specialty bakeware and tools.
Catalog available.

WILLIAMS-SONOMA
P.O. Box 7456
San Francisco, CA 94120-7456
800-541-2233
Bakeware, cookware, tools.
Catalog available.

ZABAR'S
2245 Broadway
New York City, NY 10024
212-496-1234
Bakeware, cookware, tools.
Catalog available.

FLOURS AND GRAINS

BRUMWELL MILLING
328 East Second Street
Sumner, LA 50674
319-578-8106
Stone-ground certified organic bread flour, rye and spelt flours, cornmeal.
Price list available.

BUTTE CREEK MILL
P.O. Box 561
Eagle Point, OR 97524
503-826-3531
Stone-ground bread flour, pastry flour, buckwheat flour, cornmeal.
Price list available.

GRAY'S GRIST MILL
P.O. Box 422
Adamsville, RI 02801
508-636-6075
Stone-ground certified organic bread flour, rye and spelt flours, stone-ground cornmeal.
Price list available.

THE GREAT VALLEY MILLS
R.D. 3, Country Line Road
Box 1111
Barto, PA 19504
800-688-6455
Stone-ground bread flour, pastry flour, rye and semolina flour, steel-cut oats.
Catalog available.

KING ARTHUR® FLOUR
BAKER'S CATALOG
(see EQUIPMENT)
Stone-ground bread flour, pastry flour, white whole-wheat flour, amaranth, barley, semolina, and spelt flours, cornmeal, vital wheat gluten, cracked wheat, wheat flakes.

NEW HOPE MILLS
R.R. 2, P.O. Box 269A
Moravia, NY 13118
315-497-0783
Stone-ground bread flour, buckwheat, rye, and spelt flours, vital wheat gluten, cornmeal.
Catalog available.

PETE'S SPICE AND
EVERYTHING NICE
174 First Avenue
New York, NY 10009
212-254-8773
Bread flour, pastry flour, buckwheat, rye, semolina, and spelt flours, cornmeal.
Catalog available.

SHILOH FARMS INC.
P.O. Box 97
Sulphur Springs, AR 72768
800-362-6832, *for the West and the Midwest on the East Coast.*

GARDEN SPOT
438 White Oak Road
New Holland, PA 17557
800-829-5100
Certified organic, stone-ground bread flour, and spelt flour.

STAFFORD COUNTY FLOUR MILLS Co.
P.O. Box 7
Hudson, KS 67545
316-458-4121
Hudson Cream unbleached white and whole-wheat flours.

WAR EAGLE MILL
Route 5, Box 411
Rogers, AR 72756
501-789-5343
Certified organic, stone-ground bread flour, buckwheat and rye flours, cornmeal.
Catalog available.

DRIED AND CANDIED FRUIT AND CITRUS PEELS

DEAN & DELUCCA, INC.
(see EQUIPMENT)
Dried and candied fruit, candied citrus peels, in season.

PETE'S SPICE AND EVERYTHING NICE
(see FLOURS AND GRAINS)
Dried and candied fruit, candied citrus peel.

TIMBER CREST FARMS
4791 Dry Creek Road
Healdsburg, CA 95448
707-433-8251
Certified organic, no-sulphur-added dried apples, apricots, peaches, pears, prunes, raisins.
Catalog available.

ACKNOWLEDGEMENTS

Linda Collister and Anthony Blake would like to thank the following people and companies:

IN THE UNITED STATES: Noah Alper, Linda and Ken Busteed, Alyson Cook, Cindy Falk, Betty and Abe Groff, Jeffrey Hamelman, Lucinda Hampton (Pennysylvania Dutch Visitors Bureau), Dottie and Andy Hess, Hayely Matson, Ina McNeil, Dee Dee and Jack Meyer, Will and Annette Hertz, Jim Friedlander, Lois and Ezia Lamdin, Caroll Bolton, and at Young's Pecans, Florence, South Carolina, James Swink, Susan Stephenson, Helen Watts, Diane Dorsey, Shawn Price, Mac Davenport, Henry Unruh, Rosemary Underdahl and Barbara Walker.

IN FRANCE: Kate and John Barber, Jean-Jacques Bernachon, Jean-Pierre St Martin, Clarisse and Jean Michel Deiss and Lionel Poilâne.

IN GREAT BRITAIN: Joy Skipper, Beverley LeBlanc, Janet Bligh, Sandra Bosuston, Betty Charlton, Julia Royden-Cooper, Elaine Hallgarten, Randolph Hodgson of Neals Yard Dairy, Pierre Koffman, Barbara Levy, Norma MacMillan, Joy Portch, Rachel Roskilly, Michel Roux, Louise Simpson, Jagdeesh Sohal, Anna Rollo and Cosmo Sterk, Mike Thurlow of Letheringsett, Jonathan Topps, Paul Welti, Sharon Turner and Yvonne Jenkins, Stephen Bull, Marc and Max Renzland, Brigitte Friis, Zeynep Stromfelt, Katie Stewart, Sallie Morris, Alan Hertz, Michael Sealey, Rena Salaman, Betty Charlton, Jean Bush, Alice Portnoy at Neff and Sheila Rossen.

IN IRELAND: Mary Curtis, Phoebe and Bill Lett, Veronica Steele of Milleens Dairy and Alice and Gerry Turner.

IN GERMANY: Nurnberg Tourist Office

FOR PHOTOGRAPHY: Uli Hinter at Leica Cameras.

FOR CROCKERY AND CUTLERY: Villeroy and Boch; for equipment: The Kitchenware Company; for kitchen appliances; Neff. Braun, Kenwood, Magimix.

The authors also wish to express their appreciation to the Bulgarian Wine and Tourist Agency, Kansas Wheat Commission, Nuremberg Tourist Office, Sharwoods and Trustees Philipsburg Manor.

Page numbers in italic refer to the illustrations